American Sublime

D1440891

American Sublime

The Genealogy of a Poetic Genre

Rob Wilson

THE UNIVERSITY OF WISCONSIN PRESS

The University of Wisconsin Press
114 North Murray Street
Madison, Wisconsin 53715

3 Henrietta Street
London WC2E 8LU, England

5   4   3   2   1

Printed in the United States of America

Library of Congress Cataloging-in-Publication Data
Wilson, Rob, 1947–
    American sublime: the genealogy of a poetic genre / Rob Wilson.
    352 pp.   cm.—(The Wisconsin project on American writers)
    Includes index.
    1. American poetry—History and criticism. 2. Sublime, The, in
literature.   I. Title. II. Series.
PS310.S87W55   1991
811.009—dc20
ISBN 0-299-12770-2   90-50654
ISBN 0-299-12774-5   CIP

Or to read you, Walt [Whitman],—knowing us in thrall
To that deep wonderment, our native clay . . .
                    —Hart Crane, "Cape Hatteras," *The Bridge*

After the perfect lines about the frog or cricket or eclipse we turn around and have to come to terms with the vastness of our place or our vast unspoken history.
                    —Michael Ondaatje, *The Canadian Long Poem*

Contents

Contents

Acknowledgments

Eᴀʀʟɪᴇʀ ᴠᴇʀsɪᴏɴs of chapters in this book have appeared in rougher terms in *American Poetry* 3 (1986) ("Wallace Stevens: De-creating the American Sublime"), *Early American Literature* 24 (1989) ("William Livingston's *Philosophic Solitude* and the Ideology of the Natural Sublime"), and *Prospects* 14 (1989) ("Towards the Nuclear Sublime"). I would like to thank the editors of these journals—Lee Bartlett, Everett Emerson, and Jack Salzman—for their support of my work in stages of conceptualization when faith in one's voice seemingly counts for as much as scholarly rigor.

As a product of the spiritual/ideological climate of post–Cold War America (what Robert Pinsky's National Endowment for the Humanities Summer Seminar in Berkeley, 1986, came to call "cheery pluralism"), I have tried since the early seventies in Berkeley and Honolulu—all too obsessively, I must admit—to come to more dialectical terms with nativist sentiments and a lapsed-Catholic ideality. This book may measure the conflicts and resolutions of this struggle, but certain "American scholars" have foreshadowed a commitment to articulating, as best I could, the dynamics of "the American sublime." As Longinus urged of the sublime mimetic, "These great figures, presented to us as objects of emulation and, as it were, shining before our gaze, will somehow elevate our minds to the greatness of which we form a mental image" (*On Sublimity,* 14.1). Or better said, as Emerson rephrased this competitive dynamic in his journals in 1844, "Life is so affirmative that I can never hear of personal vigour of any kind, great power of performance, without lively sympathy & fresh resolutions."

Risking such a stance of generativity at the outset, nonetheless, I would like to thank certain teachers and writers for their faith in my poetic-scholarly abilities, as well as in the difficult, all-but-bypassed splendors of American poetry: above all, as examples of this scholarly vocation, the late Josephine Miles and Henry Nash Smith of the University of California at Berkeley. My thanks go as well to the following, in differing ways embodying funds of kindness, courage, and example: Robin Magowan, Richard Bridgman, Masao Miyoshi, Dan Stempel, Roy Harvey Pearce, Susan Horton, Michael Beard, Nell Altizer, Kathy Phillips, George Simson, Barry Menikoff, Robert Pinsky, Michael Stephens, Michael Ondaatje, Stephen-Paul Martin, Stanley Fish, Michael Heller, Ursule Molinaro, Robert Aitken, Ron Silliman, Joseph Kau, Steve Curry, Reuel Denney, Howard Horwitz, Richard Grusin, Richard Burt, Amy Kaplan, Gauri Viswanathan, Mark Peterson, Kim Chi-gyu, Kim U-chang, Drayton Hamilton, Timothy O'Grady, Bruce Stillians, Robert Onopa, Wimal Dissanayake, and Peter Lee, who nourished in countless ways (as did unmentioned others) my erratic life in Berkeley, Honolulu, Seoul, and Amherst.

Frank Lentricchia was there for me, too, tasking courage and example. Allen Fitchen demanded a direct language I tried hard to accomplish. I would also like to acknowledge the textualist and materialist approaches to the sublime of Harold Bloom, Frances Ferguson, and Fredric Jameson, which (however radically opposed they now seem) have proved formative for speculations within the last decade as well as for counter-arguments and departures within this book. I thank William E. Cain for a patient, tough-minded critique, and for reminding us that "America" remains both an invigorating set of ideals and a relentless critique of them.

The interdisciplinary Theory Group at the University of Hawaii linked the tools of the English, Political Science, and Philosophy Departments together in ways that proved freshly pragmatic and helpful as I moved towards demystifying the American sacralization of force, size, speed, and grandeur as built into some machinery of progress. Here I would like to thank each member, but especially Brook Thomas, Craig Howes, John Rieder, Val Wayne, Michael Shapiro, Vicente Rafael, Tim Engstrom, and Cristina Bacchilega. Our collective agonies will, I trust, give way to saner agonistics.

I am grateful to have become part of the enclave of writers centered, more regionally, around the lively complex of place-specific poetics and local ecology that is called *Bamboo Ridge*. I would here acknowledge the friendships of Tino Ramirez and Eric Chock, "searching for his/her god off Bamboo Ridge," as well as those apprentices in Zen pool and Robocop basketball gathered on Sunday on the courts of "Roy Sakuma Productions."

The book is dedicated to the memory of Josephine Miles, whose work on the eighteenth-century sublime and the stylistics of the American sublime first attracted me to this huge and hubris-inducing topic, and whose greatness of mind and heart made Berkeley and the *Berkeley Poetry Review* lingering challenges to the reach and endurance of any toil.

American Sublime

Introduction

If there is strength in America's size and numbers, there is also a threat posed to the subject of that sublimity: "Hey you! I say to the H-bomb. / Hey you! *Miami Vice* says to me" is the way Bob Perelman stages this struggle between the democratic ego and the forces of technology and information that now threaten to magnify, dwarf, and abolish it.[1] The sense of powerlessness a contemporary poet might feel, as representative American subject, is more than just a function of wall-to-wall intertextuality or castration anxiety—unless nuclear weapons and urban terror are factored in as "texts." Humbled by overwhelming power, the self may not identify with the vast mobility of willing and collective energies the sublime is called upon to represent. How has the language of American poetry contended with representing these vast—and shifting—configurations of the material sublime?

As a poetic genre, the American sublime helped to produce the subject and site of American subjection as sublime. At least that will be one of my overall claims. Yet how does one stand, within a poststructural context of deconstruction and disbelief, to behold "The American Sublime" as a communal construct of self and national empowerment that may never have been there except as a function of those vulgarly American contexts and beliefs? The answer to this pragmatic question, posed in a little poem of canny ambitions written by Wallace Stevens in 1935, is to some extent a matter of dialogical reconstruction: to situate such question-begging assumptions of American cash-value idealism within one language-genre where they obsessively took place, that is, within the poetic genre I will term (after Stevens et al.) "The American Sublime." Stevens's metaphysical question "How does one stand / To behold the sublime?" reverts into a more genealogical one worrying the context of any such sublimating perspective: "How does one stand to behold the *Americanization* of the sublime?" The an-

3

swer to this is first, and throughout, one of historical repositioning: the conventions of the American sublime have to be reestablished and interrogated, as these emerge and get constructed in poetic discourse, just as our contemporary interest in the American sublime has to be itself historicized as a disposition no less fascinated by these representations, and critiques, of Euramerican power.

In Stevens's "The American Sublime," to return briefly to this lyric, the figure used by the poet to represent an American will-to-sublimity is Andrew Jackson, who poses as a heroic figure, resisting blankness, muteness, and mockery: "When General Jackson / Posed for his statue / He knew how one feels. / Shall a man go barefoot / Blinking and blank?" The man of national sublimity moves beyond identifying with "the weather / The landscape and that" towards the production of an exhilarating emptiness that voids nature and history of prior presences, as the American sublime comes down to affirming "empty spirit / In vacant space." Yet this sense of imaginary cleansing and uninhabited emptiness was, for Jackson, much more than a rhetorical feat or hyperbole of Adamic repression: the Indian Removal Act of 1830 under President Jackson had forcibly relocated eastern tribes such as the Cherokees to the west of the Mississippi as a national policy. The Indians were removed closer to nature, the wilderness, the west, so that "nature's nation" could produce its own forms, policies, and texts of Euramerican sublimity that might, as Stevens put it in his poem on the appropriation of Tennessee as "slovenly wilderness," "take dominion everywhere." Protesting the "Trail of Tears" to President Van Buren in 1838, not even Emerson could blithely transcend (repress) this bloody and tragic production of "empty spirit / In vacant space." Stevens remained uneasy with his own abstractly realized appropriation of the wild, aboriginal, or different into a rude figure of national self-willing: "What wine does one drink? / What bread does one eat?" he asks at the end of the poem, as if haunted by the political unconscious of the dehumanized void he, like "barefoot" Andrew Jackson, had reproduced as an American vastness (emptiness) the self might still—displacing God and indigenous mythologies—believe in.[2]

Crossing the Atlantic, the sublime underwent an ideological sea-change. If the Enlightenment sublime had represented the unrepresentable, confronted privation, and pushed language to the limits

4

of imagining the vastness of nature and stellar infinitude as the subject's innermost ground, the Americanization of this sublime rhetoric represented, in effect, the interiorization of national claims as this Americanized self's inalienable ground. The Protestant bliss of conversion and the liberal conviction of exalted subjectivity conspired to produce a widely disseminated landscape, and language, confirming and eventuating in the American sublime of Emerson's era—decades after the sublime had seemed a moribund aesthetic in England.[3] The genre of the sublime helped to consolidate an American identity founded in representing a landscape of immensity and wildness ("power") open to multiple identifications ("use").

Imagining forth vastness as a distinctly American ground, then, this landscape of sacralized force became highly conventionalized and, to us, suspect. How did one stand to behold these energies of the American sublime? As Emerson and Whitman claimed, in the Romantic dispensation, one beheld the American sublime as immense nature and force, or representations of this American sublime as technology and text—and one became, in effect, another voice representing, challenging, if not instantiating those emerging powers of the American sublime. The sublime, by converting powerlessness and a lurking sense of social self-diminishment—or historical guilt—into a conviction of dematerialized power awaiting national use, eventuated in a figure of "self-reliance," then, for whom power is not the capacity to act or to conjoin, but to convert such inaction or disjunction into tropes and compacts founded in vast scenes of dehistoricized willing. Flooded with energy and light, artistic aggression was sublimated into a national performance.

As formulated in European rhetorics and aesthetics, the sublime had comprised an experience of art-empowerment (transport) that oscillated between positive and negative convictions about poetic language (art) and the subject (poet/reader): between, on the one hand, the performative enthusiasm that immense power and light can emanate from such grand-yet-simple language and scenes, as figured in the Biblical sentence "Let there be light, and there was light" cited by Longinus and a host of others as evoking the sublime; and, on the other hand, the prescriptive warning that all such figurative representations will fail to present the infinitude of power and light they painfully gesture towards, as figured in the sentence from *Exodus* invoked by Kant as an example of how unimaginable

5

any Judeo-Christian sublime really is, "Thou shalt not make to thyself any graven image, nor the likeness of anything which is in heaven or under the earth." Kant may trump Longinus on the treachery of sublime rhetoric, and then go on to provide his own latter-day scenario theorizing how the sublime can still provide a transcendence lifting us into the moral atmosphere of the gods. But I think it is fair to say—if only recalling the exalted crossing into light-drenched empowerment in Emerson, the language claims of sublime afflatus in Whitman, if not the painterly movement of sublime tropes into American Luminism—that the positive, or Longinian, version of performative enthusiasm proved amenable to American purposes and subjects as the Old World sublime was in time appropriated, democratized, and materially transformed into what we now ratify as "the American sublime." What Anne Bradstreet early termed "the rapted wit sublime" was, throughout our poetic history, imported and installed as a native muse compelling the voice to performative claims of outdoing, overdoing, or outmoding preexisting terms.

Prior to the 1970s, however, this American sublime did not exist as anything like a recognizable literary style or entrenched tradition. Living out the terrors/wonders of modernist discontinuity and liberal individuation, American poets were read not so much as instances of a collective will-to-sublimity but as lyric monads—deracinated, anxiety-stricken, alone with their own conspicuously well-wrought terms. The aesthetic of the sublime, as a trope haunting the will to any distinctly American sensibility, was increasingly recognizable from within the formal dynamics—and discourse—of art history, on the contrary, wherein nineteenth-century American sublimity was seen to have migrated from God-drenched landscapes of national instantiation (as in Frederic Edwin Church's *Niagara* [1857]) into no less compellingly excessive and immense abstractions of ego-displacement (Barnett Newman's *Vir Heroicus Sublimis* [1950–51], say).[4] Emerging from two world wars with a moral idealism and will to greatness more or less imperially intact, the production of sublime excess seemed to have a continuing claim on the tropes and terms of the native psyche, at least within the framework of such national art. Once-embarrassing landscapes of native sublimity were dragged out of attics, libraries, stairways, and barns. Church's *The Icebergs* (1861), for example, sold for

$2.5 million dollars in the late 1970s, the highest figure ever registered at an art auction in the United States. Disturbed by technological icons, this taste for indigenous sublimity has not abated.

Post-Whitmanic poets like Emily Dickinson, Stevens, Robert Frost, and Hart Crane had recognized and indeed had long struggled with this discourse of American supremacy and distinction as founded in the sacralization of force. For the most part, such modernists displaced and deformed these claims to sublimity linked to "the weather, / The landscape and that," or to commensurable claims of self-immensity, into highly qualified vocabularies of bleak grandeur. As American poets, nevertheless, each came to terms with a seemingly blank and self-enabling bigness of place, if not confronted what A. R. Ammons called the "whit-manic" lure of textual excess and sacralized power, wild immensity, hyperbolic brag, self-deification and so on. This confrontation is enacted in the vastness-haunted lyric of "empty spirit / In vacant space" termed "The American Sublime" by Stevens, not to mention his more ambitious works of synoptic representation like "Notes Toward a Supreme Fiction" or "Auroras of Autumn." Perhaps the "*rhetoric* of exaltation" had to be undone, as Barnett Newman urged American abstractionists in "The Sublime Is Now" (1948), but this placed an even greater burden on the postmodern self to live within a sublimity of utter deprivation, imageless, unstoried, freed from the "impediments of memory, association, nostalgia, legend, myth, or what have you, that have been the devices of Western European Painting." [5]

Facing an untheorized and amorphous canon, the genealogy of American poetry has undergone, and continues to undergo, fluid reconstructions since the 1970s. Positing an "American" difference in stance and style that might be more than just the projection of Cold War exceptionality, literary scholars such as Josephine Miles and Harold Bloom situated this rhetoric of sublimity and norms of poetic excess within Romantic thematics and slowly differentiated the diction of an American great-tradition centered in Emersonian theory and Whitmanic practice. In the 1980s, subsequently, the scenario of the American sublime argued in Bloom, Joseph Kronick, David Porter, Cynthia Griffin Wolff, Joanne Feit Diehl, Mary Arensberg and others, begins with the ecstatic formulations of poetic vocation in Emerson's essays. The scenario then moves on from this "great white father of the American sublime" to generate a hugely incarnational son (Whitman), and a fiercely deconstructive daughter (Dickinson), and to filter this power-influx into increasingly self-defensive voices of "countersublimity." These poets include Stevens, Ammons, John Ashbery, and Elizabeth Bishop, though the list can be rather vacuously multiplied to include a poet of minimalist claims and miniaturist spaces such as Marianne Moore. The thematic of Native American or Afro-American formations is effectively ignored. Technological contexts are elided, and links to collective ideology are, for the most part, held in abeyance. In whatever poet, male or female, hyperbolic or ironic, plain or grand in style, this will to American sublimity is said to be founded in agonisms not so much of nature, social configuration, and technology (as I will claim it is), but of wall-to-wall intertextuality.

Existing discussions of the American sublime devolve from Emerson's self-reliant equation of "two absorbing facts—*I and the Abyss.*" Qualified to some extent by gender considerations, an important subject I will return to, the will to American sublimity is read as the ego-quest to inaugurate origins of sublime power, which is to say to evacuate some self-authenticating ground out of which the wildness/newness of power can emerge. Such a struggle for strong selfhood must take place, as the Emersonian scenario mandates, whether this I-threatening "abyss" is imagined to comprise some ahistorical vacancy or gnostic nothingness; some natural immensity in which the entrepreneurial ego can lose and find itself as in an ocean or prairie; or, nowadays, the vast intertextuality of language which codes any lyric of self-intuition with traces of otherness.

Within this discourse of lyric vocation, the representation of American vastness becomes representative not of the Over-Soul nor of the political contexts underwriting such empowerment, but of the self's ("repressive") claim to American origination: trapped in the ethos of modernity, the language and imagery of the sublime must suppress what the ego cannot long abide. This burden of the past is almost purely one of literary history, however, as if material history—as ground or absent cause—had little bearing on sublime self-imaging; and the return of the repressed is figured as strictly an intertextual issue. The iconography of Cole is displaced within Church, say, or the terms of Emerson in Whitman ironically return

8

"with a certain alienated majesty" as the language of self-dispossession. After Bloom's reading of Emerson's essays, sublime excess comes with the territory; poems of grand solipsism or of Whitmanic scope, ambition—and length—seem like fated natural occurrences.

Fitted into an oedipal framework, the American sublime is situated within a mimetic vastness that is not *geographic* (the will to dominate nature) or *social* (the will to displace Native or contiguous cultures) but *rhetorical* (the will to differentiate rival textuality). Sublimity accrues through the private production of an abyss ("vacant space") or delusion of textual displacement ("empty spirit") out of which selfhood can emerge to inaugurate claims of strong interpretation tied, as if a cultural given, to the project of self-reliance. Powerlessness is not a function of social position but of rhetorical incapacity. Poststructural concerns with textual displacement are reflected but given an oddly Emersonian, that is, self-preserving, twist.[6]

Despite the dehistoricized appeal of this Romantic equation between poetic selfhood and some blissfully American "abyss" on which the ego can rely for transcendental power, however, the construction of an American sublime does not begin nor end with the tropes of Emerson. As a discourse of national empowerment conjoining self to scene and both to moral and cash-value consequences, I will claim that the sublime is rooted in Puritan and Romantic persuasions and politically unconscious ambitions left deconstructed by the nuclear horizon. The discourse of the American sublime depends upon a distinct poetic tradition that predates Emerson, circulates through him to Whitman, and no less tellingly speaks through earlier and minor poets as their suprapersonal design to elevate nature into commodity and grand idea as well as to convert any sense of subjective powerlessness into a shared conviction of "the rapted wit sublime."

My own study of the American sublime seeks to accomplish the following large-scale ends: (1) to provide a definition of the American sublime as a poetic genre that implicates the lyric ego in the production of America as site of the sublime; (2) to track this preoccupation with achieving an American sublime back beyond the euphoric ideas and shapes of Emerson/Whitman to less-

recognized poets of the sublime mode: poets such as Anne Brad-
street, William Livingston, and William Cullen Bryant, whose dis-
course was no less haunted by the grandeur of nature and country
as tropes of sublimity empowering solitary attempts to represent
national "elevation"; (3) to situate modernist versions of the sub-
lime more fully in an emerging context of ideological deconstruc-
tion, what I call in Stevens the will to deidealize or "to decreate"
force in a way that still enables the self to create an American sub-
lime that sustains belief; (4) to embed postmodernist versions of
the sublime within a context of nuclear force that calls into ques-
tion the long-standing American sacralization of force that a poet
like Whitman all too unconsciously embodied; (5) finally, in effect,
to pluralize and to alter the American sublime so that it includes
other poets (such as Bob Perelman or Ai) and more contextually
inclusive ends (such as representing technological domination) than
those ascribed to the Emersonian master-narrative of self-reliance
that presently controls descriptions of this genre.

In the first two chapters, I move between theorizing and exem-
plifying the "minute particulars" of a poetic genre in which "sub-
limity" was contemplated, celebrated, reified, reflected upon, and
represented. In the sublime genre, the American poet not only pro-
duced "America" as a site and trope of sublimity but also, in effect,
created a representative space of discourse wherein the American
subject (whose canonical example remains "Walt Whitman, a kos-
mos, of Manhattan the son") could experience the self as dread-
and-wonder maker of the American sublime. The natural sublime,
I will claim in chapters devoted to readings of Anne Bradstreet's
"Contemplations," William Livingston's *Philosophic Solitude,* and
the vastness-haunted lyrics of William Cullen Bryant, served not
just scriptural pedagogy but increasingly American usages of ideo-
logical empowerment, self-idealization, and the control of nature.
Later, as nationally inflected and deformed, the sublime of nature,
the sublime of democracy, and the sublime of the transcendental
individual were not satisfied, as in Whitman's "Song of Myself,"
until fused into tropes of mass representation. Whitman is not so
much the cause as the effect, or discursive outcome, of this collec-
tive will to the American sublime.

Linking pious raptures of "the rapted wit sublime" to more technologically inspired euphorics and bliss-and-dread imageries pervading poets like Stevens, Crane, Ashbery, Ai, Ron Silliman, Adrienne Rich, and Bob Perelman, the goal of my chapters on the modern, postmodern, and post-ego mappings of the nuclear sublime is to posit and demystify this long-standing "whit-manic" sacralization of force, size, immensity, and speed. I will read this sublimity as a discursive complex that uneasily equates the grandeur of the American landscape (as place and as trope) with the more abstract will to technocratic domination. The poet plays a representative role, as in Stevens's "Nomad Exquisite," at times beholding (letting go of) and, later, subjugating (interiorizing) "the immense dew of Florida." These post-Whitmanic chapters are meant to help articulate, and thereby to altar/alter, this ingrained North American will-to-sublimity in ways that will better fit the emerging, postnational future. The poet is not outside the ideology of American power, but constructing, abiding, and challenging such sublimity from within.

Founded in a mythology of detextualized whiteness, the American sublime comprises, on some primary level, the all-too-poetic wish for a phantasmic blank ground, or *tabula rasa,* out of which a distinctly American poetic voice can begin. This is an incontestable subjective dimension of the Euramerican sublime. Arguably, after Emerson, any abyss does not so much threaten as exalt the American will to power, which is to say, the American will to accrue fresh sublimity. Whether the "dumb blankness" of Ishmael's white whale incarnating a dehumanized abyss, Frost's snowy spaces of solipsistic abolishment, or Stevens's "empty spirit / In vacant space," repression of prior power must give way to this Euramerican self's identification with some prior ground of surplus significance. Nature is never just "nature," but some arena of discursive augmentation. Emptiness (immensity) is troped into fullness (vacancy), silence into speech, absence into presence, circumferential irrelevance into central significance. But I would reiterate, seconding Donald Pease's New Americanist decoding of such Emersonian expansionism in "Sublime Politics," that this project is not just an ego-wish, as is allegorized in the arctic and tropical immensities of Frederic Edwin Church, but the idealized displacement into selfhood of larger, much more national and historically generated forces and preoccupations. The sublime has been conjured to serve different genders and even opposed or self-contradictory political agendas.[7]

But to oedipalize the sublime—as in the dominant mode of Weiskel, Bloom, and Hertz—is to dehistoricize its implied workings; that is, to subject the agents and contexts of the sublime to the eternal return of the same Western plot: Daddy, Mommy, and Me in poetic disguise as "precursor," "Muse," and "strong voice." Even the helpful feminist re-genderings of the sublime now underway would shift the "oedipal scenario" to a "pre-oedipal" one replete with foremothers and a desire to merge with the mother's body rather than to war with forefathers and fear-of-castration aggression.[8]

However deformed by technologies of modernization or undermined by tactics of deconstruction, the sublime comprised a mode of disenchanting and reenchanting the native ground and, thereby, refiguring the will to grandeur of the Euramerican self. The aesthetic of the American sublime helped recuperate, in shifting historical contexts, a New World aura of fresh creation as the power to create distinctively American forms/selves anew. The sublime emerged, historically, to defy the burden of history. Haunted by powerlessness, the American sublime depended upon an immense tautology, creating what it always and already assumed to be there prior to such homemade rhetoric. If prior sublimes get outmoded, and have to be abandoned or outdone, the ground of such self-elective power lingers in the landscape and language, so the sublime assumes, as the archive of grand dreams: not so much "supreme fictions" in which to believe as instruments of American power (sublimity) upon which the self can depend, and which, believing in, it can enact.

This trope of the sublime proved habitually pragmatic: immensity implied an (imagined) vacancy, and emptiness the possibility of strong and various deeds (great poems) to be outdone. Converting fullness into emptiness and vacancy into possibility, the American sublime helped generate its own sublime consequences and works—transport, aggrandizement, achievement on a Euro-competitive scale. Circularity was not so much a logical problem (tautology) or way of over-imagining (hyperbole) to be avoided, but an identity-consolidating tactic to circulate fresh transport, surplus, and self-empowerment—as in the *ur-text* of Longinus or Emerson's portrayal of writing in "Circles." "Transport" moved the scarified self to sites of the sublime as a national possession and affirmed, beyond powerlessness, exalted feelings of self-possession and the seemingly renewable language of the American sublime.

The American sublime is founded, finally, in paradoxes of national faith and the will to technological modernity that my own text will, I trust, not just enact but help make apparent: bypassing historical guilt or overindebtedness with a conviction of performative possibility, the sublime experience of huge natural forces may dwarf and empty the self, but it no less underwrites the ongoing appropriation of nature-writ-large within a giddying sense of self-empowerment that Emerson declared to be enacted as "an instantaneous in-streaming causing power." Empowering egos as heroically diverse as those of Whitman, Church, Melville, Elizabeth Bishop, Lewis Mumford, and John D. Rockefeller, the American sublime sustains multiple uses, from artistic to material, yet the same experience of tremendousness underwrites strange states of self-dispossession and affirms sheer uselessness, awesome moods of ego-dwarfing before Niagara-like powers that are awakened beyond domination or control, beyond language even, as national codes of appropriation are apparently abolished and undone.[9]

Yet on some primary level of selfhood that remains immune to deconstruction, as an operating assumption more of belief than argument, I take the American sublime to be a self-enabling and communally adhesive "supreme fiction." In a pragmatic sense, the claim perdures that an "overbelief" in power and grandeur enables the further production of power and grandeur. The aesthetic belief in the American sublime, as Church or even Whitman flagrantly realized in their careers, is a belief that, habitually maintained as theory, has moral and cash-value consequences both for self and community: Church and Whitman helped create the great sublime that created them as strong artists, a perspective of self-idealization that goes all the way back not just to William James or Emerson but, of course, to the communally demonized rhetoric of Longinus.

One beholds the American sublime, quite circularly then, by beholding "America" as the site and subject of sublime production. Can a cultural community distinguish itself or long survive without positing such a set of self-enabling fictions? How does one stand to

behold the American sublime, except as a function of one's histor-
ical positioning as an American who wills the ongoing grandeur
(and grand poetry) of his people as collective subject? How does
one stand to behold the American sublime, furthermore, without
also representing the material damages and excesses of such confi-
dently American claims to idealize power and to aggrandize the self
as the source of such ends? Admittedly, I can imagine or theorize
no context in which America, as a set of beliefs and interpretive
constraints, can or even should be wholly undone.

What I mean by positing and, later, pluralizing the American
sublime as a poetic genre should become clear from the argument
and examples of this book. What I mean by the term *genealogy* in
my subtitle was succinctly captured by its foremost postmodern
practitioner, Michel Foucault, who contended that evaluative bi-
naries such as pure/impure, high/low, sublime/vulgar, and strong/
weak must be resituated within the history of their culture-specific
formation: "Let us give the term *genealogy* to the union of erudite
knowledge and local memories which allows us to establish a his-
torical knowledge of struggles and to make use of this knowledge
today." [10] By *us* I mean, instrumentally if not prophetically, Ameri-
cans of the *fin de millennium* 1990s, whose future remains open yet
ever at risk, given the earth-shattering sublimity that was so cor-
porately revealed—by us—at the complex of Los Alamos. In the
postnuclear framework that I will elaborate, the American sublime
is deployed not just as a language-game that enables an imaginal
consensus of power/knowledge but as one that threatens those out-
side this spiritually activist construct with the terror and wonder of
technocratic domination. [11]

By genealogy, then, I mean the knowledge and struggle to recre-
ate/decreate (*alter*) the American sublime as a dialogical genre or
language-game not-so-secretly incarnating the will to national
grandeur as (seemingly) a self-relying act of "philosophic solitude."
By providing a genealogy of the American sublime, I would histo-
ricize, in culture-specific terms, the variously voiced lurch-to-
transcendence and influxes of sublimity that are ratified in this
country's poetry as well as in no less self-idealizing discourses
of American empowerment, such as religious tracts, political
speeches, travelogues, and landscape paintings.

The American sublime came early and stayed late in the grander

14

poems and paintings of this superpower climate: but Hiroshima marks one historical turning point, as does Auschwitz, after which the postmodern rapture/rupture of ecstatic forces in the landscape cannot help but disrupt and dismantle the American poet's comfortingly ethereal "transports to summer."

Part 1

The Genre of the American Sublime

ONE

An American Sublime—
"With Venom and Wonder"

"Where do I begin . . . on the heels of Rimbaud moving like a
dancing bullet thru the secret streets of a hot New Jersey night
filled with venom and wonder."
                    —Bob Dylan, liner notes to *Desire* (1976)

THAT THE SPACE-HAUNTED fantasy of the American poet has
been motivated to present some version of sublime rapture, from
our first poet, Bradstreet, to some of our recent best, like Crane,
Stevens, Rexroth, Ai, Jack Spicer, Bishop, and Ashbery, is the bur-
den of this text. Atomized into stylistic peak-moments, the sublime
has been amply theorized by literary critics since Longinus as a
facet of individual authors or single texts; by post-Kantian philos-
ophers as an aesthetic that bears "witness to the fact that there is
indeterminacy" and, as an avant-garde dynamic, cuts across whole
eras and diverse cultures; and by deconstructionists as a quality of
textual opacity "which marginalizes the literary text, takes it out
of what it literally says and gives it another dimension, renders it
more than 'literary.'" [1] But this practice has not been explained ge-
nerically, in terms of historical development, as a discourse charged
with phrases of national ideology. Mapping one continuity of the
sublime in American poetics, this study seeks to provide a more
genealogical analysis of this mushrooming European thematic as it
evinces the staying-power and habitual rhetoric (in the self) of an
overreaching consciousness spread out into local terrains of North
America. As imaginal ideology, the poetry of the American sublime
registers much more than the sublime of poetry.

Sublime landscapes of the American will-to-possess, however

Emersonian such claims of environmental transcendence or historical flight, may tell us little about nature as it is; but they reveal much about nature as men and women conceive it to be in their contextually situated representations of their own power to remake, break, and decreate their American life-world as given.

Americanizing prior mandates to sublimity, poets underwrote their own abandonment, if not the appropriation—in tones of bliss and dread—of the very ground that had inspired their loftiest influxes and flights "by blue Ontario's shore." This idea of the North American landscape as prior *ground* of transport, as place of self-enlargement if not self-abolishment, has haunted the bliss-laden imagination of American poets like an anonymous refrain, like a lyric burden that remains charged, in Bob Dylan's schizoid affirmation of a muggy New Jersey night, "*with venom and wonder.*" [2] Within the genre of the sublime, the poet uses these conflicted charges of bliss and dread to enact a mood of critical venom (critique) yet, finally, of poetic wonder (conversion). [3]

Although the beckoning prairies of Crèvecoeur or the light-drenched mountains of Bierstadt have been shorn of their redemptive aura, or the idea of nature has come to a postnuclear or greenhouse end, the call of sublime conversion for "the American, this new man" remains no less compelling than theoretical claims to stand outside ("transcend") this bliss-driven nexus of space, speed, delirious pluralism, and speculative excess. Though it by no means begins with Emerson's proclamations of possessive influx nor ends with Hart Crane's tormented affirmation of "deep wonderment, our native clay," the American sublime turns upon an *identification* with vast space and power, however imaginary this sense.

Whatever version of the American sublime poets may now propitiate, however, this mood of national exaltation is apt to be situated not so much in grace-drenched mountains nor in "the perpetual presence" of Emerson's self-exhilarating stars, but within ordinary contexts and the banality of the everyday. Even a nuclear explosion in the desert wilds of Nevada, rupturing nature and history from organic fixity and the self from interconnection, need not disturb ordinary American rounds of peace and power, dispersed and humbled into everyday ideology.

The scene of such sublimity can be a homey one: consider the TV-unified family of Paul Verhoeven's *Robocop* (1987), sitting

around the table discussing foreign policy and MX missiles, playing
NUKEUM, a game that pits family members against one another
in nuclear brinkmanship; the work ends with the luridly simulated
apocalypse of the earth exploding while OCP (Omni Consumer
Products) regenerates crime-and-waste-gutted Detroit with a post-
human hero of technological sublimity, Robocop. Punishment by
toxic-waste drenching seems a sensible act—an extreme, postmod-
ern instance of the national mood, perhaps.

But we might here invoke a quieter poem like James Haug's
"Cloud Rises Seven Miles from Observers," as a no less terror-
confronting instance of the American sublime deployed in an era
of nuclear rapture: the bliss-and-dread emanating not so much
from desert emptiness as from the same New World project of
technocratic domination from which the most ordinary labor (even
that of the poet as "distant relay") is hardly immune:

> Think of the awful dark the sky gets
> before the dawn in 1953
> over Yucca Flats, Nevada.
> The television camera is secured
> on the top of a utility truck
> and a sound man tilts his head
> toward the static of a distant relay
> inside the cups of his headset.
> All of us are waiting
> for something big to go off,
> a second dawn to bolt
> straight up and redefine the horizon, bend
> orbits, recast the universe
> to the size of a dollhouse,
> where we may examine corner to corner
> the stress points, the extent of damage
> we can sustain
> before it falls down, a future
> neat and angular, lit by a single bulb.[4]

Haunted by nature's immensity as much as by a lurking sense of
nihilism disguised as its Cold War opposite—faith in the ideology
of sublime power—the "single bulb" of nuclear power promises
not only domination of the desert and globe, earth's technocratic

measurement and control, but also that national regeneration as a "second dawn" will emerge to blast the "awful dark" of the globe into a dollhouse and history into a scientific project in stress control. The power of nature is not so much miniaturized as sublated, blasted open, wired into, and atomically outdone. Haug's tone is cool and exacting, resisting collective rapture, or trying to, as in an enclave of disenchanted language, shorn of inflated metaphors. His thoughts cannot afford to be hymns of the praise of things American, as were Whitman's; bigger may not be better, and pastoral flights offer little cure.

Haug's next stanza shifts from this extraordinary event, however banalized, to focus upon ordinary rounds of daily life, wherein the sun's returning and everyday motions seem curiously extraordinary, still empowered by a cash-value faith in the whole American project to regenerate the vacant land through feats of (spiritualized) violence:

> And over the next guy's shoulder you see
> we're not that far, as if the ferry
> will soon return to bear us
> across the river, the bank first dim
> and then bright enough
> to pierce the thin door of an eyelid.
> And there is no way to explain this morning,
> a man thinks as he drives on to work:
> how a perfect sun rose black in his eye,
> how across the desert
> a family sat down early to breakfast
> as the windows shook above the sink,
> and they lost no faith in the world turning,
> with school lunches bagged and ready
> and daylight coming for the kids.

As Haug's poem instances, the vocabulary of the postmodern sublime has quietly shifted from the "awful dark" sky to our own no less awful technologies, and yet the ego-dwarfing effect can (must) still be recoded with dread-and-wonder and emplotted into daily rounds of cash-value faith. The end of ideology emanates from within dynamics of the sublime, "and daylight coming for the kids."

Confronting the lure of American bigness, space, speed, and bulk—the virtual cultural obsession with unlocking, painting, or portraying *power* (sublimity), from Niagara Falls or Los Alamos to Mars—the mind of the poet balks, draws back, yet eventually believes. Is sublimity somehow built into the desert landscape as an idea of place? Where does this American fascination with dynamic sublimity come from, and when will it end?

Since the indigenous reimagining of place that was William Carlos William's *Spring and All* (1923) and *In the American Grain* (1925), or Stevens's more abstracted domineering of "the slovenly wilderness" of Tennessee in *Harmonium* (1923), the positing of an *"American type of sublimity"*—distinct from European sources ("on the heels of Rimbaud") yet tapping into numinous traditions wafting up from provincial grounds ("of a hot New Jersey night filled with venom and wonder")—has become a commonplace about the stylistic aspirations of post-Whitmanic poetry.

This denomination of an *American* sublime, by poet and critic alike, has slowly registered a familiar story: an anecdote bespeaking the lyric will to domination. Following upon the Emersonian claims of Harold Bloom to privatize power (sublimity) as a trope of entrepreneurial selfhood, this scenario of European repression entails that—early or late—each poet must vindicate his or her selfhood with claims to "demonization" through dialogue with indigenous forces that would belittle claims that were less than High Romantic. Whatever the lure of near beauty, the sublime is an occupational hazard. As Geoffrey H. Hartman worries this Adamic scenario in "Purification and Danger," "we have not gotten tired of hearing about the American Sublime; its capaciousness, spaciousness, greatness, newness; its readiness to take on experience and remain sublime." [5]

If poems such as Wallace Stevens's "American Sublime" (1935), Hart Crane's *The Bridge* (1935), Kenneth Rexroth's "Climbing Milestone Mountain, August 22, 1937," Elizabeth Bishop's "At the Fishhouses" (1955), Jack Spicer's *Language* (1964), Robert Pinsky's *An Explanation of America* (1979); or, less obviously, John Ashbery's "Pyrography" (1976), Adrienne Rich's "North America Time" (1983), or Ai's "The Testimony of J. Robert Oppenheimer" (1986) gave the dynamics of Western vastness a local habitation and name, American critics such as Hartman, Bloom, Josephine Miles, Thomas Weiskel, Donald Pease, Mary Arensberg, Daniel O'Hara, Joanne Feit Diehl et al. have ascribed to the sublime the components of a genre that comes down from the past as stylistic imperative, semiotic condition, and psychic mandate impinging upon any made-in-America poet worthy to lyricize his or her superpower and clime.[6]

Yet if "a humanistic sublime is an oxymoron," in that, as Thomas Weiskel's analytic mapped, *any* sublime (from Longinus to Kant, or Wordsworth to Stevens) must posit some transpersonal threshold of "heights" and "depths" beyond ordinary selfhood for such claims of transcendence to be credible as more than semiotic substitution or oceanic ego-delusion, then the *American* appropriation (or *Americanization*) of this sublime functions as an unconscious oxymoron and enacts a highly politicized trope. The transcendent emerges yet surges, by such a communal construct, into the transpolitical. Such a poetic, however Emersonian or oedipal, demands less piety or defensiveness and more interrogation as a sign of American ideology.[7]

This *"American* sublime" stipulates that what, ideally speaking, has no local habitation or proper name at all—what Longinus propagated through the height-metaphor of *hypsos* as the mind's "irresistible desire for anything which is great and, in relation to ourselves, supernatural" (35.2), or Walter Jackson Bate just as ahistorically termed the "creative and formative essentialism" of art's sublime-beyond-reach—is, by such a prior semantic turn, installed into a *national* landscape and world-competitive name. That which "knows no limits or borders" and is, in a philosophical sense, "something of a monster or, rather, a ghost" has been given an all-too-specific location and name: the American sublime comes down to positing America as ground of the sublime.[8]

The effect of this self-aggrandizing trope in the United States remains one of ideological substitution or displacement, I think, which has been partly accounted for by Weiskel's semiotic of "the Romantic sublime": "Anyone who reads into the tradition of speculation about the sublime knows in what a variety of ideologies the sublime moment finds a central place. What happens to you standing at the edge of the infinite spaces can be made, theoretically, to 'mean' just about anything. Such agreement as in fact occurs in the tradition is a precise function of a correlative ideological unanimity" (28). The American will to national power, displaced onto a landscape or technoscape of wish-fulfilling identifications—"it [the seemingly innocuous poem or art-object] took dominion everywhere"—can be made to serve "the poet's sublime" (Stevens) or "the reader's sublime" (Bloom) as these discourses of identification mingle, finally, into an *American* sublime bespeaking less the quest for selfhood and more the country's will to grandeur if not to material supremacy.

As the center of this nationalized sublime, the self of the poet becomes the site of a representative energy transformation, turning American landscape into American language; turning commodity into another sign ("symbol") of the will's power; or reconverting sign back into commodity ("wealth"), as in Emerson's sermons on American self-belief in "Nature" (1836) or "The Poet" (1844): "The breadth of the problem is great, for the poet is representative. He stands among partial men for the complete man, and apprises us not of his wealth [private capital/symbolic capital], but of the commonwealth [national sublimity/an American sublimity]" and so on. Lecturing on the conduct of American life in 1851, upon returning from a musty and smoke-filled England, Emerson was amazed yet appalled by the energy of national events, the capital-driven inventiveness and raw lack of scale: "In America the geography is sublime, but the men are not," he urged, repeating the contemptuous lesson of his own little poem, "Monadnock." [9]

Emerson's solution to this disparity between immense nature and petty humanity was simple: to will the sublimity of the self as recuperative force, as speculative faith, trumping Old World determinations of Fate or Nature with New World affirmations of power, excess, newness, wildness, that sublime "influx" whereby nature was fast transfigured into the makings of self-possibility and the market into merely another transcendental home of the Over-Soul.

This is an old story. Yet the raw power of the American sublime was manifest for Emerson, not so much as poetry or as monument, but as invention and event: the California gold rush, the opening of Texas and Oregon, the joining of vast oceans, the railroads and highways challenging this prior immensity of land, even "the involuntary blessing wrought on nations by selfish capitalists" could not be gainsaid within a merely moral calculus. The glut and glamour of American invention was not to be denied, as Whitman would vulgarly incarnate as "body electric."

Emerson urged in the giddying maxims of "Circles" (1840) that the past must be swallowed, and cultural memory disburdened of its "once hoarded knowledge, as vacant and vain": infinitudes of nature and art are reduced by Wallace Steven's enactment of the American will in "The American Sublime" (1935) to "empty spirit / In vacant space." It is only appropriate, indeed foundational, for any scenario of sublime self-empowerment to forget American history, bypass any mediations of society, and reduce prior poetry to so much Eurocentric moonmash on the dump.

The American sublime has a prior and much more deeply embedded history, however, one that makes this Emersonian transfiguration of America's technocratic activism in "Circles" no less spooky or ideologically enchanting, especially in the postnuclear era:

> New arts destroy the old. See the investment of capital in aqueducts, made useless by hydraulics; fortifications, by gunpowder; roads and canals, by railways; sails, by steam; steam by electricity.

It is as if our homespun sage of Sublime Influx were here ratifying any politically promiscuous conclusion, "electricity by nuclear power," "poetry by video," "nuclear power by Star Wars," and so on.

Thinking through some of the categorical impertinence that still clusters around this overbelieving "ideologeme" of the sublime, my definition of "the American sublime" seeks—through attending to and quarreling with such historical passages of the sublime and theories of literary strength that emerge to explain them—to track the genealogy of this "correlative ideological unanimity" by which the sublime moment came to be read as a distinctly "American" projection. Registered as a conversion scenario of self-empowerment, the moment of the American sublime will be read not so much as a sign of personal fulfillment (or abyss of "textual sublimity") but as a sign of national grandeur and collective empowerment, as when Brigadier General Thomas Farrell at Los Alamos—invoking sublime poets and an unspeakable vision of the Christian godhead—reads the first atomic bomb as a disclosure of America's moral grandeur and scientific capacity to reign as superpower on earth.[10]

Supplementing Bloom's ego-centered model of the sublime as a struggle between will-to-power (typically male) subjects for agonistic priority (or, in Pierre Bourdieu's impious terms, for greater "symbolic capital"), and assuming that Josephine Miles's stylistics of sublime diction perdure in the American literary unconscious, as well as taking into consideration the largely oedipal master-narrative of Mary Arensberg's helpful collection (1986), we still need to articulate the "Americanness" of this American sublime. We still need to situate this poetic sublime in the "minute particulars" of its idiom and practice.[11]

This demand for a more broadly historical description remains because, as Jerome C. Christensen contends in a fine critique of Weiskel's *Romantic Sublime,* "a semiotic model of exchange cannot explain readers' and poets' ideological investment in particular forms of sublimation; it cannot predict either the 'god-terms' which will be substituted for indeterminacy nor the channel in which the metonymic expansion [of sublime discourse] flows."[12] The language-genre of the sublime must be regrounded in history where it was formed, and not just left within the claustral purities of poetic diction. We still need to articulate not only *how the sublime works,* but also, as Christensen suggests, *what it is for* in more than a subjectivist sense of the quest to accrue originality, identity, or greatness.

I approach the sublime, then, as a poetic genre disseminated in America from Bradstreet's Puritan times through Whitman and Stevens, and on into more "hysterical" refigurations in postmodernism, which functions less as a private trope and more as a social site wherein poets render the "totality" of the American landscape/environment representable—or at least symbolically less opaque—to a collectivity which is working to engender a response of democratic autonomy in its more-or-less blissfully interpellated ("self-reliant") subjects.

Inner and outer forces conspire, as willing selfhood in Whitman's lyric of American sublimity, for example, into a song of atomic bliss not so much immune to as incarnating depths of this New World ideology of capitalist expansion: "I celebrate myself, /

And what I assume you shall assume / For every atom belonging to me as good belongs to you." Embracing and ratifying his culture's technological activism and entrepreneurial vigor, Whitman supplanted fits of anxiety or self-emptiness with a grand "language experiment" in democratized sublimity, *Leaves of Grass*: "His thoughts are the hymns of the praise of things." Stevens can be no William Cullen Bryant of homiletic woods and skies, of course, affirming vastness-skimming egos as in "To A Waterfowl" (1815). The trope of the natural sublime became harder to assume as discursive certainty, influx of "perpetual presence," or self-corresponding metaphor to glorify an Ideal Deity shedding grace—and colonial empowerment—upon the land.

As a diachronic construct persistent in American culture from 1650 to the postnuclear present, the sublime remains one language-genre which can give us access to representational versions of the American project to "behold"/"subjugate" nature, those ambivalent verbs from Stevens which I will use to suggest the passive and active extremes of a textual enterprise which transformed the archival imagery of the sublime object and seductive bulk of space "into a 'libidinal apparatus,' a machinery for ideological investment." [13]

The sublime remains one of those literary genres which, persisting in usage over time as an imaginal construct—as New World dialogue between "Americas" past and future—permits a purchase on both diachronic/synchronic dimensions of collective history. A literary genre does this (implicitly) by foregrounding the concrete mediations between the individual literary text and the social subtext the poem assumes—and transforms—as a precondition of its own existence. As Fredric Jameson argues in a critique of romance as a narrative genre sedimented with ideological/Utopian class aspirations and social resentments which are more than personal choice, "The strategic value of generic concepts for [post-] Marxism clearly lies in the mediatory function of the notion of genre, which allows the coordination of immanent formal analysis of the individual text with the twin diachronic perspective of the history of forms and the evolution of social life" (105).

A "genealogy" of the genre, furthermore, must relate such formal/close analysis of individual poems not only to tropes and conventions of the sublime genre but also to evolving forms of social power and "voice" which they symbolically refigure into "poems of our climate." I want to track the Puritan and Romantic origins of this power (sublimity) into its dictional lairs, so to speak, the better to decreate/recreate this power-quest into an altered sublime befitting the post–Cold War future if not the ethnically plural present. Power is not just a function of the lyric ego willing and commanding private possession.

Whitman proclaimed in the 1855 preface to *Leaves of Grass* that the American poet's "spirit responds to his country's spirit . . . [and] incarnates its geography and natural life and rivers and lakes." This provincial American landscape became ideologically reinvested by such poetry into a cultural imperative or power-sign. The landscape of national sublimity functioned as a shared discourse urging poets to achieve a grandiloquence which, after the Americana-omniverous "Song of Myself," compelled subsequent poets to later, longer, stranger, blissed-out registers of an incarnational sublime.[14]

The ideology of the sublime form, with its premonitions/admonitions reducing the self to (seeming) insignificance before natural or technological spectacles of American power, persists as a speech-genre, then, wherein the poet can appropriate shifting historical content. The genre of the American sublime functions as a site expressive not so much of originality (selfhood) but of intertextual materiality (history). Sublimity registers these American values which are more than a diction of individual choice or syntax of solipsism. Even Poe's purist sublime, like Whitman's heteroglossic outreach, is formulated to counter the ideological, middle-class aspirations which came to be registered in the sublime vocabularies of Emerson and Whitman: the latter not so much a lyric isolato (like Poe's "Usher") but a Homeric incarnation of preexisting codes that would express an "American" or "western" brand of the sublime.

If "The American Sublime" came to be reduced by Stevens to a rhetoric of "empty spirit / In vacant space" in the canonical poem of that title, producing an *imagined* vacancy like that of Bryant's western plains or some Indianless "desert" akin to Thomas Hooker's Hartford, can the modernist poet surrender tropes of transcendent selfhood to decreation and still write? "What wine does one drink? / What bread does one eat?" in an age of mockery, conformity, plainness, diminishment—an age in which grandeur has become embarrassing on a personal or, worse yet, an imperial scale? Chastened of illusions of transcendence, should the poet empty the sublime of its self-infinitizing claims, the supreme fiction that "man can, in feeling and in speech, transcend the human"?[15]

Have we reached a terminal state of irony in which no General Jackson can gesture sweepingly against the sky, no Whitman appears to engorge the technologized landscape like a "ten-foot poet among inchlings," no Frederic Edwin Church emerges to paint the immensity of "the landscape and that" on a panoramic scale? History muted into the elegiac vacancy of Elizabeth Park, does the sublime, as a landscape of American self-empowerment, really vanish with the gods and with the Whitmans?

Stevens refused to settle for any such minimalist reductions of self and style. He claimed in "Notes Towards a Supreme Fiction" that "there is a month, a year, there is a time / In which majesty is a mirror of the self." By imperatives of the sublime genre, that is, American space demands that there *must* be a time when another "majesty"—or some synonym for transcendent power in self and country—regenerates history and serves as the proper trope of the subject: a time in which the sublime comes down to reside in the expansive self and so, by maneuvers of correspondence and projection, in the national landscape itself.

If a *literary ideology* represents—if not helps to enact—"modes of feeling, valuing, perceiving and believing which have some kind of relation to the maintenance and reproduction of social power," then an ideologically overinvested genre such as the American sublime can be seen to articulate power structures and power relations of the colonial subject within American society as it breaks away from British possession, circa 1760–1860.[16] In one context, as I will claim, this will to the *American* sublime becomes a way of doing battle in the nineteenth century with the hegemonic British tradition. The quest for sublimity registers an attempt to wrest a cultural and social priority corresponding to the transformations of the American Revolution, decades after the sublime had seemed an Augustan curiosity or Victorian joke in the land of Burke, Arnold, and Milton.

The discourse of the sublime helped to underwrite a vision of lyric self-determination propagated on idealist grounds. Even

Emerson's self-reliant will to the sublime is more than just personal mandate to analytical greatness or peculiarity; his quest, in essay and lyric, for strong energy informs a more broadly cultural preoccupation with "power," which he represents to himself as self-made property from the terrible "influx" of metaphoric newness into the Over-Soul. Enjoined into libertarian selfhood, the poet obtains further linguistic capital ("symbols") by refiguring the landscape from real estate into the site of the poet's imaginative unity and motility.

As idealizing agents of "disalienation," poets of the American sublime perform a kind of ideological labor within the colloquy and symbol-making of American culture. They do this by representing imaginary relationships to their environment as refigurations of the historical "real." That this real was coded in Emerson's and Whitman's era with shapes and mandates conducive to a cultural sublime is quite apparent in painters of national empire like Cole or Church, and later manifest as well in the "hyperspace" of New York City skyscrapers which panicked Henry James in *The American Scene*.

This idealist life of the American mind must endure historical deformations into Hiroshima and beyond, surely, yet Perry Miller's late formulation (1965) of the Romantic quest for an American brand of sublimity, as formulated during Emerson's "take-off" era of industrialist development, reeks too much of transcendental idealism to be of much help as cultural description. Miller, like Melville or Mailer, is as much symptom as sign of this all-engulfing sublimity:

> Hence America, led by science out of Colonial isolation into National magnificence, has discovered, more than anybody else, the TRUE SUBLIME behind the obvious SUBLIME of the immense pageant of Technology. This is MIND itself.[17]

Miller's hypothesis of a "general [American] conviction that ultimate Sublimity in the creation is human Mind (especially when dependent entirely on sense impression), because it can demonstrably cope with the infinite expanse of Nature, can keep pace with further discoveries, can follow the dynamic flow" (321) reads less like a post-Kantian description of the sublime—which, of course, it is—and more like some deep credo of faith in the mentalistic

31

origins of American technology as a benign force.[18] The sublime here encodes an idealized consensus serving power.

Miller's Americanist positing of a scientific/legal "community of sublimity" (271), grounded in native idealism and Puritan piety, no longer suffices as description; it inhabits the very idealizing power-quest it should seek to distance. Instead, the American Scholar begins to participate in the rhetoric of cultural empowerment, enacting an American troping of the will to spiritualize technology and to dominate the Massachusetts wilderness.

Arguing for the emergence of an American sublime in landscape painting from Thomas Cole (centrally in 1825–1829) through Church and the Luminists, Bryan Jay Wolf shows the persistence of sublime conventions in later, self-conscious variations of the genre: "For luminism is another form of the American sublime—not the sublime of Burke or even Cole, but the sublime of a generation uneasy with the grandiloquence of past painters and in search of a counter-rhetoric at once simple in its gestures and yet arresting in its power." [19] Wolf's "textualizing" approach, as his literary metaphors and mirror-stage scenario taken from Lacan's Imaginary Order suggest, argue the prior and *literary* (sign-based) nature of the sublime genre. Liberating forbidden or even illicit forces ruled out by painterly empiricisms, the sublime is posited as that "moment of psychological reversal when an oppressive burden is lifted and the soul receives an influx of power, which it experiences in an ecstasy of liberation and release" (177).

When Wolf concludes that "the mantle of the sublime will pass as destiny and doom to other painters, most notably Church and the luminists" (247), we may not be able to substitute literary names like Rexroth, Crane, Stevens, or Ai for such a rhetoric-based paradigm of "destiny and doom" to work for American poets. But the persistence of this sublime genre—in painterly and in literary manifestations—through some 150 years surely argues the persistence of a cultural form, or genre, that serves transpersonal ("ideological") aspirations and calls out for a language of "counter-love, original response." [20]

In final chapters on the "postmodern" and "nuclear sublime," I invoke writers as diverse as John Ashbery, Ai, Jack Spicer, and Norman Mailer in *Of a Fire on the Moon* to claim that the "natural sublime," as a dialogue between man and God within the discourse of the will-to-power over the manifest landscape, has been superseded in American poetics by an implied dialogue between man and various technologies. Such sublimity takes place within the bliss-and-dread discourse of submission to a naturalized system—Capital—which has become the "always-already-given" of global vastness that the ego must now contend with through gestures of alienation, transcendence, nature retreat, hypertextual decreation, flights into Vermont silence—that whole romantic vocabulary of self-representation and implied critique which is still at work, at times hysterically, in newer versions of the sublime.

Poets of the Deep Image School, for example, with their mystique of "the poetic image" from wry depths of the unconscious and a seemingly antihistorical attraction to animal or mineral states of being, can be seen to offer a nostalgic, neoprimitivist retreat from a tech-glutted postmodern environment into some subjective sanctuary of image worship and romantic discourse. Such poetry leaves the reified social totality recalcitrantly in place. Robert Bly's politicized poetics would conjure images from the associative depths of Minnesota farmlands as if a priori indictments of the desacralized environment of the Pentagon and the shopping mall. Yet as language-poet Ron Silliman laments of such poetically hysterical tactics in *Lit* (1987), "The militant syntax of the surrealists has begun to froth." [21] Even pastoral poets are getting attacks of nervous paralysis.

By regrounding poetic forms in the dynamics and stylistics of history where they were forged, we can better see that American poets (and painters) reproduce the concept of the sublime as a way of representing the "real life-process" and "the unceasing sensuous labor and creation" through which countless anonymous Americans have produced a relationship of material mastery over their New World surroundings. If the sublime remains a phrase of American ideology in "the poems of our climate," this is because, as Marx must remind us in our highly Emersonian occupation, even poetic diction is not just subjective prattle or flight but the ideational refraction of some prior historical ground: "The phantoms formed in the human brain are also, necessarily, sublimates of their material life-process, which is empirically verifiable and bound to material premises." [22]

The American sublime is one such "sublimate" of historical matter. The American sublime functions as a trope of empowerment emanating, in part, from a will to reimagine the American ground. This takes place within the idealizing ("supernal") language of poetry which, however privatized and inward, remains the real language of "practical consciousness that exists also for other men" in their colloquy with nature, God, and themselves. Speaking in another context of the furious modernity transforming Emerson's America, Marx observed that the "feverishly youthful pace of material production" in the States was creating uncanny conditions in which there was "neither time nor opportunity . . . to abolish the old spirit world." Gothic demons, material fetishes, uncanny tropes, and Romantic sublimities would linger on in the collective psyche and its reified by-products (commodities) in the nineteenth-century urban landscape and arcade. Such sublimity lingered on no less in the pneumatic sedimentations of literary forms wherein the repressed abides (and returns) as "heightened" discourse.

As poets, we invest the sublime object with the "aura" of our own greatness, which comes back to the subject as if involuntarily, mysteriously, through some cosmic agency (or "Over-Soul") working beyond the disunited ego. As in Baudelaire, if not in the polymorphic eros of Walt Whitman, the cost of any postmodern sublime must be both pleasure and pain; the ambivalent "shock" of a (materialist) illumination from the vast environment to the interiorized subject who walks inside the city as in his "body-electric" skin: "He [Baudelaire] indicated the price for which the sensation of the modern age may be had: the disintegration of the aura in the experience of shock."[23] Yet, for American poets called upon to replicate commonsense ideologies of bliss, this shock was recoded into another occasion of democratic self-authentication, as (massively) in "Song of Myself."

Even in the conventionalist terms of Jonathan Culler, readers are now urged to theorize beyond the sublime of single texts or Longinian scraps to inhabit the "intertextual space" and "semiotic codes" which inform the presuppositions of literary genres: "To engage in the study of literature is not to produce yet another interpretation of *King Lear* but to advance one's understanding of the conventions and operations of an institution, a mode of [social] discourse."[24] The sublime registers just such a transpersonal discourse, I think, functioning as a generic space of social embodiment and carrying "norms and expectations which help the reader to assign functions to various elements in the work."

Decoding the sublime, Culler stigmatizes Bloom's over-psychologizing of the sublime into a warfare between ego-subjects: "Bloom transforms intertextuality from an endless series of anonymous codes and citations to an oedipal confrontation, one of whose effects is to preserve the integrity of his poets as agents of the poetic process" (111). In this misreading of poetry as eternal *agon* of Emersonian fathers and sons, the literary text is granted discursive and historical immunity from tonal mediations and social determinations apart from those of poetic diction, as if poetry perpetuated its own lofty monologue through the labor of a few heroic egos. Even using the ego-model of oedipal selfhood that obtains in Bloom, to this "imaginary couple" of the sublime poet mirroring selfhood through his image of an idealized precursor must be added the monstrous *third* of social reality, which mediates imaginary *duality* into mimetic *triangularity*. As one critic objects to this male-centered model of greatness, "If the face-off between two opponents or polar opposites always backfires and misfires, it can only be because 2 [to invoke some overused American examples, Emerson/Whitman, Whitman/Crane, or Stevens/Ashbery] is an extremely 'odd' number. On the one hand, as a specular illusion of symmetry or metaphor, it can be either narcissistically reassuring (the image of the other as a reinforcement of my identity) or absolutely devastating (the other whose existence can totally cancel me out)." [25]

Applying the post-structuralist model of selfhood in Louis Althusser, sublime poets can be seen not just to *reproduce* but, at times and with conceptual struggle, to *distance* the reign of idealist "ideology" in their *materia poetica*. They are able, that is, to produce *"a 'Representation' of the Imaginary Relationship of Individuals to their Real Conditions of Existence."* [26] As *"illusion/allusion,"* such representational structures of the sublime allow individual American subjects (poets) to imagine, by means of such constructs, a more liveable relationship to self-dwarfing realities such as Niagara Falls, the Grand Canyon, the Mojave Desert, the euphoric prairies of Bryant (nature as historically coded with self-liberating attributes of "the sublime"); or, in later versions, the enchantments of the Brooklyn Bridge, the Empire State Building, or

Los Alamos (technology recoded to represent later "sublime" manifestations of American dominance over space).

In a negative sense, ideology comprises the collective fictions and poetic enchantments which a culture tells itself as a way of sustaining its own interests and power over others, within history. Yet, in a more positive sense, by alluding to the ideological construction of the sublime object, poems such as "Anecdote of the Jar" or "To Brooklyn Bridge" can make us see (*"nous donner à voir"*), by an act of *"internal distantiation,"* the very climate of ideology from which they emerge; symbolically enacting "in some sense *from the inside,* by an *internal distance,* the very ideology in which they are held." As a dialogue on the shifting terms of sublimity, the American poem represents not only fictional structurations that circulate through unspoken ideology (what Bakhtin calls "behavioral ideology") of social relations, but also structures of God/Capital which get daily inscribed as free speech in the democratic subject—"by traces and effects, negatively, by indices of absence, *in intaglio (en creux)."* [27]

If ideology in (literary) action is what a group takes to be freely and willingly natural if not self-evident, "both the condition and the effect of the constitution of the subject (of ideology) as freely willing and consciously choosing in a world that is seen as background," [28] then the American sublime developed—as liberal poetics—into just such a "natural" convention of the romantic soul: the self crossing vast and beckoning spaces, alone with his or her great American enterprise before God and nature. This lyric "I" helps to impart the cash-value trope of autonomy and self-determination in the American subject and hence aids in propagating an *imaginary* relation to power before configurations of the material sublime.

American modernity, which would recognize no traces of "ideology" as operative in determining spiritual or cultural formations such as poetry, allows this sweeping assumption of identity between subject and nation to be so, implying as it does the lack of critical distance between high-literary formations and social formations. The sublime is a representative American trope. As Sacvan Bercovitch puts the case for theorizing such "American" cultural formations—or "American" notions of exceptional selfhood:

> America, as it was thus conceived before and after the Revolution, from the *Magnalia Christi Americana,* through *The Rising Glory of America* and "The American Scholar" to *The American Dream*—America, in all these various forms and contexts from Mather to Mailer is quintessentially an ideological term.[29]

Literature measures the grip of liberal ideology upon such poetic constructions. "America" becomes the pragmatic rhetoric in which its citizens have come to believe and, believing, enact into fulfillment: the "sublime" of this America remains one of literary ideology's unconscious tenets.

The American landscape, as site of collective sublimity, has transported poets from Bradstreet to Bryant and beyond into whitmanic tropes of expanded power and higher energy. This continental sublimity, signifying at some semiotic bottom line the project of American expansion (will) taking "dominion everywhere" from Florida to India, has helped to entrench the tropes of a liberal nation legitimating its own innermost terms. Is it surprising, then, that major American poets of the sublime, with Whitman as canonical example, write *within* phrases of American ideology, as if providing a poetic "mythology" (Stevens) of the whole American enterprise? Even the "decreative" tactics of a more severe modernist like Stevens cannot wholly undo or "distantiate" the idealism of this American will-to-sublimity, taking "dominion everywhere."

As a place/sign of numinous power converted into self-empowerment, the vastness of the American landscape—for European immigrants like Anne Bradstreet and urban ethnics like Walt Whitman; for insurance lawyers like Wallace Stevens and brigadier generals like Thomas Farrell of the Los Alamos project; for language-shapers like Ron Silliman and latter-day visionaries like Ai or Bob Dylan; for compassionate explainers like Robert Pinsky or aesthetic sign-drifters like John Ashbery—has been, in effect, variously recharged "with venom and wonder" by the poet: "America" not just as material presence (place of catastrophic grandeur) but as cash-value idea (sign of expanded power).

The "self" of this lyric poet may not equal "America," as Whitman lyrically reimagined in 1855 Brooklyn; but this self, variously inflected, has played some imaginal part in inventing America as an idea of place and a place of expanded power: as the locus of a self-empowering sublimity enjoining others to reinvention, expansion, risk, excess, endless mobility, "language experiments" of the Puritan-coded soul. The vanguard function of the poet as register of this sublime mood (transport), ratifying vast space (immensity) and projects of imaginative excess, is merely indicative of the collective will; a symptom of large-scale trends by Euramericans to interiorize and, hence, to valorize this place of vast power by repeated acts of imaginative possession.

Alexis de Tocqueville long ago observed that collective ideology is much more operative than critical philosophy (what we would call *theory*) in the shaping and interiorizing of American values: "I think that in no country in the civilized world is less attention paid to philosophy than in the United States. . . . Yet it is easy to perceive that almost all the inhabitants of the United States conduct their understanding in the same manner, and govern it by the same rules; that is to say, without ever having taken the trouble to define the rules, they have a philosophical method common to the whole people." [30] This "philosophical method common to the whole people," which came to fruition in the discourse of transcendental idealism (Emerson) and the cash-value pragmatism of William James, assumed as one of its phrases what we can only now distance, within the altered terrain of postmodernism, as an "ideology of the sublime." A poetics of an Americanized sublime emerged to articulate so many "ideologies of bliss" which assumed and depended upon, in romantic dissemination, what Weiskel called "the grand confidence of a heady imperialism, now superannuated as ethic or state of mind—a kind of spiritual capitalism, enjoining a pursuit of the infinitude of the private self." [31]

Writing in the aura of nuclearized sublimity and of nature-decentering conquests of outer space, Weiskel theorized this "romantic sublime" as a semiotic of British Empire which had played out its heady, prestructuralist day: "It is against this sense of an increasingly constricted and structured world," he wrote, "that the ideology of the sublime looms up retrospectively, as a moribund aesthetic." Yet as critics of postmodern society have been increasingly pointing out in the United States (and, even more so, within the *ideologiekritiks* of Europe), the sublime is not so much "moribund" as it is blissfully/anxiously latent and reborn in the panic-stricken and commodity-glutted aesthetics of postmodernism. This is notably the case, for example, in the post-Kantian dynamic of sublimity that Jean-François Lyotard foregrounds as a formal/ethical mandate linking Romanticism to avant-garde experiment: "to represent the unrepresentable" of the sublime as the agonistic and self-dwarfing language-game of "the postmodern condition."[32]

Lamenting the small-themedness and retreats into domesticated solipsism that now humble American poetry into beauty or irony, Terrence Des Pres has claimed that this inability to evoke sublimity is partly a response to nuclearized forces that beget new terrors defying representation, as well as a political credulity that passes over into ego-indifference or despair. At the end of "Self/Landscape/Grid," Des Pres finely (and in a Longinian mode) invokes the *great poems* of Whitman and Wordsworth as a power with which to face and contain forces of ego-negation:

> The human spirit draws its strength from adversity, and so do poems. Examples like *The Prelude* or *Song of Myself* incorporate and thereby transcend that which, if they ignored it, would surely cancel their capacity for final affirmation. And having mentioned poems of this caliber, I might also add that the "American sublime," as critics call it, has been missing in our poetry at least since late Stevens.[33]

Though I will return to quarrel with Des Pres's Bloom-like and inadequately theorized claim that this "American sublime" has exhausted its very power of imaginative resistance in "late Stevens," and I will flesh out exactly how this nuclear anxiety threatens the "supreme fiction[s]" of American poetry with evacuation, I can only second his eloquent call for a national poetry essaying the sublime. Des Pres argues for a poetry of the sublime whose terror emerges from engaging with nuclear "terror[s] beheld and resisted": "The sublime, as observers like Burke and Kant and Schopenhauer insist, arises from terror, terror beheld and resisted, the terror of revolution for Wordsworth, of the abyss for Whitman, of nuclear annihilation for any poet today who would make a language to match our extremity."

If categories of *the sublime* as "a language to match our extremity" perdure and coalesce beyond the land-and-crowd-intoxicated pipedreams and proletarian identifications of "Walt Whitman, a kosmos, of Manhattan the son," the term *sublime* fittingly eludes any lasting delimitation. Totalization is the lure yet failure of any sublime. Charged "with venom and wonder," the sublime takes us up to unsayable limits of American rapture and collective belief. Yet within a postmodern context of nuclear power and the pious entrenchment of liberal terms/forces globally dispersed, it is time to start altering (decreating/recreating) this American sublime—of Walt Whitman—into a stance of empowerment that better fits the post–Cold War future. Poetic immunity is played out. Claims of American exceptionality—or national grandeur—are not enough.[34]

In the following chapter, "Preliminary Minutiae: Pluralizing the Genre of the American Sublime," I will further negotiate between overviews—and redefinitions—of the American sublime as it has materialized in particular imageries and sublimations. I want to analyze more concretely the post-Whitmanic sublime as expressed—"with venom and wonder"—in recent poems of this American climate. As the mind "dilates with the grandeur of the universe" into tropes of self-proclaimed power, the American poet all too unconsciously imbibes a climate of bigness, speculative excess, success, continental mobility, and superpower. Such poetry must now take into ego-calculus as voice or style the shifting sublime of waterfalls to interstate highways to cybernetic machineries to widescreen orientalist epics to Superbowls to laser-beam visions to telematic unities and "Star Wars": "Here the theme is creative and has vista."[35]

TWO

Preliminary Minutiae

Pluralizing the Genre of the American Sublime

Great-enough both accepts and subdues; the great frame takes
   all creatures . . .
The navy's new-bought Zeppelin going by in the twilight,
Far out seaward; relative only to the evening star and the
   ocean
It slides into a cloud over Point Lobos.
                                        —Robinson Jeffers

Michele Bonuomo: Is the erupting Vesuvius the image of a
catastrophe for you?
Andy Warhol: Oh yes! I think it's a bit like the atomic bomb.
Yes, I think it works just like that. . . .
Michele Bonuomo: Should New York have the Vesuvius?
Andy Warhol: No, I can't imagine a thing like that. Perhaps
here in New York there is only one thing that may look like
the Vesuvius: the Empire State Building. If it should catch on
fire.
                         —Interview in Andy Warhol, *Vesuvius* (1985)

DEVOID OR AT LEAST more wary of any theosophic under-
gridding in an "Over-Soul" or *uebermensch* of higher energies, the
sublime remains a language-genre that, in particularized effect, still
seeks to unleash a "voice that is great within us [that] rises up / As
we stand gazing at the rounded moon" (Stevens). The sublime typ-
ically occurs in some charged-up tone of "high speech" (Baraka)
that, feeling itself "great-enough" to contend with dynamical forces
such as Big Sur hawks or navy Zeppelins (Jeffers), if not the Vesu-
vius of Longinus or the flaming skyscrapers of Andy Warhol, would

move consciousness beyond deadening constraints and imagined blockages of style, ideology, or form. Such a sublime voice—carried in awe/terror across portals, lifted above panic threats of material violence, *transported* out of the stodgy self—would impose upon its convention-ridden audience (those "mickey mockers / And plated pairs" of a commodity-glutted culture) the counterforce of transfigured language: to invoke Stevens again, a poetry of "ghostlier demarcations, keener sounds" to match the plashing grandeur of sky and sea at Key West.[1]

This is to maintain that the sublime still comes down to our own text-glutted era as that speech-genre or "form of seeing and interpreting"[2] in which the grandest concepts and shared representations of the "self"—space, God, nation, identity, language, form—break down before antagonistic forces of materiality (confronted as landscape, technology, or even as "Capital") and monuments of textual sublimity (Whitman), into a sensation of emptiness, languagelessness, some zero-space of empty signs in which the signifying chain is (seemingly) halted and the self (seemingly) ends.

This recurring mood of blankness in the text (or self) is overcome, again and again, as in the bare-commons grandeur of Ralph Waldo Emerson, by crossing over into a renewed sense of utterance, speculative excess, dialogical response, a power emanating from mergers of self and place: that sudden sense of egress from the sensuous world in which the beautiful would hold us captive. The sublime depends upon some conviction that, despite terrors, privations, overloads, or the threat of any abyss, the sublime is happening again, now and here: as Barnett Newman avowed in an essay of that title in 1948, with New World certitude outlasting poverty and war, "The Sublime Is Now."

Before tracking the genealogy of the American sublime, I want first to articulate some of the *countervailing* forces and tones that make the continuity of any poetic sublime seem unlikely and out of place, "wrong from the start." I will go on to delineate some of the components of the Whitmanic sublime that nevertheless endure, haunt, and inhabit the practices of twentieth-century American poets, some of whom—like Robinson Jeffers, Adrienne Rich, and Jack Spicer—have successfully altered and transformed the sublime by engaging the antagonistic forces, both linguistic and technological, that poetry must now confront.

If "the cistern contains whereas the fountain overflows," as

Blake's aphorism against Pope urged in advance of the Whitmanic incarnation of America's will-to-sublimity, to evoke the sublime would be to alter/altar beautiful decorums and forms (couplets, sonnets) into a miming of power's unsituated influx. The sublime claims to implode into space or to speed up language to some liminal threshold of resistance (free verse, automatic writing): one effect is to make poetic form *overflow* molecular limits, as in Gertrude Stein's *Lectures In America* and *How to Write* or Ron Silliman's *Ketjak*.

Even as a word-shattering emotion, the sublime entails terms of egress or domination: raptured excess, the lyric self lost into the landscape, decentered, or absorbed into the attributes of God or incorporated into Capital, as later dwarfed by techno-structures of nuclear power. The tradition of the sublime underwrites thinking aloud in rapt superlatives or terms of sensuous excess, as in this spectacle of a custom paint job described in *Car Culture:* "Sublime paint finish on a 1934 Ford." [3] As a fellow American redneck, you cannot pass beyond *this* paint finish, this fire-red metal which gleams like a California godhead exactingly achieved. Or pass beyond—to invoke another vernacular instance—the basketball performance of Boston Celtics forward, Larry Bird, as portrayed by Michael Madden in the *Boston Globe* (May 23, 1988): "Words fail where Larry Bird didn't. Basketball can be no better than this, nor a seventh game, nor a fourth quarter, nor Dominique Wilkins and most of all, Bird. It all was sublime and Larry Bird was beyond even the sublime."

If at times Larry Bird plays "beyond even the sublime," perhaps there is a sublime beyond the sublime. Less breathlessly considered, the source of such transformations through intensified art-mood (transport)—of language, form, game, norm, rule, precedent—is still, from a romantic point of view, simply the power of the imagination to generate and regenerate, ad infinitum, the soul's "meter-making argument" and posit energy of will. Form shatters and is transformed, as in Emerson's enactment of this will to revolutionary newness, "Circles."

Perhaps sustained by what Heidegger theorized as the "rapture of form-engendering force" and Nietzsche the strong forgetfulness of the will's "hope-filled striving," the genre of the sublime valorizes these rule-breaking energies that would break the domination of history, tradition, or habit. Imaginative forces, moving not so much

43

"under" as "up to or against" prior boundaries and material block-ages, create a rupture, or break, from more solacing formations of "the beautiful." Each boundary is experienced as self-made, but reconstituted by an influx of new energies, as in Nietzsche's very Emersonian passage from "On the Uses and Disadvantages of History for Life" (1874), which recalls the sublime-mimetic of Longi-nus: "Draw about yourself the fence of a great and comprehensive hope, of a hope-filled striving. Form within yourself an image ["will a self"] to which the future shall correspond, and forget the super-stition that you are epigones. . . . Satiate your soul with Plutarch and when you believe in his heroes dare at the same time to believe in yourself."[4]

In this economy of art-raptures, strong willing makes the great style; but, at least for Emerson, the God-relying sublime makes the man (or woman) who is and makes, however traumatized, that "great style." As earlier claimed, the American sublime functions as a cash-value idea that would engender power—in the self if not in the grandeur-seeking community—through a trope which one comes to believe in and practice. As Emerson, Nietzsche's forever-young master, phrased the form-shattering "Spontaneity or In-stinct" animating any American sublime in "Self-Reliance" (1840): "And why need we copy the Doric or the Gothic model? Beauty, convenience, grandeur of thought and quaint expression are as near to us as to any, and if the American artist will study with hope and love the precise thing to be done by him, considering the climate, the soil, the length of the day, the wants of the people, the habit and form of the government, he will create a house in which all these will find themselves fitted, and taste and sentiment will be satisfied also."[5]

According to this can-do Emersonian faith in strong willing, the European sublime, in effect, constitutes one huge "utterance brave and grand" that calls out for, indeed evokes, a counter-response "in the same pitch of voice" (sublimity) that is, if not equal to Dante or Shakespeare, at least interesting, because verbally *differ-ent* and *new*, as a self-made utterance resisting outside structures: "There is at this moment for you an utterance brave and grand as that of the colossal chisel of Phidias, or trowel of the Egyptians, or the pen of Moses or Dante, but different from all these. Not possi-bly will the soul, all rich, all eloquent, with thousand-cloven

44

tongue, deign to repeat itself; but if you can hear what these patriarchs say, surely you can reply to them in the same pitch of voice; for the ear and the tongue are two organs of one nature" (165).

If the beautiful calls for imitation and sensuous seduction, the sublime threatens, dwarfs, yet enables the production of—or at least the belief in the power of—cultural difference, urging out the singularity of a grand-yet-simple style, as in the "parole" of Emerson's bullet-spray essays or Moses' God-inspired sentence (atomized as grandeur by Longinus and latter-day American critics): *Fiat lux.*

As the site of industrial transformations and social mobility, modernist America, however, produced a climate in which the inflationary rhetoric of poetry's power to "maintain 'the sublime' / In the old sense" had been *brought down,* leveled, if not dispersed through contact with ordinary utterances and workaday tones. In a "half savage country" given to inventing structures of impermanency and mobility, given (at least *in theory*) to a dense plurality and multiplicity of voices and styles, the sublime seems credible only if stumbled upon in a landscape or intoned as a gesture or image rather than maintained in the stubborn, class-legitimated manner of a grand style such as that crafted by Mauberly/Pound or, at times, Wallace Stevens or Robert Duncan. As in the linguistic austerity of Mallarmé, the modernist sublime had hollowed out into a compound of hyperbole and irony, rhetoric hedged by self-mockery, as the sublime comes to refer less to superlative revelation than to the circumstances in which such a revelation might have taken place.[6]

Rather, as George Oppen conceived of his own tenacious, anonymous labors—within the materiality and noun-thickened syntax of "Objectivism"—as a San Francisco poet whose work is akin to that of *any* skilled American laborer,

> One makes a life, a place. as, a tool and die maker. One
> may be the greatest of poets; one is certainly not the
> greatest of tool and die makers. Just one's life—in which
> one cannot be 'great.'[7]

Given such terms of marginal production and technological displacement, the hunger for transport, infinitude, and what Robert

45

Duncan had called some landscape "of first permission" which had animated the Romantic sublime must come to terms with conditions of banal selfhood and failed promise, "Of Being Numerous" in scenes of urban vastness and corporate grandeur, eluding private articulation. Oppen spoke over and over, nonetheless, of poetry's high moral purpose: to achieve a language (even within the glutting materials of New York City) "showing a sense of awe"; showing the kind of euphoria one might feel, say, before the human reach and sky-challenging energy manifest in the Empire State Building—of which cityscape Oppen would affirm, "Obsessed, bewildered // By the shipwreck / Of the singular // We have chosen the meaning / Of being numerous." [8]

What kind of sublimity as displaced earth-awe could survive—pious superlatives unscathed—in a country with the following roadside attractions on display as monuments?
1. A replica of the Great Seal of the United States, made out of sharks' teeth;
2. A wax model of Superman using x-ray vision to look at Lois Lane's panties;
3. Jayne Mansfield's death car;
4. Rock touched by Helen Keller;
5. Plastic replica of the world's largest hailstone. [9]

If this Americana entails a young poet's "learning from Las Vegas," such postindustrial simulacra can beget a mock tonality of pseudo-awe (if not disgust) before formations of national culture, a countersublimity tenaciously ordinary and ugly in its terms. We can notice the rise of such tactics as "mock description" and "mock discursiveness" as ways of cooling off the tone or claims of mastery and commitment in postnuclear poems of wonder, as in Kenneth Koch's parodic sublimity of wilderness America in "A Poem of the Forty-Eight States":

The electric chair steamed lightly, then touched
Me. I drove, upward,
Into the hills of Montana. My pony!
Here you are coming along with your master!
Yet I am your master! You're wearing my sweater.
Oh my pony. [10]

Groping towards Las Vegas and Hollywood to be reborn, the American sublime can come down to outsize "monster trucks" like "Bigfoot" flying across wrecks and junks or colliding with super-dome walls as the crowd cries out for the thrill of macho mastery or technological disaster, or down to the panic of shopping-mall and police-car demolitions in *The Blues Brothers*.

One result is the mock-sublimity and wary tone, for example, of Marvin Bell talking to a paranoiac friend from the 1960s "who talks too fast and is now teaching *Moby Dick* / according to ju-jitsu." Bell resorts to a just-one-of-the-guys jocularity that under-mines big statements and sweeping images as embarassing, the hy-perbolic readymades of his culture's transcendentalism, its "tall tales":

> Moby Dick, you damn whale,
> I've seen whales.
> America, though—
> too big to be seen.

Against Rilke's space-terrorized cry, "Who if I cried out would hear me among the angelic orders?" we have the ponderously ordinary voice of Philip Levine in "Last Words," say, which actually opens: "If the shoe fell from the other foot / Who would hear?" The shared terms of such banality and poverty seem gruff, flattened, tied down to a dailyness bleaching the terrain of awe:

> But in this part of the midwest,
> the land is flat and monotonous,
> there are no good restaurants,
> and even our friends seem to leach out
> each year, or become flattened
> by the terrain. So,
>   I've stopped
> believing that the birdfeeders
> could yield surprise . . .

Whatever beauty exists in a paired-down domestic scene like that in Wakoski's "A Snowy Winter in East Lansing" (and it *does* exist) is interior, prosaic, tentative, wary, muted, wry—"if looked at / with certain eyes." [11]

A contrast with the stronger flights of Romantic poets can only suggest, at this point, a *further* diminishment of voice and an American stricturing of the high style—Oppen called his own "Objectivist" language "a going / down middle voice"—that turns away from lofty terms and sweeping predications. Poetry becomes that obsolete genre maintaining a central or major self's (or, worse yet, a great country's) vision of *the sublime*.

In the pluralized and regionalized poetry of the 1980s, then, these whiny, zany, whimsical, or even flat tones (as in Wakoski's poem) can seem more trustworthy than claims to whit-manic exaltation. Exalted landscapes and perspectives such as the High Sierras ("A stage of granite swept for meditation— / Irrelevant to the saunas, Volkswagens and woks" [Pinsky]) remain credible only if hedged by historical ironies or the modulated tone in, for example, Robert Pinsky's *An Explanation of America* (1979), while evoking the natural and social grandeur of America's "Great Emptiness" and "Everlasting Possibility" to his daughter:

> A boundary is a limit. How can I
> Describe for you the boundaries of this place
> Where we were born: where Possibility spreads
> And multiplies and exhausts itself in growing,
> And opens yawning to swallow itself again?
> What pictures are there for that limitless grace
> Unrealized, those horizons ever dissolving? [12]

Pinsky's sweeping abstractions (such as "limitless grace" and "Possibility") and curt predications ("A boundary is a limit") are played off against an implicitly Whitmanic multiplication of instances and an enjambed sense of limitlessness ("and, and, and"). He qualifies such illusions of sublimity through more self-conscious tactics of nervous hyperbole ("opens yawning to swallow itself again"), multiple questioning, blank-verse stability, and the plain diction and shared ideas a child might understand. Finally, the vista of the landscape is evoked *against* historical ironies of Viet Nam that had "aged" his voice.

This anchoring of the American sublime within tactics of everyday speech and shopping-mall *kitsch* suggests, furthermore, that any Poe- or Mallarmé-like deformation of language into high, symbolic diction which only a handful of poets could understand would by now seem willfully *pure*, self-absorbed, monological in its sterile claim to elevate "the poetic" from other language-genres such as (in Pinsky's poem) the classroom lecture or the bedtime story. For, as Mikhail Bakhtin claimed of postnovelistic poetry, "The speaking subjects of high, proclamatory genres—of priests, prophets, preachers, judges, leaders, patriarchal fathers, and so forth—have departed this life." [13] Left behind to speak, not *proclaim*, is simply *the writer*, overburdened heir to romantic irony, occupational alienation, and a warehouse of contradictory styles supporting, at best, the sublimity of pastiche or the grandeur of the vulgar (as in Robert Venturi's laconically poetic *Guild House*).

Yet behind self-ironic voices such as Bell's or that of the more aerial Pinsky stands the textual example of Whitman, claiming to express ("incarnate") America's bulk, brag, promise, raw energy, and half-baked ideas. In "By Blue Ontario's Shore," he confronts would-be poets of American immensity ("*too big to be seen*"?) with an on-the-job interview of their stylistic credentials, testing their tones of language *and* national ideology. If Nicaraguan poets can still look to Rubén Darío as model for an indigenous poetic rooted in vernacular *exteriorismo* (the voice of the everyday, of real objects), this is because, as Margaret Randall explains, "His [Darío's] work is at the very roots of poetic experience in the country in much the same way that Whitman's *Leaves of Grass* shaped poetry in the United States." Or as Kuo Mo-Jo captures the *global* sway of this Whitmanic sublime in China, his democratic equalizing of natural with textual forces: "Whitman! Whitman! The Pacific that was Whitman!" [14] Whitman's voice, amazing as it remains, nevertheless comes stockpiled with American ideology and dream, a sublimity hazing over its imperial sources and goals.

Would American poets remain lofty in spirit, Whitman asked, in touch with mandates and street tones of democracy, hence capable—in *new* idioms and "language experiments"—of inaugurating an American sublime as sweeping as his own?

Are you he who would assume a place to teach or be a poet
  here in the States?
The place is august, the terms obdurate.

(349)

Whitman's sublimity, at once grand and naive, would dwarf *any*
speaking self with determinations of landscape and language, prior
structures inducing blockage and awe: *The place is august, the
terms obdurate.* Yet didn't the tradition-thin situation of poetry in
America—as place and as convention—demand something this big
and gripping, a sublimity radically supple, open to plural energies,
common images, and modes of concretized realization like Whit-
man's own, knowing the self "in thrall / to that deep wonderment,
our native clay" as Hart Crane enthused of his American *Meister-
singer* in *The Bridge?* Whitman's declamation of national grandeur,
by the immensity of Lake Ontario as along the multicultural streets
of New York City, has proved *obdurate* as a shared vocabulary and
a set of poetic conventions proclaiming, beyond wasteland defor-
mation or lament, what Hart Crane termed our "deep wonder-
ment, our native clay."

Bodily rapture, spilling over into vast space: all well and good
for the inner self. Yet thinking on the displaced rapturism of the
"nuclear sublime" that confronts American poets in the 1990s, ter-
rifying diverse voices into idealist credulity if not into technological
awe, Whitman's centrist utterance (*the place is august, the terms
obdurate*) has lingered on in my mind as signifying a key tonality.
Whitman's poetry remains burdened with the energy *and* limits of
sublimity as a native tradition, in the best and worst senses, prop-
agating shared terms/tones of "deep wonderment": Whitman,
"Our Meistersinger, thou [who] set breath in steel." The terms of
the American sublime have remained ones of obdurate rapture en-
coding the individual voice with awe ("*gleaming cantos of unvan-
quished space . . .*") before Niagara Falls and Brooklyn Bridge as
before the moonlanding, if not the wonders of a massively re-
searched and cinematically engendered Star Wars.

However ironized or repressed, Whitman's voice—seeking to
"raise aloft" the contemporary, at once bragging and culture-
specific—has lingered into the twentieth century as a mandate to
tonal grandeur and long-poem bulk, to accents and genres of com-
mensurate wonder. *August, immense, grand*—the sweeping adjec-

50

tives and fleshly details of his paratactic intoxication have added up, even critically, to the persistence of a landscape called *the American sublime* in poets as diverse in culture as Allen Ginsberg and Stevens himself, as descriptively eclectic as Frank O'Hara or Elizabeth Bishop. Even a master-ironist of theological anorexia and blasted hymnals such as Emily Dickinson can now be seen to offer deftly "calculated" versions of her country's will-to-sublimity and negative mastery, her idiosyncratic quest to outdo Emerson, Higginson, and God.[15]

Charles Newman's disclaimer against modernist grandeur (in the postmodern novel) and romantic mastery—"Self-absorption in the grand manner: Elitism"—cannot dissuade American poets from reaching towards what has been called "a high lyric grandeur"[16] or postabstract American painters such as Rodney Ripps or Mark Tansey from reaching after bigness or abstract space, a vastness of design creating "beauty through intimidation" and an ego-absorption which need not be separated from the cultural quest to invent further versions, amid junk and cultural glut, of our "neo-sublime."[17]

A sublime spunkiness survives in the voice of Frank O'Hara lifting up out of the banality of "ugly NEW WORLD WRITING" and the colossal textures of New York City to affirm how Billie Holiday "whispered a song along the keyboard / to Mal Waldron and everyone and I stopped breathing"—his elegiac metaphor (from nowhere) lifting her singing (his poetry) to a death-of-the-self. Or it even survives crazed and full-bodied in the voice of Anne Waldman in "Makeup on Empty Space," filling atomic "emptiness" through a barrage of antic images fighting off the bomb—desert spaces never to be empty (in quite the same *textual* way) again:

> Look what thoughts will do Look what words will do
> from nothing to the face
> from nothing to the root of the tongue
> from nothing to speaking of empty space
> I bind the ash tree
> I bind the yew
> I bind the willow
> I bind uranium
> I bind the uneconomical unrenewable energy of uranium
> dash uranium to empty space . . .

I build up the house again in memory of empty space
This occurs to me about empty space
that it is never to be mentioned again . . . [18]

Like a conjured cosmogony, Waldman's poem moves from proclaiming a quasi-Buddhist emptiness and filling it with myriad objects—natural and technological—even claiming (shamanlike) *to subjugate nuclear power* ("I bind uranium") by antic hyperboles, wild tropes cast out into the mass-media void. In "Anti-Nuclear Warheads Chant," Waldman solidifies her antagonism to the false sublime of nuclear power, emptying the self of beauty and driving the poet to cast out an inflated rhetoric ("makeup") of high vision, blatantly sublime in its run-on mode: "I pour words over empty space, enthrall the empty space / packing, stuffing, jamming empty space / spinning necklaces around empty space."

Given the buildup of nuclear technology which now turns the landscape into a grid of terror rather than a haven of pastoral comfort, not even the fences and shrouds of Christo, with his parodic megabucks and high-tech projects such as *Running Fence* or *Wrapped Coast,* can surround and capture nature's desacralized being. The mock-sublimity implied by Christo's wrapping of the Biscayne Bay islands in 6,500,000 square feet of flamingo-pink polypropylene *mimics* the technological outreach of America's global energies, turning the immensity of once-wild nature into a colossal commodity, ready-to-take-out. Christo's agitprop tactics of postmodernity suggest, in ephemeral images costing millions, such a "neo-sublime."

Alone with the immensity and Muse of the Great Lakes in 1856, Whitman had mulled over a poetics of grandeur that could claim the substance of natural and industrial power he found in the buildup of America as "heroes," to pump them into more accessibly sublime forms—"Chants Democratic," as he proclaimed in a title inverting high and low. As a pastiche of his own terms from the 1855 preface to *Leaves of Grass,* "Poem of Many in One" became "Chants Democratic" became "As I Sat Alone by Blue Ontario's Shore" became "By Blue Ontario's Shore." The poet labored—alone with the landscape as symbol of his own grandeur and, projectively, of his North American continent—to suffuse the

52

content of ideological elevation (the still-blue lake and egalitarian masses as hero) into fresh forms of poetic language, "chants" democratic in substance and style.

Even after the Civil War traumas and the buildup of Gilded Age Capital, the sublime Muse ("A Phantom gigantic superb, with stern visage") demanded of American poets a new grandeur, proclaiming an identity of power between self and country (if not world). Whitman's language registers the sublime of collective ideology: "*Chant me the poem*, it said, *that comes from the soul of America, chant me the carol of victory, / And strike up the marches of Libertad, marches more powerful yet, / And sing me before you go the song of the throes of Democracy.*"

One hundred years later, such a tone sounds solipsistically aloof, deafened to the idolatrized march of its own tropes of *power* over the landscape. Poetry enacts the rhetoric of a nationalism that can only suggest the buildup of toxic waste and nuclear weaponry by Blue Ontario's shore. (Only the Spanish term *Libertad* lingers as a curious dictional token of Whitman's openness to alien cultures and class undertones, the languages of North and South America dreamily conjoined in the dialectical march of Liberty to elevate the masses from Europe.)

Whitman's declaiming, in bulky, China-wide lyrics of ideological impurity such as "By Blue Ontario's Shore" (or, even more blatantly, "Song of the Redwood-Tree," in which a giant California sequoia gives up its Indian spirit to the chainsaws of national progress) would render the landscape of modernity *august* and the language of national rapture *obdurate,* as it is, later, in Galway Kinnell's *The Avenue Bearing the Initial of Christ into the New World.* Whitman's is the voice I have heard dragged out at poets' weddings or seminar farewells, bespeaking a comradely accent of generous openness and patriotic love urging towards communion: consecrating the humblest American scene by evoking some peculiar mixture of dailiness and shared ideal.

Yet if the would-be poet of sublimity affirmed, "Yes I will make an American poetry august in substance and obdurate in terms," Whitman tosses off blatantly *political* questions on his or her overall fitness to lyricize such an "august place," as if to induce the information overload that informed Kant's concept of a "mathematical sublime" marching, beyond cognition, to infinitude:

Who are you indeed who would talk or sing to America?
Have you studied out the land, its idioms and men?
Have you learn'd the physiology, phrenology, politics,
  geography, pride, freedom, friendship of the land?
  its substratums and objects?
Have you consider'd the organic compact of the first day of
  the first year of Independence, sign'd by the
  Commissioners, ratified by the States, and read by
  Washington at the head of the army?
Have you possess'd yourself of the Federal Constitution?
Do you see who have left all feudal processes and poems
  behind them, and assumed the poems and processes of
  Democracy?

(349)

The terms of such grandeur are not just *studied* but *studied out*—
caught living from "the land, its idioms and men." Such *obdurate
terms,* sprung from the unconscious shapes of the vernacular as
much as from any intertextual storehouse of poetry, keep their
freshness and exactitude.

For Whitman, poetry registered the sense that a great landscape,
site of collective dream-projection within, and a "great Idea," were
speaking through the ego of the personal self, choosing loftier tones
and terms, commingling ordinary language with spectacular goals
left unfinished by Western history: "I harbor for good or bad, I
permit to speak at every hazard, / Nature without check with orig-
inal energy." It is this kind of ideological intoxication with father-
hood, mastery, and native place which a poem like Adrienne Rich's
"North America Time" (1983) would set its counterlanguage
against and would undermine through countervoices that have
been silenced and toxic details that have been idealized (if not re-
pressed) by the macho ego of the Whitmanic stance:

> The almost-full moon rises
> timelessly speaking of change
> out of the Bronx, the Harlem River
> the drowned towns of the Quabbin
> the pilfered burial mounds,
> the toxic swamps, the testing-grounds
>
> and I start to speak again.[19]

54

Rich sees that the all-American mind has to be cleared—at the end of the poem—of the gilded-age rhetoric and high abstraction of such poetry (the moon "timelessly speaking of change"), just as the terrorized Bronx landscape has to be cleared of arrogant history and incorrect ecology, before this *North* American poet can "start to speak again"—of damages wrought, margins blotted out, women ignored and injured, whole subjects and peoples missing from what Tracy Chapman calls "the dream of America."

As a discourse of the expansive self, Whitman's work lingers on in the literary unconscious to register a central version of the American sublime: at once model and threat to subsequent voicings of august mountains and lakes, streetwalkers and blades of grass, silencing past attempts (such as Joel Barlow's *Columbiad*) and future efforts (such as Crane's *The Bridge*) as epic mishmash, not sufficiently rooted in the body nor in the scene.

Need we settle for such a purely subject-centered account of the American sublime as a battle of male egoes for mastery, centrality, and originality? At this point, two questions must challenge such a monological view of the sublime genre: (1) Did Whitman just spring up out of the landscape, like a gigantic *genius loci,* emerging godlike from his own self-conception? (2) Did "the Whitman" play out any sublime mode, turning later versions of democratic elevation into empty reruns and ennervated odes, like Ginsberg, shopping in the Berkeley Coop in the somnambulent 1950s, reduced to ogling the grocery boy as some campy version of his own folk-bard?

If "All Sublimity is founded on Minute Discrimination," as William Blake fumed in response to Sir Joshua Reynolds's *Discourse* on the sublimity of art's grand ideas (1808), I take my cue for a more socially attuned poetics of the sublime genre from the dialogism of Bakhtin/Medvedev/Vološinov: "Poetics should really begin with genre, not end with it. For genre is the typical form of the whole work, the whole utterance."[20] Such poetic genres develop as dialogical responses ("whole utterances") that must be situated—quote, mime, echo, reaccent—within concrete social horizons, as ways of shaping utterances and coding them with the language of imagination and the conflicts of ideology. Genre is not the invention of one man or voice, but a dialogical construct and group invention miming a shared vision of imaginal longing.

Poetry remains one of those "little behavioral *genres*" that, however opaque or elevated ("pure") its diction, is continuous with language-games of ordinary speech seeking to convey *utterances*—threats, encouragements, visions, dreams, warnings, transports, pleas. Critics must reconstruct the social contexts and implied horizon of ideology, contested and conveyed. This reveals poetry's coding in of larger tones and themes—shared "heroes." Even poetry, uttered in continental vastness, implies sympathetic readers, allied in irony—or in awe,—"Or to read you, Walt,—knowing us in thrall / To that deep wonderment, our native clay."

To invoke a troubled example of sublime resistance open to discursive flux, to cite just one more counterexample, I would read Jack Spicer's deft meditation on "this ocean" in *Language* (1964) as a depiction, bravely discontinuous, of the emerging post-Sausurrean incommensurability between natural forces and human structures ("Language") imposed upon Romantic vastness: the *gap* between natural and textual sublimes which Whitmanic ego-boasting by Lake Ontario can no longer heal. As a material "hero," the sublimity of the ocean does not mean nor intend; it need not trope into something else, it need not answer any whit-manic will to incarnation:

> This ocean, humiliating in its disguises
> Tougher than anything.
> No one listens to poetry. The ocean
> Does not mean to be listened to. A drop
> Or crash of water. It means
> Nothing.
> It
> Is bread and butter
> Pepper and salt. The death
> That young men hope for. Aimlessly
> It pounds the shore. White and aimless signals. No
> One listens to poetry.[21]

In Spicer's wry collocation of "whole utterances" lifted from discrete contexts of contemporary speech, the Pacific Ocean wavers between signifying another vast metaphor (*this ocean* as source of sublime power, as in "Starting From Paumanok") or an indifferent energy flatly separated from human discourse (*this ocean* as massive static, "White and aimless signals").

The pathos inhabiting the recurring line, "No one listens to poetry," takes on accuracy within the technoscape of postmodern America, where against conditions of geographical vastness only a small audience does, in fact, listen to poetry as mask or force of sublimity "tougher than anything." Given this solitude, regionally glued together at best, the poet must listen to the ocean as he would to any poet (called later a "counterpunching radio"): as structural model for message-making and a source for the widest metaphor the mind is capable of, signaling material life ("It / Is bread and butter") or the transcendence of ego ("The death / That young men hope for").

Stripped of context, however, the ad-like phrase "tougher than anything" denotes multiple (and disjunctive) contexts of force, meanings for *this ocean* apart from nature-as-symbol. As Ron Silliman comments, " 'tougher than anything' can be understood in a variety of ways, depending on whether the ultimate referent is Mount St. Helens, Krazy-glu, or Bette Davis".[22] That is, Spicer *ungrounds* any Whitmanic sublimity of force from its determinacy in Nature and God by multiplying the implicit contexts of structure, language, and relevance in which such a phrase might make strong (that is, awe-inspiring) sense.

Spicer's poem, like an enactment of its own ocean-language, goes on churning out affirmations of "Thing Language" without any sure audience, even without an ego design or intention to will grandeur. Somehow, in a cold tone miming structural play, Spicer achieves the remoteness and force of an immense ocean, his own version of a textual sublime which will later sustain, as one model, Silliman and certain Language Poets of the 1980s in later quests to articulate a *total syntax:* the sublimity of social-aesthetic forms embedded in the claim "What I want when I write is a total engagement with language." [23] Spicer alters and pluralizes the prior language of the Whitmanic sublime.

Spicer's poem deforms and enacts the creation of a new sublimity that is more poststructurally based, one founded in structures of language as against more reified idealisms of natural or technological force that are seductive in American poetry. For, in *Language* or *Book of Magazine Verse,* it is not any private language or "voice" which is implicitly ego-sublime, but the massive structure of *language* itself, apart from individualized meanings and intentions such as those the poem goes on to generate while "No one listens to poetry." As Silliman worries this conflict between natural forces and vast overdeterminations of language in "No one listens to poetry," Spicer's sentence "presents syntax, if not language itself, at its most tangibly oppressive, admitting no possibility of difference or doubt" ("Spicer's Language," 181). More than an august landscape of nature, Spicer presents terms envisioning *any* sublime within postmodern conditions ("language") of cultural glut and ideological encoding.

In contrast to this language-centered version of the sublime, consider the vatic landscape of Robert Duncan, as it blurredly shifts from an outer condition of nature (meadow) to an inner space of neo-Platonic infinitude, imparting an energy of the mind generating new forms "against chaos":

> Often I am permitted to return to a meadow
> as if it were a given property of the mind
> that certain bounds holds against chaos,
> that is a place of first permission,
> everlasting omen of what is.

Against the boundaries of stanza and meadow, the mind is said to overflow daily limits ("bounds"), as the language lifts into a hyperbole affirming some "first permission": a priority—or sense of infinitude—that is at once formal and psychological, equalizing outer (nature) and inner (form). In such a spatially driven poem as Duncan's, as Robert Hass has written, "you can actually watch, as the words are laid down on the page, the process from which the perception of the thing gets born into its numinous quality as a word, an abstraction out of the thing." [24] The disappointment entailed in the gap between word and nature, consciousness and substance, desire for union as against displacement into abstraction, seems forgotten and elided in the moment of the sublime, as if the meadow were the inalienable property of the poetic ego.

Decrying an idealistic impatience with dailiness that haunted American poets (such as Duncan) in the 1950s, Robert Lowell labored to avoid, in an exactingly confessional voice, that "leap for the sublime," or any Ahab-like will to declaim the visionary. Hence, his own poetry struggled, as James Breslin argues, to move away from its lifelong fascination with "an elevated, a grand style—a gnarled sublimity" packed with myth and literary allusion. "Beyond the Alps" (which opens *Life Studies*) mock-accepts such a pious stance equating the mind and grand landscape, compounded as it was of natural immensity and (more latently) the surplus grandeur of Capital on which the self relies:

> I envy the conspicuous
> waste of our grandparents on their grand tours—
> long-haired Victorian sages accepted the universe,
> while breezing on their trust funds through the world.

Such a Niagara-like scenery of self-immensity when even "Everest was still / unscaled" gives way, in "Waking Early Sunday Morning" [1965], to Lowell's more outraged lament against such idealizations of American power. This overreaching ego—now reduced to a whine—confronts the political (and technological) formations which superintend and police this ancient grandeur of mountains and skies:

> Pity the planet, all joy gone
> from this sweet volcanic cone;
> peace to our children when they fall
> in small war on the heels of small
> war—until the end of time
> to police the earth, a ghost
> orbiting forever lost
> in our monotonous sublime.

Such a fall into "the monotony of the sublime"—which Lowell early feared as a stylistic peril—is decried as one consequence of our American will-to-sublimity, now displaced from natural ("sweet volcanic cone") or human centers ("our children") to soul-dead icons such as satellites and nuclear warheads—hence comprising, in all dread and terror, *"our monotonous sublime."* [25]

More caustically than Robert Lowell, Robinson Jeffers summoned the majestic forces and ego-dwarfing immensities of the natural sublime around Big Sur to evoke a landscape arctically cleansed of a humanity "drunk with machinery":

> I strain the mind to imagine distances
> That are not in man's mind: the planets, the suns, the
>   galaxies, the super-galaxies, the incredible voids
> And lofts of space: our mother the ape never suckled us
> For such a forest. The vastness here, the lonely horror,
>   the mathematical unreason, the cold awful glory.
> The inhuman face of our God: It is pleasant and beautiful.

Such "pleasures" might efface the human ego in immensities of space and time, concepts and words pushed recklessly beyond all manageable limits or emotive measures. Jeffers could be no less tactlessly local and political in confronting the engines of technology reshaping earth and ego, as in his ranting evocation of "holy awe" before the infinitudes unlocked at Hiroshima:

> It is ruthlessly indecent, certainly, to have used the uranium-
> Derived explosive to clinch any war with,
> And then in holy awe removing it, hoping to prohibit
> Its future use. It makes us damned hypocrites,
> Besides being impossible.
>   So the thing will kill cities.
> We shall all be well without them, I think.
> But as for an improbable chain-reaction in the common
>   elements
> Of earth and air; that at least has no terrors;
> To become star-flame,
> A transfiguration too fine for man's fate.

It is within such an impossible-to-articulate horizon that we now live, dwarfed by the sublime of nuclear power that threatens to annihilate the lyric ego into star-flames—atomic radiance without form or end. (And Jeffers is all too gleeful at this prospect.) The postmodern sublime is not merely Vesuvius, but the Empire State Building in flames.[26]

The sublime recurs—less bitterly—in two contemporary writers whose struggles within and against communal materiality and narcissistic tactics of "poetical" language have resulted in their alliance with the Language Poets: Michael Amnasan and Robert Glück.

Michael Amnasan recontextualizes any idealist sublime by locating his evocation of awe *not* in "the sight of unlimited distances and heights lost to view" (Schiller) or under "the starry firmament" forever evoking moral law (Kant), but in a tool factory. He claims that "The sublime is a sensation, a feeling of irreconcilability with that which has provoked this sensation. My identity as a divergence from the world at large is sensational and unreasoning, a disharmony within my very soul with the blank this divergence has generated." [27] For Amnasan the sublime occurs in the very gap between who he is as a welder or toolsetter, immersed in processes of matter, and who he is as a thinker, abstracted and lifted out of history.

Recording a struggle between the body and its dematerializations into words and ideas, the sublime seems built into the human condition as some inner *need,* a displacement of the self from given bodily and social conditions which would capture this immensity. Amnasan's next paragraph presents this "irreconcilability": "Waiting to be dispatched to another job. Noticing my tool box and green bucket filled with my most often used tools sitting just inside the front door, I feel the immaturity that has been generated in contrast to the use of those same tools." The sublime has been the (narcissistic) moment of disembodiment: the self contemplating its own immensity, apart from "those same tools." By resituating the experience of the romantic sublime in the workplace, Amnasan deforms the tradition into new relevance, strange sense.

As "immature" reverie, the sublime is *not* a use-value: it defines the self as interior infinitude, as a blank soul abstracted from history into spatial sensation. The sublime affords the mind an egress from the world of force, from the violence of matter: as in Schiller's post-Kantian scenario in *On the Sublime* (1801), the sublime affords an intuition of the soul's infinitude, hence indeterminacy. "Thus the sublime affords us an egress from the sensuous world in which the beautiful would gladly hold us forever captive. Not gradually (for there is no transition from dependence to freedom), but suddenly and with a shock it tears the independent spirit out of the net in which a refined sensuousness has entoiled it, and which binds all the more tightly the more gossamer its weave." [28]

What binds Amnasan is physical entoiling, day-laboring, that labor within and against materiality which for Schiller is merely a metaphor of "weaving" and "netting." The struggle between sensuousness and freedom, polarized in the older vocabulary as the gendered opposition between *the beautiful* and *the sublime,* becomes in the later writer the opposition between physical and mental labor. This sublime intuition of indeterminacy recalls him to his vocation as writer, confronting a total syntax.

For Robert Glück, the sublime is posed against claims of the local and communal, body and not-self: "The local is a necessary component of any community, and an allegorical poem can be local and at the same time claim or recover that other component of community life: the sublime. By local I mean: intimacy, the circumstances of knowing others and being known, being the subject of one's story, sharing gestures over a period of time, sharing ideology. By sublime I mean: transgression of ego boundaries, merging, transcendence, horror/awe, discontinuities of birth, sex and death." [29]

In Glück's refiguring, the American sublime entails a confrontation between locality and otherness, that which calls the self and community out of shared limits—in rapture, excess, awe, even death. The sublime moment is instigated out of disjunction, enjoining a double awareness and double coding, yet not inflected with Old World cynicism: the self as bound in foreign materials, the self as freed through fictions of mastery.

As the cash-value instrument of a mobile people not particularly given to self-ennervating theory, the sublime was located *outside* as empty space (wild landscape as access to goodness, productivity, and God); and *inside* as a vacancy whereby the mind resonated with experiment, as a space of cognitive infinitude. The American sublime remained a trope of pragmatic possibility, as in Whitman's "Song of Myself," with the ego seeking to know this sublime (in Thoreau's catch-phrase from *Walden,* "*by experience*") not by textual rumor or derived authority but first-hand, here and now giving voice to the vastness of mass, crowd, and place.

We can grasp the sublime poem as a refiguring of history within the minds of our poets, voicing what Stevens called "The Poems of Our Climate" in some full aesthetic/ideological sense; that is, troping Althusser on interpellation, as "effect[s] of [American] structure." The escape from contingency and struggle into aesthetic perfection ("complete simplicity") and imagery, "Of clear water in a brilliant bowl," was not enough in 1938 to satisfy the "never-resting mind" of Wallace Stevens as he imagined—in schizoid bitterness and delight ("in this bitterness, delight")—interior paradises of "flawed words and stubborn sounds" to compensate for the imperfect real he lived within and transformed as "Hartford seen in a purple light." [30]

"The Poems of Our Climate" registers this self-relying and insatiable heart ("vital I") and "never-resting mind" of America, willing excess if not urging towards a new grandeur ("One desires / So much more than that"):

> Say even that this complete simplicity
> Stripped one of all one's torments, concealed
> The evilly compounded, vital I
> And made it fresh in a world of white,
> A world of clear water, brilliant-edged,
> Still one would want more, one would need more,
> More than a world of white and snowy scents. [31]

Stevens, like many a displaced modernist, here retreats into the ironic sublime of language: the delight which "lies in flawed words and stubborn sounds." [32] The American sublime was, in this way, not a matter of place or self—"the evilly compounded, vital I"— but of decontaminated language.

The sky over America was both immense and limited: the sky as great space, the sky as seen. Slowly localized, the sky became a concept of luminous space, a perception of the ego within limits of its own region and neighborhood (history). Yet the nuclear sublime now threatens to evacuate this homey concept of the sublime: an excess without transport. No "transport to summer" if there is no more summer. Just nuclear fire, in which myriad selfhoods get absorbed: the sublime lifting out of history which Americans have been awaiting, and poetically endorsing, building structures towards (and beyond) the sky.

To deconstruct the allure of such "nuclear rapture," we need to go back, warily, into the *materia poetica* of the American sublime as this emerged in pre-Whitmanic poetics, Puritan to Romantic, as well as in its "whit-manic" stance as globe-incorporating ego in "Song of Myself." The development of the sublime as a style and set of verbal conventions provides the semantic preconditions for even seemingly singular or privatized poets such as Wallace Stevens or Anne Bradstreet.

Mapping the energies of an American sublime, we need not follow the poetics of excess and strong forgetting that Emerson recklessly urged upon American artists of any age, voiding history into so much dematerialized bunk: "When we have new perception, we shall gladly disburden the memory of its hoarded treasures as old rubbish." [33]

Part 2

Early American Precursors:

Landscape as Transport

THREE

"Enrapted Senses"
Anne Bradstreet's "Contemplations"

"Getting the Grandeurs"

When I identify my self, my work, and my country, you may
think I've finally got the grandeurs: . . .
  —A. R. Ammons, *Sphere: The Form of a Motion* (1974)

When the imagination of a whole people has once been turned
toward purely quantitative bigness, as in the United States,
this romanticism of numbers exercises an irresistible appeal to
the poets among business men.
  —Max Weber, *The Protestant Ethic and the
Spirit of Capitalism*

UNLIKE THE double-toned textuality of Mexican poets, who
remain tragically torn between Eurocentric traditions imputing
style, power, and a will to formal innovation as posited against the
more animistic lure of "indigenous [pre-Hispanic] traditions" va-
lorizing blood, death, Aztec earth-myths, and sacrificial rites, Early
American poets such as Anne Bradstreet, Richard Steere, or Wil-
liam Livingston were initially fortunate to encounter a kind of
double-emptiness that permitted just about anything to pass as po-
etry of this New World. Such a Euramerican sense of vacancy had
to be produced and vindicated, of course, as a self-enabling, glib, if
not illusory, condition. Repression would prevail where identifica-
tion with prior powers had traumatically faltered.
  Given the smallness of the self as measured against the vastness

of this new space, however, the poet soon turned her or his vocation of self-making towards identifying with what Max Weber diagnosed as the representative lure of "quantitative bigness" and material bulk. The result became some Protestant troping of this physical sublime into an exalted state of "election" (via the rapture of conversion) that might link the vastness of this geography to some vastness of spirit, if not, finally, to the speed, power, and influx of Capital.[1] An energy of the spirit became transacted in, if not as, the liberal American self brazenly seeking to stake out a place of empowerment in this New World grandeur and, thereby, to solidify and ratify America as site and substance of an emerging sublime.

Convinced by the presence—if not the metaphor—of vast space as well as by a kind of self-willed emptiness towards this New World landscape that might void the chattering languages and "aristocratic jargon" of Anglo-European traditions, American poets can suffer from the occupational hazards of trying to invent and colonize such an American sublimity. (If they are not, say, James Russell Lowell, John Hollander, or Peter Viereck, more or less content to retool European elegancies of form, irony, and metaphysical wit.) The result can be conflictual yet enabling, begetting in such poets a case of "venom and wonder," as place enjoins upon the lyric self the unconscious dynamics of continental vastness and "whit manic" mastery—*"getting the [poetic] grandeurs."*[2]

Like Allen Ginsberg, Norman Mailer, or even Gerald Stern in *Lucky Life* (1973), such "puny democratic egos" can become language-hungry for continental vision and bigness of voice; for tones and image-flights to native grandeur released in expansive forms and frames positing new selfhood, "omniverous lines,"—"getting the grandeurs" from place if not tradition. Emerging out of any region or ethnic voice, "The Great American Novel" could at least find a post-Whitmanic contender for the "Great American Poem."

As A. R. Ammons diagnosed and tried to distance his own case of sublimity in *Sphere: The Form of a Motion* (1974), "what do they [my readers] / expect from a man born and raised in a country whose motto is E / *pluribus unum*: I'm just, like Whitman, trying to keep things // half straight about my country." But the imperial outreach is surely there, if idealized into an occupational hazard:

                        I am not a whit manic
to roam the globe, search seas, fly southward and northward
with migrations of cap ice, encompass a hurricane with

a single eye: things grown big, I dream of a clean-wood
shack, a sunny pine trunk, a pond, and an independent income: . . .[3]

Ammons's pastoralism and yeomanlike ethic of autonomous land-
holding at Ithaca would fight against this lurch towards incarna-
tional outreach, towards some whit-manic bigness of form and a
God-drenched voice (the poem, after all, is written *"For Harold
Bloom"*) that would ratify such national projects. This authority
depends upon high mastery and a style resonant with a self-incor-
porating and all-but-imperial reach to absorb puny others and to
domineer slovenly space. Ammons must try to distance this whit-
manic sublime, all the more so because he is so indigenously drawn
to it, as threat and possibility, as his encompassing colons and ro-
mantic flights divulging "radiance" in *Sphere* suggest.

Does "getting the grandeurs" really begin with "Whitman," or
might some rudimentary *poetics of transport* be there at the Eur-
american origin, deployed as a possibility of wonder at the New
World which our first poets, in a more austere Puritan context, had
begun to realize, ratify, and transmit? Consider the acceptably Pu-
ritan rapture ("Raptur'd Contemplation") and tone of moral uplift
animating Richard Steere (1643–1721) in *Earth Felicities, Heavens
Allowances*, for example, "one of the first blank-verse poems writ-
ten in America":

When we the Azure Cannopy Survey,
Deck'd *with those bright* and Glorious Rouling *Torches;*
It mounts our minds in Raptur'd Contemplation,
With Rev'rence, up to the Admired Author.
With Awe, *with* Joy, *with* Fear . . .[4]

Granted Steere's images and metaphors seem epithet-laden and ge-
neric, and lead all too inevitably to God; but the tone and mood is
latitudinarian and sensuous, hardly one of "innate depravity" or a
shrinking distance refusing ego-identity with what came to be
widely legitimated, in Boileau's era, as the natural sublime. This
Christianized sublime emerged as God withdrew from landscapes

and texts into some wry, belated, imaginary interaction between the two.

This is to ask a genealogical question that might connect our present to its past, power (as rhetoric) to its initial "eruptions" as discourse. Where—as a poetic tradition—does this "American sublime" begin? Scholarship of our era has nominated a contradictory list of scrappy grandeurs heading in a centrist direction—that is, towards and away from the self-reliant sublimity of Emerson and Whitman: (1) the epic desperation of the Connecticut Wits to "raise to sublimity the aspiring Muse"; (2) Bryant's expansively moralized prairies; (3) in theory, Emerson's self-empowering vision of the Poet overflowing ecstatic infinitude into mountains, railroads, John D. Rockefeller, and even ants; or (4) the startlingly vernacular yet representative "language experiment" that was Whitman's "Song of Myself."

The *dominant* answer to this question of sublime origin, after the modernist polemics of Pound, Williams, and Emerson himself, and the oedipal model of will-to-power enunciated by Harold Bloom and his followers which now prevails in American criticism, continues to be the language of *Leaves of Grass* (1855). In such a foreshortened view of literary tradition, it is as if, at one stroke, the "westerning genius" of Whitman (boiling over with what he himself called an "Emersonism [which] breeds the giant that destroy[s] itself") annihilated two hundred years of native poetry, reducing the prior rhetoric of the American sublime to so much moonmash on the dump: to so many "rocks, roots, pottery shards and skull fragments," as Margaret Atwood described early Canadian poetry's equally scrappy attempts to claim and to ratify, for shared use, the northern wilderness.[5]

Post-Emersonians by cultural necessity as much as by any hermeneutic choice, self-reliant Americans hunger for some version of a native sublime, different, credible, expansive, great; and such a tradition of majesty, we know from the speculations of Longinus's *Peri Hypsos,* is credibly founded by the incarnational nationalism (or epic ego) of a Homer. Such a voice of culture-summarizing mastery creates an intertext whose shaping gestures and contagiously mimetic influence (like Milton's in England, or Dante's in Italy) need not be a blight, inducing parody or silence, but can be a voice of radiant "influx," that most Emersonian of terms for the spark of genius coaxing would-be originality into self-greatness, through mediations of text and place (as a westerning *genius loci*). Such a voice of collective representation installs and instantiates the components of a central genre.

Compiling the *New Oxford Book of Canadian Verse in English*, Atwood termed her own anthology " 'a collection of rocks, roots, pottery shards and skull fragments' " yet claimed that Canadian poets had sprung up early and abundantly in the wilderness as if to alleviate the vastness and to garrison off any sense of threat. Poetry emerged to fill the unwritten terrain and the traumatic solitude, generating poets like Al Purdy, who would later dig down through archives of soil, blizzard, and bedrock to find their own place in a fledgling tradition. At first, originality would be beside the point to these poets, a luxury of Europe. But the analogy between textual vacancy and vast solitude holds for other early poets in the Northern Americas, I think, and Atwood goes on to draw a compelling moral: "These poets [Hayman, Stansbury, O'Grady, Goldsmith, McLachan] are important not for their elegance or originality but because they were there first, and they said something. There is no more need to apologize for their presence than there would be for beginning a survey of American poetry with Anne Bradstreet. We read them as we would read travel writers, for their reports of a strange country that later became our own." Anne Bradstreet, in generic respects, needs no such apology.

Anne Bradstreet's Puritan Sublime

> That there is a God my Reason would soon tell me
> by the wondrous workes that I see, the vast frame
> of the Heaven and the Earth, the order of all things,
> night and day, summer and winter, spring and autumne . . .
> The consideration of these things would with amazement
> certainly resolve me that there is an Eternal Being.[6]

Anne Bradstreet (c. 1612–1672) was surely *there first*, but we still don't know how, poetically, to situate or claim her. The strange country of the Indian wilderness which her courtly/Christian poetry helped to domesticate and to legitimate conveys traces of a tone and tradition which later signaled, no less explicitly, *the transport of the sublime*. Bradstreet "said something" of her new country: she invented and indulged in "rapt senses" of place that, later, turned into a kind of commonsense and commonplace of the American will to remake the material landscape into a locus of spiritualized awe and self-empowerment. I take "Contemplations" to reveal such a pious landscape of American "election"—of self-election into the "rapted wit sublime." Bradstreet's poetry remains exemplary, it seems to me, of an awe-stricken sublimity struggling to be born in an inhospitable climate of "desert wilderness" and a cultural landscape of hegemonic plainness, as her woman's voice becomes marked with anxious transgression exactly as it is lifting into rapture.

As an early and even oxymoronic incarnation of such a *Christianized* sublime, Bradstreet is both blasted to mute admiration by the grandeur of the past yet enabled by the sublimity of this radical tradition—the "other tradition" of her beloved Du Bartas and, later, of John Milton—to achieve some version of an original voice. Worshipping the poetic sublime, Bradstreet says something from *New* England by which to supplement and make new the Nine Muses of tradition. American poetry is often caught (as in Bradstreet, from the start) in this fruitful tension between an indebtedness to prior languages silencing the self before the burden of the European past, and hyperboles of inventiveness, or vacancy—the will to modernity marking a displaced self struggling to innovate poetry in a future-haunted landscape of emptiness and bulk, as a way to voice what John Cage would later proclaim is "knowing nowness."[7]

As a Puritan woman given to the very *male* art of English poetry which had come down to her, as she realized, "shod by Chaucer's boots and Homer's furs"; as a would-be poet of high feeling before the creatural world, whom Nathaniel Ward rightly praised in the "Introductory Verses" as an "Auth'ress [who] was a right Du Bartas girl," sporting her own brand of stylistic "spurs";[8] and as a woman of "unweaned" maternal attachments to her own flesh and blood touchingly portrayed as "eight birds hatched in one nest," Bradstreet wrote from the curious position of a marginalized subject permitted to aggrandize and *to feel*. That is, she could as such a poet succumb to sudden, transgressive flights of rapture (yet thereby produce out of these moods her own convictions of faith and grace) before the creatural world. Indeed, this storehouse of natural images was fast becoming (after Du Bartas and the awakened European interest in Longinus) the basic substance of the sublime mode, as *humilitas* gave way to a divinely sanctioned *sublimitas,* anywhere on earth.[9]

Just registering such poetic moments of "feeling knowledge" (sublime transport) in poetic "contemplations" or prosaic "meditations," Bradstreet was (by gender) already outside the law of *plain-style* subordination; her voice of sensuous rapture was secretly operating, as we might now say, "from the peculiar *sub rosa* position of the doubly-displaced subject" who is never fully present to the (male) interpretive community as plain sign nor as self.[10] The sublime seemingly ratified such illicit moods and motives outside, or beyond, the law. Such power, at least, came with the occupational territory.

Postfeminist revisionings of American poetics now underway might allow us to rescue Bradstreet's verse from the hegemony of Perry Miller's New England Way as anti-fleshly and characteristically "plain," as monological and metaphysical in its poetic mode. For, if the dissemination of the vaunted "Plain Style" worked to restrain male egos into stylistic plainness, or shackled and bloated the energy of Edward Taylor into nervous excess, say, the female poet as *Tenth Muse* could spring up in the Massachusetts wilds from inhabiting, by contrast, the secret space of her own recurring rapture. Bradstreet early suggests the locus of an American countertradition, the making not only of what Wendy Martin and Cheryl Walker have tracked and differentiated as "a female counter-poetic" to the reign of phallo-logic (see notes 11 and 27), but also, from a more genealogical point of view, of the generic possibility of an American sublime not wholly displaced by anxiety towards the past, a mood of which, as a scribbling woman and wilderness poet, she had an impressive dose.

Empowering herself as poet, Bradstreet installs and instantiates the genre of the American sublime. Yet Martin oddly disqualifies Anne Bradstreet—if not American woman poets more generally—from innovating such a sublime mode, stipulating, almost like Edmund Burke, that these privatized poets tend to write at the level of the domestic, the ordinary, and the beautiful. "Because these

73

women writers [Bradstreet/Dickinson/Rich] reject the male hierarchies that accord more importance to public than to private life," Martin claims, "their poetry is not a narrative of sublime moments but a chronicle of the quotidian." [11]

Writing palpably within a Protestant tradition of exalted feeling and high truths modeled after the *Devine Weekes* of the Calvinist poet, Du Bartas, Bradstreet nevertheless *could* and indeed did, I will claim, write a sublime poetry of "feeling knowledge" towards that very quotidian which, in an instant of transport, linked the "rapt contemplation" of nature, as item and framework, to the contemplation of God. Surrounded by privations and dread, the American sublime is emergent, seemingly stranded, yet *there* in the poetry of Anne Bradstreet. The ingredients and consequences of this event have gone largely unrecognized, at least as instantiating the makings of a poetic genre.

Like latter-day American and equally Christian poets, such as William Livingston, William Cullen Bryant, Walt Whitman, Emily Dickinson, or Frederick Goddard Tuckerman, Bradstreet registers "the sublime" as a moment of pious awe before the landscape in which the poet is dislocated, undone, yet perilously uplifted into regions of spirit. The poetic result is, quite often, an elevated tone of praise and a sense, more materially speaking, of symbolic self-empowerment where the ego fits in a scene of its own self-constituted unity. The sublime, as Bradstreet early glimpsed, might have cash-value consequences if sustained through faithful labor. This scenario of *conversion,* heights and risks of ecstasy in an indigenous setting, is memorably depicted in "Contemplations," a poem which suggests the emerging genre of an American sublime in its tone of "rapted wit" and master narrative of conversion.

Displaced from community power into the no-place of poetry, this hyperbolic *Tenth Muse Lately Sprung Up In America* (London: Bowtell, 1650) was presented to her largely male readers by amazed male critics ("To force a woman's birth" in such a labor of "pleasant witty poetry," the book was printed in London not by herself but by her brother-in-law, John Woodbridge)[12] as a "right Du Bartas girl." That is, Bradstreet emerges as an amazing (and threatening) offspring of the Protestant sublime which was increasingly legitimating such private "rapture" to supplement the textual mediations of the Bible and the Church. The mood seemed necessary to the settlement of New World havens.

The Puritan sublime of this "right Du Bartas girl," as depicted in "Contemplations, could be conjured to serve the rapture of conversion: representing the moment as an interiorized opening of "rapt senses" to natural creatures of the Massachusetts wilds such as birds, brooks, and trees, of which woman herself was a salient embodiment after the figural fall of Eve. Her "rapt," if not sun-raped, senses were made into signs of exalted feeling, of course, and (more latently) into signs transgressing the very plainstyle *limits* (in the *sub/lime*) which the poem went on to moralize. That is, however evocative of New World powers, the mood of the sublime had to be converted into a credible metaphor of divine law and of man's fall into sensuous subjectivity, a legitimate *figura* for the collective (male) project to subdue a beast- and Satan-filled wilderness.

Relegated by gender to the *humilitas* of lowly domestic productions (the textual slogan of this "Feminist Bradstreet" emerging in the 1980s, as in Martin, becomes "In better dress to trim thee was my mind, / But nought save home-spun Cloth, in the house I find") and, as a Calvinist, hyper-cognizant of her own reprobation, Bradstreet subjected herself to moods of recurring stylistic anxiety towards representing any such elevated subjects or attitudes beyond reclamation. This anxiety yet reveals her deepest aspiration to evoke the *sublime* style in a cultural code of Puritanism which largely constrained her voice to use the "home-spun Cloth" of lesser modes of lyric/ domestic production. Needless to say, these quotidian lyrics are deft and local, such as those love poems to her Christ-like absent husband or ones keeping track of her chattering flock.

In the larger frame of "Contemplations," however, she blames this lingering sense of stylistic inadequacy and any smallness of voice (*humilitas*) on her own female "imbecility." But this self-definition is surely overdetermined by the Puritan consciousness of womanhood as inferior, as well as of sinfulness as a perpetual threat (as is exposed in stanzas 10 through 17, where figural men pursue base instincts and vain pleasures, and "The Virgin Earth, of blood, her first draught drinks"). This drive to settle upon a humbled voice of textual austerity is also urged upon her by the sermon-induced hegemony of "the Puritan Plain Style," which would downplay the raptures of selfhood and the richness of nature. The "inner feminist world" of Bradstreet was fully mediated by such Puritan strictures and a discourse of piety which subjected this brilliant poet to the laments of a *failed sublime*. Unsponsored by props of tradition or genre, this can make for a voice of perpetual anxiety and seemingly idiotic awe before prior and surrounding shapes of textual grandeur.[13]

If the sublime of Bradstreet emerges blasted and torn, and her drive to write poetry is hemmed in by anxiety and threatened by a self-humiliating sense of modesty and scorn, this is because the sublime comes down to Bradstreet as already gendered in voices of mastery and empowerment that are fully Eurocentric and not her own. Courting female power, this "right Du Bartas girl" Bradstreet must enter into if not invent a genre of permitted trespass in which women such as herself can seize or inhabit roles formerly alotted to the strength of men.

As Patricia Yaeger theorizes in "Toward a Female Sublime," without in any way considering the untimely figure of Bradstreet, the forces that would conspire against a woman inhabiting any sovereign sublime have made for what Yaeger calls a "failed sublime." "In texts where it occurs," she theorizes, "we witness a woman's dazzling, unexpected empowerment followed by a moment in which this power is snatched away—often by a masculine countersublime that has explicitly phallic components." Though women poets like Bradstreet are surely capable of miming and joining the great, we must go on to recognize, as Yaeger argues, "that something in the social order (either something external, or a set of beliefs internalized by the actant herself) intervenes, and the heroine finds herself not only stripped of transcendent powers, but bereft, in a lower social stratum than before."[14] The context and ideological hegemony of Puritanism would mitigate against claims of selfglory or threats of female empowerment; hence they must be smuggled in and questioned, if not explained away, by Bradstreet herself as "poetic rapture" or as merely the inflated claims of the bewildered, brazen, and dispossessed.

To evoke one telling example, Bradstreet's "bleating" strain and "rudeness" of style as she contemplates the "royal hearse" of Queen Elizabeth would yet register, rather outrageously and with all the anxious power-dynamics towards self-anointed queenhood of Emily Dickinson, her own *rapture* before that British "rex" who had already, in quite worldly terms, invalidated the (very sexist) claim that "our sex is void of reason" and incapable of such precedent-making grandeur:

> Although, great Queen, thou now in silence lie
> Yet though loud herald Fame doth to the sky
> Thy wondrous worth proclaim in every clime,
> And so hath vowed where there is world or time.
> So great's thy glory and thine excellence,
> The sound thereof rapts every human sense,
> That men account it no impiety,
> To say thou wert a fleshy deity.

(195)

This wonder-struck elegy "In Honour of that High and Mighty Princess Queen Elizabeth of Happy Memory" is coded with *rapture* if not divinization before female *power/grandeur,* that exalted consciousness of the specular model's superiority. No less so emerges Bradstreet's humility, which this poet was forever feeling, even before a fellow woman who might model her own empowerment and will to elevation. Bradstreet is transported to incarnate a mode of elevated praise, however, by a woman herself elevated into a "fleshy deity," a highly un-Puritanical creature of political grandeur subjecting England to a reign of happiness who had sent "Her seamen [subversive pun on textual *semen*] through all straits the world did round" (197).

As a poetic stance, nonetheless, Bradstreet aspires to mime the fleshly grandeur of her subject—here the praise of a female sublimity—which paradoxically inspires her to a rapture that humbles if not annihilates the emergence of her own voice: "Her personal perfections, who would tell / Must dip his pen in the Helaconian well, / Which I may not, my pride doth but aspire / To read what others write and so admire" (197). So blasted, the voice falls off into that of a *readers' sublime:* that is, Bradstreet becomes dwarfed by the prior sublimity of England and France, which only male "pride" could aspire to emulate (as does her emulous cock son). But her effusive praise for this "glorious sun" as son/rex of England is motivated by a sense that woman can and will instance this power, this "excellence" and majesty, which the Queen like a *fleshly* deity had once embodied. Through Elizabeth, Bradstreet models yet disables the emergence of her own American sublime.

Not surprisingly, the affect-rich and over-allusive textuality of *Tenth Muse* had inspired in Nathaniel Ward his own quite misogynistic warning, distanced in the timeless voice of Apollo, "Let men look to't, lest women wear the spurs." Or as John Woodbridge warns readers concerning woman poets *too* ambitious of such grandeur, unlike his "modest," "solid" and "comely" Mistress Bradstreet, "Some books of women I have heard of late, / Perused some, so witless, intricate, / So void of sense, and truth, as if to err / Were only wished (acting above their sphere) / And all to get, what (silly souls) they lack, / Esteem to be the wisest of the pack" (5). Such "silly souls" (Puritan females) would aspire to lord it above their subordinate workaday sphere ("in better dress") writing intricate sense and even voicing "truth," that is, the logocentric perogative of the governing male. If these souls aspire to the esteem and envy of the phallic pack and somehow style themselves sublime, they will prove incapable of those "pleasant witty strains" Woodbridge attributes to his scribbling sister-in-law, whom he yet forcibly publishes (and advertises, as in colonial travelogues) as a New World wonder, a goddess lately (somehow) sprung up in crabbed *New* England.

Bradstreet depicts these very sublime moods of "amazement," against all odds, as a self-made labyrinth of enraptured feeling in which sensuousness exceeds moralization, or public recuperation, yet is interpreted as a sign of God: "The consideration of these things would with amazement certainly resolve me that there is an Eternal Being." "These things" of which Anne Bradstreet speaks to her children are the "wondrous workes" of nature, which present to the senses the vast and orderly evidence for God's existence. Such works, moralized, provide the basis for an *immense* metaphor of correspondence between earth and heaven. The New World is not necessarily, thereby, a place of hermeneutic deprivation. Contemplating nature in such rapt moods of election, faith is possible, indeed inevitable—a "feeling knowledge" fitfully obtained. Nature awes Bradstreet into faith in God as the source of vastness and as author of her own potential greatness on earth. Not alone "the verity of the scriptures," not extraordinary events like miracles or tempests, not analytical meditation on the state of the self, but nature affectionately *beheld* fills the mind with the self-subjugating idea of God. Vacancy could be converted and moralized into poetic immensity. However shorn of creature comforts, surely colonial America had that.

"Feeling Knowledge" in "Contemplations"

Such a scenario of sublime election is recorded in "Contemplations," the Bradstreet poem that best serves as a Euramerican prototype of this Puritan sublime, which would "with amazement" use nature as sensuous means to affirm sensations and concoct ideas of Nature's God. For Bradstreet, as for diverse American Puritan poets such as Richard Steere and Edward Johnson, sensuous images of nature, beheld "in Raptur'd Contemplation," could lead to ecstatic convictions of faith and provide some basis for a metaphor linking this "under world" of nature with a transcendent world of the spirit.[15] The body of nature evoked affections which convinced the poet's senses and, rather too inevitably, her reason of God's existence in and beyond nature. Such had been Du Bartas's Calvinist vision of rapt self-election, as this French poet had generated a new poetics of the senses which all the more befitted, albeit generally and abstractly, the landscape of the New World.

Between the publication in 1650 of *The Tenth Muse Lately Sprung Up in America* and the revised edition of *Several Poems* (Boston: John Foster, 1678), Bradstreet wrote "Contemplations," a 33-stanza poem on beholding nature which met with lofty praise from contemporaries and enthusiastic commentary from later generations, most of whom rightly treat the poem as a "Romantic" precursor in feeling and genre, several even citing the self-divided flights of Keats's "Ode to a Nightingale."

"Contemplations" opens with a twilight scene of natural and autumnal wealth, spiritually beheld in a rather self-produced state of exaltation which would somehow remain "void of pride":

> Some time now past in the autumnal tide,
> When Phoebus wanted but one hour to bed,
> The trees all richly clad, yet void of pride,

Where gilded o'er by his rich golden head.
Their leaves and fruits seemed painted, but was true,
Of green, of red, of yellow, mixed hue;
Rapt were my senses at this delectable view.

(204)

Bradstreet is moved ("rapt were my senses") by the autumnal majesty of nature to mimic some visual-aural majesty in her own style. She urges her discourse of rapture towards an adjectival indulgence that risks violating the ascesis of Puritan plainness. For, as Norman Grabo has pointed out, her "rapture" remains a dangerous feeling, suggesting sexual oneness with earthly Phoebus and his natural artistry. However, despite our modernist clichés, such as those in William Carlos Williams's *In the American Grain,* tender moods of transport and touch were not wholly idiosyncratic for American Puritans, Indian-hating and devil-fearing of the "desert wilds" as they well might be.[16]

In the influential Puritan devotion manual outlining an amazingly *worldly* mode of Christian self-interpellation and interiority, *Saints' Everlasting Rest* (1649–1650), for example, Richard Baxter disseminated a process of *contemplation* which used "sensible objects" (Bradstreet's imagery of sun, trees, fruit, rivers, fish, birds, say) to stimulate moods of spiritual happiness ("Consolation") and, later, "Heavenly Contemplation."[17] Like Milton's transport-hungry drifter in "Il Penseroso," Baxter recommended pensive hours of twilight as the natural and Biblically endorsed setting to intensify the "solitude of contemplative devotion": "I have always found that the fittest time for myself is the evening, from sun setting to the twilight. I the rather mention this, because it was the experience of a better and wiser man; for it is expressly said, *Isaac went out to meditate in the field at the even-tide.*" Seeking solitary communication with the sublimity of this God, Bradstreet imitates the figural pattern of the meditating Isaac by delighting in sensible objects. In doing so, she loads every stylistic rift with adjectival ore and hints that the masculine Phoebus has "rapt" (ravished or raped) her with not-so-pagan delight.

The poet presents this transport and surplus feeling in response to the landscape, creating two correspondingly *rich* surfaces to be interiorized as the makings of spiritual capital: that of nature and that of the "painted" text. In so doing, Bradstreet enacts what she means by her Baxter-like title, *"Contemplations"*: (1) sustained focus on the elevated splendor of nature can lead to (2) a heightened mood of transport before the divine artistry of nature, and (3) the poet ultimately goes on to transcendence of nature through an affective recognition of the "immortal" and "vast" beauty/power of God.

In effect, the self can achieve this faith-drenched exaltation in a mood of *rapt appreciation* that is self-engendered: the poet is alone with the landscape, but thoroughly interpellated by the fledgling community. Such a poem can really go nowhere, however, for the self only affirms its preexisting set of beliefs in that Christ whose sublimity is, unlike that of rivers and autumnal trees, immortal and infinite: "But he whose name is grav'd in the white stone / Shall last and shine when all of these are gone." The American sublime, in this early incarnation, is always located in the same place: not so much in the landscape as in the power implicit behind that landscape and selfhood, namely, in God. So Christianized, the sublime has to be separated from the objects and characters that seemingly instigate and inspire such moods.

In the next stanza, then, Bradstreet undermines this ecstatic union with nature by connecting such attributes of earthly "power and beauty" with more properly supernatural sources:

> I wist not what to wish, yet sure thought I,
> If so much excellence abide below,
> How excellent is He that dwells on high,
> Whose power and beauty by his works we know?
> Sure he is goodness, wisdom, glory, light,
> That hath this under world so richly dight; . . .
>
> (205)

As in the neo-Platonism of Longinus, then, Bradstreet can celebrate "power and beauty" as sources of sublime rapture only if she redeems them mentally as analogous to the sublime excellence of God, that ultimate poet "whose power and beauty by his works we know." Sublimated into God or Queen, the poet can identify with sublime power.

If the "under world" calls, the self must uplift nature and sublimate the mind to a higher affirmation of faith. In the *Devine Weekes and Works*, Joshua Sylvester's vivid translation into English of Du Bartas had given Protestant poets a kind of new authority to view this sublime of nature with rapt "spectacles of Faith," in a more sensuous style, one charging the self with moods of a very Christian transport:

> God, of himselfe incapable to sence,
> In's Works reveales him t'our intelligence:
> There-in our fingers feele, our nostrils smell,
> Our Palats taste his vertues that excell:
> He shewes him to our eyes, talkes to our eares,
> In th' ord'red motions of the spangled Spheares.[18]

If the Puritan eschewed "painted" forms of worship in his purified temple, in accord with the sense-denying norms of the "plain" style, she yet could worship, in the manner of Du Bartas, by portraying ("seemed painted, but was true") high-minded rapture in God's natural temple, "rich" with materials for a sublime poem. The material of the Earth, "richly dight," evoked the contemplation of "works" in an immediate apprehension of God, through fingers, nose, tongue, eyes, ears.

Imitating sublime Du Bartas, Bradstreet surveys the panoramic cosmos of God in her equally long-winded and lush *Quaternions,* showing "How divers natures make one Unity," in an avowedly "lofty stile" "Where Art, and more than Art, in nature shines." Imitating Du Bartas's transport to the "rapted wit sublime," Bradstreet sought, in effect, to survey if not to localize the natural whole as a divine whole, and to make the sensible object (tree, sun) contribute to a spiritual effect (transport), and so to increased vocational power.[19]

Bradstreet starts up her very worldly machinery of "Contemplations" by focusing upon a natural scene, responding affectively, and later reflecting back upon her transport as a means to what Baxter termed "heavenly-mindedness," the joy of transcending sensuous for spiritual unions. She enacts, in an exemplary solitude, how such focus upon nature can impress the mind with sublime "amazement," a devotional awe that inspires deeper belief in God, the self's articulate power, and the new world's lushly reworkable wealth.

In her prose confession, "To My Dear Children," the Massachusetts poet echoes this very sublime process of Puritan "contemplation," showing how fits of rapture had overcome more bitter moods of infidelity (described, even before Kant, as a "block") towards these "wondrous workes" of God: "That there is a God my Reason would soon tell me by the wondrous workes that I see, the vast frame of the Heaven and the Earth, the order of all things, night and day, summer and winter, spring and autumne, the dayly providing for all this great household upon the Earth, the preserving and directing of All to its proper end. The consideration of these things would with amazement certainly resolve me that there is an Eternal Being" (243).

This passage clarifies what remains sublime for the senses of Bradstreet and what will remain so for early poets of the American sublime: the objects and affections of nature; the harmonious correspondence of local sense to cosmic spirit; the orderly, even aesthetic, progress in the cosmos; vertical heights and transports of spiritual union, and lesser forms of union (as with her husband); lofty piety carried into exclamation and praise; a tonality of wonder and appreciation; the happiness self-produced in birdlike flights of the spirit "into a country beyond sight." And all these wonderworks of God and subjective excess are threatened by bitter blockages and moods of sudden disbelief as well.

"Contemplations" presents this recurring experience of *transport,* suggesting that for Bradstreet the Puritan conviction of supernal grace (what Weber calls the self-conjured "election" to a calling that is both worldly and world-denying) came at such solitary moments of passionate perception. For if the Puritan placed a rather compulsive emphasis upon the purification of public forms of worship (as in "A Dialogue between Old England and New"), this cultural code also emphasized the individual's self-purification or "preparation" for an often passive experience of ecstatic conversion. Perry Miller defined this Puritan ecstasy as the quasi-Augustinian "moment of aesthetic vision" when the rapt believer receives "supernal" grace (justification) and the sense of faith and godliness (sanctification): "The one pure, unqualified, and absolute beatitude was the inward ecstasy of regeneration." [20]

In stanza 4, Bradstreet shifts the focus from a growing oak to an experience of the powerful sun so as to intensify the emotion of "amazement":

Then higher on the glistering Sun I gazed,
Whose beams was shaded by the leavie tree;

> The more I looked, the more I grew amazed,
> And softly said, "What glory's like to thee?"
> Soul of this world, this universe's eye,
> No wonder some made thee a deity;
> Had I not better known, alas, the same had I.
> (205)

She must resist seductive enchantments of nature, oddly, by experiencing them to the ecstatic hilt, the better to transcend them for consolations of spiritual beauty. Going beyond "feeling knowledge" of the sensuous, Bradstreet imagines the excellence of the Creator authoring these creatures, using ecstasy merely as foreshadow:

> How full of glory then must thy Creator be,
> Who gave this bright light luster unto thee?
> Admired, adored for ever, be that Majesty.
> (206)

"Musing thus with contemplation fed," she leads the self to mental reflection, new transport, and tones of reverence befitting spiritual Majesty. The sublime installs a power beyond trees or suns or metaphors.

Bradstreet can load her poetic lines with adjectival ore, indulging in the stylistic lure of "rich golden" suns and "in the darksome womb of fruitful nature dive," I think, as she aspires towards the "higher lay" of a melopoeic poetry bordering on the ineffable. She can do this because her natural world is made over into sensuous evidence for God's existence and a rapt stimulus towards contemplation. Mystifying or displacing the source of her own lyric power, such a voice would celebrate not nature, not herself as sublime maker, but "my great Creator":

> Silent alone, where none or saw, or heard,
> In pathless paths I lead my wandering feet,
> My humble eyes to lofty skies I reared
> To sing some song, my mazed Muse thought meet.
> My great Creator I would magnify,
> That nature had thus decked liberally;
> But Ah, and Ah, again, my imbecility!
> (206)

84

Bradstreet's "mazed Muse" would sing in tones befitting and miming the sublime God. But the blockages of her feminine humility ("But Ah, and Ah, again, my imbecility") and an American stylistic anxiety compel a rather nervous and broken syntax. Her voice is emerging, though, shorn of Eurocentric tradition or model. The result in such moments is the compulsive *modesty topos* of a self-limited poet, anxious to voice aesthetic grandeur but incapable of linguistic freshness or singularity of stance. The American sublime seems all but blocked and blasted at its solitary birth.

If, to invoke the Weber-like reading of Larzer Ziff, "Piety, the possession of grace, freed man to treat the material world as wholly mediate, a malleable set of circumstances that would yield to their sanctified condition," "Contemplations" shows that such aesthetic transport remains, at this early point, problematic.[21] The image and effect of autumn trees *are* moving, but finally transient, whereas the image and effect of God are both "excellent" and "everlasting." Any *natural sublime* must here, as later in William Livingston's equally pious *Philosophic Solitude* (New York: James Barker, 1747) give way predictably to a spiritual sublime through transcendence in consciousness and subjugation of the self to the ideology of moral codes. Even Kantian discourse will emerge to rope in such energies of the sublime, rather fitfully, to serve this Christian pedagogy.

Just as transport before nature remains problematic for any Puritan, however womanly or outside the law, so is any full sublimity of poetic style. For is not a richly artificed ("painted") style an act of *worldly* vanity, and a sensuous poetry an implicit allegiance more to sense and wealth than to spirit? Perry Miller, who first reconstituted the conventions of the Puritan "plain style" for our own era, oddly suggested that Bradstreet's poetry yet had struggled towards the "sensual delights" we now term sublime:

> Of course, the Puritan aesthetic restricted the Puritan poet. He could not surrender himself to sensual delights, and the code of the plain style would apply to his rhythms as well as his prose. Consequently little of this production speaks readily to the modern reader, but every collection of American poetry must salute the lyrics of Anne Bradstreet.[22]

Miller works hard to repress his lurking sense that Bradstreet's lyrics might show how one could intensify one's "feeling knowledge" of the "Glory of God." Of course, the elevation of her poetry remains strictly pious, as she explained to her children in works such as "Meditations Divine and Morall": "I have not studied in this you read to show my skill, but to declare the Truth—not to set forth myself, but the Glory of God" (240).

This needs to be so because, for Puritan poets, the glory of God could be celebrated in what Milton—having early incorporated Longinus into his poetic/rhetoric with everything else under the Cambridge sun—oddly termed the "simple, sensuous, and passionate" medium of poetry, which puts the world's majesty into the service of glorifying, not the imagination nor the artifact itself, but God as source and end of any natural sublimity.[23] If Bradstreet's coupling of sublime ecstasy with religiosity seems odd or automatic to us now, we need only recall that even in the moody locus of "Il Penseroso," Milton allows his contemplative poet a vision of self-transport in "twilight groves," where religious splendor can "Dissolve me into ecstasies, / And bring all Heav'n before mine eyes" (lines 155–66).

In Bradstreet's dialogue of "The Flesh and the Spirit," Flesh mocks the claims of such sublime unions, Spirit's habit of transcending sensual wealth and delight for the imagined consolations and "happefy'd" unions of "contemplation":

> Sister, quoth Flesh, what liv'st thou on
> Nothing but Meditation?
> Doth Contemplation feed thee so
> Regardlessly to let earth goe?
>
> (215)

Enduring the temptations of this unregenerate voice, Spirit presents the counter-argument as a smugly contemplative voice:

> My thoughts do yield me more content
> Then can thy hours in pleasure spent. . . .
> Mine Eye doth pierce the heavens, and see
> What is Invisible to thee. . . .
>
> (217)

The mind experiences celestial vision in terms of earthly splendor, however, transacting a metaphoric process of worldliness in which sensuous images glorify the spiritual. Baxter had urged the contemplating mind to "compare the objects of sense with the objects of faith," as in the poetry of *Revelations*. Contemplation was exactly such a process of rising "from sense to faith by comparing heavenly with earthly joys." In this scenario of ethical self-interpellation according to the Puritan code, the earth's body is not denied but purified, subsumed, consecrated, or *sublimated* through a self-created affect of transport linking such states of excess to signs of spiritual fulfillment. Empowerment has to be vocationally conjured, yet explained away.

When, in stanza 8 of "Contemplations," Bradstreet transcends the immediate scene to wander amazedly "in pathless paths" of interior consolation, she nevertheless returns to nature to heighten such affections:

> I heard the merry grasshopper then sing.
> The black-clad cricket bear a second part;
> They kept one tune and played on the same string,
> Seeming to glory in their little art.
> Shall creatures abject thus their voices raise
> And in their kind resound their Maker's praise,
> Whilst I, as mute, can warble forth no higher lays?
>   (207)

If even the modest artistry of pagan/natural creatures contributes to the glory of God, what inhibits the emerging sublimity of Bradstreet's "higher lay"? Her doctrinal answer is presented in stanzas 10 through 17, a meditative "composition of place" in which the figures of the Fall are reimagined to refresh her consciousness of sin, which only the justification of Christ can efface. Bradstreet imagines herself present in Eden, and watches "glorious Adam" fall from his harmony with nature into a bickering state of alienation and labor. Two lines of Edenic happiness (stanza 11) give way to five lines of pain.

If the grasshopper and "black-clad cricket" contribute to the harmony of divine order, "seeming to glory in their little art," Bradstreet is determined by the Calvinistic burden of original sin and her own recurring sense of stylistic impoverishment before the painted glories of nature and Du Bartas. Hence, seemingly, she "can warble forth no higher lays." Aspiring to maintain a voice of poetic sublimity, Bradstreet early—indeed *first*—undergoes what Harold Bloom has termed "the anxiety of influence" as the danger and possibility of a "counter-sublime" (self-demonization): the sense that prior poetic sublimity cannot be transcended by the language of the present American voice, however transumptive, canny, or hyperbolical.[24] She recalls the prelapsarian harmony of Adam and nature, but such "contemplation" is marred by her renewed preoccupation with limitation and sin. Adam's blackened "Progeny" now lead lives of "pleasures vain" and spurious liberty (stanza 17), akin to the enchanting but lesser sense-transports of "L'Allegro." The sublime seems otherwise and elsewhere.

In stanza 18, Bradstreet again turns from self-examining reflection (*meditation*) to behold (*contemplate*) the natural "heavens as in their prime" and the seasonal earth "still clad in green," in order to recuperate her response of rapt wonder (stanza 1), despite inherited guilt, occupational anxiety, and the vanity of worldly pleasures (stanzas 10 through 17). As Ziff finely comments, "Like the great nature poets she does not condemn the changes brought by time, but, rather, expresses a deep longing to submit to them as if the beauty of seasonal rhythms was in itself divine" (13). A creature of nature, she cannot will the rebirth of Spring or the felicity of birds, but is condemned to anxiety, labor, and the often alienating burden of self-reflection on the "oblivion" of the grave or the slightness of her own works.

Having moved from contemplation of "the heavens" to affirmations of faith, Bradstreet again (as in stanzas 1 and 18) focuses upon nature as starting-point for renewed wonder through further "musings." To accrue a misplaced sublimity, the poem seemingly starts again:

Under the cooling shadow of a stately elm
Close sat I by a goodly river's side,
Where gliding streams the rocks did overwhelm,
A lonely place, with pleasure dignified.
I once that loved the shady woods so well,
Now thought the rivers did the trees excel,
And if the sun would ever shine, there would I dwell.

(210)

Opting for the solitude of an oddly sublime grotto, where "Il Penseroso" received his own imagined dream of airy transformation (lines 131–55), Bradstreet focuses upon the force of a river; not as a source of sublime vision, however (as in Longinus), but as a perceived emblem of the soul's journey (the river) to the union of paradise (the "longed-for ocean"). The poetic saint's everlasting rest is obtained ultimately in eternity. But when the Puritan mind imagines this fulfillment, it does so in images of earthly splendor, accruing figurative *and* real wealth ("vast mansion").

After focusing with self-conscious nostalgia upon the "felicity" of fish ("You wat'ry folk"), Bradstreet presents yet another climactic experience of sublime transport before the delights of nature, this time before the "melodious strain" of a nightingale:

> While musing thus with contemplation fed,
> And thousand fancies buzzing in my brain,
> The sweet-tongued Philomel perched o'er my head
> And chanted forth a most melodious strain
> Which rapt me so with wonder and delight,
> I judged my hearing better than my sight,
> And wished me wings with her a while to take my flight.
>
> (211–12)

Nourished by "feeling knowledge" of sensible objects in Massachusetts (such as elms, river, rocks, and fish), and "buzzing" with fancied analogy, Bradstreet hears a nightingale evoke through music (Poe's "supernal" or sublime art) an ecstasy which deepens and renews her sense of harmony between mind and place. The transport occurs not through the stimulus of the plain and powerful *logos* of the converting sermon, however, but through the worldly lyricism of a (mere) bird's chant. Again rapt/raped with the sublime emotion of wonder, she imagines her consciousness to ascend with, if not as, the female nightingale, becoming a sensible object at once of celestial spirit and of terrestrial might.

Such a transport in a solitary locale (later valorized as the "contemplative" grotto of sublimely imaginative vision, as in Thomas Warton's "The Pleasures of Melancholy") can be termed a "romantic" convention, effecting the nostalgic fusion of mind and object as a means to self-transcendence. Such New World locales of spirit occasion, like tiny cathedrals, the private yet religious quest for moments of liberating "flight" towards a happiness of spirit. This flight upward (transcendence) is brought about in the interior of the Puritan self through *transport*.[25]

In "The fifth Day of the first Weeke," Sylvester's translation of Du Bartas had presented, earlier, a no less "rapt" response to the nightingale:

> But all this's nothing to the *Nightingale*,
> Breathing so sweetly from a brest so small,
> So many Tunes, whose Harmonie excells
> Our Voice, our Viols, and all Musike els.
> Good Lord! how oft in a greene Oken Grove,
> In the coole shadow have I stood, and strove
> To marrie mine immortal Layes to theirs,
> Rapt with delight of their delicious Aiers?[26]

Bradstreet's reworked and reworded sublimity keeps the elm and oak and shade of rapt contemplation, wherein a lyric nightingale (unknown to the New England landscape, as realist critics mockingly noted as far back as the 1840s) could transport her with sudden rapture. Unlike Du Bartas, if a bit more like the incarnational Whitman, the Puritan poetess integrates such raptures into the context of a sustained poem by positing and fleshing out exactly the relationship between such natural ecstasy and that desired union with the sublimity of God.

Alienated to a life of "cruciating" self-doubt, melancholy thought (like Keats), and anxious toil (like Adam), Bradstreet early emulates the freedom of the "sweet airy legion." Whatever the consolations of nature, the Puritan woman remains subject to a life of self-examination and self-rebuke, to pains in body and mind and a seemingly endless state of "vexation" within and without, caused by "knowledge ignorant" of truly spiritual consolations (stanza 29). Bradstreet's ecstasies and "feeling knowledge" of such creatures must move towards consolations and a "feeling knowledge" of God. But the landscape has been sanctified and made malleable to human usages (such as transport) through the language of the poem. The sublime empowers and uplifts the voices of poets whom it otherwise might break.[27]

Bradstreet would be a "merry Bird" and sing a sublime lyric of divine praise, in a summer of bliss. Such, however, cannot be her woman's lot in that sin-conscious version of Christianity disseminated as American Puritanism. Having risked sensuous, if not sensual, rapture in a natural setting, Bradstreet merely (and even boringly) reiterates the vain pleasures of "sinfull man" to make him "deeply groan for that divine Translation" into immortal spirit, and to undermine prior illusions of worldly delight. Man cannot remain a merry bird in rapt harmony with divine works, but must *journey* (like Whitman's adventuring Soul) through time to the "vast Mansion" and secure "port" of eternity as an ever-questing mariner (stanza 31), whose plot is marred by delusion and adversity as he "saileth in this world of pleasure." All nature secretly *groans* for redemption in the body, and the body in "Contemplations" is finally redeemed only through a kind of ecstatic death, a surrender of the egotistical river to the cosmic ocean, the "translation" of suffering body into rejoicing spirit. The earth's body must be transcended, but not before it has been consecrated as a stimulus to sublime contemplation.

When Bradstreet mocks the "fond fool" who "takes this earth ev'n for heav'ns bower," the crude irony casts a self-demystifying light upon her own sublime bowers of bliss wherein she had sought to expand moments of transport into secure consolations, resting spots in the movement of time into eternity. Moving from sensual response to affirmation of doctrinal precept, the result is all too didactic. Yet Baxter defined the aim of such "contemplation" as a way to get spiritual truth "from thy head to thy heart," and to experience the notion of faith with "the bloud and spirits of Affection." Having felt the necessity of earthly transcendence through contemplation, Bradstreet can now affirm that "only above is found all with security," a sublimity immune from the ebb and flow of grandeur in such a world and as such words.

Shifting in the final stanza (33) to leave-taking (didactic) couplets, Bradstreet reiterates this sublimity of spirit by drawing upon an image (later beloved to Emily Dickinson) not from nature but from the types of *Revelations*, the "white stone" which Christ imparts to the justified:

> Nor wit nor gold, nor buildings scape times rust;
> But he whose name is graved in the white stone
> Shall last and shine when all of these are gone.
> (214)

Of course, the light of *Phoebus* (which opened the sublime scenario of the poem) has been surpassed by the inner light of *Christ* who, in this self-election of mind, will shine forever.

"Contemplations" mimes the splendors of the world in ecstatic praise, then transcends them in imagination to approach more closely to their Creator in amazed union. The sublime poem in America is, at its generic origin, typically such a nature lyric of quiet rapture and pensive praise. Like Bradstreet, the American poet often retreats to a solitary grotto to evoke, but really to self-create, a vocational sense of sacred presence and her or his own elected power. Like "Contemplations," later versions of the sublime will depict some imaginative union with a vaguely sketched-in place, ending with transcendence of those beloved powers and presences of sun and river and bird.

In a prefatory imitation of the *ababccc* stanza of "Contemplations," John Rogers (1631–1684) of Ipswich aptly commended *The Tenth Muse* to readers in an ecstasy of praise which nicely (like a tonal mimic) complements the poet's own ecstasy in "blissful bowers":

> Madam, twice through the Muses' grove I walked,
> Under your blissful bowers, . . .
> Twice have I drunk the nectar of your lines,
> Which high sublimed my mean born phantasy,
> Flushed with these streams of your Maronean wines
> Above myself rapt to an ecstasy: . . . [28]

While not exactly a "tenth muse" surpassing European modes of textual sublimity, Bradstreet does help to install a muse of *sublimated sublimity* ("which high sublimed my mean born phantasy") next to the locality of American rivers and trees. She humbly invents a lyric form, in "Contemplations," which remains appropriate to the contemplation of nature as an act of rapt, anxious, and lonely beholding. Awed by nature, God, Queen, as much as by her great poet of the Puritan sublime, Du Bartas, and terrified by an almost pagan worship of the sensuous sun as Phoebus, Bradstreet successfully evokes and negotiates the sublime of nature, in a mode of worried rapture. She helped make this "rapted wit sublime" a tonality fit for the climate and place. We might, at least as generously, say of her as she said of Du Bartas, giving vent to such wonder: "My ravished eyes and heart with faltering tongue, / In humble wise have vowed their service long" (192).

This Early American mode, conjugating and sublimating the landscape into the site of a lone transport, is fitfully plain, nervously sublime. Terror, emptiness, or the threat of abasement is not the whole story. Flip-flopping between heights of grandeur and depths of sudden imbecility and cliché, the poet might, through sheer effort and energy of will, supplement the Nine Muses of European poetry with tropes from "the Tenth Muse"—as the male blurbs for Bradstreet's poetry and place hyperbolized—and prove capable of a new, lyric reportage vindicating the (seeming) vacancies and sorry solitudes of American grandeur.

If the Puritan sensibility of Anne Bradstreet all too nervously depicted a landscape more of *mind* than of *Massachusetts* and gave birth to a poetry more of *topos* and *tropos* than of *locus*—as we might wish after the thickly descriptive and culture-glutted poetry of place such as Williams's *Paterson,* Ammons's *Sphere,* Olson's *Maximus,* Robert Pinsky's "Long Branch, New Jersey," Richard Hugo's immensely lonely Missoula, Montana, Thomas McGrath's spunky odes to the cowboy proletariat, or Diane Wakoski's place-absorbing obsessions in *Greed*—still, Bradstreet's voice rose up and expanded before the prospects of conversion amid the bleak loneliness of such American bowers and forests. "America" early served Bradstreet as a place/metaphor of seemingly vast "emptiness" and plural "possibility" where the colonial poet must ask herself, like any businessman amid the mobile multitudes, paranoid crowds, swirling numbers, and giddying speeds of the Capitalist's eagerly spiritualized New World sublime,

"Am I one of the elect?"

Poems like "Contemplations" created representative landscapes and scenarios of selfhood that, however threatened or deprived, helped the community of such sublimity fitfully to answer, "Yes."

FOUR

William Livingston's *Philosophic Solitude* and the Ideology of the Natural Sublime

On the contrary, a spacious horison is an Image of Liberty . . .

—Joseph Addison, *Spectator*, No. 412

Beyond the Religious Sublime

IF, AFTER THE stylistic monitions against *false sublimity* and self-inflated pomposity in Alexander Pope's "Peri Bathous" (1728), or Mather Byles's watered-down Loyalist version mocking sublime Bostonians entitled "Bombastic and Grubstreet Style: A Satire" (1727), only scribbling fools could still *admire* where men of sense merely *approved,* American landscapes of vastness and wildness, nevertheless, were stimulating diverse poets to adopt neo-Longinian conventions of wonder, ravishment, reverence, and rapture, and tones of would-be sublimity. As David S. Shields has documented, a "religious sublime" founded not only in the marvels of Biblical imagery but also in this newer mood of landscape elevation, as epitomized in a poem such as Sir Richard Blackmore's *Creation; a Philosophic Poem* (1712), permitted (if not *compelled*) New England poets of the 1720s such as Jane Turrell, Roger Wolcott, and John Adams to aspire to an indigenous Christianizing of the sublime poem. Even the sober poet-critic, Mather Byles, for example, felt compelled to imitate this palpably empiricist genre of sublime poetry wherein sensory surveying of nature could lead to benign emotions of pious transport—moods set, rather woodenly,

94

in a heightened landscape of enthusiasm "Where JESUS Flames with everlasting Rays" even in the sunrise of Boston, say, as John Adams lyrically proclaimed.[1]

Such hyperbolical signs of "sacred rapture" and of a responsive heightening of language and landscape, in various (and often tonally mixed) genres of American poetry, can now be read as imported variations on that mood of "sublime transport" (*hypsos*) which neo-Longinian aesthetics were endorsing in post-Lockean England as pleasures of imagination not to be avoided but invoked. This fashionable shift towards a new poetics of vastness was spreading, in British literary circles, through the affective-centered criticism of such works as Joseph Addison's "The Pleasures of the Imagination" (1712), John Dennis' *Grounds of Criticism in Poetry* (1704), and John Baillie's *Essay on the Sublime* (1747). Great literature functioned (according to this affect-drenched hermeneutic) like mountains, volcanoes, and oceans, and caused the poet-reader to engender, by linkages of sensation and association, a special mood of *pious rapture:* this mood of literary *sublimity* would lead almost invariably to affirmations of God's existence, even in the world-weary Addison. Poems, like sunrises or mountains, promoted a state of exalted "transport" that the Calvinist stress on the passive reception of grace had made even more crucial to poets of reformed Christianity in the years of the Great Awakening.[2]

Given the historical vacancy of America as measured against its vast geographical grandeur and an emerging social dynamic valorizing "liberty," this expanding interest in *domesticating* such modes of sublime contemplation for as-yet-unconscious or dimly perceived *political* purposes was given pre-Revolutionary expression in William Livingston's youthful poem, *Philosophic Solitude: or, The Choice of a Rural Life* (New York: James Barker, 1747), as I will detail. A colorful if wooden poem mingling contradictory tones from both pastoral and sublime modes, *Philosophic Solitude* yet sketches in and deploys the natural sublime of the American landscape of New York. In so doing, it signals a figurative movement towards articulating an emerging Whig ideology of liberation, on Lockean and Miltonic grounds, evoking the sublime not just as *natural* but as *social/political terror* that can be made to work to liberal American purposes.

Understandably in an era of deconstructive irony and anti-sentimentality, *Philosophic Solitude* has received meager contemporary commentary, yet Livingston's poem was widely hailed and reprinted in the eighteenth and nineteenth centuries. This was partly so because, despite its code of sentimentality and diction drawn from minor poets such as John Pomfret and major ones such as John Milton, this pastoral lyric succeeds in depicting "sublime transport" in a rural setting. Livingston uses a mode that became especially congenial to the American wilderness topography, shorn as it was of the rich associations and legends such as those displayed in Pope's thickly descriptive "Windsor-Forest." Attacking the time-killing games and frivolous pleasures practiced by what he called the New York City "Beau-Monde," Livingston (1723–1790) held out in an essay called "Of the Waste of Life" (*The Independent Reflector,* October 25, 1753) for the more "sublime Pleasures" of philosophical conversation and natural contemplation, kindred to what his critical model of greatness, Joseph Addison, had called the "pleasures of the imagination": "The Mind, that superior Part of Man, evidently designed by the wise Author of Nature, for more excellent and sublime Pleasures, is suffered to lie idle, and contract a Rust which can scarce ever be worn off."

Miming the poetic bliss of Protestant sublimity in Milton, Dryden, Pope, and Watts in England, Livingston had quite conventionally, at the outset of the poem, urged upon his friends from Yale a mood of sublime transport in which "Our eyes are ravish'd with a sylvan scene." As the colonial poet emotes over his "green retreat" to nature in upstate New York, the natural sublime as presence (or, better said, as *stimulus* to "loftier" voice) is used to serve as one means of evoking the infinite and even trans-social force of Jehovah, praising a power that can somehow empower (through mimetic contemplation not so much of literary texts but of nature's *boundlessness*) this aspiring poet from the city:

None but a Pow'r omnipotent and wise
Could frame this earth, or spread the boundless skies . . .
Jehovah's glories blaze all nature round,
In heav'n, on earth, and in the deeps profound; . . .
But Man, endu'd with an immortal mind,
His maker's image, and for heav'n design'd!

To loftier notes his raptur'd voice should raise,
And chaunt sublimer hymns to his creator's praise.

(23)

This *natural sublime,* read with post-Lockean enthusiasm to cele-
brate the "maker's image" by contemplating His blazing immensi-
ties coded in the landscape, tellingly functions here as mandate to
evoke a *poetic* or *rhetorical sublime,* which must be expressed in
"loftier" tones that can better display the power of Nature's God
with suitably "raptur'd voice." The sublime, ironically become
such a blithe mood of sublimation, can work to stabilize the self
within structures of moral (if not social) omnipotence, engendering
a mood of rapt submission. Politically ambidexterous and still up
for grabs, the sublime has to be made (read) to serve libertarian
purposes.

So it is that, more perilously, evoking the sun as evidence of
God's sublime power, Livingston (later in the poem) goes on to
threaten earthly potentates and their civic toadies with cosmic an-
nihilation, the specular death-of-the-self which the sublime depends
upon for its materially terrifying shock-effects of hurricane, vol-
cano, earthquake, *and* (as spelled out into "dread majesty" by
Burke and Kant) social revolution:

Thou bow'st the heav'ns; the smoking mountains nod,
Rocks fall to dust, and nature owns her God;
Pale tyrants shrink, the atheist stands aghast,
And impious kings in horror breathe their last.

(26)

Feeling the dread power of the sublime as dynamic force and as
cognitive anxiety, Livingston comes close to invoking, in such pas-
sages, that half-conscious political dread ("terror") that was never
far from the self-dwarfing experience of social domination and
magisterial submission evoked—"openly or latently" (58)—in Ed-
mund Burke's *A Philosophic Enquiry into the Origins of Our Ideas
of the Sublime and Beautiful* (1757) and propagated (as in the
gothic fiction of Edgar Allan Poe) as his "ruling principle of the
sublime": "Thus we are affected [with *sublime terror*] by strength,

which is *natural* power. The power which arises from institution in kings and commanders, has the same connection with terror" (67). As dread power, God terrifies the king into moral submission; and the king can equally terrify his mute subjects.

That is, this terrifying threat to self-preservation of Burke's sublime depends upon both *natural* and *institutional* power-imbalances between loving subject and admired object, as the Burkean ego can be equally subjugated by that which is natural (a volcano or tiger) or that which is social (a general or the king). All but shunning images of social beauty, Livingston's radicalizing of the fear evoked by the sublime is not so much *of the King* (the humbling power for Burke embodied in the British King's *"dread majesty"* [67], or in the even more terrifying Revolutionary image of "the late unfortunate regicide in France" [39]), however, but *of that God* who empowers such earthly potentates and hence can topple their tyranny and impiety in the dynamic flash of an instant. This is because, living in the virtual wilds of America, Livingston implicitly can wield the sublime as a political threat to terrify unnamed tyrants and "impious kings" (of Europe) with the moral force of nature and of nature's God: "Rocks fall to dust, and nature owns her God." (Not until Kant's more imperiously transcendental "analytic of the sublime" in the *Third Critique* of 1790 will the neo-Romantic ego find any egress, in the moral autonomy of sublime experience, from the latent subjugations of the ego-body to nature *and* to royal society that obtain all too comfortably in Burke.)

Governor of New Jersey under its Revolutionary constitution of 1776—a position of social power he held until his death in 1790—Livingston bravely outlined his political philosophy in polemics of liberal dissent centered mostly in "the inestimable value of liberty" and written with William Smith, Jr. and John Morin Scott for the weekly *Independent Reflector* (1752–1753) of New York City. In this American version of *The Independent Whig,* these radical lawyers from Yale articulated a Whig ideology of moral imagination and national independence, which would lead more forcefully to their resistance to the Anglican establishment and Governor De-Lancey over the governance of King's College (Columbia) and other acts of British hegemony prior to the Stamp Act's broadening of such colonial resistance.

Assuming as ethos the sublimity of God and nature throughout his political career, Livingston's moral stance depended upon the quasi-Lockean right of "liberty of conscience" as centered in an individual's unmediated relationship to God. As he wrote to Noah Welles in 1747, "true Religion consists in the internal purity of the heart, and the soul's being as it were moulded into the image of God" and not in a multitude of Anglican rites or Papist interpretations.[3] Livingston courageously articulated such a libertarian stance, for example, in his spirited defense of the Moravians and Quakers in the *Reflector*. Dubbed "Don Quixote of the Jerseys" by the *Royal Gazette* and (ridiculously) an "atheist" by his rivals, Livingston and his legal-literary circle comprised a group of "sturdy Calvinists" and Presbyterians who objected to the more centrist moves and power-broking by the Anglican gentry and their Loyalist allies in provincial politics.[4] The poet of *Philosophic Solitude* remained, throughout his political career, a "Friend of civil and religious Liberty" by opposing imperial impositions as commander of the New Jersey militia and as a member of the Continental Congress during the American Revolution.

While Livingston later longed, in the equally *pastoral* fashion then in Republican vogue, to retreat to his garden at "Liberty Hall" in rural Elizabethtown, New Jersey, nevertheless he remained until his death a political activist caught up in the civic themes and contradictions of social power that effected the American Revolution. If read in such a historical context, the natural sublimity of his "pastoral" poem can better reveal its political dimensions as a latent critique of social power and, beyond that, as a representative authorizing of the natural rights of the awe-struck subject before God as model sovereign.

Although *Philosophic Solitude* does suggest the pastoral genre in its all-too-conventional opposition between rural virtue and urban luxury, as well as its ethic that proposes rural nature as locus for liberty and foundation for social engagement, as has been finely argued by Frank Shuffelton, the poem can also be read as a Whig primer in what to read—if not *how to experience*—as some conversionary moment to sublimity in the American landscape.[5] If, in Livingston's essays on religion and government, the Colonists will later find a textbook in Whig political theory amenable to Revolutionary uses of liberation, I would go on to claim that, in his youthful book-length poem, the liberal-minded Livingston presented the sublime in a way that might at least imply and instantiate a landscape of natural liberty adaptable to American uses.

As Livingston urged, invoking God's sublime in "Patriotism," "We are accountable to the Supreme Beneficient Governor of the Universe, as the Donor of these Blessings" (*The Independent Reflector,* 220); hence our allegiance should be to "public Spirit" and not to self or to an arbitrary temporal law. His spiritual vow in *Philosophic Solitude* remains, "For sovereign GOLD I never would repine, / Nor wish the glittering dust of monarchs mine" (27). This resistance to social follies—based in natural rights and the power of God as manifested in nature—helps to explain, I think, the poem's early popularity. For if his lyric records, as Shuffelton claims, "less a defense of private life than a charting of the relationship between private and public virtue," the poem can also be read as a movement from sublime contemplation to political action, charting a relationship between the natural and the moral sublime in an appropriately elevated diction.[6] Preferring the "downy fleece" of the lamb to "dazzling vestments" of woven gold, Livingston can justify stylistically this putting of the high (sublime) into the lowly (pastoral), or the philosophically complex into simple diction, through invoking the figure of Adam as Christian model for displacing what Erich Auerbach in *Mimesis* termed *sublimitas* (high) into *humilitas* (low):

> Thus the great Father of mankind was drest,
> When shaggy hides compos'd his flowing vest."
> (28)

Interestingly, Livingston's socially empowering linkage of natural to moral sublimity, expanded in the physico-theological contemplation that serves as the poem's lengthy center, was *not* used at all in Livingston's British model, Rev. John Pomfret's "Choice" (1700). Pomfret's much-imitated pastoral representation of "the Good Life," according to what Raymond Williams terms "the small independent freeholder" of rural England, did celebrate a neat but simple mansion, unluxurious furniture, the company of high-minded friends, a reading list of poets (with "sublime Milton"— that is, radical Puritanism—notably absent), and the tender companionship of a female friend "'(for I'd have no wife)'"; all of which the "Gentleman educated at Yale College" dutifully repeats. However, Livingston indigenizes the pastoral lyric, so to speak, by making his Penseroso-like solitude into a fit locus for one-on-one dialogue or sublime apostrophe with the Deity, and by propagating a reading list founded in exaltations of Protestant sublimity, making for a potentially radical displacement of the more genteel British conventions. In W. H. Auden's terms, Livingston's version of "pastoral" is "*Utopian*" (future-oriented) rather than "*Arcadian*" (past-oriented): it evokes a political ideal (narrative) of simplicity that needs to be realized in the future rather than lamenting a falling-off from some natural past presumed as golden norm, as does Pope's "Windsor-Forest" (1713), wherein "The Groves of *Eden*, vanish'd now so long, / Live in Description, and look green in Song."[7]

If *Philosophic Solitude* is *pastoral* in form, then, it remains would-be *sublime* in tone and style, resulting in a curiously hybrid mixture that speaks beyond its sophomoric production of an American sublimity that will emerge rife with genteel contradictions, promoting and evoking *both* landed stability and social liberation—a contradiction Ralph Waldo Emerson later expresses in his will to evoke the sublime of nature both as fixed "commodity" and, by power-trope, as self-liberating "symbol." In Livingston's poem, at least, the sublime experience is portrayed as a potentially liberating moment that is (explicitly) both *Lockean* in epistemology and *Miltonic* in Puritan amplitude and tone, if derivative in form and sentiment from Pomfret and Pope.

The sublime moment is read, teleologically, as a moment coding the construction of an awe-struck Christian subject who finds evidence for God's existence in the natural world and can act—*morally and politically*—upon these rapt impressions of place. As Shuffelton concludes insightfully of such poetic nature-worship, "Livingston's turn inward has led to a vision of sublime action able to prepare him for a meaningful re-encounter with the world" (48). In Livingston's quasi-Lockean scenario linking the private pursuit of happiness with the social pursuit of liberty—that is, of imagined happiness as a basis for virtuous action on a social scale—poetry can precede politics by linking the freedom experienced in the natural sublime to the liberty that should be experienced in the social state. The poetic sublime, in other words, is produced as part of and prelude to a political dynamic of change. Defending himself against rather silly Deist charges of "atheism" in the *New-York Mercury*, Livingston had urged in a discussion of Immortality for *The Independent Reflector* of November 1, 1753, that the sentiment of the moral sublime should be linked to "great and glorious Actions": "The Belief of the Immortality of the Soul, imparts an unutterable Dignity to human Nature. It inspires us with sublime Sentiments of our future Grandeur, and affords the strongest Incitements to great and glorious Actions" (414).

Considered as another indigenous appropriation of the pre-Romantic sublime, then, *Philosophic Solitude* becomes as revealing in its pursuit of high-minded pleasures of the Christian imagination as was Anne Bradstreet's "Contemplations," a poem from the 1678 edition of *Several Poems* that Livingston echoes blatantly enough to suggest that he knew it, as did Edward Taylor (1644–1729) in rural Massachusetts. Shuffelton laments that our century has assured the obscure status of this long poem by almost never anthologizing it and by neglecting (or mocking) its overtly imitative habits of elevating the topography and tone. Yet as Milton M. Klein has established, "As a separate publication it [*Philosophic Solitude*] went through thirteen editions, the last in 1790. It was a favorite of magazine editors and anthologists during the Revolution and the early years of the Republic; and it made its author colonial New York's first and principal poet." [8] Livingston is no William Carlos Williams, but he did try to generate sublime poetry out of the lowly terrains of New York and New Jersey.

"Sacred Transport" and Livingston's Will to Liberty

To grasp the conventions of sublime rapture ("sacred transport") with which the colonial poem was produced, we can begin by looking at the prefatory poem to *Philosophic Solitude,* wherein Noah Welles brashly commended the poem of his former Yale classmate with those overenthusiastic and epithet-ridden terms before a New World creation that had first greeted/inflated Bradstreet's *Tenth Muse.* Oddly declaring that the verse is "smooth, yet sublime," Welles specifies his overgenerous Longinian response—mere transport into a "reader's sublime" [9]—to Livingston's effort to *elevate,* as if by poetic fiat, nature in America as a scene of sacred presence, whereby a lowly "rural scene" yet can yield the vaunted affects of "sacred transport" and sublime persuasion:

> While in your verse with transport and surprise,
> We see the rural scene sublimely rise; . . .
> To nature's God you tune the warbling lyre;
> The sacred transport every power controuls. . . .
>
> (iii-v)

For Welles, Livingston in effect presents "sacred transport" as movement—in good Lockean fashion—from sensuous contemplation of nature to a more complex perception of "nature's God" as source of sublime presence and power. The poem, like a secondary nature, can itself function as the scenery of a conversion affectively induced, as it was for Welles. The sublime is encoded as a moment of teleological inscription: the moment wherein to encode the subject with intimations of moral liberty through that wild natural scenery in which, both Locke and Addison admitted, America abounded.

William Smith's prefatory lyric is equally *emotive* in tone and fitted to the sublime mode:

> Rapt by your Notes, from maze to maze I rove,
> And hear soft music echo thro' the grove
> . . . But when your lofty numbers reach the skies,
> Th' excursive soul thro' every region flies;
> Reads nature's volume with supreme delight,
> And joyous roams the boundless fields of light.

While Livingston can make the "gilded landskips rise," Smith remains rather struck in the "thick town" and its vista not of natural immensity but the cluttered streets of New York City, where even the "Chairs, carts, drays, coaches, dirty pavements lie."

Livingston's prefacing "Argument" no less blatantly suggests, in a prose outline befitting a lawyer, his own sublime use of natural "contemplation" and sense impression to construct an idea of God's attributes: "Hymn to the Sun. Contemplation of the Heavens. The Existence of God inferr'd from a view of the Beauty and Harmony of the Creation. Morning and Evening Devotion . . ."

103

(12). As Shuffelton claims, such "Devotion" could indeed cut across denominational lines because, "in pluralistic New York, Livingston needed to create a compelling moral imagination outside the limits of denominationalism" (52). I would claim he does this— as his "Argument" suggests—by creating a one-on-one with the Deity through using the ideological apparatus of nature; that is, nature portrayed as higher than and prior to any state. Withdrawing to a sequestered grotto of nature ("Me to sequester'd scenes, ye muses guide, / Where nature wantons in her virgin-pride"), Livingston depicts his ceremony of response, in the exclamatory manner of Milton's Penseroso, figure for the lone Puritan invoking sublime power and revolutionary vision:

> Welcome ye shades! all hail, ye vernal blooms!
> Ye bow'ry thickets, and prophetic glooms!
> Ye forests hail! ye solitary woods!

Alone with the landscape, Livingston would remain no hermit of splenetic contemplation; instead, he would communicate his new-found "prophetic glooms" and vision of seasonal order to high-minded Yale friends such as Welles and Smith who walk with him through the landscape. The "Penseroso" poet, having been granted the material of "sacred transport" in virgin America, must convert the *black* melancholy of contemplation into a *golden* rapture that is nonetheless "philosophical" in its reach beyond nature towards divine affirmation. For such God-relying *solitude* to become "philosophical," as the title promises, a moment of transport must be posited in which the conversion experience can be located as the conversion to depths of subjective feeling for nature and to theological appreciation of God, as aesthetic feeling becomes ethical mandate—the dynamic of the natural sublime which Burke (and especially Kant, or Emerson) will later objectify as the not-so-hidden vocation of the sublime to bring about recognition of one's moral grandeur.

If the majestic beauty of the autumn sun and trees had stimulated the Puritan senses of Anne Bradstreet to moods of rapture in a proto-nature lyric such as "Contemplations" from *Several Poems* (1678)—"Rapt were my senses at this delectable view"—she inevitably went on to transcend any such ecstatic charges from sen-

104

suous objects of "this under world so richly dight" by affirming a higher world of spirit as source of any earthbound sublimity:

If so much excellence abide below,
How excellent is He that dwells on high,
Whose power and beauty by his works we know?
(205)

Given the still-Calvinist horizon in which the poem was produced by this "Yalensis" son (vi), Livingston just as vividly (if not American-generically) presents a hymn to the sensuous sun, only to save "sublimer hymns" for his contemplation of that ultimate source of sublime power, God:

Hail Orb! array'd with majesty and fire, . . .
Jehovah's glories blaze all nature round,
In heav'n, on earth, and in the deeps profound;
Ambitious of his name, the warblers sing,
And praise their maker, while they hail the spring,
But Man, endu'd with an immortal mind,
His maker's image, and for heav'n design'd:
To loftier notes his raptur'd voice should raise,
And chaunt sublimer hymns to his creator's praise.
(21–23)

Impressed by the majesty of nature in detail and scope, the American poet yet reserves "loftier" strains and affections for the God of immortal mind, in that adjectival "raptur'd voice" that is, at this time, the touchstone of any thickly descriptive sublime style: "Father of *Light!* exhaustless source of good! / Supreme, eternal, self-existent God!" (29).

Such a line was clearly overstuffed with an abundance of "supernumerary epithets" that drove antisublime Byles to splenetic mockery, as he tried to exorcise a stylistic habit all too notable in his own early verse. Mocking the "exorbitant Style" of Richard Stentor's panegyric to Beacon Hill, Byles seconds Longinus and Pope in distinguishing a *"true Sublime"* from this unwitting parody of such rhetorical elevation (*hypsos* become *bathos*):

It appears plainly that he heaps his Subject with improper and foreign Thoughts; that he strains those Thoughts into the most unnatural and ridiculous Distortions; and, last of all, that he clouds them with so many needless supernumerary Epithets, as to fling the whole Piece into this unaccountable Huddle of Impertinence and Inconsistency.[10]

The hyperbolic adjective of sense impression, which we now recognize from the stylistic countings of Josephine Miles as the dominant *sign* and substance of the sublime mode in Blackmore, Thomson, and a host of others, drives Byles into vivid fits of religious parody in 1727, way before the Connecticut Wits made this a norm in nationalistic epic and rapturous odes at Yale: "I my self counted in Fifty Six Lines of it, three *Celestials,* eight *Immortals,* eleven *Unboundeds,* six *Everlastings,* four *Eternities,* and thirteen *Infinites;* Besides *Bellowings, Ravings, Yellings, Horrors, Terribles, Rackets, Hubbubs,* and *Clutterings,* without Number" (692–93). (Needless to say, it did not take Burke's treatise on the production of the sublime [1757] to disseminate the literary conventions of such wonders, terrors, and horrors before nature's infinitude as the basis for the generation of a would-be American sublime.)

Despite such stylistic monitions against the bathos of a *failed sublime,* Livingston still posits and negotiates his own lofty space of "lone grotts for contemplation made," for in such pastoral retreat from society he can best pursue inspiration and even prophecy, making "sacred themes" his lofty subject in a once-lowly setting. To render solitude "philosophical," he advises that "reading should be to contemplation join'd," especially the reading of sublime Milton, of course the major poet (with Du Bartas) of any Puritan sublime:

> Great Milton first, for tow'ring thought renown'd
> Parent of song, and fam'd the world around!
> His glowing breast divine Urania fir'd
> Or God himself th' immortal Bard inspir'd.
>
> (32)

Inspired to awe-struck moods and hero-worshipping tones by the sublime stance of "Urania-fir'd" Milton, just as the Puritan Bradstreet had been by Urania-inspired Du Bartas, Livingston is elated merely to evoke this great Protestant tradition of sublime poetry, however minor his own lyric contribution must remain.[11]

106

Neither the vexed questions of superior influence and hostile audience that Wallace Stevens posed, for example, in "The American Sublime" (1935)—"How does one stand / To behold the sublime, / To confront the mockers / The mickey mockers / And plated pairs?" (114)—nor the fear of a failed sublime evoking deflation and mockery were much of an *anxious* burden of literary greatness for William Livingston: one simply (that is, idealistically) beheld that poetry of Virgil, Milton, Dryden, Pope, and Watts in order to behold, through their foreign language, the sublime of nature and of God.[12] The American sublime emerged as a matter of shared beliefs. There was little question of seeking textual originality, or worry over the "mockery" that befits the derivative condition of writing like another pseudo-British "plated pair," or (in Byles's deadly pun) another "Observe-a-Tory." The real threat from Milton's lofty voice to Livingston's line would be parody or silence, the death even of exclamation or adjectival imitation, in the total turn away from idealized poetry to more practical politics that he later made. But the incentive is that, like Dryden translating Virgil into English, the derivative American poet can displace the sublime original, if only in certain native lines:

> With more than native lustre *Virgil* shines,
> And gains sublimer heights in *Dryden's* lines.

Lacking in Dryden's differential force of "original genius," surely lacking in the poetic genius of a Whitman or Poe, Livingston's stance towards any prior sublimity of language remains kin to that talent-bounded one in Blackmore's *Creation*, as in W. Jackson Bate's portrayal in *The Burden of the Past* (London: Chatto & Windus, 1971): "Oppressed with the burden of such high and apparently diverse ideals, Blackmore staggered under the weight, but bravely wrote on" (43). The hope remains that, through emulating the greatness of the past *and* of nature, this sublime of nature and artistic greatness can serve as a counterforce to release what is "below the threshold" for personal fulfillment and the freedom to create—to evoke self-sublimation if not in poetics then in politics. Though Livingston is indeed a minor poet, the discourse of the sublime is carried on in his poetry, indeed constitutes his poetry as nature and norm of "sacred rapture" (conversion).

Livingston's proposed reading list of influences within his poetic grotto (or lyric ghetto of freedom) reveals the epistemological master of any sensory-based sublime, Locke, as the center of a still-Christian empiricism that can piously link private sensation to moral idea:

> Sagacious Lock, by providence design'd
> T' exalt, instruct, and rectify the mind.
> (36)

Although, tellingly enough, Livingston does include the reading of Longinus and a host of classical models of greatness from the "learned dead" (36), Milton and Locke remain mastering influences upon the poetic impressions of *Philosophic Solitude,* a poem that in its very imitativeness and banality reveals the sources and intentions of an emerging American sublime. Like Philip Freneau (1752–1832) later in, say, the lushness that calls the ego back to political power in "The Beauties of Santa Cruz" (written in 1779), Livingston can represent the liberal and Puritan origins of a sublime rapture towards nature or another self, as in Bradstreet, providing its poetic ratification, especially as this will-to-sublimity became displaced later into less idealized forms of power (waterfalls, bridges, airplanes, and so on). Through such enthusiasm of "sacred raptures" (30), Livingston would somehow contemplate the "supernal" in bird, forest, sun, friend, and wife—images which can only remind the solitary poet of "supernal grace and purity divine." Contemplating a lowly landscape in the wilds of America, Livingston yet aspires to convey the "sacred rapture" of his own sublime, that is, to evoke an elevated style appropriate to religious transport before such scenery.

The Sublime of Nature and Nature's God

According to Locke in *An Essay Concerning the Human Understanding* (1690), subjective knowledge came wholly "from *Experience*"; hence this entailed the experimenting mind's pursuing a compound of sensations plus reflection upon those sensations to form both simple and complex ideas. Our idea of God's *immensity*

or *infinitude,* to use the sublime example, came initially from con-
templation of his manifest attributes; but this impression was com-
pounded to maximal extension, at which point the mind balked in
an experience of awe. For, as W. Jackson Bate explains of Addison's
natural sublime, "Locke's sensationalist psychology had encour-
aged the belief that the greater the size of the object contemplated
or recalled, the greater is the feeling or thought which results." [13]
Without resorting to innate ideas or extraordinary faculties (as in
the *a priori* scenario of the mind's autonomous sublimity in Kant),
the human mind could derive the concept of God wholly from the
experience of the senses, especially when attuned to this new sen-
sibility of nature as vast space, as felt immensity.

We can arrive at an empirical notion of God's *infinity,* for ex-
ample, through the following natural scenario "of expansion," ac-
cording to Locke (book 2, chapter 17, "Of Infinity"):

> 'Tis true, that we cannot but be assured, That the Great GOD, of
> whom, and from whom are all things, is incomprehensibly Infinite:
> but yet, when we apply to that first and supreme Being our *Idea* of
> Infinite, in our weak and narrow Thoughts, we do it primarily in
> respect of his Duration and Ubiquity; and, I think, more figuratively
> to his Power, Wisdom, and Goodness, and other Attributes, which
> are properly inexhaustible and incomprehensible, *etc.* For when we
> call them Infinite, we have no other *idea* of this Infinity, but what
> carries with it some reflection on, and imitation of that Number or
> Extent of the Acts or Objects of God's Power, Wisdom, and Good-
> ness, which can never be supposed so great, or so many, which these
> Attributes will not always surmount and exceed, let us multiply
> them in our Thoughts, as far as we can, with all the infinity of end-
> less number. [14]

If God can fill the immensity of natural space, He yet remains be-
yond felt space or any astronomical mapping of it. However, by the
mind's enlarging upon its very idea of natural space as immense, it
can eventually arrive at the idea of boundless space as "infinite,"
and ("more figuratively") as a helpful if still-limited representation
of God: "So that wherever the mind places itself by any thought,
either amongst or remote from all bodies, it can in this uniform
idea nowhere find any bounds, any end; and so must necessarily
conclude, by the very nature and idea of each part of it, to be ac-

tually infinite" (210). No transcendental loophole needs to be figured in, as in Kant, to provide an egress for the ego from material (and social) domination.

From the sensuous experience of the finite and natural, then, the lonely mind can arrive at an idea of God as that which is properly "inexhaustible and incomprehensible," as Locke (like many sublime poets) must inevitably admit. Hence, after Locke's empirical psychology validates a rational use of the imagination as a means to grace, natural space can function, in the subjective mind, as the locus of religious conversion: "For it is the observation of space as limitless and the experience of time as endless that give us the sensations which constitute our ideas of God's existence." [15] That is, our idea of God as a complex of "power," "knowledge," "goodness," "immensity" and so forth, is "originally got from sensation and reflection." As Livingston argues his own conception of the self's "immortality" in the *Reflector*, his model for deriving this "idea" remains fully Lockean, as befits the liberal wilds and contracts of America: "Again, it appears that all our Ideas are either received by the external Organs, or compounded of those, by the internal Operations of the Mind. The former are called Ideas of Sensation, the latter of Reflection" (416).

According to such an empiricist (*pre-Kantian*) scenario, religious affirmation can become linked to poetry, especially through the subjective mediation of vast landscapes. In works such as Joseph Burnet's *The Sacred Theory of the Earth* (1697) and Joseph Addison's *Spectator* essays on "The Pleasures of the Imagination" (1712), the immense vortex of astronomical space and vast configurations of mountains, deserts, and volcanoes can be invoked to serve as images of moral grandeur and inner freedom: "We are flung into a pleasing astonishment at such unbounded views, and feel a delightful stillness and amazement in the soul at the apprehension of them" (Addison, *Spectator* No. 412, June 23, 1712). The mind can be transported ("flung into a pleasing astonishment") by wild images of "*Greatness*" such as those of "a vast uncultivated Desart, of huge heaps of Mountains, high Rocks and Precipices, or a wide Expanse of Waters, . . . [and] that rude kind of Magnificence which appears in many of these stupendous Works of Nature."

Based upon this new poetics of imagination and vastness disseminated into the wilderness-great colonies by Addison and others, even *the horizon* (as limit or threshold) could function not as neutral emptiness nor as aesthetic deformity, but (in these colossal terms taken again from *Spectator* No. 412) as an "Image of Liberty": "The Mind of Man naturally hates every thing that looks like a Restraint upon it, and is apt to fancy itself under a sort of Confinement when the Sight is pent up in a narrow Compass, and shortened on every side by the Neighbourhood of Walls or Mountains. On the contrary, a spacious horison is an Image of Liberty, where the eye has Room to range abroad."

Hence, though sequestered in a grotto-like space in upstate New York, far from Yale and England, Livingston presents the immensity of the natural sublime as a vehicle of awe—tellingly enough— through using the modern technology of a telescope, that post-Ptolemaic instrument (also invoked by Kant to arouse awe at the macrocosm, before the mind entered such a scene as more truly sublime in moral infinitude), to *spatialize* God's infinitude:

> Oft' would I view, in admiration lost,
> Heav'ns sumptous canopy, and starry host,
> With levell'd tube, and astronomic eye
> Pursue the planets whirling thro' the sky:
> Immensurable vault! where thunders roll,
> And forky lightnings flash from pole to pole.
>
> (22)

From such a yeomanlike survey of cosmic immensity invoking the sun as "globe of fire" and the planets as agents of spiritual vastness, even a "railing Infidel" would be converted to faith-states or over-beliefs in this conventional God. For, by such Lockean premises, who could look upon "Th' harmonious structure of this vast machine, / And not confess its architect divine?" The spatialization of God, which to later designs could signify Frost's "desert places" of vast absence and loneliness, still represents an immense presence and even comfort. Nature has become for Livingston's mind not just a "vast machine" but a machinery to produce sensations / ideas of vastness by which the Protestant poet can directly commune with God and "confess"—through a sacramentalized landscape— his faith in God's sublimity as the only legitimate source of power.

What *awes* Livingston is not only nature, of course, but also prior texts of sublime influence, Milton and Locke, who lead him towards a sensational poetics linking sensuous contemplation to ethical affirmation. His form becomes a curiously hybrid one, what might be called *sublime pastoral,* an old form in which new feelings of transport can be generated from a New World setting. God, we would have to conclude, is his ultimate source of awe, an amplitude of feeling he constructs (as God-drenched ego) in "philosophic solitude" by enthused contemplation of sun and planets. His enclosed pastoral landscape can barely accommodate such sublime feelings of vastness, but he piles on adjectives in a haze of awe before the sun's "Darting ... deluge of effulgence round" (21). He moves from a soft rapture to a kind of earnest humility, an unabashed effusion of sentiment and a moral embrace of the sublime as a feeling appropriate to the new geography, which (it can be said in support of Byles) was having a fatal influence on his use of descriptive and hyperbolic adjectives such as *raptured, exhaustless,* and *immortal.*

The sublimity of Livingston's poetry remains, however, like that of Bradstreet's, still much too *optative* and *wish-fulfilling:* one dependent on the grace of religious transport more than on difficult feats of original imagination or achieved form, of spectacular "blockages" overcome (as in Kant), or places adequately rendered (as in Whitman's polymorphous identity with New York City). Such a sublime poetry is so faithful and intense in naive aspiration that it all-too-easily borders on rapt *inexpressibility,* bloated figuration, or a stock diction of hyperbolic adjectives (pseudo-sublime tropes) that render the scene all too remotely and make the affective communion one of mere willed exclamation. Seeking the happiness of the "nature-taught" in another poem, "A Morning Hymn" (*American Museum,* Jan. 1789, 100–101), Livingston would later aspire from the landscape to "transport rise" by invoking sense impressions of copse, bird, and sun, as seen in the still-conversionary light of "nature's renovating day":

Sacred to HIM, in grateful praise,
  Be this devoted, tranquil hour;
While him, supremely good and great
  With rapt'rous homage I adore.

112

Yet again in the nature-worship of "A Morning Hymn," Living-ston's Protestant-liberal tone remains one of "rapt'rous homage," linking the contemplation of nature to affirmations of "nature's God." His is a stance not of natural subjugation but of awe-struck moralizing (transport) that moves the poet to epithet-laden praise for what is "good and great" as legitimate sources of power (terror, awe).

Through such overenthused contemplations of nature and the nationalizing of "Nature's God," later and stronger poets such as Barlow, Trumbull, Bryant, Whitman, Stevens, and Rexroth would present stronger transports of more panoramic imagination, mak-ing/mainstreaming the sublime into a more central norm out of our cultural ambition to "raise to sublimity the aspiring Muse" of America. Nevertheless, in my view, Livingston had helped to de-velop a tradition (or at least *tone*) of transport that, in the regen-erative wilds of space-vast America, became increasingly valued in eighteenth-century poetics as the theme, affect, even the style of a distinctly American poetry. This eventuated especially as such po-etry came to terms with a moralized geography of magnitude and then the possibility of social regeneration within subjective climates of bliss: "As the immense dew of Florida / Brings forth hymn and hymn / From the beholder / . . . So, in me, come flinging / Forms, flames, and the flakes of flames," even if the post-Hiroshima sky's rays are forever shorn of Jesus.[16]

113

Part 3

Romantic America: Ideologies of Bliss

FIVE

William Cullen Bryant
Domesticating the Natural Sublime

It is not drum-taps
For a lost race of giants,
But perhaps says something, here
In Mr. Bryant's

Homiletic woods,
Of the brave art of forage
And the good of a few nuts
In burrow-storage; [. . .]

Of the plenum, charged
With one life through all changes,
And of how we are enlarged
By what estranges.
    —Richard Wilbur, "A Wall In the Woods: Cummington"

Wнеn william cullen bryant (1794–1878) reflected upon the pomp and scantiness of "Early American Verse" for *The North American Review* in July of 1818, he assessed that the patriotic but all-too-British-modeled attempts of the Connecticut Wits to achieve an American sublime in various genres was lacking in several enduring senses. Finding John Trumbull utterly imitative, Timothy Dwight deficient in "inventive and poetical fancy," and Joel Barlow's *Columbiad* falling off miserably from "that calm, lofty, sustained style" which befits such topics of morality and philosophy, Bryant concluded that the would-be American sublimity of the Yale Wits was hollow, rhetorically mannered, and monotonous in its patriotic overreaching to achieve some native "elevation of style":

117

> One material error of taste pervades the graver productions of these
> authors, into which it would seem they were led by copying certain
> of the poets of England, who flourished near the period in which
> they began to write. It was their highest ambition to attain a certain
> lofty, measured, declamatory manner—an artificial elevation of
> style, from which it is impossible to rise or descend without abrupt-
> ness and violence. . . . [1]

Sublime mannerisms that were beholden to the Miltonic epic and
neo-Pindaric ode, and imported (by the Connecticut Wits at Yale)
along with a self-sublimating taste for such lofty pleasures (and
anxieties) of the imagination from pre-Romantic England, could
no longer suffice to materialize an American poetry able to link
the contemplation of nature's sublimity—that "encircling vast-
ness" which Bryant felt abounded in the American wilderness as
in the "homiletic woods" around the vistas of his native Cum-
ington—with representative forms and voices. As Bryant's own
poetry of moralized sublimity would go on to show, the American
sublime had to be courted and invoked through miming wilder
landscapes and affects of self-transport. The effect aimed at was
neither epic nor heroic, but a more subjectivized one of sublime
conversion.

With "unbounded" adjectives and competitive hyperboles all
their own, the Connecticut Wits had sought, in Miltonic epic as in
Pindaric ode, to achieve, by collective fiat if not wholesale Euro-
pean importation at Yale, a *sublime* style that would endure as
commensurate with the American landscape and high social des-
tiny. Such a poetry proved all the more necessary, Romantic poets
would agree, as the United States moved towards installing modes
of Liberty and Equality trumping those of the past. All too me-
chanically, as Bryant saw, these erudite poets had tried to "raise to
sublimity the aspiring Muse" of American verse, by stylistic fiat, as
Trumbull (1750–1831) outlined in his *Essay on the Use and Ad-
vantages of the Fine Arts* (New Haven, 1770).

That Trumbull—so-called "poet of the American Revolution"
as the sign rather mystifyingly proclaims in Watertown, Connecti-
cut, his birthplace—assumes that American poetry should at least
aspire to the sublime, despite the anti-Longinian neo-classicism of
Mather Byles or the "plain-style" Puritanism of John Cotton's gen-

118

erations, can be seen in the rapt criteria dominating his critical language. Trumbull predictably admires Milton's "sublimity of conception" and Joseph Addison's "sublimity of sentiment," yet finds "moral rapture" even in the ironical Pope, and dilates with grandeur before the nature-energized imagery of vastness of James Thomson's *Seasons*—"The liveliness of his paintings, his sublime morality, and his delicacy of thought justly raise him to the highest rank of genius."[2]

Tracing the imperial migration of the poetic Muse *westward* from Greece and Rome, through England, to the green and vaster terrains of Revolutionary America, Trumbull boasts (on neo-Longinian grounds) that because of a widespread "natural genius" unfettered by inherited "rules of method" or aristocratic decorums of "false taste," America will soon attain to supremacy "both in arts and arms." This nationalistic (and given our nuclear horizon, *spooky*) argument will resound stridently into the 1840s and 1850s, of course, leading to and confirming the more "original" sublimity of Emerson and Whitman as American incarnations. It would take the more fiercely post-Romantic irony and gendered sense of dispossession in Emily Dickinson, furthermore, even to begin to distance, defer, qualify, or undo this will to collective mastery implied by such a stance of pious, ideologized sublimity.

In a high-minded, if highly conventional, poem concluding this *Essay* on poetics, Trumbull urges these wits at "fair Yalensia" to aspire nonetheless to a poetry of the America sublime. Suppressing all signs of mimetic rivalry, jealousy, or sense of collective dispossession, Trumbull uses terms far more euphoric than the warily oedipal ones of Yale's latter-day critic of the America sublime, Harold Bloom. "Beneath a solemn grove's delightful shade," Trumbull's poet of this superlatively "happy land" cannot help but brag with "joy entranc'd" and feel "Long visions rising in the raptur'd mind."[3] (Anybody who has read, or tried to finish, Joel Barlow's *Columbiad* (1807) or Timothy Dwight's *Greenfield Hill* (1794) might at least agree, "Yes, *long* visions of the American sublime.") Surrounded by the "boundless" materials of the natural and religious sublime and aspiring to write "heav'nly themes," as with the "rapted wit sublime" of Bradstreet and Livingston, the America poet (in Trumbull's view) must somehow achieve a "soaring" tone to represent this elected land and confederated people:

In mighty pomp America shall rise;
Her glories spreading to the boundless skies . . .
Sublime the Muse shall lift her eagle wing;
Of heav'nly themes the soaring bards shall sing.

Such "soaring bards" of patriotic glory leave local causes and scenes far beneath the haze of ideological sublimation. Indeed, Trumbull's penchant for a Biblically bloated poetry, with tone *soaring* and adjectivally laden lines *singing,* as voice lifted into Miltonic pomp and Thomsonian boundlessness, affirming eagle-coated ideality, was doubtlessly—as Bryant early saw—part of the stylistic problem. The Connecticut Wits spent too many lone and long hours creating a *false* American sublime, overloaded with allusions and ready-made myths better suited to the high-style taste of aristocratic Europe (or to pre-Wordsworthian England).

Bryant more shrewdly claimed in his own poetics that "new modes of sublimity, of beauty, and of human emotion" would have to be invented to claim, if not interiorize, such New World immensity. However influenced by prior forces and models, native originality of form and risks of imagination had become an issue. Such a poetics of sublime association he went on to outline for national uses in *Lectures on Poetry* (1825).[4] Defining the nature and value of poetry in the psychological terms he had claimed from Common Sense aesthetics, especially Archibald Alison's *Essays on the Nature and Principles of Taste* (1790), Bryant sought on such principles of grounded association to write a poetry which would, in predictable effect, impress a "poetic exaltation of mind" and a "sense of sublimity" upon the American reader.[5] The immensities of American space had to be cornered into cathedrals and enclaves enacting claims of first possession.

Representing this sensuous imagery, especially if tied to natural immensity as well as to historical details of time and locale (as in "The Prairies"), became Bryant's primary technique to evoke or "suggest" the pious effect of sublimity uniting poet and reader alike. The transport of Bryant's poet was meant to be representative of a *common sense of sublime rapture* any American might feel in contemplating vast space, moreover, whether instigated in the Berkshires or (even more so) out west: the boundlessness of nature and of God that humbled and sublimated the ego to solidarity and liberal-hearted belief. If in the United States men were equal, they were equally exalted and united by the same, common materials (fields, birds, mountains, crowds, and so on), and by the same humble-yet-sublime language as in the Longinian model, *Fiat lux*.

This image-plus-feeling formula of poetry worked in Bryant to "suggest[s] both the sensible object and the association." Poetry arranges words as God arranges wondrous items (like space-swimming waterfowls) in nature, to solicit moods of pious arousal: "Poetry is that art which selects and arranges the symbols of thought in such a manner as to excite it [the imagination] the most powerfully and delightfully." [6] If poetry, as an elevated genre of language, aims "to excite the imagination" to transport, this rapture remains pious and pure, moral at its core, *mildly* Kantian: "There is something pure and elevated in the creations of poetry. Its spirit is an aspiration after superhuman beauty and majesty and virtue." [7] Longinus would be made to feel at home in the American wilds, in the simple poetic language of *fiat lux*. Whatever terrors of dispossession might surround the Adamic subject, the natural sublime, at this point, still instigated a kindred, American sense of belonging to the place. The poet, in Bryant's moral scheme, ratified and policied such Euramerican claims through acts and tropes of credible possession.

Like some dread-and-wonder machine droning on (waterfall-like) to provide earnest encouragement to the self-elected poet, poetry must derive the association of *moral sublimity* from vast, sensible images of nature. The poem processes a sublimity all too inevitably "leading the mind of the beholder to the contemplation of the Almighty." We can recognize the competitive scale of such sublimity as voiced, however belatedly idealized, in "western" landscapes of self-possession and hyperbolic outdoing such as Thoreau's "Walking":

For I believe that climate does thus react on man,—as there is something in the mountain-air that feeds the spirit and inspires. . . . [and] I trust that we shall be more imaginative, that our thoughts will be clearer, fresher, and more ethereal, as our sky,—our understanding more comprehensive and broader, like our plains,—our intellect generally on a grander scale, like our thunder and lightning, our rivers and mountains and forests, . . . [8]

121

Circulating American power and displaying supersensible might, such sublimity conspires to instigate and to ratify acts of poetic possession. Poets were enlarged by that which, otherwise, might seem inhumanly estranging.

In Bryant's most famous nature-lesson in power/knowledge, "To a Waterfowl," which became the model of moralized sublimity for Fireside poets, early and late, boundless sky and geographical vacancy conspire to suggest not so much human isolation or democratic pettiness (as they do in Tocqueville's evocation in 1835–1840 of wilderness vastness and the potentially violent tyranny of mass-thinking), but the infinite and sustaining power of God confirmed in space, for bird as for man. The ironic result of such a piously *domesticated* wildness, encountered as an uplifting wilderness trauma, is that finally, as Harold Bloom claims, "Bryant's ecstatic beholding has little to do with what he sees." [9] Bryant's sublimity is scarcely "whit manic."

Yet such a poetry is rather a generic necessity. A libertarian stance, such as William Livingston's in *Philosophic Solitude,* and the resulting sense of self-empowerment from the wild as from the good have become, by this time, automatic, an "over belief" immune to historical contradiction. Somehow the earnestness of Bryant's voice and the neatness of his poetic forms and polite terms are meant to stabilize, or at least to make lastingly credible to his liberal community of readers, the vastness of such claims to possess American grandeur and to install a difference from prior sublimations.

As a "suggestive art" evoking elevated moods, such poetry of the natural sublime uses novel effects and fresh scenes to build up towards rarefied yet common associations. The American poet can still learn from the vast storehouse of traditional poetry "the secrets of the mechanism by which he moves the mind of his reader." [10] In "On Originality and Imitation," Bryant claims that these "new modes of sublimity" he seeks in the American wilds must push the limits of these inherited terms and forms into more original applications: "The poet must do precisely what is done by the mathematician, who takes up his science where his predecessors have left it, and pushes its limits as much farther, and makes as many new applications of its principles, as he can." Like a tamer version of Emerson in "Circles," Bryant urges the American poet to push prior languages of "excellence" into new, original applications and terrain: "He must found himself on the excellence already attained in his art, and if, in addition to this, he delights us with new modes of sublimity, of beauty, and of human emotion, he deserves the praise of originality and of genius."[11] Though Bryant was no Whitman of the American sublime nor a Wordsworth moving towards claims of poetic autonomy, he headed towards, if not into, this more *democratic* and *vernacularized* terrain. Bryant at times credibly evoked a sublime language and mood—as Asher B. Durand depicted in the thoroughly domesticated, dark, yet preachy New York wilds of *Kindred Spirits* (1849).

Unlike the forced "elevation" and soaring tonalities of the Connecticut Wits, which had inexpertly estranged poetry from natural imagery and common language, the sublime poetry of Wordsworth, Bryant saw, was more genuinely based upon "a certain fearless simplicity," hence akin to that unaffected yet ever-forceful sublimity of nature that he himself would aim at. Going more directly to nature for his imagery, if not to common people for his diction, Wordsworth had corrected the deadeningly false neoclassical taste and self-consciousness of style which assumed "that a certain pomp of words is necessary to elevate the style and make that grand and noble which in direct expression would be homely and trivial." The imagery of nature, both in its immensity and little details, might unlock a source of *new sublimity* if contemplated freshly and directly: "What a profusion of materials for poetry Nature offers to him who directly consults her instead of taking his images at second-hand," Bryant urged, miming and domesticating Wordsworth for local use.

Communing with such visible forms of Nature in western Massachusetts, Bryant was early hailed by *The North American Review* and the *United States Democratic Review* as the foremost American poet because poems like "Thanatopsis" ("It is sublime throughout") were piously (that is, semi-wildly) both contemplative and sublime in effect. Bryant typically moved from subjective contemplation of natural imagery to an expansive mood of *associated sublimity* in which the idea or "high sentiment" of God emerged as the ideological trump card of any American sublimity. Here, alone with the landscape, poets confronted a moral power and standard of topographical greatness to be invoked in and be-

123

yond Nature's Nation as unifying sign of "Nature's God." As William Joseph Snelling claimed, evoking neo-Longinian terms of a "greatness" that is both natural and moral, simple yet sublime, while reviewing "Bryant's Poems" in the *North American Review* [34 (April 1832):505]:

> The bent of his mind is essentially contemplative. He loves to muse in solitude, in the depths of the forest, and on the high places of the hills. Whatever is great, whatever is fair, is felt by him as soon as seen. His thoughts go beyond external appearances to dwell upon things not visible to common mortals.

Snelling sees that Bryant achieves this native sublime through linkages of natural simplicity and common piety. The poetic sublime emerges in and as a mood of moralized rapture: "His thoughts are natural and simple, seldom common-place, and often sublime." Earlier poems such as Bradstreet's "Contemplations" had moved from natural imagery to such a mood of self-elected awe. American critics in Bryant's era more widely endorsed this mode as a sublime well suited to the vastness and vacancy of place, which felt more and more like a country elected to provide global, if not cosmic, redemption. Strong selves were needed for such contests, and Bryant moralized and calmed their invention.

Like a watered-down and cheerier Wordsworth, then, Bryant domesticated the material of this natural sublime. He made vastness and wildness resonate with pious and national purposes. A sense of material and westward expansion had to be spiritually ratified, and poetry remained one genre in which such discourse took unconscious effect. In mild and flowing manner, Bryant sublimated the possession of power and thereby fulfilled the long-standing American criterion to effect a sublime which equated wild poetic transport with imperatives of spiritual election, as grandeur within matched the lure of material grandeur without. A *Democratic Review* [5(1839):525] critic, for example, claimed that "Thanatopsis" "administers welcome nurture to the contemplative mind" through its sublime effect: " 'Thanatopsis' is not so sublime as Coleridge's 'Hymn in the Valley of Chamouni,' but its effect on the imagination of the reader is scarcely less grand." National intentions could be elided in such grand, dematerialized designs.

124

Another sublime-hungry American reader expressed his own response to "Bryant's Poems" (*Democratic Review* 6 [1839]:274–79) in terms of correspondingly lofty emotion, poetry filling the mind with commonplace metaphor reifying a commonsense mood of exaltation: "Certain of his poems it is impossible to read without gliding unconsciously into a thousand trains of associated thought." Yet the thoughts associated by such a neo-Longinian reader were mostly the sublime ones of vastness and an elevation suggesting the infinite wealth of this world as transformable to ideal human usages such as poetry: "The themes are vast, giving scope for the boldest and broadest flights, exciting the highest sense of sublimity, treated with a corresponding grandeur of language and thought." The poet's language had to be big, spendthrift, spread out like the dematerialized power of God's vast scenery: the sublime of Capital's elected country was fast generating the symbolic capital of the poetic sublime, in a moral dialectic of transport connecting (in the poet's post-Puritan symbols) mutual election to spirituality as well as to worldly vocation. This sanctified wealth (symbolic, material) of sublimity might be renewed in each self-made poet, in any locale.

In a review of "Dana's Poems" for the *North American Review* (26[Jan. 1828]:242), Bryant himself argued that the will to poetry was not at all so vulgarly material but grandly *contemplative* in nature and pious in transport: "The contemplative nature of poetry, also, its love of plaintive themes, the liberty it allows of dwelling long and enthusiastically on the emotions of the heart, and the depth and intensity of coloring it requires, are all in our author's favor." The art critic Henry Theodore Tuckerman agreed with such criteria, finding this mingling of contemplative mood and sublime affect admirable in Bryant: "Bryant is eminently a contemplative poet. His thoughts are not less impressive than his imagery." Tuckerman went on to observe that Bryant's sublimity depends upon a new, paradoxically *lofty simplicity* of language, as in the language of *fiat lux:* "A noble simplicity of language, combined with these traits, often leads to the most genuine sublimity of expression" ["The Poetry of Bryant," *Democratic Review* 16(1845):189]. In other words, ordinary words and commonplace sites could serve as American locales for "genuine sublimity of expression."

In "To A Waterfowl" (1815), to invoke a Frost-like chestnut of

homemade Americana, Bryant moves from pensive contemplation
of a solitary bird traversing natural space ("the abyss of heaven"),
beyond terrors of solitude, to a comforting recognition that some
infinite Power sustains the flights of both bird and poet through a
boundlessness tersely evoked:

> He who, from zone to zone,
> Guides through the boundless sky thy certain flight,
> In the long way that I must tread alone,
> Will lead my steps aright.
>
> (27)

This natural sublime, contemplated as a landscape of immensity
and negotiated as the site of self-empowerment, suggests (all too
inevitably) the immanent power of God to prop up and underwrite
the ego's loftiest flights to didactic realms of transport. Yet unlike
the egotistic sublimity of Wordsworth on Mount Snowdon, say, or
Whitman incarnating the bulk of national geography into amped-
up songs of himself as wider than democratic masses, Bryant's con-
templations lead not to affirmations of the mind's sublimity or to
self-estrangement from birds, but to self-humbling reaffirmations
of religious precepts. Ironically enough, such sublimity tails off and
ends up recycling merely *beautiful* sentiments and home-grown pie-
ties, domesticating wildness into closed form and sublimity into
obviousness. Bryant's sublime is commonly one of prefabricated
sublimation. As Richard Wilbur notes (see chapter epigraph) in the
"homiletic woods" around Bryant's Cummington, even a mere bird
song can only remind the American self "of how we are enlarged /
By what estranges." [12]

Viewing the "haunts of Nature" in strictly solitary contempla-
tion, however, Bryant can proclaim a "deep contentment" and
"kindred calm," in which the poet, like a spontaneous creature of
nature, can again "enjoy existence" and exult in being alive within
such natural vastness ("Inscription For the Entrance to a Wood"):

> Throngs of insects in the shade
> Try their thin wings and dance in the warm beam
> That waked them into life. Even the green trees
> Partake the deep contentment . . .
>
> (25)

126

Terrors and threats are held too much in abeyance. This natural sublime is humanized and negotiated without risks of sudden devastation. Yet in "A Forest Hymn," contemplating vast forest groves as signifying "God's first temples," Bryant contends that the "sacred influences" of natural space suddenly overtook him as

> All their green tops, stole over him, and bowed
> His spirit with the thought of boundless power
> And inaccessible majesty.
>
> (79)

Here, better, Bryant faces the threat of submission and the risks of blocking off a power inaccessible to the subjective mind. Again emerges Bryant's reigning convention that the natural sublime—contemplated as immensity and in freshly perceived detail—can lead to renewed convictions of the diety, apprehended (repeatedly) in a conversionary mood of rapture. Through the "continual worship" of Nature, that is, the poet can enjoy the *accessible* presence of God through his life-world's vast yet local attributes. Through such awe, wildness is tamed and interiorized in the heart, linking the wild to the good, and power to ethos:

> But thou art here—thou fill'st
> The solitude . . .
>   Grandeur, strength, and grace,
> Are here to speak of thee. This mightly oak—
> By whose immovable stem I stand and seem
> Almost annihilated—. . .
>
> (80)

Anxious before images that might become "tremendous tokens" of God's power as deployed against his own thoroughly democratic puniness,"*almost annihilated*" [emphasis added], Bryant trumps up another sublime hymn to the influx of his own shareable power, as self and scene are made to correspond as unitary incarnation:

> My heart is awed within me when I think
> Of the great miracle that still goes on,
> In silence, round me—the perpetual work

Of thy creation, finished, yet renewed
Forever.
(80–81)

Such an American sublime, like God's primary creation, must be renewed in fresh acts, though it has long been finished as mountain or as epic.

"The Prairies" (1832) is even more furiously localized and associative, yet builds upon this commonplace convention of transport. The poet confronts the natural sublime as a material malleable to the ideological dreams of power and self-making in Romantic America, as it poetically breaks away from England and is called upon by mandates of the sublime-mimetic to forge some vaguely realized American version of the sublime:

These are the gardens of the Desert, these
The unshorn fields, boundless and beautiful,
For which the speech of England has no name—
The Prairies. I behold them for the first,
And my heart swells, while the dilated sight
Takes in the encircling vastness.
(130)

In this recurringly "dilated" mood of national amplitude, Bryant summons up barely repressed associations of Indian and ancient civilizations which such American sublimity, however Romantic, must empty out in order to emerge. He views the landscape of vast dirt with quickened perception, in a fine image and apt epithet:

sliding reptiles of the ground,
Startingly beautiful.
(133)

To the "startlingly beautiful" imagery of nature, Bryant goes on to supplement this ground with the moralized association of God as "the quickening breath." Such an unlocalized Being sustains the vast forms of nature and power, in country as in city.

"The Prairies" remains a rather picturesque poem *trying to be*

128

sublime, it seems to me; that is, a poem *trying* to use the landscape to invoke an anxious, empowering source of the poet's self-expansion, as Bryant remembers past associations of history, ruins, Indians who once inhabited this vast space (seemingly) aeons ago. A sublime emptiness is fitfully produced. Later, like a watered-down Frank O'Hara in New York City, even in the "vast and help-less city" Bryant can, according to the free-floating conventions of this emergent American sublime, "commune with Heaven" and a "present Deity": "Even here do I behold / Thy steps, Almighty!— here, amid the crowd, / Through the great city rolled" ("Hymn of the City" [1830]). Such pious transports amid city streets and crowds recall Whitman's urban sublime and, later, Louis Simpson in "The Hour of Feeling," (1976), which does the same for the skyscrapers of modern New York City, importing sublime feeling from a rural to an urban context, making even advertisements of Capital's details (whiskey signs) glow with the radiance of his own immense feeling.[13]

Such a radiant image of the American wilderness Bryant had memorably urged upon American painters of national landscapes in "To Cole, the Painter, Departing for Europe" (1829) as mandate to circulate sublimity:

Thine eyes shall see the light of distant skies:
   Yet, Cole! thy heart shall bear to Europe's strand
   A living image of our own bright land,
Such as upon thy glorious canvas lies;
Lone lakes—savannas where the bison roves—
   Rocks rich with summer garlands—solemn streams—
Spring bloom and autumn blaze of boundless groves.

                 (127)

As a member of the Hudson River School of landscape painting, the first indigenous painting-style of distinctive force (sublimity) in America, Cole had done much to represent these "boundless groves" of American sublimity in paintings of vast (and pietistic) scenes. Yet Bryant warns his *kindred spirit* of Catskill bliss and pious awe not to be taken in by the merely *"picturesque"* scenes and associations of overcivilized, form-deadened Europe:

129

> Fair scenes shall greet thee where thou goest—fair,
>   But different—everywhere the trace of men,
>   Paths, homes, graves, ruins, from the lowest glen
> To where life shrinks from the fierce Alpine air—

The essential image of Bryant's America remains bright and wild, however, abounding in a sublime tied to natural energies and forces and legitimating huge claims:

> Gaze on them, till the tears shall dim thy sight,
> But keep that earlier, wilder image bright.
>   (128)

In a poetics of transport and poems of natural sublimity where daily selfhood and ordinary reference to God *almost* break down, such as "The Prairies" (1830), "contemplative" Bryant had lovingly represented this "earlier, wilder image" of America as a place of self-exalting transport. The landscape was conjured into a mandate to exalted tonalities that might somehow remain natural (not "artificial" like Trumbull's sublime) yet compete with Europe. Both Bryant and Cole, as Asher Durand's painting *Kindred Spirits* (1849) didactically depicted, did emerge and commune as "kindred spirits" of the American sublime: brothers communing with the spirit of the sublime in nature, tapping into the wealth-begetting power of the Godhead in the Catskills, and thereby unlocking (through this mode of dynamogenic self-imaging) the magnitude of their own cash-value art and potentiality to invent "new forms of sublimity." Circulating belief and sustaining such grand actions, the sublime proved to be a fully pragmatic trope of self-instantiation. For, as Gary Lee Stonum has written of the "Romantic sublime" as installed, instantiated, and transformed within scenarios of American poets from Emerson to Dickinson and beyond, "The prestige of the sublime depends not upon penetrating reflections about why it works but upon the self-legitimating and self-authenticating fact that it does work." [14] As a visionary compact, the American sublime generated the American sublime.

Bryant, then, provides one lastingly genteel version and pious domestication of this American sublime. As such, he still shines forth as a poet of natural forests, of peaceful, calm, ancestral places

130

where the mind can evoke, moralize, and finally control, reverent associations, if not root its sense of shared (mainstream) history in some imagined vacancy of place. However committed to a theory of the sublime, he often adheres to a merely "picturesque" tradition of association which is exactly the lower mode (a version of "the beautiful" with legends and ruins thrown in) that he advises Cole against as a tradition more suited to Europe, with its burden of history and legacy of forms, classes, and myths. As a supple poet and democratic editor, Bryant promoted forest hymns, lyrics to God set in wilderness locations, as well as reforms of equality set in his equally beloved vastness of American cities. Yet Bryant's sublime-seeking poetry all too conventionally, like a homemade and more banal version of Wordsworth, did fulfill the norm of the American sublime circulating in an era of Common Sense. This sublimity equated poetic transport with the terrors and wonders of sacred suasion (conversion).

For such artists, seemingly exhilarated by the very dearth of tradition and precedent, an imagined vacancy of place shorn of Indians as well as of sin, the living image of America must beckon the lone self into what Cole calls the "sublime wilderness" of mountain, lake, and waterfall. The sublimity of art was enjoined if the technologies of progress were vaguely impeded. Such banal sublimity of national aggrandizement lives on in the heart (and language) of Bryant as on the "glorious canvas" of Cole's art. Talking also to himself in the poem as he ages and hence falls off into mannered versions of his own earlier sublimity, Bryant must remind the painter of this sublime legacy as he leaves for Europe to study Old World models and monuments. The material of the American sublime is proclaimed as preexisting *in the landscape* like a spiritual mandate calling the artist to generate sublime self-election: those lone lakes, vast savannas, rocks, streams, "skies where the desert eagle wheels and screams," "boundless groves" which for Bryant functioned like primordial cathedrals, evoking awe and faith as in spaces of worship. One question must linger in his own mind, seeking that essentialized greatness of the ages: Was the Romantic sublime really that abundant, freshly deployed, or "original" in his own poetry?

He brags to Cole (in his little sonnet) that Europe is not so much *sublime* in vastness and potentiality, as it is *picturesque* in associations, a place of timeworn achievements and ruins, domestications, objects bleared with the touch of human history. If such a European world "is charged with the grandeur of God" as an energy ("charge") of vast force *and* moral responsibility ("charge"), it may soon be irreversably "seared with trade; bleared; smeared with toil" as Gerard Manley Hopkins was to depict it in the English/ Irish landscape of "God's Grandeur" (1877).[15] (This theme of wilderness contamination indeed informed the cyclical paintings of Thomas Cole as it did his own ecological polemics.) Nevertheless, if Americans can still (in the self-reliant, not yet full Capitalized raptures of 1829) *expand* the freshness of the self in such a sublime space, dwellers in the Old World somehow *shrink back* from solitary heights and Catskill communions. They better abide in park-like glens, "where life shrinks from the fierce Alpine air." Such is Bryant's polemical opposition of the beautiful and the sublime, anyway, as he invokes the sublime to do battle against the limits of the British picturesque, taking "greatness" out of the ideal spheres and making it (as an *American* sublimity) do battle in history and emerge as wild form.[16]

Bryant's *sonnet* form, however, is all too well-wrought, hemmed in, and closed off from the possibility of original phrasing or tonal accent: that passionate utterance growing out of sublime feeling yet tapping into vernacular language that we denominate as rhetorically sublime. Walt Whitman's "Song of Myself" enacts such a *wild* image of the self as keeper of nature's original energy and America's massiveness, generating new modes of utterance, unexpected diction, unprecedented rhythms and incarnational connections. Yet Bryant's heart is in the right place, moved by the actual landscape, freshened by liberal sentiments, even if his poetic form and all-too-poetic diction of "the beauteous" holds him back from a language of pragmatic sublimity commensurate with this American vernacular and democratic ground.

As Stevens said in praise of his overidealized precursor, Whitman, "he wrote naturally, with an extemporaneous and irrepressible vehemence of emotion." Whitman displaces these prior or Longinian commonplaces of the American sublime. The negativity of the material sublime had to be mastered and outdone. As a voice of representative mastery, however, Bryant merely *hints* at such a wild vehemence in a marvelous phrase like "skies, where the desert eagle wheels and screams." This remains a good figure for any American poet of such traumatic landscapes who remains ecstatic (and tiny) in an immense and self-consecrated space, yet keeps "that earlier, wilder image bright."

SIX

Walt Whitman

The American Sublime as "Song of Myself"

The élan of the essential Whitman is still deeply moving in the
things in which he was himself deeply moved. . . . The good
things, the superbly beautiful and moving things, are those
that he wrote naturally, with an extemporaneous and irre-
pressible vehemence of emotion.

—Wallace Stevens

Whitman's "Vast Egotism": "One Vast Democracy"

As a song of "vast egotism" in which the "poetic idea" of
continental America as well as the "antipoetic" materiality of daily
life could, to invoke Tocqueville's terms, be envisioned as "one vast
democracy" subsuming national grandeur and unity into a single
citizen, Walt Whitman became the American sublime in 1855.[1]
Through an unfathomable act of self-invention and discursive col-
lage, ["Walter"] Whitman forged *Leaves of Grass* (Brooklyn, 1855)
into a model of textual sublimity fit to convey America's landscape
of august mountains and great lakes, railroads, dynamos, and red-
necks. This material was done up as self-election into rapture,
wholeness and *wellness,*

> At length let up again to feel the puzzle of puzzles,
> And that we call Being.[2]

If "the place is august [and] the terms [of sublimity] obdurate" as
Whitman boasted to future poets in "By Blue Ontario's Shore"
(349), his democratized mode of the sublime deployed "omniver-

134

ous lines" of itemized incarnation that displaced prior attempts (such as Joel Barlow's *Columbiad*) if not future efforts (even Hart Crane's *Bridge*) as so much Eurocentric poetic-diction, epic moon-mash, ersatz grandeur.

In the trope of "Walt Whitman," sublime rapture found *American* terms and expressed what Bryant theorized as "new modes of sublimity." The American sublime emerged, beyond tamer worships of Bryant or the meter-making arguments of Emerson, as an egalitarian voice representing big feelings and commonplace ideas. "Song of Myself" linked landscapes of transport to self-empowerment and fused into imaginal wholeness a poetics of sublime exultation ("sacred rapture") that had been developing, as I have claimed, for two centuries. All prior American versions seemed wishful tonality more than earthy fact: an olden sublime insufficiently rooted in body, language, or national scene.

As with the oral-epic tradition for Homer, or patristic commentary for Dante, an amorphous (and highly ideological) mix called the *American sublime* was there coding Whitman's poetic ego with collective thematics; or, better said, there constituting what Bakhtin called a *speech-genre* or "way of seeing and interpreting."[3] "Walt Whitman" emerged from the literary unconsciousness of Puritan and Romantic America, that is, to incarnate and to voice, as seeming "origin," these ready-made terms, overbeliefs, and myths of social and self-regeneration in that brash, "western," charged-up way of speaking that is "Song of Myself":

> Creeds and schools in abeyance,
> Retiring back a while sufficed at what they are, but never
>   forgotten,
> I harbor for good or bad, I permit to speak at every hazard,
> Nature without check with original energy.
>
> (29)

"For good or bad," one result has been that Whitman's voice, at once bragging and culture-specific, has lingered on into modernism to serve as generic mandate to national grandeur, American brag and bliss, furthering accents of such scope: *august, immense, grand.* These sweeping adjectives and ideologically underwritten transports before material sources have added up, even critically, to the persistence of a genre called, after an anecdotal poem from 1935 by Stevens, "The American Sublime."

Each line of "Song of Myself" seemingly emerges as a raw, unprecedented utterance through which, as Stevens saw, "vehement" feelings overflow extemporaneously and find new forms, open rules, utter hyperboles that seem natural and credible because they are so faithfully uttered and rhythmically sustained.[4] Each moment of utterance, each object or self of perception, can become a new sign of transport, generating high feelings and representative claims. Whereas Emily Dickinson cultivated a lifelong stance of radical inwardness and gnomic privacy which, hovering and hesitating in traumas of unbreachable otherness, refused to give "the Romantic sublime" any positive location or proper name, Whitman's song of American mastery enacted, circulated, and reified the far more public claim: "I troop forth replenish'd with supreme power, one of an average unending procession" (72).[5]

Leaves of Grass can be read as "only a language experiment" in the sublime mode. As the voice of this "average unending procession" into liberal empowerment, Whitman moves to derive sublimity from American substances and vernacular forms—"to give the spirit, the body, the man, new words, new potentialities of speech," words charged with magnitudes of the American democracy, landscape, and spirit. Despite Whitman's quest for quotationless autonomy (he advised himself in his notebooks in the self-formative stage of the early 1850s, "Make no quotations and references to any other writers")—that is, for a wholly unmediated or "self-trusting" sublimity—his poetry is shaped in and emerges as the sublimity of language. Whatever his struggles with the vastness of nature or the vulgarity of democracy, these words (as diction and syntax) inhabit selfhood with the discourse of the prior and other whose more "feudal" sublimity Whitman must encounter with the timely/untimely grandeur of self-expression, "Walt Whitman, a kosmos, of Manhattan the son" (52).[6]

As Whitman boasts in the first Preface to *Leaves of Grass*, "His [the American poet's] spirit responds to his country's spirit . . . he incarnates its geography and natural life and rivers and lakes" (iv). In this rather desperately reiterated dialectic of big (*sublime land*) and small (*humble individual*), a common self from a carpentry family on Long Island "troop[s] forth replenish'd with supreme power" to generate troops of self-grandeur who can interiorize the outside world, from New York City to California to India and beyond, into enclaves of immensity which he calls the "Me myself" of the Over-Soul. Whitman identifies with and represents this American immensity. Otherwise, the frontier and swarming city seem too external and immense, too "monstrous without a corresponding largeness and generosity of the spirit of the citizen" (iv). "Song of Myself" embodies, on a grand scale of Emersonian self-intoxication, this attempt to represent sublime space by remaking the ego into a selfhood capable of blessing place and globe like a shamanized Columbus fusing "America" into an India of his own imperial design.

Hardly the island of *haiku,* or compact Hondas, or of Phillip Larkin's "unfenced existence" forever out of reach, America generates in the Whitmanic ego (in Ammons's diagnostic, the "whit manic") an "élan" imparting haze, vista, scope. Linking details to vast conceptions, Whitman's poems are driven to assume those overreaching tropes of "gigantism" that Tocqueville argued would afflict democratic authors when they turned away from the pettiness of the ego ("a very insignificant person, namely himself") or towards the dullness of business life. This was especially so "when they attempt a poetic style" beyond the prosaic round of their banal, unglamorous existence.[7]

Even a midwestern farmyard in "A Farm Picture" can be refigured, for example, beyond pastoral stability or closure, into a framework of grand acceptance. Door, cattle, peace, and horizon link to comprise "democratic vistas" of immensity. Near and far, small and big are interconnected by the self-made radiance of consciousness, "and that we call Being":

Through the ample open door of the peaceful country barn,
A sunlit pasture field with cattle and horses feeding,
And haze and vista, and the far horizon fading away.
(274)

Such American farm doors, surrounded by bigness, do not close and shut off, but open to "haze and vista."

Whitman, like any other "puny democratic ego," is just a *tiny* body in space—like the country barn or his characteristic images of himself as child, bird, oak, spider, Columbus, a leaf, or blade, of grass. Barely six feet, he remains a lonely figure set off against "vast wildernesses" and the lurking threat of social mass or erotic devastation. As poet, however, he projects a counterimage or "countersublime" to dialogize and to match the material forces that threaten this American mastery. He thereby confronts the geographical immensity and pluralistic maze of America and makes it more malleable to human industries such as farming or poetry.[8]

"Song of Myself" negotiates these overlarge feelings and overbeliefs of the Romantic self to enunciate Whitman's own origin (originality), "with original energy," and announce a landscape (and country) possessed by materials of wonder: "knowing us in thrall / To that deep wonderment, our native clay," as Hart Crane enthused of Whitman as the American *genius loci* in *The Bridge*. The cash-value result of such libidinous self-imaging is a poetry that overflows laws of ordinary syntax, as Stevens wrote, in neo-Longinian terms, "with an extemporaneous and irrepressible vehemence of emotion." For, as Nietzsche claimed of "Homer," dispersing the genealogy of this authorial genius into the genre of the Greek epic, "We believe in a great poet as the author of the *Iliad* ["Song of Myself"] and the *Odyssey—but not that Homer* [Whitman] *was this poet.*"[9]

Like his *Over-Soul* and *over-man* influence, Emerson, who had begun to democratize and to vernacularize the sublime into more material trenches of the humble, Whitman refused to see the sublime *only* in or as the immense; as he chided his theosophic friend, R. M. Bucke, with the overbelieving claims of his own imagery, "After all, the great lesson is that no special natural sights—not Alps, Niagara, Yosemite or anything else—is more grand or more beautiful than the ordinary sunrise and sunset, earth and sky, the common trees and grass."[10] Grass was for Whitman as miraculous as a mountain, waterfalls, or stars. Each object could instigate fits of mental grandeur, vast conceptions of self and self-as-divinity, that state of self-transcendence which Bucke credited as "cosmic consciousness," and which Whitman (in Bucke's hero-worshipping view) had embodied (like Blake and Balzac) as an exemplary case. For Bucke, this was Whitman's essential poetic doctrine, simply put, as spiritual mandate: "that the commonplace is the grandest of all things."

138

In this radical equation of *sublimitas* and *humilitas,* Whitman furthered the libertarian/Christian dynamic of Emerson, for whom the sublime entered into everything: a multiplication table, a privy, even an ant or a bee was sublime. *Sublimity* obtained for Whitman, furthermore, not only in the "higher" life of the idealizing mind ("soul") but also in the "lower" instincts ("body electric") as much as in the lower classes from which his pedagogics of grandeur had emerged, as shown in "Starting From Paumanok." The Whitmanic sublime existed in the most humble, or degraded object. Such an insouciant overturning of aesthetic hierarchies made for lines of startling juxtaposition, colliding dictions of high and low, as inner and outer spontaneously merged, with forces precious and gross: "I hear bravuras of birds, bustle of growing wheat, gossip of flames, clack of sticks cooking my meals" and so on, in a way that continues to amaze.

For Bucke, as for Emerson, this *democratic* perception of the sublime in the lowly, and the miraculous in the vulgar or vernacular, depended on a highly sublimated consciousness Bucke called a "more or less supernatural faculty, separating [the poet] from other men." This conflict of empathy and superiority translated, as poetic subject matter, into the drama of double-consciousness between empirical and transcendental selves. The will to achieve such sublimity Whitman presents as the bliss-and-dread scenario of regeneration that is "Song of Myself."

Within Enlightenment poetics, the "sublime poem" had emerged as that speech-genre which, in Martin Price's eloquent summary of the pre-Romantic tradition, "seeks to convey the experience of transcendence. To do so it must dazzle us with its freedom from constraints of time and space, or, conversely, it must present the limited object as radiant with a more than natural presence. This may be achieved by hyperbole, by the extension of the vast to the illimitable, by the evocation of plenitude in a welter of images, often mixed, discordant, oxymoronic, paradoxical." [11] As the imagination strains to depict shifting versions of material vastness or cognitive infinitude, prior terms of "ordinary" selfhood and "poetic" form get pushed by the overreaching ego to some liminal breaking point.

The sublime poem induces some blockage or collapse, as Price claims, tracing and enacting the limit between the *sublime* (Words-worth) and the *visionary* (Blake): "In each case the poet moves towards the unimaginable; measure falls and pictures are dissolved. . . . In all these cases language confesses its bankruptcy, and the drama consists precisely in the imagination exhausting words and straining beyond them." Price's generic model seems to predict or to summarize Whitman, who expanded commonsense notions of selfhood and country in "Song of Myself": "The sublime was an experience of transcendence, a surpassing of conventions or reasonable limits, an attempt to come to terms with the unimaginable. The moment of the sublime was a transport of spirit, and at such a moment the visible object was eclipsed or dissolved." [12] Whitman pragmatized the dynamics of this genre to American ends.

For, building on the revolutionary energies of European Romanticism by indigenizing this *Romantic sublime* for national purposes and distinctly Capitalist ends, Whitman's America was exactly that "western" space of Empire wherein the poetic mind might experience, in rapt conversion to self-possibility, such *transcendence* of inherited limitations and aristocratic forms. Poets of Whitman's sublime are called upon to recognize, with intense faith, and "much more vast conception [s] of divinity itself," the radiance of power pervading mind and cosmos, making nature malleable, even eclipsing it through tropes assuming mental grandeur. Whitman's goal, as announced in "Starting From Paumanok," was to elevate and sanctify the "real and permanent grandeur of these States" (20); to open up the democratic self to futurity, possibilities of self-exaltation adjudicated in the common tongue: "Still the present I raise aloft, still the future of the States I harbinge glad and sublime" (26).

Overexclaiming and all but pushing these vocational delusions of self-grandeur and self-as-country wholeness to an (inevitable) breaking pint or "blockage," as in the emergency of abysmal vastness that is "As I Ebb'd With the Ocean of Life," Whitman's voice rendered the empty landscape *august,* and the language of such Bible-like rapture *obdurate.* Yet void of such transcendental tropes, Whitman is neither the mountain nor the ocean but a minute particular, like the live oak growing in the solitary wilds of Louisiana: "all alone it stood and the moss hung down from the branches, / Without any companion it grew uttering joyous leaves [*Leaves*] of

140

dark green" (126). The self stands alone in nature, *alone with America* (as Richard Howard spookily troped the poetic vocation here),[13] like the solitary thrush or a traumatized child confronting undefined space. Crossing into the sublime, the mind is filled with swirling images and unlocated voices dispersing identity into the crowd.

As Tocqueville warned such unsponsored poets of the egotistical sublime in "Why American Writers and Speakers Are Often Bombastic," they might be deluded by these very claims of commensurate grandeur:

> Each citizen of a democracy generally spends his time considering the interests of a very insignificant person, namely, himself. If he ever does raise his eyes higher, he sees nothing but the huge apparition of society or the even larger form of the human race. He has nothing between very limited and clear ideas and very vague conceptions; the space between is empty.[14]

Almost swallowed by this social emptiness, "empty spirit / In vacant space" (Stevens), Whitman emerges to project his poems as representative enactments of national sublimity. He breaks the dread of ego-solitude by "uttering joyous leaves of dark green" and hymns to "manly love" and democratic community (126). The live oak in "I Saw in Louisiana a Live-Oak Growing" is treated as a *hero* of the natural sublime in its isolate confrontation with American vastness ("a flat wide space") and social indifference: "the live-oak glistens there in Louisiana solitary in a wide flat space / Uttering joyous leaves all its life." This treelike "uttering [of] joyous leaves" is done in vast solitude, without a companion-reader to confirm its sense of slow grandeur: "I knew very well I could not" utter leaves alone, Whitman admits in the companionable love poems of gender-mingled sexuality in *Calamus* (1860).

Manically defensive and warding off lyric solipsism, this Whitmanic self in "vast wildernesses" of space *needs* human others, not just the vastations and consolations of the sublime. Each influx of vastness is threatened by an efflux of emptiness. The poems serve as symbolic links, "filaments," "bridges," "leaves" to other Americans negotiating the lonely present and vacant future. Yet the assumption abides that beneath the abyss of nature or disintegration

141

of death, there is a "well-join'd scheme" of unity which the dispar-
ate unity of the poem only reflects, or at best enacts. The sublime
functions as a visionary compact or erotic glue by fusing the poetic
ego to the massiveness and alienating power of the prairies or a
Broadway scene. Vastness comprises a spectacle by which to absorb
items and forms into some self which is bigger than America, can
command chaos and life to flow on, can instigate nature to expand
and contract into itself while Whitman journeys on the "open
road" of vista, speed, and space beyond anxious gender-identity as
"the body." Each object gets used up by Whitmanic sublimation,
absorbed into bliss-wrought unity of the self ("You furnish your
parts towards eternity") and interior vastness of the soul, which
transcends time (the Over-Soul may still be looking) and place (it
is bigger than Manhattan) (165).

Risking Mockery and the American Sublime

> The very experience of this limit [in "a bliss of colors"] is a bliss
> greater than my bliss, it exceeds both myself and my sex, it is sub-
> lime, but without sublimation. If there is a sublime, it would be there
> where there might be no more sublimation, *n'est-ce pas?* And in or-
> der to be sublime, sexual difference must no longer be subject to
> dialectics.[15]

Who more omniverously than Whitman merged into and became
the sublime essentiality/ideality of the American landscape and
spirit? Stimulated by democratic mandates as well as by tropes of
American "self-reliance" as a trust in vast energies of God and
Capital flowing through the land, and the national quest for liter-
ary magnitude on a world-competitive scale, Walt ["Walter"] Whit-
man yet seems to have sprung from some imaginal conception of
himself. This remains so—source studies of the imagery of George
Sand, the prosody of Martin Tupper, or the dialectic of Hegel,
Marx, or Paul de Man notwithstanding. Considering the stylistic
transformations of diction and form-as-event in the *language ex-
periment* that is "Song of Myself," it seems mean-spirited to ponder
this American free spirit in relation to *any* continuities of genre or

142

language, no matter how mediating such conventions remain for the "inner speech" or "intuition" of the most self-reliant self.

Whitman yet transforms the genre (frames/limits) of the sublime by becoming his own rule. He becomes a *transitive* origin of I-centered expression. A spiritualized sexuality is given the desublimated shape of unprecedented form. This happens in the *Calamus* poems, surely, a gender-merging form which may have alienated Emerson but secured future disciples such as Allen Ginsberg (or Robert Pinsky), who must absorb this transgressive language to become their greatest American selves. From the perspective of Nietzsche's *The Will to Power,* the Whitmanic sublime can be read as an aspiration to agonize the "Great Style." Such mastery assumes the channeling of huge force—not just material but male. This is achieved through imagined overflowings of vitality, will, sexual energy, blood, and breath, into a form (the fifty-two sections of "Song of Myself," most notably) of unprecedented unity that threatens to overwhelm the "rapt" listener with new plenitudes of language.[16]

The American sublime here occurs from states of self-intoxicated power in which the will orders nature, commands sensual flux to take on democratized forms of utterance in a vulgar or "*impure*" diction transgressing the decorums of Poe or pieties of Emerson.[17] In the shattering of sublime bliss that is "Song of Myself," the "I" of the poem ("I celebrate myself, and sing myself / And what I assume you shall assume" [28]) not only identifies with but merges into huge powers outside itself. He achieves this unity through tropes of grand, itemized incorporation ("I lean and loafe at my ease observing a spear of summer grass"[28])—what we would now try to demystify as "identification," "displacement," or "sublimation." Yet through these tactics of overbelieving, the ego can unite with an imagined *whole* and help create and circulate (for others) that pragmatic conviction of cash-value wellness and wholeness in the country supporting this "American" self:

> Swiftly arose and spread around me the peace and knowledge
>   that pass all the argument of the earth,
> And I know that the hand of God is the promise of my own,
> And I know that the spirit of God is the brother of my own,

And that all the men ever born are also my brothers, and the
women my sisters and lovers . . .

(33)

In this oscillating flux of merger and isolation, Whitman's eroti-
cized sublime enacts a scenario of self-intoxication that seeks to
transfigure the materiality of the States, exalt matter into some-
thing malleable to the workaday will and dreams of self-
expression. As Harold Bloom avowed of the American sublime ex-
pressed in early Stevens, "The American reality is sea and sky, the
immensity of space, and like Emerson and Whitman, Crispin [Ste-
ven's poetic alter ego in "The Comedian as the Letter C"] beheld
and became that new man, the American." [18]
  Whitman's version doubtlessly records a machismo of the sub-
lime. Sperm, blood, and breath are stored up only to overflow com-
monsense limits, to invest wilder forms, to secure radical "habits
of the [American] heart." Sperm, yoga-like as in some "body with-
out organs," circulates as image and trope of phallocentric power
and sublime mastery in Whitman, as in the pan-sexuality of "Song
of Myself," wherein "Something I cannot see puts upward prongs /
[and] Seas of bright juice suffuse heaven" (54). Confronting this
sexualized version of "expressive individualism," fusing (through
acts of corporate merging) soul into body, self into other, opposi-
tion into unity, we can *sublimate* Whitman, as does Bucke. Or the
reader can *desublimate* him, as does Nietzsche on art's figurations
disseminated "beyond good and evil" or "truth," or Derrida (as
above) on gender-transgression. Whitman is *large* (at least his self-
image of "voice" is). He comes bragging like a hero from the coun-
try of Big Sky and Rocky Mountain High and (later) Big Macs. His
poems encompass both sublimations and are able "to contain mul-
titudes" and myriad contradictions relating self to/from other.[19]
  Offspring of American ideology as much as his own Hindu-like
imagination ("both in and out of the game and watching and won-
dering at it" [32]"), Whitman creates a sublimity of rapt selfhood
(mastery) as both origin and tradition. He is the singular yet inter-
pellated embodiment of the American whole.[20] If Whitman does
not originate the American sublime, he embodies its heterogeneity,
becoming "America" in all its sexual, ideological, and ethnic excess
and contradiction. At times he is *beyond or without sublimation,*

merging colors, genders, generic codes, beyond the law of framed (binary) opposites. He can withstand both a pious *sublimating* of his sublime (as in stylistics) and an impious *desublimating* of his own grand terms (as in psychoanalytic demystifications) and textual sublime. Neither initiating nor foreclosing the genre, Whitman became the American sublime that he imagined and saw, inside the self and in the *genius loci,* and that remains a literary feat immune to ridicule or destruction.

Whitman's Americanized Sublime as "Song of Myself"

To exist as the "afflatus surging and surging" (52) that is poetry for Whitman, the sublime must *come down* to enter into the American spirit and land, its mores, its clashing language, its words of simple magnitude. Still, what comprises the components of this sublime for Whitman? Admittedly, to speak of any *national* sublime (British, French, Indian) is to reify an ideological oxymoron, here a trope mixing pragmatic idea and spiritual rapture (as appropriated in the 1840s and 1850s during the take-off of industrial capital in the States). This trope of national sublimity gets historically fitted to political purposes and social concerns that have much to do with the engendering, at once on a private and collective scale, of material *power.* But to declaim this *American* sublime is to assume a necessary hyperbole of mental, verbal, and physical grandeur, as Whitman detailed once and for all time in "Song of Myself." This is the historically accurate term, furthermore, not merely a rhetorical projection back from our sign-glutted era in which a forest of new sublimities now proliferate as panic, as hysteria, as camp, and so on.

Besides writing, printing, and later reviewing the first edition of *Leaves of Grass* at the Brooklyn press of his friends James and Thomas Rome, Walt Whitman fabricated a document of Americanized sublimity as the prose preface to the (all-but-textually-unbroken) 1855 edition of *Leaves*. Whitman is seemingly more interested, as an aesthetic policy, in the grandeur of *self* and *country* than in matters of literary *style,* high or low. But his claim is a disarming gesture which, as Susan Sontag explains, is "a standard ploy for ushering in a new stylistic vocabulary." [21] Yet Sontag exaggerates the uniqueness and discontinuity of Whitman, as if any poem could achieve "originality" in diction, syntax, or tonality in (dialogical) relation to the constraints of language as cultural system or sign.

Even the most jaded poststructural reader *is* still struck by the freshness and surreal oddness ("I believe the soggy clods shall become lovers and lamps" [59]) of Whitman's poetic language, however, as this displaces the anterior sublimity of British or Early American poems: as one Marxist critic summarizes, "Indeed, it is a truism, and a truth, that Whitman all but invented American poetry, or at least finally made it possible." [22] I would go beyond Jerome McGann's "truism" of literary history to claim that the heteroglossic plenitude and semiotic overload of imagery and phrases in "Song of Myself," to use the central example of the sublime genre, becomes *more,* not less, representative of prior American poetics. He does not invent so much as transform conventions and materials of American poetics. The Whitmanic sublime becomes more resonant with history and ploys of textual materiality when considered in the context of Early American poems such as Bradstreet's "Contemplations," Livingston's *Philosophic Solitude,* or Bryant's "Prairies."

Seeking to solidify the sublime, "Song of Myself" moves through states of *terror* and *horror* to renewed affirmations of spiritual *wonder,* rapt awe, and plenary union with the vastness of God. Whitman's staging of transport before item and whole represents and reaccents the whole genre of the American sublime, as Hart Crane dangerously realized in *The Bridge.* Whitman's "deep wonderment" and "native clay" emerges from the very language and ground: Whitman becomes the great sublime he draws. "America does not repel the past or what it has produced under its forms or amid other politics or the idea of castes or the old religions," as Whitman claims in the first sentence to the 1855 printing of *Leaves of Grass* (iii). The poet refigures these class-ridden terms/forms to suit newer, American purposes, as Whitman goes on to show.

The 4 July 1855 preface to *Leaves* highlights *three* ingredients of the sublime which will be presented in the "Song of Myself," which immediately follows. First, his country's elevated substance, echoing Emerson et al. in paragraph 2: "The Americans of all nations at any time upon the earth have probably the fullest poetical nature. The United States themselves are essentially the greatest poem. In the history of the earth hitherto the largest and most stirring appear tame and orderly to their ampler largeness and stir" (iii). Second, the poet must make himself into a grand, wholesome, hard-working if not entrepreneurial figure of self-mastery who will be commensurate with and empowered by these dynamics of scope and depth. He emerges as "Walt Whitman, an American" of laboring-class origin who will yet encompass (in language and imagination more than body) the immensity of America: "His [the American poet's] spirit responds to his country's spirit . . . he incarnates its geography and natural life and rivers and lakes" just as "he spans between them also from east to west and reflects what is between them" (iv).

Third, all this American "magnitude of geography" and "native elegance of soul" demands, finally, "the gigantic and generous treatment worthy of it"—that is, a poetry more liberated in style and verbal gesture, able to *heroicize* the place as theme and style. "For such the expression of the American poet," Whitman boasts, "is to be transcendent and new" (iv). Such lofty ("transcendent and new") American poetry should not so much be given to metaphysical argument ("A morning-glory at my window satisfies me more than the meta-physics of books" [54]), or to classical satire ("I have no mockings or arguments, I witness and wait" [32]), but to the sublime tonality of wonder and national praise: "As he [the poet] sees the farthest he has the most faith. His thoughts are the hymns of the praise of things" (v). Before the grandeur of this "superb nation," even the Old World language donates: "The English language befriends the grand American expression" (xi). Whitman defended against the past, typically, by opening himself more fully and vulgarly to it.

Even Wordsworth's sublimity can appear "tame and orderly" compared to the subsuming of self and modern man "En-Masse" (as urban crowds, for example) depicted in "Song of Myself." Whitman brings forth, through overbelief in the self, something like an internalized romance of self-and-soul, attaining to national consummation and achieving cash-value efficacy as "Walt Whitman," cosmos and son. As Bloom phrases these dynamics, "Whitman, having married himself, goes forth as an Emersonian liberating God, to preside over the nuptials of the universe."[23] Transfiguring

the genre of native sublimity, "Song of Myself" reaccents that
transport and awe-struck contemplation which circulated in the
American sublime as "the rapted wit sublime," which Bradstreet et
al. had less outrageously incarnated.

Whitman's presentation of poetic transport as "sacred rapture"
assumes that through self-possession as God-intoxication, "you
[the reader] shall possess the origin of all poems, / You shall possess
the good of the earth and sun, (there are millions of suns left" [30]).
This stance is more *panoramic* and *astonishing* than anterior Amer-
ican poems in style, as well as more visibly threatened with empa-
thies of horror ("What is removed drops horribly in a pail" [42])
and terror ("Steep'd amid honey'd morphine, my windpipe throt-
tled in fakes of death" [56]). Yet Whitman again assumes that self-
regenerative *wonder* is, finally, the appropriate tonality and stance
towards the American life-world:

> Do you take it I would astonish?
> Does the daylight astonish? does the early redstart
>   twittering through the woods?
> Do I astonish more than they?
>
> (47)

The tone before daylight and redstart is simple yet grand, each line
a recycled chant of astonishment, like *fiat lux*.

Spending a scant two dollars on Whitman's book (though it did
cost more than Longfellow's best-selling *Hiawatha* published the
same year),[24] the American reader is urged to participate in self-
regenerative "astonishment" (*hypsos*). He does this by beholding
the world through the awe-struck ego-identity of a common man
who has earned this ecstasy through a defiantly *physical* union with
the vastness of God and America. "At length let up again to feel
the puzzle of puzzles, / And that we call Being" (as in the central
union of stanza 26), Whitman-as-poet ("I skirt sierras, my palms
cover continents" [61]) emerges as an I-voice "troop [ing] forth
replenish'd with supreme power, one of an average unending pro-
cession" (72). Through such an experience of sublime empower-
ment, or the passionate tropes engendered out of that experience,
it is as if Whitman has become—or made himself into, through
such language—a fully humanized (that is, fully *Americanized*)

148

God, who can "celebrate" the body (the seen) and soul (the unseen) as one. The vulgar has become a credible locus of sublime habits.

Moving from contemplation of a "spear of summer grass," Whitman becomes increasingly "intoxicated" with the particulars, energy, scope, and materiality of America and cosmos until he can affirm the immensity of each object, as extensions of himself: "And limitless are leaves stiff or drooping in the fields, / And brown ants in the little wells beneath them" (33). Merging his solitude outward, not just into prairies but everywhere, Whitman would have limitlessness emanate from even the lowliest item in the American democracy, until from a perspective of plenary "Being," he can Christ- or Nietzsche-like affirm his trans-nihilistic credo, "And a mouse is miracle enough to stagger sextillions of infidels" (59).

"Song of Myself" is founded in "the meditation, the devout ecstasy, the soaring flight" which Whitman claimed was *the* source of great-style poetry in "Democratic Vistas."[25] Transport occurs as a movement, in "Song of Myself," from a commonplace wonder, through threats of horror and terror, to a newly earned "positive wonder," as outlined in a prose note which Whitman transformed into the music-induced ecstasy of stanza 26:

> I want the chanted Hymn whose tremendous sentiment shall uncage in my breast a thousand wide-winged strengths and unknown ardors and terrible ecstasies—putting me through the flights of all the passions—dilating me beyond time and air—startling me with the overture of some unnameable horror—calmly sailing me all day on a bright river with lazy slapping waves—stabbing my heart with myriads of forked distractions more furious than hail or lightning— lulling me drowsily with honeyed morphine—tightening the fakes of death about my throat, and awakening me again to know by that comparison, the most positive wonder in the world, and that's what we call life.[26]

Impressed to voice *the most positive wonder in the world* by a "chanted Hymn" (as through poetry or nature), Whitman moves beyond "terrible ecstasies" and "some unnameable horror" impinging on consciousness by instigating a union with Being with effects the death of the unregenerate self. Replenished with power, finally, if not jetting forth the erotic stuff of unimagined republics,

Whitman is reborn into a renewed sense of awe at mere being. The New World terrain rebegets a new form of selfhood, as well as sublime forms of poetry issued from and as this male selfhood.

In "Song of Myself," whirled by an orchestra in stanza 26 "wider than Uranus flies," Whitman passes beyond "fakes of death" to experience sublime union with Being. Material limits seem suddenly transgressed:

> At length let up again to feel the puzzle of puzzles,
> And that we call Being.
>
> (56)

Whitman's positive wonder confirms reigning nineteenth-century American conceptions of the sublime as a mood of sacred suasion and moral bliss—as in Bryant, or Longfellow's "Excelsior"—which commonly reclaimed horror and terror into a quality of wonder at the presence of God in mountain and lake. Part of Whitman's "colossal grandeur and beauty of form and spirit" comes from representing this typically American reclamation of the sublime into the imaginal process of "Song of Myself." [27]

Merging with "puny democratic egos," Whitman moves beyond self-isolation, through absorption, towards a sense of mastery and identity. He troops forth replenished as the grandiose "Walt Whitman, a kosmos, of Manhattan the son," whose "omniverous lines" can incorporate his surroundings into poetic speech ("song") and exalt the common (*humilitas*) into the miraculous (*sublimitas*). Whitman would have the reader, too, undergo a transport which regenerates (through experiencing its exalted language) the self with *wonder* and *belief*: "I believe a leaf of grass is no less than the journeywork of the stars" (59). The initial item of contemplation, "a spear of summer grass" (stanza 1) here (in stanza 31), amazingly enough, takes on the magnitude of stars.

Longinus had proposed in *On the Sublime* (36) that sublimity raises man "near the majesty of God." The sublime claims to transcend, in feeling and in speech, the deadening limits of the human. It is the democratized *sublimity* of "Song of Myself" not only to proclaim the Godlike potential of any consciousness, or huge things, but also to elevate the "mossy scabs of the worm fence, heap'd stones, elder, mullein and poke-weed" as small-but-equal

150

items of wonder within his American sublime. Not even contemplation of the whole universe would suffice for the Whitmanic spirit of this American sublime, as depicted in the open-road vista of stanza 46:

> This day before dawn I ascended a hill and look'd at
>   the crowded heaven,
> And I said to my spirit *When we become the enfolders*
>   *of these orbs,*
>   *and the pleasure and knowledge of every thing in*
>   *them, shall we be fill'd and satisfied then?*
> And my spirit said *No, we but level that lift to pass*
> *and continue beyond.*
>
> (83–84)

America was not "empty spirit / In vacant space"—but an early strength of self, mastering the energies and flows of nature, leveling them into a spirit which answered laments of self-pity with the mandate to "continue beyond" and transcend even the poet's own greatest achievements. This sublime has to empty itself out, desublimate itself, yet still posit a grandeur recoverable beyond that of any prior sublime—"Ebb, ocean of life, (the flow will return)" (255) remains, even after 1860, the motto of this positive, whitmanic sublime.

The sublime genre gets radically transformed in the "language experiment" of *Leaves of Grass:* not only in that American Protestant mode of raptly responding to sensuous item and spiritual whole which was there from the start in Anne Bradstreet, but also in Whitman's adept usage of epic, ode, and patriotic hymn for national purposes, as in the Connecticut Wits. More idiosyncratic in energy and style than such anterior American poets, Whitman assumes and re-presents that American literary convention which equates poetic transport with sacred rapture as the ravishment of the mind by natural and social facts. American poets, intoxicated by the sublime of land and language, represent a vision of faith in globally expanding settings, until Whitman as "divine literatus" can behold his version of God everywhere, from California to India: "I hear and behold God in every object, yet understand God not in the least / Nor do I understand who there can be more wonderful than myself" (86).

Beholding and wondering at the sublimity of himself—the self, the self, the great American self—Whitman fulfilled his culture's long-standing norm to invent a democratic sublimity that was simple yet energetic in style and to project a mood of unity with collective energies through accruals of natural imagery in a vernacular voice. Wonder and elevation (*hypsos*) emanated not from any artifice of fantastic image or purification into symbol as in Poe; but from energies and slangs rooted in the libidinous personality. The energy of sublime impression carried over into the shape of each line, expanding it, freeing it from prior rules of meter or poetic decorums, making I-centered utterance an act of speaking-singing: a rhythmical argument (song of selfhood) suggestive of the spirit grand and unseen behind the "body electric."

"Song of Myself" continues the production of the sublime poem in America, then, putting its conventions of self-power (rapture) close to the center of the "American" genre. Whitman maintains the epic scope and bardic vision of the eighteenth-century sublime tradition (which, as Bryant saw, the Connecticut Wits had aspired to achieve) as well as that stance of rapture before concrete item and synoptic whole which is crucial to indigenizing the sublime. Whitman's democratic "song" of sublimity, as this attempts to embrace even the most humble Americana, befits the earlier convention of valuing the high importance (sublimity) of the merest bird, tree, brook, or prairie.

Forgetting Whitman?

"No one will get at my verses who insists upon viewing them as a literary performance, or attempt at such performance, or as aiming mainly towards art or aestheticism," Whitman warns in "A Backward Glance O'er Travel'd Roads" (1888).[28] He is trying to forestall reading *Leaves* as a complex of genre and style, at the expense of its ideological/spiritual content. Why invoke the Greek category of the "sublime," then, to describe the language experiment of *Leaves*? We need not interpret American poetry as an *entelechy* towards and away from Whitman, as if he "finalized" American poetry as Homer did the epic for Aristotle or certain neo-classical poets. But we can link the theories and practices of earlier poets with the realizations of *the Whitmanic sublime:* a model that needs to be historicized and perhaps even (as pre-Hiroshima ideology) *forgotten.*

As Whitman claimed in the prose jottings of *Specimen Days,* he had early sought to minimize the influence of "precious" forms and traditions ("the stock 'poetical' touches") by composing his sublimity in the presence of sea and sky. However idealized these feats of repression, Whitman thought of himself as an American artisan, a "builder" or exalted "language-shaper," fusing the phrases of the American vernacular and older forms of poetry into an "exalté, rapt, ecstatic" language ("Eidólons") linking soul and world. The stunning neologisms, the syntax of immediate and seemingly infinite parallel-equation, the lifetime of textual experiment—all testify to Whitman's preoccupation with transforming poetic discourse to convey the presence of the American poet as declaimer of highest faith. His American sublime opens "democratics vistas" that would *revolutionize* the Old World on a more democratic-Capitalist model, East and West, present and future.

In "By Blue Ontario's Shore," Whitman's recapitulation of bardic themes from his 1855 Preface, the poet acknowledges that any such distinctly American *grandeur* had to be earned in relation to, yet "surpassing," built-up conventions of past eras and feudal lands:

> Ages, precedents, have long been accumulating
>   undirected materials,
> America brings builders, and brings its own styles.
> The immortal poets of Asia and Europe have done
>   their work and pass'd to other spheres,
> A work remains, the work of surpassing all they have
>   done. . . .
>
> Land of lands and bards to corroborate!
>
> (342)

Inspired by the scenery if not by the sublime of Capital as one nature-transforming labor, as was Frederic Edwin Church in instantiating the god-drenched bliss of Niagara Falls in 1857, the poet of indigenous "styles" and vernacular mores is charged by this dream-vision of the sublime to construct ("build") a trope of national and global unity. The poet is called upon to provide, as poetic image, a "Rondure" of spiritual frame more vast than the natural panoramas of Thomson's *Seasons*.

As James Thomson advised British seekers of the sublime in *The Seasons* (1726), "A genius fired with the charms of truth and nature is tuned to a sublimer pitch, . . . I know no subject more elevating, more amusing; more ready to awake the poetical enthusiasm, the philosophical reflection, and the moral sentiment, than the works of Nature. Where can we meet with such variety, such beauty, such magnificence? All that enlarges and transports the soul!"[29] Musing by the sublimity of Lake Ontario's shore, Whitman abstracts beyond the material scene to give voice to a "Phantom gigantic superb" who urges the poet to chant in unfettered "rapt verse" the "audacity and sublime turbulence of the States" and the elevating (yet equalizing) idea of Democracy. Arrogantly seeing America as "land of lands" and an emerging global power linking up the yogas of the Old to the technologies of the New Worlds, Whitman pumps up the rhetoric of the sublime into ideological intoxication. The American sublime may have done so all along, unconsciously, but Whitman's demand is that American poets incarnate this geography and polity in "omniverous lines" freed of syntactic subordinations as of social submission.

A *brash* example of this open-road sublimity linking Long Island to India is the opening to the 1860 text of *Leaves,* the "Proto-Leaf" of his initiation as American chanter, wherein ordinary syntax is atomized into free-standing units glued loosely together by the I-voice:

> Free, fresh, savage,
> Fluent, luxuriant, self-content, fond of persons and
>   places,
> Fond of fish-shape Paumanok, where I was born,
> Fond of the sea—lusty begotten and various,
> Boy of the Mannahatta, the city of ships, my city,
> Or raised inland, or of the south savannas,
> Or full-breath'd on California air, or Texan or
>   Cuban air,
> Tallying, vocalizing all—resounding Niagara—
>   resounding Missouri,
> Or rude in my house in Kanuck woods,

154

Or wandering and hunting, my drink water, my
    diet meal,
Or withdrawn to muse and meditate in some deep
    recess,
Far from the clank of crowds, an interval passing,
    rapt and happy,
Stars, vapor, snow, the hills, rocks, the Fifth
    Month flowers, my amaze, my love,
Aware of the buffalo and peace-herds, the bull,
    strong-breasted and hairy,
Aware of the mocking-bird of the wilds at daybreak,
Solitary, singing in the west, I strike up for
    a new world.[30]

Defining self through this startling amassing of adjectives and par-
allel phrases ("fond . . . fond") in equal ("or . . . or") left-branching
arrangement which all modify the "I," Whitman resorts to a soul-
"tallying" syntax of democratic equalization: one liberated from
restricting habits (limits) of analytical awareness which might sepa-
rate rather than fuse qualities and identities. He speaks this way to
suggest a style of self-speaking that would inaugurate a "new
world" in the West by generating nomadic forms of "rapt"
articulation.

Such *open* lines and *free* forms signify that here is an original
self who can absorb the sublimity of America ("resounding Niag-
ara—resounding Missouri") into the movement of his voice, as if
"vocalizing" all the grandeur of Nature through such private har-
monics ("stars, vapor, snow"). The result is a tonality of rapture
that he nicknames, wonderfully enough, "my amaze." Again, Whit-
man sees the American sublime in high and low places, city and
country, East and West, persons and places, creating a submerging
effect of textuality through which the reader might participate in
new awareness from a viewpoint of "democratic vista" and self-
faith.

Earlier American poets had confined their transports to one or
two rural locales, which is just one of Whitman's spiritual "or"s,
and they used the closed perfections of artifice as part of a cere-
mony to induce pious effect. Whitman fuses such impressions from
many American locations, often visited only through imaginative
self-projection, finding an American aura of power everywhere: "I

am afoot with my vision" (61), he affirms. David Humphreys had earlier claimed of American poets seeking the sublime, "Our minds, imperceptibly impressed with the novelty, beauty or sublimity of surrounding objects, gave energy to the language which expressed our sensations."[31] Whitman realizes, through freshness of phrasing and a striking new realism, this stylistic ambition of the Connecticut Wits to make the "energy" of sublime sensation carry over into the shape and movement of each line. He invents a free and parallel syntax patterned into a rhythm charged with the blissed-out energies of response to natural magnitude as well as to collective ideology.

In a review of "New Poetry in New-England" which we know Whitman read in the *Democratic Review* 21 (May 1847):300), an anonymous critic looked beyond the intellectual verse of New England (as in Bryant or Emerson) to the more expansive regions of the west for a stronger brand of sublimity about to emerge:

> Moreover, the American Poet is not in our view to be born in New-England, but in a broader and more genial region, where nature is less restricted. The great men of this country are to appear beside the mighty rivers and amidst the fruitful fields of the West. Thence too will come to us the poets of immortal name; great, world-embracing souls, who shall weave all things into their strains, and paint as in fire all forms of passion, opening up for man the blessedness of Paradise and the glories of the New Golden Age.

As wild-child of "Paumanok" and "Mannahatta," Whitman identified with this mighty scenery of the west, conventionally enough, "singing" or "weaving" into himself (as this critic advised) not only the west but, *in* the bold style of the west, subsuming American forms into the bragging song of himself. Whitman commanded such indigenous codes of liberal sublimity, as I have claimed, in the language experiments of *Leaves of Grass*. As Thomas McGuane has avowed of his own latter-day vocational "rebirth" under the Big Skies of Montana, "The air of the fresh start is alive here. People are willing to accept the idea that you can pull your life out of the fire and turn it around completely. It's an echo of gold mining days."[32]

The request for a poetry of indigenous sublimity, elevated to match or outdo the scenery and destiny of America itself, was a long-standing one going back to the Revolution and, more immediately, to the literary nationalism of the 1830s and 1840s. The geographical magnitude of America mythically if not in fact inspired these sublime sensations, awaiting only what Whitman called in his 1855 Preface "the gigantic and generous treatment" worthy of them. Understandably enough, Emerson early recognized in *Leaves* the "courage of *treatment*" as befits the "large perception" of these "western wits." [33] In the Whitmanic calculus, as Emerson seconded, the American poet must be the ego of most faith whose ecstasy before the natural sublime is typical and shareable, whose forms seem democratic and new, whose "thoughts are the hymns of the praise of things" ("By Blue Ontario's Shore" [348]).

Benjamin T. Spencer has called this American "assumption that grandeur in scenery would issue in sublimity of poetic vision and loftiness of style" the *topographical fallacy* at the thematic core of Romantic literary nationalism. [34] If such critical reasoning was unsound, however, it proved helpful and pragmatic. Such ideological dream-thinking surely influenced Whitman to "incarnate" the American geography in his style and yawping voice. Periodical criticism widely promoted this *natural sublime* as a means to stimulate a poetry of ideological transport, or to ponder as a standard of greatness, as this telling review of "Recent American Poetry" in the *Democratic Review* (5 [June 1839]: 541) declaims:

> The poetical resources of our country are boundless. Nature has here granted every thing to genius which can excite, exalt, enlarge, and ennoble its powers. Nothing is narrow, nothing is confined. All is height, all is expansion. . . . prairies meet the wide horizon all around with undulations of magnificent verdure. Here, too, are forests in whose vast, dim cloisters the mind may feel a sense of loneliness and an overwhelming awe, which no fabrics of human rearing could impart. . . .

Exalted into self-hyperbole by this Bryant-like sublime, Whitman goes beyond such domestications to invent a "democratic" poetic line itself wide and free. His sublime issues, at times, from depths of his own sexuality. Whitman's gender-crossing achieves a new sublime, one *without sublimation,* as Derrida has suggested in another context as a limit of imaging any trans-sexual sublime. Whitman's poetry emerged charged with such energy but serving sentiments and pieties of his own era.

Consider the tactical lyric from *Good-Bye My Fancy* (which Pound admired for its "deliberate artistry"), "To the Sun-Set Breeze" (1890):

> (Distances balk'd—occult medicines penetrating me
>   from head to foot,)
> I feel the sky, the prairies vast—I feel the mighty
>   northern lakes,
> I feel the ocean and the forest—somehow I feel the
>   globe itself swift-swimming in space;
> Thou blown from lips so loved, now gone—haply from
>   endless store, God-sent,
> (For thou art spiritual, Godly, most of all known to
>   my sense,)
>
>   (546)

The expansive response ("I feel . . .") to vastness ("the prairies vast"), a feeling-knowledge that the senses suggest in transport and amazement at an ordinary sunset or breeze, elevation to praise of God and country—such are the *mainstream* signs of the American sublime. In a word, finally, this is a poetry of *my amaze*.

When Whitman considered the transport of William Blake, he contrasted his own American norm of using simple, sensuous imagery as a means to balance and imply such moods of vision, or "intoxication":

> Of William Blake & Walt Whitman. Both are mystics, extatics but the difference between them is this—and a vast difference it is: Blake's visions grow to be the rule, displace the normal condition, fill the field, spurn this visible, objective life, & seat the subjective spirit on an absolute throne, willful and uncontrolled. But Whitman, though he occasionally prances off, takes flight with an abandon & capriciousness of step or wing, and a rapidity and whirling power which quite dizzy the reader in his first attempts to follow, always holds the mastery over himself, &, even in his most intoxicated lunges or pirouettes, never once loses control, or even equilibrium.

158

"Song of Myself" remains Whitman's greatest attempt to balance claims of spiritual transport and physical form, the abstract and the concrete. The poem represents a movement between the egotistical sublime of the mind's power to transcend natural limits or to install the sublime of common recognition and liberal sense. Whitman defines himself as a poet of the world's body, not of the mind's visions: "The main character of his poetry is the normal, the universal, the simple, the eternal platform of the best manly & womanly qualities." [35]

Against Poe's "technical and abstract beauty, with the rhyming art to excess," Whitman contrasted his own affirmation "of the perennial and democratic concretes at first hand, the body, the earth and sea, sex and the like"—balancing if not fusing the sublime of outer and inner, body and soul, without compromising either unseen spirit or seen sense, or dehumanizing poetry into a mechanics of aesthetic technique. [36]

Whitman achieved this capacity for sublime projection in space and identification with the American scene through what William James would soon theorize as a "dynamogenic" outreach of the Protestant imagination. Whitman enacts overbelieving ideas and balances location (identity) with transcendence (union), infusing daily business with faith. The sublime worked to produce a vision of the self as power become fate and realized as cash-value consequence. Imagery functioned as a symbolic rehearsal of the bodily states the willing subject sought to achieve:

> Abstract yourself from this book; realize where you are at present located, the point you stand that is now to you the centre of all. Look up overhead, think of space stretching out, think of all the unnumbered orbs wheeling safely there, invisible to us by day, some visible by night. . . . Then again realize yourself upon the earth . . . pass freely over immense distances. [37]

Through such gymnastics and pragmatic methods, Whitman sought to expand the ego-scope of being, seeking to convey that state of "meditation, the devout ecstasy, the soaring flight" so as to become a grand poet of his own Americanist design.

"Devout ecstasy" as experienced by communing with God

through objects of nature and society was *the* founding act of religion and "original" poetry for Whitman. The "grand style" appropriate to such material was achieved, as he argues in *Democratic Vistas* (1871), not through mechanisms of art (as in Poe's language-purified sublime) but through achieving states of elevation in the poet himself. Magnitude and health had to be created as consequences unifying body and soul: "Much is said, among artists, of 'the grand style,' as if it were a thing by itself. When a man, artist or whoever, has health, pride, acuteness, noble aspirations, he has the motive-elements of the grandest style. The rest is but manipulation (yet that is no small matter)." [38]

Whitman's assumption is that the "grand style" emanates from the self's high ethos-pathos rather than from rhetorical manipulation or deracinated trope. This idea accords with Longinus's earlier Greek view that the sublime is generated from high-mindedness as much as from figurative secrecy. Whitman's sublime style is founded in a myth of the organic phrase emanating instantly, too, like the *fiat lux* from God, whose speech is charged with a "dilating" energy of the spirit, writer into reader. But this latter-day Moses remains a man *en masse*.

Crucial to this sublime style was the experience of "devout ecstasy," the transport inhabiting the "rapted wit sublime." Whitman articulates the transport basic to the American sublime in *Democratic Vistas* in the following terms:

> I should say, indeed, that only in the perfect uncontamination and solitariness of individuality may the spirituality of religion positively come forth at all. Only here, and on such terms, the meditation, the devout ecstasy, the soaring flight. Only here, communion with the mysteries, the eternal problems, whence? whither? (398–99)

Only by withdrawing to some privatized space or de-Capitalized enclave of power and first permission does this "devout ecstasy" of conversion-via-transport take place in the ego-self, however. Still, "on such terms," this American sublime is here and now.

Whitman goes on to affirm this transport to "interior consciousness" as a mode of venerating awe, defending a solipsistically American sense of the self ("identity") as sublime and prior to church, state, or mountain:

Alone, and identity, and the mood—and the soul emerges, and all statements, churches, sermons, melt away like vapors. Alone, and silent thought and awe, and aspiration—and then the interior consciousness, like the hitherto unseen inscription, in magic ink, beams out its wondrous lines to the sense. Bibles may convey, and priests expound, but it is exclusively for the noiseless operation of one's isolated Self, to enter the pure ether of veneration, reach the divine levels, and commune with the unutterable.[39]

This consciousness of divinity as power and as language-flow within the self gets embodied in "Song of Myself." "America demands a poetry that is bold, modern, and all-surrounding and kosmical," Whitman argued, so he took it upon himself to invent a made-in-America *grand style* and *grand self,* immune to beauty or elegance: "To take expression, to incarnate, to endow a literature with grand and archetypal models—to fill with pride and love the utmost capacity, and to achieve spiritual meanings, and suggest the future—these, and these only, satisfy the soul." [40]

Yet to experience this sublime in nature (as self) is by no means the same as to achieve stylistic transcendence (as language), the surpassing of outmoded "poetic" habits of form, as the Du Bartas-dwarfed moves of Bradstreet and the Wordsworthian manners of Bryant had attested. Undaunted, like Nietzsche or Emerson, Whitman cultivated sublime *elevation* through states of physical well-being generating moods of self-intoxication, as he outlines in "Health, (Old Style)":

In that condition the whole body is elevated to a state by others unknown—inwardly and outwardly illuminated, purified, made solid, strong, yet bouyant. . . . A man realizes the venerable myth he is a god walking the earth, he sees new eligibilities, powers and beauties everywhere.[41]

Stylistic transcendence was achieved, rather, by lifelong feats of language-shaping, as Whitman's famous comment to Traubel in *An American Primer* assumes: "I sometimes think the *Leaves* is only a language experiment—that is an attempt to give the spirit, the body, the man, new words, new potentialities of speech." [42]

Whitman's "language experiment" in sublimity took much invention. Each poem is as much a singular finding of *the new* (as in his technologized vocabulary of the "body electric") as a ponderous remaking of *the old* to serve American mores. In "Out of the Cradle Endlessly Rocking", for example, the Grand Ode of Europe consecrates not the birth of an aristocratic hero but the emergence of the depressed poet ("solitary singer") from the lower-class depths of America, as Leo Spitzer claimed:[43]

> The boy ecstatic, with his bare feet the waves,
>   with his hair the atmosphere dallying,
> The love in the heart long pent, now loose, now
>   at last tumultously bursting . . .
> Now in a moment I know what I am for, I awake,
> And already a thousand singers, a thousand songs,
>   clearer, louder and more sorrowful than yours,
> A thousand warbling echoes have started to life
>   within me, never to die.
>
> (251–52)

Sublime form (*ode*) and response (*transport*) are invoked to heroicize, not to mock, a *humble* lyric-subject: the awakening of a commoner poet, alone with some oddly operatic birds by the Atlantic Ocean, to intimations of his own strength and to his vocation as language-shaper of this democratic polity through a heavily eroticized art. Amazingly, again the poem opens with a series of adjectival phrases twenty lines long (as in "Proto-Leaf"), a radical syntax suited to evoke bliss if not *shock*.

Whitman, then, experiments with a *new language* to represent exalted consciousness ("identity") and invents a syntax suited "to exalt the present and the real." He also conjures the *old language* of poetic elevation and deforms it to American purposes, celebrating not the *epic warrior* but a *sublime beholder* who is both cosmos and native son. As he jokes in "Song of the Exposition" (1871) while admiring American gadgetry and a mightily industrial landscape of "steamers, coming and going, steaming in and out of port" with "long pennants of smoke" (204), Whitman installs the Muse of Old World Europe "smiling and pleas'd with palpable intent to stay" amid such banality:

> She's here, install'd amid the kitchen ware!"
>
> (198)

Less humorous is the *indiscriminate* American sublimity of poems such as "Song of the Redwood Tree" (1873), in which the trees give themselves up, like so many cheery Indians, to the "progress" of the American axe, or "Song of the Broad-Axe" (1867), with its Capitalized bliss at ongoing industrial production and commodity-worship, fully national if not global in outreach:

> The shapes arise!
> Shapes of factories, arsenals, foundries, markets,
> Shapes of the two-treaded tracks of railroads,
> Shapes of the sleepers of bridges, vast frameworks, girders,
>   arches,
> Shapes of the fleets of barges, tows, lake and canal craft,
>   river craft . . .
>
> (193)

This bliss before technology seems better fit to incarnate Soviet realism in the 1930s or to inaugurate a gigantic damn in North Korea. It verges euphorically into what Leo Marx called "the rhetoric of the technological sublime."[44] Seldom are these poems quoted anymore; but these odes do constitute, and reflect, the stance of liberal ideology animating Whitman's omniverous American sublime.

In "Poetry To-day in America—Shakespeare—The Future" (1881), however, Whitman claimed to see a distinctly American *esthetik* (his term) emerging from such "autochthonic poems and personalities" (*Prose Works 1892*, 474–75) especially his own. *Leaves* is fully "autochthonic" if situated in the context of earlier American poetics of the sublime. Reading *Leaves* or Emerson's *Nature* in their generic and national contexts, these works seem less singular and more representative. Their "greatness" and "mastery" become part of the place, bespeak "poems of our climate," in Stevens's phrase. As Virginia Woolf rightly noted of any literary sublime, "masterpieces are not single and solitary births; they are the outcome of many years of thinking in common, of thinking by the body of the people, so that the experience of the mass is behind the single voice."[45]

"The mountains, rivers, forests and the elements that gird them about would be only blank conditions of matter if the mind did not fling its own divinity." When Whitman read this (fully Emersonian) sentence that the mind, not nature, is the primal ground or onto-logical source of any sublimity, he wrote in the margin of *Graham's Magazine*, "This I think is one of the most indicative sentences I ever read." Responding to—yet resisting—the natural sublime, the self recognizes an immensity of consciousness, moral and literary, if not the immortal divinity of mind contending against—yet com-muning with—these dynamic forces of nature (the sun) through metaphors and hyperboles of excess ("sun-rise out of me"). The key lines of such resistance occur in section 25 of "Song of Myself":

> Dazzling and tremendous how quick the sun-rise would
>   kill me,
> If I could not now and always send sun-rise out of me.
>
> We also ascend dazzling and tremendous as the sun,
> We found our own O my soul in the calm and cool
>   of the day-break.
>
> (54)

In Whitman's earliest notebook extant (1847), he entered a cu-rious passage on "Dilation" (later rewritten as section 46 of "Song of Myself") which reflects this *dangerously* American predisposi-tion to cognitive transcendence, the self's going beyond any mate-rial limits. The "I" ascends from natural forces to immaterial es-sences with the courage of a "voyage" and the "open road":

> When I walked at night by the sea shore and looked up at the count-less stars, I asked of my soul whether it would be filled and satisfied when it should become god enfolding all these, and open to the life and delight and knowledge of everything in them or of them; and the answer was plain to me at the breaking water on the sands at my feet: and the answer was, No, when I reach there, I shall want to go further still.[46]

Whitman's programmatic sublimity, as it degenerated into pub-lic rhetoric in his later life, as in the technological euphoria that is "To a Locomotive in Winter" (1876) affirmed the fully capitalist sublimity of factories or railroads as a "Fierce-throated beauty"

164

(472), should not be separated from earlier, equally vulgar produc-
tions of the American soul: "I guess I am mainly sensitive to the
wonderfulness and perhaps spirituality of things *in their physical*
and *concrete expressions*—and have celebrated all that," he reaf-
firmed to William D. O'Connor, on 18 April 1888.[47]
Whitman's sublime assumes and affirms the accumulation of
concrete Americana in overstuffed, Sears, Roebuck-like catalogues
with a glee that is fully material. Yet there is also the *tender* resolve,
as well—vivid, cameralike, to consecrate materiality:

> That I walk up my stoop, I pause to consider if it really be,
> A morning-glory at my window satisfies me more than the
> meta-physics of books.
>
> (54)

Whether projecting *"my amaze"* across continents, globe, galaxy
("The orchestra whirls me wider than Uranus flies"), or cosmos, or
contemplating the tiny divinity of a fieldmouse ("And a mouse is
miracle enough to stagger sextillions of infidels"), Whitman consti-
tutes "America" by accruing varied materials of the sublime. Like
Bryant, too, Whitman called the western prairies "America's char-
acteristic landscape" because such scenes of natural vastness "fill
the aesthetic sense fuller" with moral power, thereby evoking—by
stimulus and as standard—"new and transcendent" forms of
American reality if not the emerging grandeur of Capital as such—
"Even their simplest statistics are sublime."[48]
In the latter half of his career, Whitman turned back to propa-
gate the more conventional machinery of the sublime poem: cere-
monious invocations of phantom abstractions and the *genius loci*
of the landscape; the affirmative framework of "God's scheme,"
wonderful in item and whole; melopoeic odes of exclamation and
harmony; the seasonal procession of "God's calm annual drama";
the graveyard sentiments of moral terror ("This Compost") used
by Bryant and Freneau; odes to American liberty in the manner of
Thomson or Joel Barlow; panoramas and transports into angelic
ideality, as in "The Mystic Trumpeter" (468–71).
Yet through such "language experiments," Whitman further ex-
aggerated and installed the Tenth Muse of the poetic sublime for
interlocking American purposes, both spiritual (to achieve strong

selfhood) and ideological (to achieve national superpower), by Niagara Falls, along Broadway, or even shining "amid the kitchen ware!" like an ad-poem for American sublimity. As reinflected and ratified by American artists such as Whitman, Bryant, Emerson, and Church, "the ideology of the sublime constituted and sustained a community of readers who could contemplate the commodification of nature as an elevation of nature into grand ideas." [49] Blissfully and anxiously, "Walt Whitman, a kosmos, of Manhattan the son" had strengthened, through superb feats of democratic imagination, the resolve of American exceptionality and liberal selfhood voiced at the—yes, still astonishing—end of "Song of Myself":

> I hear and behold God in every object, yet I understand God
>   not in the least.
> Nor do I understand who there can be more wonderful than myself.
>
> (86)

Part 4

Alter Sublimes: Beyond Los Alamos

SEVEN

Wallace Stevens
Decreating the American Sublime

I don't think that the United States should enter into the next
world war, if there is to be another, unless it does so with the
idea of dominating the world that comes out of it, or unless it
is required to enter it in self-defense.
—Wallace Stevens (1939)

Framing the Sublime

UNLESS HISTORICIZED, the *sublime* can degenerate into one
of those vapid critical terms which, like *auratic* or *demonic,* one
inflects nowadays mostly in italics. Sublimations still threaten the
framing power of critical discourse like the abyss imagery of a Poe
short story. The etymology of *sublime* in the Latin word *sublimis*
suggests this straining towards a limit: not so much a ridiculous
sinking (though this risk remains) but an imperious rising or ele-
vating of self to some *limen* (threshold) of greater consciousness.
As a genre of empowerment, the sublime both threatens and in-
vites, enables yet eludes. As Derrida contends of Kant's Romantic
sublime, deconstructing any segregation of this tremendousness
into purely *aesthetic* genres, "If art takes form by limiting, indeed
by framing, there can be a *parergon* [an inside/outside framing] of
the beautiful, the *parergon* of a column or the *parergon* as column.
But there cannot be, it seems, any *parergon* of the sublime." [1]

In the limit-threatening experience of the sublime, so textual-
ized, prior terms and tropes of representation break down, give
way to semiarticulate intuitions of wonder or ideas of "freedom"
and "infinity" that cannot find adequate expression or settle down
into orderly art-enframing. This is why Longinus could claim in the

169

proof-text of *On Sublimity* (9.2) that "a mere idea, without verbal expression, is sometimes admired for its nobility—just as Ajax's silence in the Vision of the Dead is grand and indeed more sublime than any words could have been"; or why Kant could even find the terrors of the French Revolution—and regicide—*sublime* in half-evoking "the 'presence' of the unpresentable Idea of freedom." [2]

Challenging social framings of nature and language-games of art, the poetic sublime developed not only as the numinous substance of noun and adjective, *the sublime*, but as the transaction-ality of the verb *to sublime*. The sublime sublimated by risking states of transcendence which would transform the habitual self through a transport or ecstasy variously induced. In the frame-breaking moment of transport, the sublime threatens to trespass some boundary line of consciousness, or prior normality, as in the central American ecstacy of Whitman's "Song of Myself" (section 26), begetting self-aura and outgoing plenitudes of bliss:

> Steep'd amid honey'd morphine, my windpipe throttled in
>   fakes of death,
> At length let up again to feel the puzzle of puzzles,
>   And that we call Being. [3]

The prefix *sub* of *sublime*, the Longinian term for Whitman's self-transfiguring ecstasy, suggests this ontological force of "letting up-ward," a movement of the mind not so much *under* as *up to*, or *against*, thresholds of higher power ("Being").

The Whitmanic sublime clearly sanctions such transport, but it risks the mockery of mundane others by contesting conventional boundaries of consciousness and form. The poet must war against these falsely imagined limits of a period's style which serve as an-tagonists of any original sublime. If the legacy of the natural sub-lime was fading, and the frontier had closed, such Romantic config-urations had seemingly evacuated what Frederick Jackson Turner called the era of free and unlimited horizons. [4] Yet even in the vast-ness of America, as Wallace Stevens enacted in "Notes Towards a Supreme Fiction," the sublime occurs mostly along a mental limen or frontier, "a point / Beyond which thought could not progress as thought." [5] Risking this subliminal boundary in sweeping poems like "Notes Toward a Supreme Fiction," the language of poetry breaks down at overreaching extremities of metaphor, or turns against prior claims of its own word-thick grandeur.

Employing tactics of modernist decreation, Wallace Stevens struggled both to demolish and to extend the idealisms and metaphors inhabiting the "deep wonderment" and overreach of an American sublime. Throughout his career as a poet, Stevens labored to become a major American voice who could obliquely embody the reach for sublimity of his own culture. He would do this, as in Whitman's *Leaves,* by comprising a *Harmonium* of language-grandeur he almost called, in a panic-stricken letter to Alfred Knopf, *The Grand Poem: Preliminary Minutiae.* If the African mythology and climate might eventuate in "the black sublime" of lions, jaguars, serpents, and bones, as Stevens imagined in the dense textuality of the section on "The Greenest Continent" in "Owl's Clover" (1936), then America had eventuated, and still could, in "The American Sublime" of this climate and place.[6] At least that was at risk, allegorically, in Stevens's struggle to confect a sublime of rapt contemplation in which Americans could still believe.

Sublime transport comprises a threat to self-possession, a "fall upward" that brings about an awesome/terrifying disorientation from the ordinary, as if the poet had to pay for grandeur with loss of "sensibility" in any common sense. Locked within actuarial rounds warding off risk and securing the self against future damages, Stevens needed such contests of strength. Speculation proved a domain putting sublimity in motion and at risk. For, in the agonistic terms proposed by Harold Bloom and others, the sublime entails a power struggle against authority, as if the poetic master-builder had to clear a space for his own "original" majesty by countering the sublimity of a precursor, a "giant" like Milton or Whitman, the father-bard looming over belated creations with his beard of fire, solar chants, and staff of flame.[7] "Uplifted by the true sublime" to a recognition of his own spirit circulating in the text of greatness and its soul-great maker, the poet—in a Longinian reading—must vaunt a way to commensurate productions and flights, or be silenced by nature and his own languagelessness. His native landscape can become reduced to what Robert Frost confronted as a *desert place,* "with no expression, nothing to express" of those terrifying/wondrous spaces between stars.[8]

By a consensual (heavily idealized) definition derived from Longinus, Burke, and the Scottish Common Sense tradition that remained dominant in American criticism until around 1870, we can say that the sublime is that which in nature or in art impresses the subject with a consciousness of elevation (*hypsos*). This occurs in a transport contrarily marked with *terror* at the loss of ordinary selfhood and *wonder* at the promise of expanded being. The poet becomes, in Stevens's phrasing, that *noble rider* of imaginative outreach for whom an "occasional ecstasy, or ecstatic freedom of mind" is a property of his vocation at its most exalted.[9] Paul Valéry, whose work on the "elevation of aesthetics" Stevens later wrote canny prefaces for, theorized that the poet was a citizen who, through transport, undergoes "a hidden transformation" from everyday boredom to exalted states of wonder:

> I have . . . noticed in myself certain states which I may well call poetic, since some of them were finally realized in poems. They came from no apparent cause, arising from some accident or other; they developed according to their own nature, and consequently I found myself for a time jolted out of my habitual state of mind.[10]

Jolted from habitual perception by "some accident" of nature or art, the poet tries to re-evoke this "poetic" effect of *transport* in the reader through estranging artifacts of word and symbol—a theory of the poem as a sublime language-mechanism evoking special sensations which was elaborated in Valéry's *symboliste* master, Poe.

Towards an American Sublime

After the will-to-poetic-power exaggerations of Transcendentalism, which had rendered rainbows, bumblebees, or an ant (as in Emerson) into visitations of supernal glory, or made Niagara Falls into an environmental symbol of American omnipotence and moral supremacy, the cultural arrogance of the American sublime more credibly comes down to spirit itself: "The empty spirit / In vacant space." Still, modernist man hungers amid such decreative negotiations for that transcendental experience which art, like religion, once provided, if only in a statue of Andrew Jackson gesturing against the empty sky. Still, the landscape, as numinous site of transcendental transactions, can at times suffice to provide an ecstatic identification between self and environment: it was this "blissful liaison" that Stevens labored to ratify in his Crispin-like colonization of North America (see "The Comedian As the Letter C," in *Collected Poems of Wallace Stevens*, 34).

Seeking grandeur of expression much more than minimality of image or tone, Wallace Stevens reclaimed this sublimity as a mood of self-exaltation, being "Happy rather than holy but happy-high," as in a line from "A Thought Revolved" in *Man With the Blue Guitar* (1937). These terms of beatitude suggest that poetry carries a quasi-religious burden for post-Romantics who remain in need of a *credible* sublime which can survive the revolutions of thought and need. Seeking to present some latter-day sublimity in "The American Sublime" (1935), from *Ideas of Order* on, Stevens was wary of pomposity and the mickey-mouse mockery of democratic, plain-speaking peers when opening towards the sublime. The result is a stripped-down poem, composed in a telegraphic style and tentative tone. The poem reads in full:

How does one stand
To behold the sublime,
To confront the mockers,
The mickey mockers
And plated pairs?

When General Jackson
Posed for his statue
He knew how one feels,
Shall a man go barefoot
Blinking and blank?

But how does one feel?
One grows used to the weather,
The landscape and that;
And the sublime comes down
To the spirit itself,

The spirit and space,
The empty spirit
In vacant space.
What wine does one drink?
What bread does one eat?[11]

If the American sublime is leveled to "empty spirit / In vacant space," an immense emptiness of consciousness contemplating a dehistoricized vacancy of space, the poet asks for transport with diminished hopes for *religious* transcendence (or public communion): "What wine does one drink? / What bread does one eat?" How does one stand to behold the sublime, in an age of mockery, conformity, plainness, and wholesale diminishment, an age in which American grandeur has become embarrassing on a personal or, worse yet, on a national scale? So the poet, chastened of Romantic illusions, would empty the sublime of Longinian claims, the belief that "man can, in feeling and in speech, transcend the human"?[12]

How can anyone proclaim transcendence (self-transport) in a commodity-glutted American landscape without measures of self-irony? If American culture reaches toward the *big* and the *super* in everything from comic book heroes to hamburgers to skyscrapers to shopping malls, as if bigness could itself compensate for a missing greatness of style, "mickey mockers" (like the Disney folk-culture of Mickey Mouse?) would rather protect themselves against art-intoxication, the elitist delusion of self-grandeur on the poet's part, with the safer, neo-classical irony of a Robert Burns in "The Whistle":

Come—one bottle more—and have at the sublime.

In a debunking context, the sublime may come down to even less than a vast landscape, to reside in the simplicity of one word aptly spoken: "It may come tomorrow in the simplest word, / almost as part of innocence, almost." Numinous words serve to reverberate with being, glow like so many stars that "are putting on their glittering belts," as in the textual motions into (and out of) eloquence in "Auroras of Autumn," which is often adduced as a chilling example of Steven's American sublime (*Palm*, 315).

In the second stanza of "The American Sublime," the focus shifts from a reader's reception of the sublime to a hero's creation of it, personified in the gesture of General Jackson, who rose from humble Southern origins to the democratic sublimity of being president:

When General Jackson
Posed for his statue
He knew how one feels.
Shall a man go barefoot
Blinking and blank?
                    (*Palm*, 114)

This telegraphic gesture of the American sublime is based on re-
sponding to the 1853 statue of Andrew Jackson by Clark Mills in
Washington's Lafayette Square, which Stevens discusses in his
Princeton poetry address of 1942. He claims in "The Noble Rider
and the Sound of Words" that Mills's statue is a work of *failed
grandeur,* an American try at Eurocentric greatness in "the noble
style" which hovers between evoking passion and ridicule: "One
feels the passion of rhetoric begin to stir and even to grow furious;
and one thinks that, after all, the noble style, in whatever it creates,
merely perpetuates the noble style." Yet the continuity of a nation's
"noble style" and an artist's will to sublimity was for Stevens, how-
ever tenuous, a supreme good: "something in the mind of a precar-
ious tenure." [13]

This American reach towards monumentality of style was
meant, in Alexis de Tocqueville's view, to compensate for the puni-
ness and humility that must be felt by the ego within democratic
masses: "Nowhere else do the citizens seem smaller than in a dem-
ocratic nation, and nowhere else does the nation itself seem greater,
so that it is easily conceived as a vast picture." [14] As with Walter
Whitman become the cosmic "Walt" of exalted imaginings, Stevens
intimated that Andrew Jackson's pose of nobility must repress, by
force of Euramerican will, any "barefoot / Blinking and blank"
expression of poverty where Jackson, like many Americans, had
begun. (Mills himself was a self-taught artist sculpting his own sub-
lime; and Stevens, the insurance lawyer, is another instance—
caught up in the quest for social mobility, "elevation" in a class
sense.) Cognizant of plain style and humble origins, Stevens could
not long tolerate a winter "plainness" in which man remains an
unheroic dwarf of himself and no giant, or "central man," from
whom the sublime emanates in "unexpected magnitudes." In such
moments, the "voice that is great within us" rises up and matches

the majesty and dynamic force of nature with what he termed "mountain-minded" utterance:

> Yet there was a man within me
> Could have risen to the clouds,
> Could have touched these winds,
> Bent and broken them down,
> Could have stood up sharply in the sky.[15]

By such potency of self-belief and a pragmatic stance that would make concrete these consequences, "A Weak Mind in the Mountains" might overcome the *natural sublime* of cloud, wind, and mountain which is so abundant in America—as in the landscapes of Cole or Church—with a *rhetorical sublime* of voice.

In the third stanza of "The American Sublime," Stevens cannot abide the prior idea—or fiction—of Jackson as idealized hero, posed in the heroic stance of eighteenth-century portraiture, so he shifts the focus toward "the weather, / The landscape and that," that *materia poetica* of natural sublimity which the Hudson River school of painters and the Luminists had appropriated as substance of any American sublime.

The convention that Stevens is *decreating,* or reducing, of imaginative illusion is the idealized notion that vastness of place demands a corresponding vastness of spirit on the poet's part. This truism of American poetics was one which Whitman among a hundred others gave voice to in the 1855 preface to *Leaves of Grass* and poems such as "By Blue Ontario's Shore": "The largeness of nature or the nation, however, were monstrous without a corresponding largeness and generosity of the spirit of the citizen."[16] The poet, then, had to produce cures for the largeness of the ground and the massiveness of a self-equalizing democracy. But were they credible, even to himself?

Writing in the wake of Whitman's deluge of vastness, Stevens's stance is less illusioned, more chastened to humanist dimensions, but still sublime in scope: "And the sublime comes down / To the spirit itself, // The spirit and space." Stevens will not settle for a simple equation of the natural sublime ("space") with the sublime of consciousness ("spirit"). The American sublime must also come down, via decreation, to a zero degree of rhetorical emptiness, to "empty spirit / In vacant space," a tallying of abyss plus abyss which equals sublime perception.

This sign-alteration of adjectives from *full* and *vast* to *vacant* and *empty* is for Stevens a trope which alters nature, as is later claimed in "An Ordinary Evening in New Haven": "It was the same, / Except for the adjectives, an alteration / Of words that was a change of nature, more / Than the difference that clouds make over a town" (*Palm,* 350). If the American sublime had existed (even in Whitman) by a striking accumulation of adjectives, the sublime comes to exist for Stevens in a subtle decreation ("difference") of adjectives from the infinite to the finite and near. The American sublime must come down to "the nothing that is," the mutuality of empty spirit in vacant space.[17]

A "grim little poem" with large claims, "The American Sublime" makes little assertion of sublime presence, affirms no overbelief in a cash-value sublime; it ends with two wary questions, phrased in the language of religious mediation: "What wine does one drink? / What bread does one eat?" Through later and longer poems, Stevens would attempt to answer these mid-career questions *affirmatively* by attempting to mime a "bread of faithfull speech" from often tacky American idioms. Such a sublimely confected textuality would yet suffice as the "thesis of the plentifullest John" did for prior, less uneasily logocentric poets such as Emerson and Whitman.

Decreating the American Sublime

The spirit of the sublime—American or otherwise—can only exist for Stevens through countermovements of the spirit which negate ("decreate") false or prior notions of the sublime, even if they are images from his own earlier poems declaiming majesty, as in the austere, postnuclear seeings of "The Rock." What he called the "enormous a priori" of consciousness in an essay called "A Collect of Philosophy" had to be evacuated again and again. Hence, negations (*decreations*) reoccur from text to text, as if each poem must try to forget poems where majesty of spirit existed in nature or in words: as this poetic destruction is re-enacted in "The Auroras of Autumn," "Farewell to an idea . . . The cancellings, the negations are never final" (*Palm,* 310). "The American Sublime" presents the crisis of absence without claims of strong presence, except to imply that poems such as this must become a means of finding a sublimity that will, for the modern mind, suffice.

Still, "What wine does one drink?" to have at the American sublime? For Stevens, the natural sublime—in all its immensity and particularity—came to be supplemented by a word-thick, or *textualized,* sublime. Poetry enacted an interplay of mind and nature tangled into "heavenly labials" of sublime language. He presents this claim for the supremacy of language in the hyperbole that outrageously opens a poem from 1952 where the stance is not so testy:

> There it was, word for word,
> The poem that took the place of a mountain.
>
> He breathed its oxygen
>
> > (*Palm,* 374)

If the *genius loci* of America was plentiful with mountains and waterfalls bulking bliss-laden around the Hudson Valley and the wild Rockies, it was not all that laden with sublime poetry, excepting (in Stevens's *one-on-one* reduction of influence) the figure of Whitman. Into this imagined "nothingness" of space, Stevens projected a chastened version of the American sublime. The "ultimate elegance" of his project was to create an "imagined land" with the oxygen, climate, and scope of a poetry able to complement a supreme or once-supreme land. Tough-minded and ambitious, Stevens theorized an America-based poetry "filled with expressible bliss," the bliss and power of climate, in more representationally demanding shapes which surpassed, say, the more Bryant- or fireside-like mode of Robert Frost (*Palm,* 186, 231).

From the word-lush *Harmonium* (1923) to the chastened terms of *The Rock* (1954), Stevens labored apart from (and within) his workaday life to leave behind a wilderness-dominating jar, a labial artifact, a radiantly tenanted house-of-being: in short, some *mundo* affirming a world harmoniously contrived from sublime imaginings on the way to the bus. But "rock" and "ice" are not, finally, the sublime for Stevens; they are the natural *ground* or locus of spirit upon which a sublime art in tune with American ideology could be reclaimed. Stevens projected an origin of "nothingness" which he needed to keep positing in order to construct the "great mansion" or *"mundo"* of sublime art. Nature stimulates, moves, transports, gives a high atmosphere of majesty, an affluence of sun, wind, and leaves. But the vastness of nature must be reimagined in the "cry" of poetic eloquence.

Caught up in an ideology of capital and global power, Stevens representatively wavered between the American will to contemplate nature as moral idea and transporting mood (his recurring verb for this is *to behold*); and, contrariwise, the American will to take possession of the landscape as a material resource subservient to mental designs (his recurring verb for this potency is *to subjugate*). To invoke a colorful example of this will to behold the American sublime as a rapt mood of letting-go, if the "immense dew of Florida" brought forth palms, vines, and alligators "angering for life," so did this climate of bigness, wildness, and freshness generate a sublime response (transport) in this "Nomad Exquisite" from the actuarial heart of Connecticut:

> As the immense dew of Florida
> Brings forth hymn and hymn
> From the beholder,
> Beholding all these green sides
> And gold sides of green sides. . .
>
> So, in me, come flinging
> Forms, flames, and the flakes of flames.
> (*Palm,* 44)

On "blessed mornings" in Florida, surrounded by natural green and the economy of infinitizing gold-and-green, the American sublime found a "beholding" poet, transfiguring the twists and terms of nature into his own traditions and altering the sublimity of a common ground. "Anecdote of the Jar" enacted the will to take American dominion, but was countered in such poems as "Nomad Exquisite" by an equally compelling will to let go, to become self-dispossessed, to merge ego-voice into the shapes, sounds, and influx of natural grandeur.

As a latter-day Transcendentalist, Stevens had to surmount the sublime in what he calls, in "Esthétique du Mal" from *Transport to Summer* (1947), the language of *dark italics,* "hermeneutic as

well as pneumatic" signs which would somehow evoke the pres-
ence of a vast force kept at a distance through irony, half-ridiculed,
negated, defied.[18] Seated by Vesuvius near Naples, writing, and con-
templating the self-dwarfing threat of a volcano which, for Longi-
nus and Romantics such as Church, had represented a natural force
overwhelmingly sublime, the aesthete of this world-weary poem re-
flects upon the *inhumanity* of such force, that potential for catas-
trophe which threatens to overwhelm the *ego* at a geological whim:

> He was at Naples writing letters home
> And, between his letters, reading paragraphs
> On the sublime. Vesuvius had groaned
> For a month . . .
>
>   His book
> Made sure of the most correct catastrophe.
> Except for us, Vesuvius might consume
> In solid fire the utmost earth and know
> No pain (ignoring the cocks that crow us up
> To die). This is a part of the sublime
> From which we shrink. And yet, except for us,
> The total past felt nothing when destroyed.
> *(Palm,* 252)

Shrinking back into inner resources, Stevens knew that a destruc-
tive effacing ("decreation") of the past was often, however painful,
a necessary step in the creation of a modernist sublime. Out of the
fires of the volcano and the nothingness of European history, none-
theless, a new sublime would have to be conjured on American
grounds of self-reliance.

Yet Vesuvius, as a darker Italian *genius loci,* stands inhospitable
to American notions of new energies and fresh starts. It has Old
World catastrophe and "dark italics" on its mind. That part of the
sublime from which we "shrink" in Romantic delusion is the rec-
ognition of Nature as an alien "Not-Me," destructive of minute
particulars like poets, and certainly no "lovely cure" for that hal-
lucinated pain of self-pity and rhetorical diminishment which cir-
culates like a floating anxiety through this poem. For Longinus,
Nature itself does encourage rhetorical sublimity by "implant[ing]

180

in our souls the unconquerable love of whatever is elevated and more divine than we" (*On Sublimity* [35.2]); but admiration for the power of Etna, which Longinus encourages, can engender the poet's subjugation before an alien force. This is a catastrophe all too correct. Like a reader submerged into admiration by "alien majesty," the tiny poet beholds nature and he is subjugated, terrified, silenced. Such a momentary loss or death of the ego can lead to silence, nothingness, death—or, better yet, a more chastened poetry wary of negations, as it did in Stevens after *Transport to Summer* (1947); or it can generate the equally compelling will to dominate and subjugate this volcanic sublime.

The more benign, place-specific fireworks of "The Auroras of Autumn" (1947) would suggest for Stevens not the presence of the demonic, finally, but an emptiness or "innocence" of nature where manmade sublimity can emerge again. His tone reverts to one of promise, spontaneity, awe before the grandeur of nature and man, in a poem replete with depths and heights to match the stellar fireworks on the dessicated beach:

> So, then, these lights are not a spell of light
> A saying out of a cloud, but innocence.
> An innocence of the earth and no false sign
>
> Or symbol of malice.
>
> (*Palm*, 314)

Stevens here claims to speak the sublime in a *sublimated* language, "in the idiom / Of the work, in the idiom of an innocent earth, / Not the enigma of the guilty dream" (*Palm*, 315). Any critical attempt to read such a sublime will-to-power of the self, in its reach to equal the innocent idiom of the natural sublime, in terms of a displaced sexual energy would be for Stevens reductive, as one reference to Freud makes clear: "Freud's eye was the microscope of potency" ("Mountains Covered with Cats," *Palm*, 286). This would be a reductive and self-falsifying lens. There can exist an innocent time for the "sense sublime" to occur (in childhood, say). But there can be no innocent place unless it exists in our idea or "description" of place (*Palm*, 314), whereby the *genius loci* of the

American climate can compel the creation of a poetic imagery (Whitmanic "leaves") by which to cover the "nothingness" of empty space.

"The Rock" (1950), a late and stunning example of figurative decreation, begins in a "vital assumption" or "first idea" of nothingness in order to create a textual space in which the poet can cover the rock with imagined "*leaves*" and "*icons*" of poetry. These are terms for the logocentric tropes of poetry which Stevens takes from Whitman and the Christian church. The poem itself becomes the "cure" of *false* sublimities, even of the prior fictions of Stevens's own imagery ("The sounds of the guitar / Were not and are not. Absurd") (*Palm*, 362). The poem effects the cure of Stevens's own anxiety of silence when the poet is "too dumbly in [his] being pent" (*Palm*, 51). The wry, impotent voice of "The Man Whose Pharynx Was Bad" cannot achieve a poetry representative of a nature-dominating culture.

For the post-Romantic poet of "Esthétique du Mal," the sublime energy of nature provides little cure for a hallucination of pain and the "satanic mimicry" of self-pity and creative anxiety. The precursor poem that emplots confronting the natural sublime with ego-grandeur is probably Matthew Arnold's "Empedocles on Etna" (1852), wherein "lovely mountain paths" are supposed to keep the mind "from preying on itself" in fits of Romantic self-consciousness; in that poem, mind literally surrenders to the sublimity of the volcano, and thus to banal terrors of self-annihilation. If "lakes are more reasonable than oceans" (*Palm*, 262), and mountains like Snowdon more reassuring in their presence and force than volcanoes, then Stevens—as a petitioner of the sublime—would prefer to live, "merely in living as and where we live," in a credibly ecstatic consciousness purified of false imaginings and yet transcendent, still suggestive of a *beyond* or *threshold* of potency which can stimulate fear and wonder nearer home: "The scholar of one candle sees / An Arctic effulgence flaring on the frame / Of everything he is. And he feels afraid" (*Palm*, 312).

In "Notes Toward a Supreme Fiction," valorizing *moments* of "sensible ecstasy" and "accessible bliss" over the more voracious stormings of the sublime found in Whitman and Poe (*Palm*, 221,

228), Stevens tried to invent, against skeptical or outmoded notions of "false" sublimes, poetry of a daily majesty that could emerge in silences of its own, like that "influx" of self-reliant energy which Emerson had credited to the Over-Soul's household visitations. "Notes" represents the crisis of a sublimity which can assume no beyond, no God to confer the crossing of art's thresholds and frames; and so Stevens must embrace, and confer—as in a comical act of self-canonization as the Canon Aspirin—the fiction of his own sublimity: "I have not but I am and as I am, I am" (*Palm*, 231). The candle may glow with intimations of transcendence, but it sits staunchly in a room: "There was no fury in transcendent forms. / But his actual candle blazed with artifice" ("A Quiet Normal Life") (*Palm*, 369)

Despite the sublimity of terrorists and volcanoes which, correctly contemplated, give the lie to celebrations of natural potency in the "Planet on the Table" that is any text, Stevens seeks a "promenade amid the grandeurs of the mind." His center remains not a natural but a rhetorical sublime. While bordering on non-sense, the speech of sublime poetry can find the ear pitting the powers of Language against the Giant of unimagined nature. His texts unleash "heavenly labials in a world of gutturals" (*Palm*, 23). "The luminous melody of proper sound" becomes one means to achieve an appreciative yet subjugating stance full of testy imperatives and breathless superlatives. Moving towards the sublime, the poems halt all too often at a Crispin-like play of language bordering on textual idolatry: "Chieftain Iffucan of Azcan in caftan / Of tan with henna hackles, halt!" (*Palm*, 75).

This self-disgusted halting at an extremity proclaiming a "gaiety of language" (*Palm*, 260) is a *false* sublime: a dead end in which language wallows in its own exuberance, as "The Comedian as the Letter C" shows.[19] A reified *textual* sublime can provide little defense against that state of "poverty" or "nothingness" in which the imagination (seemingly) surrenders to the priority of nature and otherness. The poet must resist this reduction of overbeliefs to a sense of banal "plainness." Therein lurks a profound ennui of winter's nothingness that Stevens attempts to cure through positing supreme fictions, as in "The Rock." As a poet of the American sublime, however, the impotent cry of "The Man Whose Pharynx Was

Bad" (1921) from *Harmonium*—"I am too dumbly in my being pent"—must give way to the self-empowering chant of "Hoon" (*Palm*, 55)—"Out of my mind the golden ointment rained"—if Stevens is to survive as a maker for whom the legacy of "Song of Myself" and the American sublime is not a total influenza of spirit beyond credible notions of the human or the new.[20]

America is encountered as open space ("vacant space"), a blank wilderness, rather than a brutalized, industrializing, war-torn history, but the poet must evoke something "major" and self-enabling in this fix on vast nothingness shorn of tradition as is affirmed in "Notes Toward a Supreme Fiction":

Out of nothing to have come on major weather,

It is possible, possible, possible.

(Palm, 230)

If Stevens cultivated an originary state of vacancy ("empty spirit / In vacant space") seated by Vesuvius or by the pond at Elizabeth Park after his corporate labors, he willed larger states of feeling and imagery by which to supplement such ego-emptying moods. Plainness had to be countered by a will to the sublime.

Whatever man-as-poet makes in this huge landscape becomes part of the weather, the major climate, a presence of language "smeared with the gold of the opulent sun." Stevens's late indigence, his human need in "Lebensweisheitspielerei," "is an indigence of the light." Amid Big Sky mountains, triple rainbows, and fish-filled lakes, each person can only move us "in the stale grandeur of annihilation" (*Palm*, 384). What we need, Stevens claims in his cryptic poem on Emerson, "Looking Across the Fields and Watching the Birds Fly," is "a sharing of color and being part of it": a responsiveness or letting-go of the will that is obtained through an influx of creative light that comes merely in watching birds fly— "A daily majesty of meditation, / That comes and goes in silences of its own" (*Palm*, 380). If "what one believes is what matters," as Stevens affirms like many a poet of the sublime, then what he believes in are "ecstatic identities" between self and place as he preaches in "Extracts from Addresses to the Academy of Fine Ideas" (*Palm*, 183).

The Imaginative Rabbit as Social King

Reflecting on the modernist poet's burden of creating in the wake of "an enormous a priori" of the sublime, the weight of a tradition which demands not imitation but emulation and surpassing, Walter Jackson Bate recurred to the sublime mimetic of Longinus:

> The essential message of Longinus is that, in and through the personal rediscovery of the great, we find that we need not be the passive victims of what we deterministically call 'circumstance' (social, cultural, or reductively psychological-personal), but that by linking ourselves through what Keats calls an "immortal free-masonry" with the great we can become freer—freer to be ourselves, to be what we most want and value; and that by caring for the kinds of things that they did we are not only "imitating" them, in the best and most fruitful sense of the word, but also "joining them." [21]

Such a "vision of greatness" transmitted by sublime poetry can become not just an anxious burden but a stimulus to further majesty, opening the self to a dialogue with tonalities and imageries of greatness.

At the height of the American influx stands Emerson's "Fate," where similarly the "noble creative forces" of self-reliant power allow the poet to overcome *any* limiting (material) circumstances or (textual) blockages. This is brought about by identifying not with an artist but with the dematerialized power that enabled that prior voice or stance. The God-intoxicated self opens to a transcendental union with the inspiring spirit: "The beatitude dips from on high down on us and we see. It is not in us so much as we are in it." In response to the interpellated majesty of nature and spirit, Stevens would have the poet mime—and "rise" in sublime language—the oracular substance of the natural sublime: "Or we put mantles on our words because / The same wind, rising and rising, makes a sound / Like the last muting of winter as it ends" (*Palm*, 380).

Emerson was, like Whitman, the air that Stevens breathed. But that Stevens was familiar with Longinus's original notion of the sublime we know from one incontestable source: he read with great care, at mid-career, I. A. Richards's study, *Coleridge on Imagination* (London: Kegan, Paul, 1934), annotating for future reference on the flyer a passage where Longinus is adduced by Richards to argue how the creative imagination "goes beyond, outdoes reproduction to present to the mind what has not and cannot be known." The passage quoted as influence on the Romantic imagination is a famous one affirming the imagination's power to transcend limits of nature to achieve an inner greatness which is the mind's self-imagined approximation to the divine:

> Wherefore, not even the whole universe can suffice the reaches of man's thought and contemplation, but oftentimes his *imagination oversteps the bounds* of space, so that if we survey our life on every side, how greatness and beauty and eminence have everywhere the prerogative, we shall straightway perceive the end for which we were created.
>
> (*On Sublimity* [35.3])[22]

Both the greatness of the past and forces of nature ("beyond all, the sea") demand greatness on such a poet's part. Like Whitman, Stevens was aware that the oceanic majesty of the sea nourished but threatened to overwhelm the Romantic imagination with its own "meaningless plungings," unless the spirit fought back with ideas (and symbols) of imagined order. The poet countered with fictions of the mind's supremacy: "Crispin was washed away by magnitude / . . . Could Crispin stem verboseness in the sea?" (*Palm*, 59). Like his voracious if not imperialist *alter ego*, Crispin, Stevens's "violence was for aggrandizement." Like Crispin, he worked to achieve a "blissful liaison / Between himself and his environment" that would generate a credible American sublime in the Colonies and tropics (*Palm*, 64). Into the Tennessee wilderness of "slovenly" America, Stevens posited the "domineering" jar of his art as sovereign center of the only majesty that counts—human (*Palm*, 46).

However hedged round with negations, qualified with irony, or buried in seemingly endless and self-denying appositions, the sublime *had to exist* for Stevens, as "A Rabbit as King of the Ghosts" (1937) intimates:

> The difficulty to think at the end of day,
> When the shapeless shadow covers the sun
> And nothing is left except light on your fur—

There was the cat slopping its milk all day,
Fat cat, red tongue, green mind, white milk
And August the most peaceful month.

To be, in the grass, in the peacefullest time,
Without that monument of cat,
The cat forgotten in the moon;

And to feel that the light is a rabbit-light,
In which everything is meant for you
And nothing need be explained;

Then there is nothing to think of. It comes of itself;
And east rushes west and west rushes down,
No matter. The grass is full

And full of yourself. The trees around are for you,
The whole of the wideness of night is for you,
A self that touches all edges,

You become a self that fills the four corners of night.
The red cat hides away in the fur-light
And there you are humped high, humped up,

You are humped higher and higher, black as stone—
You sit with your head like a carving in space
And the little green cat is a bug in the grass.

(*Palm*, 150)

This beast fable on the American will to transcendence (if not global supremacy) represents an attempt to recover a potency of the sublime. Stevens posits a sublime so egotistical that it is, finally, vacant of others. The rising rabbit of the poem becomes self-proclaimed "King of the Ghosts," omnipotent ruler over a self-made kingdom of empirical spirits, which is truly a kingdom of ghosts. This fiction of democratic selfhood, as in Whitman, sub-sumes the reality of others. The household cat serves as an ad-like image of sensory fulfillment, by contrast, a being with little con-sciousness of anything beyond property-possessive fear: "There was the cat slopping its milk all day, / Fat cat, red tongue, green mind, white milk."

But the daydreaming poet, hovering between household facts and thoughts of being a Capital-rich Fat Cat, would rather reima-

187

gine the "green" mind more transcendentally as a rabbit whose consciousness provides the core of immensity in which the cat is an unthreatening and utterly minute particular, "the cat forgotten in the moon" of ordinary nature. The rabbit may be Whitman or Emerson, but the cat is surely a rival, minor poet or a socially conditioned being who is satisfied with the world-as-given. The cat is Americana without the gloss of a blue guitar.

The persona of the rabbit, like some orientalist "Hoon" or Whitman himself, sees the world only as a vast projection of his consciousness, signed with the signature of his own Emersonian luminosity: "And to feel that the light is a rabbit-light, / In which everything is meant for you / And nothing need be explained." For the "it" which "comes of itself" reenacts Emerson's influx of the creative spirit in which thought can shape commodity-nature over in the mind's vast image: "The grass is full / And full of yourself." The presence of the grass (as in *Leaves of Grass*) becomes filled with being, as does the presence of the self, constituting a globelike consciousness ("No matter"), seamless with nature even in its threatening aspects.

The poem concludes with the song of a self that has bypassed the threshold of ordinary perception, as if in flight upward, *filling all space,* from earth to heaven: "You become a self that fills the four corners of night." Robert Penn Warren once filled vacant American space with a much more fearful, paradox-conscious self, in "Homage to Emerson, On Night Flight to New York," making a mock-affirmation of stellar grandeur dispossessing the ego:

At 38,000 feet Emerson
Is dead right.[23]

Less fearful because *more Emersonian,* the Rabbit's transcendental imagination moves beyond fact to become otherworldly, stationed beyond the "fur-light" of those who abide in limits of four-corner rooms and not in the self-dispossessing boundlessness of night. Humped in the immensity of space like Emerson's "Over-Soul" or Whitman's "Me Myself," by such symbolic capital (sublimity) the rabbit can dominate a socially conditioned cat who would rather slop milk than become a transcendental ghost for whom consciousness alone is world-transforming and supreme. Steven's poem

188

enacts the "double consciousness" of a poet equally worldly and transcendental, given to harmonizing both empirical fact and ontological thought, with "incandescence" given to the overreaching rabbit and not to the business-like cat.[24]

It is, finally, hard to figure out the tone of this poem: half-mockery, half moral-seriousness, a kind of pyrrhic victory for the American sublime? The rabbit is a too-eager Canon Aspirin who represses the fact of the cat in order to assert the hyperbole of all-inclusive selfhood. He celebrates an oceanic consciousness that can take pride in a world without objects. But for Stevens, as Helen Vendler has argued (see note 19), the sublime had to be *livable* and *credible* within humanist limits, without any Emerson-like security in a consciousness beyond the human.

As I claimed at the outset of this chapter, however, invoking Derrida on limits and frames, any genuine sublime, as a trope of ecstasy, must extend inert notions of *limit*. To invoke Emerson again from "Circles," "The only sin is limitation." The poet crosses limits by representing, or claiming to represent, a moment of consciousness which can disclose higher power in no more and no less than human speech, "the the." Such a figure of the sublime poet, "impatient for the [idealist] grandeur that you need / In so much misery," is presented by Stevens in the guise of the dying aesthetic idealist, Santayana, his Harvard mentor, in "To an Old Philosopher in Rome" (1952). In this late poem, it is *as if* for once the American idealist hunger for "total grandeur" of self and globe were satisfied, exactly upon the *threshold* of the body's limits.

In Stevens's portrayal of Santayana, the old philosopher envisions Rome in a triumph of idealized sublimity as willed design:

> [The] total grandeur of a total edifice,
> Chosen by an inquisitor of structures
> For himself. He stops upon the threshold [of heaven],
> As if the design of all his words takes form
> And frame from thinking and is realized.
>
> (*Palm*, 373)

For once not fearing *totalizing* the American sublime, Stevens urges that the earth, not heaven, is the locus of majesty. Furthermore, Stevens claims that the poem's language can capture this union of

189

consciousness and form. It is not the *philosopher* Santayana, but the *poet* Stevens, after all, who articulates "without speech, the loftiest syllables among loftiest things" (*Palm*, 373). Stevens is the poet who achieves a version, however qualified or undercut, of the American sublime.

Reimagining the Sublime: "Loftiest Syllables Among Loftiest Things"

As a terse portrayal of Stevens's response to the sublime rhetoric of earlier artists—this time expressed as the European "dark companion" of Brahms's music in a great-style opus of "single majesty"— "Anglais Mort à Florence" ([1935]; *Palm*, 117) is unrivaled. Bloom reads it (self-reflectively) as a poetic elegy for an earlier self, a higher tone when Stevens was capable of Hoon-like proclamations of his own majesty. Emptied if not overwhelmed by the majesty of another self (through the transporting music of Brahms), Stevens almost dies in the remote silence of Florence, annihilated by a European majesty evacuating him to silence and dust. The profounder strength of American self-reliance almost deserts the ego, leaving him ravished by the alien majesty of prior art. Art-as-majesty here threatens to silence the poet with the terror of a volcano, reducing his poems to so many postcards from a volcano, and the sublime "mansion" of his art to "a dirty house in a gutted world" (*Palm*, 127). But the "blockage" of this timid reader's sublime must give way (by metaphor) to the poet's sublime, as he counters the European grandeur of Brahms with American poetry which can install the majesty (or what in self-reliant illusion, "seemed to be") of further creation, as new "particles of order."

The familiar companion of Brahms's music walks apart, like a self-sufficient art, disdainful of disciples. Uncertain of his own gifts, the poet can recall the majesty of creation as an earlier self, which offers little consolation. But glib "coherences of moon and mood" no longer suffice at midcareer. Somehow, mysteriously, the sublime art of Brahms goes on to become the sublime speech he needs. The sublime empowers Stevens in a dialectic of empowerment: he moves through yielding to (*beholding*) outside grandeur to resisting (*subjugating*) the harmonium of another's music:

He used his reason, exercised his will,
Turning in time to Brahms as alternate

In speech. He was that music and himself.
They were particles of order, a single majesty:
But he remembered the time when he stood alone.

He stood at last by God's help and the police;
But he remembered the time when he stood alone.
He yielded himself to that single majesty;

But he remembered the time when he stood alone,
When to be and delight to be seemed to be one,
Before the colors deepened and grew small.
                                        (*Palm*, 118)

Repeating three times that "he stood alone," an Ariel-like Stevens is transported out of himself and networks of the state or God by the mimic majesty of Brahms. But he is also unified with the energies of music and thereby with his own central self. The poet recalls his former grandeur, when being was a source of delight ("When to be and delight to be seemed to be one") and grand poetry.

The tone here is too self-qualified and elegaic to sustain an American sublime, however, as is often true in the fragmentary sketches of grandeur in *Ideas of Order* (1936). The Stevensian sublime remained a series of "notes toward" its supreme instantiation. Threatened by nothingness and deprivation, the sublime did arrive. If not in the music of Brahms, where did the spirit of this sublime abide for Stevens? In a vast landscape, another person, a room, in weather, sculpture, painting, in God or Nietzsche, in rock, stone, tree, in bread and wine, in leaves of grass?

Was the sublime—now thoroughly Christianized and democratized into American recesses of *the humble*—anywhere and everywhere, as Emerson had urged upon his Concord brethren? I would claim, qualifying Vendler's austere reading (see note 19), that the sublime resided for Stevens not in primitive *rock* nor in Puritan *ice*, those barren items of nature; but in an edifice, a *mundo* of art and textuality. Stevens evoked the sublime as a house or self-wrought "mansion" in which glimpses of being could dwell and, seemingly, speak: a house for consciousness. The American sublime came to exist for Stevens not only in mountains like Chocorua or in Cris-

191

pin's "verboseness in the sea," but also in feats of architecture. A garden-encompassed mansion can stand as one figure for its supreme-fiction-maker, that hero of "blissfuller perceptions" whose positings would abstract a "man-sun" representing our "highest self."

Though the poet viewed the cathedral-grandeur of "St. Armorer's Church From the Outside," for example, he constructed his "lofty" and "massive" construct out of linguistic magnitude, creating a post-Emersonian "chapel" of "newness":

> The chapel rises, his own, his period,
> A civilization formed from the outward blank,
> A sacred syllable rising from sacked speech, [. . .]
>
> In an air of newness of that element,
> In an air of freshness, clearness, greenness, blueness . . . [25]

To assert the sublime of *architecture* is to say, in social terms, *art*— that secondary environment generated through recreations of the real, if only in one mantralike "sacred syllable" rising out of the sacked vernacular to disclose fullness of being. The sublime comes to exist through overbelieving acts of rapt consciousness elevating not mountains and oceans with the "golden ointment" of Hoon or the "metaphysical metaphor" of mountain-minded Chocorua, but consecrating small, domestic items as in an "immensest theatre" of grandeur.

For Stevens, finally, the American sublime did not abide in the heroic sculpture of Andrew Jackson, nor St. Armorer's Church, nor just in the weather or that nineteenth-century paraphernalia of landscape painting but in "empty spirit / In vacant space." This is to affirm, as American difference, that the sublime abided in a kind of vast nothingness or a textually purged consciousness wherein art could begin again to generate new structures of elevation. Paradoxically, working through threats of emptiness and of nothing further happening, the American sublime came to exist as "newness," even forgetting its own tradition or history.

This impulse to subdue and to remake the once-European environment over in a more pragmatically American image is depicted by Stevens in his poem on the dying Santayana, whose imagination confers whatever beatitude there is upon the room:

It is a kind of total grandeur at the end,
With every visible thing enlarged and yet
No more than a bed, a chair and moving nuns,
The immensest theatre, the pillared porch,
The book and candle in your ambered room, . . .
("To an Old Philosopher in Rome" [*Palm,* 373])

The sublime came to exist, in this late seeing, as the "total gran-
deur of a total edifice, / Chosen by an inquisitor of structures / For
himself." As in the claims of this poem, the Americanized sublime
abided for Stevens not just in nature or language but in a mansion,
a theatre, a park, a room, a house, a structure wherein being could
dwell and speak, self-forgetfully, in that radiance of central con-
sciousness which is love.

Architecture serves, too, as Stevens's synchronic trope for the
intertextual language of poetry as it mediates between mind and
nature by fabricating (half-collectively) a dwelling place, a *mundo*
wrought from "sacred syllables" wherein being can disclose itself
anew in transcendental transactions. Language installed "heavenly
labials in a world of gutturals." A poem called "The Pure Good of
Theory" affirms such poetic *felicity,* as "*Dry Birds Are Fluttering
in Blue Leaves*":

    . . . the beast of light,
Groaning in half-exploited gutturals [. . .]
Touched suddenly by the universal flare [. . .]
                              (*Palm,* 268)

This "flaring" is due to some power of universal consciousness,
which posits no beyond, but inhabits a room, an edifice, a park.
On the threshold of heaven, Santayana's room becomes "ambered"
by such sublimity, just as Hartford is seen "in a purple light."

Stevens must work *beyond* decreation toward fresh creation, as
is suggested in a crucial passage from "The Relations between Po-
etry and Painting" (1951) on modernist *decreation:* "She [Simone
Weil] says that decreation is making pass from the created to the
uncreated, but that destruction is making pass from the created to
nothingness. Modern reality is a reality of decreation, in which our
revelations are not the revelations of belief, but the precious por-

tents of our own powers" (*Necessary Angel*, 174–75). If the poet cannot affirm planetary "affluence," he can at least renew the expressive power of the self to find such sublimity ("unexpected magnitudes"). Beyond nothingness can emerge "the precious portents of our own powers." This recurs as a mode or stance of affirmative beholding:

> The way the earliest single light in the evening sky, in spring,
> Creates a fresh universe out of nothingness by adding itself,
> The way a look or a touch reveals its unexpected magnitudes.
> ("Prologues To What Is Possible" [*Palm*, 378])

Stevens seldom wavered in his will to create a sublime worthy of the American idealist climate which had nourished Whitman and Emerson, which had elevated himself and his family. If the sublime lingers on as a " 'cash-value' idea" or *supreme fiction* like "wealth," Christian "truth," "power," and "health," it worked for Stevens as overbelief generating its own consequences: the production of an American sublime that is *The Collected Poems of Wallace Stevens*, the *grand poem* willing no less than grandeur on a representative scale.

Stevens's lifelong question, "How does one stand to behold the [American] sublime?" suggests the deeper uncertainty of any decreative stance. His is a disenchanted modernist viewpoint which recognizes that the sublime has existed in the past but realizes that American society is fast rendering the natural sublime unavailable to ordinary experience, except as a poetic diction infused with nostalgia. We confront this in the pious "ideality" of Santayana, who still spoke—on his deathbed amid the fading Catholic grandeur of Rome—"loftiest syllables among loftiest things" (*Palm*, 373). (A summary vision, the poem seems to be a precognition of Stevens's deathbed conversion in 1955 from postnuclear nothingness to the sublimity of God and Rome.)

The decreated sublime came down to what the subject could produce in the pathos of internalizing the "landscape and all that" from the infinitizing heritage of nineteenth-century art. The "empty spirit / In vacant space" which Stevens "found" was really what he had invented in the "ghostlier demarcations and keener sounds" of each poem. The decreative poem works to undo prior symbolizing

194

of the natural object so that some credible version of the sublime can be preserved, if only through a stance of self-purification claiming to undo the American ideology of the sublime, only to reinstate its contradictory hold over the contemporary subject:

In this plenty, the poem makes meanings of the rock,
Of such mixed motion and such imagery
That its barrenness becomes a thousand things

And so exists no more. This is the cure
Of leaves and of the ground and of ourselves.
                    ("The Rock" [*Palm*, 364])

Internalizing forces of nature as a "nothingness" of space, the aging poet recapitulates American dynamics of beholding/subjugating nature. He renders the poem itself an "icon" of the mind encompassing space. He then reduces such tropes of union from Whitman to "nothingness." Finally, he produces *new* images and tropes of leaving, flowering, and blooming as a way of refiguring the American ground. "The Rock" attempts to cure consciousness of sublime figurations as a kind of fortunate fall into delusive imagery—"The stone from which he rises, up—and—ho, / The step to the bleaker depths of his descent"—only to reassert the hold of such "icons" over the subject as a "cure" which can give back the tropological majesty it appears, terrifyingly, to take away.

Stevens confronted modernist terrors of nothingness, emptiness, deprivation, and disaster. He represented the possibility and staked the risk that, as Lyotard has argued, "the sublime is kindled by the threat of nothing further happening." [26] Moving beyond austerities of decreation, the poet as "silent rhapsodist" had, like a recycled Whitman, reposited (for his culture) a "tranquil self" to reabsorb the particular rock and vast distances of space which engender the desire for a vision of *totality:* "That in which space itself is contained" (*Palm*, 365).

However strong was Stevens's will to purify poetry of its illusions or hyperboles of autonomy, "He could neither live with the sublime, as Harold Bloom has remarked, nor live without it and remain a poet." [27] Beyond negative dialectics or rhetorical deconstruction, the American sublime was installed as "empty spirit / In vacant space." Stevens had to evacuate prior claims to grandeur, even if the "nothingness" that emerged was the poem itself rising up from the "void" or "bunk" of history as icon of the self's grandeur.

If the sublime took on "cash-value" as an American idea with self-empowering consequences, Wallace Stevens had realized both the grandeur and risks of these language-claims. However fitfully, he had renewed Emerson's native conviction that "we are all of us very near to sublimity."[28] The "nothingness" his austere, late poems like "The Rock" evoke is more than a neo-Nietzschean trope of semiotic emptiness or nature's fleetingness: it is the ground of American nature poetry after the infinitude of Hiroshima has threatened claims of "the supreme fiction" and the modernist poet (like Santayana) has turned back from Cold War agonistics to the Church of Rome for postnihilist direction.

EIGHT

Postmodern Sublime

New Admonitions/Premonitions
of the Vast

Shakespeare and Byron possessed 80,000 words in all:
The future genius poet shall in every minute
Possess 80,000,000,000 words, squared.
— Mayakovsky

In your dream we never saw each other again.
In mine worlds collide.
— James Tate, "Cosmology," in
The Oblivion Ha-Ha (1970)

IF THE ALPINE scenery of mountains and waterfalls could awe an atheist into belief, as Thomas Gray affirmed in 1739, the horizon-dominating hyperspace of Sears Tower threatens to induce a new form of ego loss and credulity in the contemporary subject drifting along Michigan Avenue. The props have changed from natural mountains to urban megastructures, but Thomas Gray's response of awestruck conversion in an Alpine setting remains paradigmatic of the sublime moment, as in his letter to Richard West, 16 Nov. 1739: "In our little journey up to the Grand Chartreuse, I do not remember to have gone ten paces without an exclamation, that there was no restraining: Not a precipice, not a torrent, not a cliff, but is pregnant with religion and poetry. There are certain scenes that would awe an atheist into belief, without the help of other argument."[1] The postmodern landscape has changed and emerged more densely textured, but the recoding of such sublime conversions to a reigning *telos* remains much the same in the liberal

197

subject—speaking not so much of a pantheistic God but of the globally beneficent forces of American power.

Confronting the decreative flux of history taking place under the sway of this technological modernity, Wallace Stevens affirmed in a 1935 letter on Marxist transformations facing Western society that,

> The only possible order of life is one in which all order is incessantly changing. Marxism may or may not destroy the existing sentiment of the marvelous; if it does, it will create another.[2]

Poets of the American sublime, their lyrics formulated under accelerating processes of speed, efficiency, utility, and standardization, tried to carry on in their Emersonian vocation much like the tenacious Stevens: recreating and destroying ("decreating") shared senses of a sublime grounded in, as he said, "the existing sentiment of the marvelous." Like that other son of Hartford, Frederic Edwin Church, Stevens secured his notes towards a *Grand Poem* within the assumption that to be great meant to be national and that the natural sublime, by some kind of metaphorical equation not so easily abandoned, had carried this burden of a will to domination over this light-drenched, God-given vastness.[3]

Whether blazing into transcendental selfhood at Key West, or drifting inside the solipsisms and crowds of New York City, the lyric "I" served Stevens as the site of an energy transformation, refiguring "the immense dew of Florida" into an "idea of order" and regenerating, thereby, "supreme fiction"[s] of purpose and design by which the agent could represent/act within a technocratic horizon increasingly dwarfing a once-self-reliant infinitude. Forging splendors of natural imagery and oracular sound—which run through Stevens as "heavenly labials in a world of gutturals"—the poet would, through ancient sublimities of language, link, mime, and awaken some chorus of aesthetic-minded readers who, "like damsels captured by the sky, / [are] Seized by that possible blue."[4] An American sublime of vast space, inner emptiness, and a speculative will to excess glutting that vacancy would be again possible; it still came down to that.

Before Auschwitz and Hiroshima had evacuated grander claims of the aesthetic imagination to renew the collective life-world, how could any American poet get beyond the whit-manic energy of con-

198

sciousness before the sublime that abided in desert spaces, huge skies, mountain grandeur, continental drift, and stellar dreams? Emerson struck the representative note for this poetic of vastness when he affirmed, in a journal entry for 1844, that "the idea which I approach & am magnetized by—is my country." Beyond Old World irony, wonder remained for Stevens a stance crucial to such poetry: a tone bespeaking the modernist urge to refigure "the existing sentiment of the marvelous" beyond natural forces. Or should poets like Stevens, Crane, Williams, and Marianne Moore continue down the byways of force opened by Whitman in poems such as "Passage to India" and effectively "transmut[e] the rhetoric of the technological sublime into poetry"?[5]

Volcano (as in Matthew Arnold), ocean (as in Whitman), mountain and rock (as in Robinson Jeffers at Big Sur) still serve Stevens as recurring images of the material sublime as a premonitory force enabling fresh signification, "new senses in the engenderings of sense," as in these lines from "A Duck for Dinner" in "Owl's Clover":

In an age of concentric mobs would any sphere
Escape all deformation, much less this,
This source and patriarch of other spheres,
This base of every future, vibrant spring,
The volcano Apostrophe, the sea Behold?[6]

This "sentiment of the marvelous" is generated not only in the mass, speed, and force of nature, but in the vertical materialization of a moral idea ("America") in space which benevolently effects the domination of the urban horizon, if not material nature itself.

The reified aftereffect of this dynamic, which is urban architecture or urban space itself, can subject the postmodern streetwalker—drifting under the toxic sunsets of Los Angeles in which garish chemical colors get synthesized, as in Elvis Presley's deathbed liver—to a condition of material "decentering." One need only walk out under the Wrigley Building or loftier skyscrapers of Michigan Avenue to exclaim, against Stalin and Mao, "I believe, I too believe!" Some theorists of pan-American culture would call this sign-glutted mood coding the bliss-and-dread subject a "panic sublime."[7]

Taking postmodern twists upon the Dynamic Sublime, the response to shifting configurations of American grandeur remains one of awe-struck credulity in "God" or that equally vast source of American infinitude reified into power, "Capital." The lone self of vast forces, semiotic-overload, and media-driven bliss ("ecstasy of communication") opens up to awesome otherness like Thomas Gray in the "religious" Alps. The ego is still transported into a mute autumn of theological acceptance. There can be little space for psychic indifference; no enclave of lyric privacy; little territory in which commodification has not already spread its icons and ad-poems, bespeaking some aura of new infinitudes, new powers—not even in the remote terrain of Fitzcarraldo's Amazon or the sleepiest agrarian villages of Australia or South Korea. The freedom-loving subjects of Hartford out on a Sunday stroll, "keep to the path of the skeleton architect / Of the park. They obey the rules of every skeleton. / But of what are they thinking, of what, in spite of the duck, / In spite of the watch chains aus Wien?" [8]

These fellow-Americans ("skeletons") may hunger for the sublime of ego-grandeur or collective uplift (like Emerson), Stevens's "Bulgar" sees, while they work assiduously in the marketplace (like Franklin, or his fellow Pennsylvanian, Stevens). But the American sublime can degenerate into something "elevating" you meet on weekends in museums or stumble upon as stars and sunsets, moon rockets or urban vistas, on the way home from corporate work.

Contingent upon the inertia of discursive frames and the persistence of idealist terms coming down through Bradstreet, Whitman, Emerson, Bryant, Tuckerman, and a host of others, the vocabulary of the sublime in American poetry—as an intuition of indeterminate boundlessness—has migrated from configurations of natural power and symbolic immensity (as in Bryant, Emerson, Frost, Rexroth, and Stevens) to ones recentered in technological power, mass mediation, and urban energy (Hart Crane, Williams, O'Hara, Oppen, Ashbery, Ai, Rich, Bob Perelman). The conversion scene of the postmodern American poet—overcoming known boundaries and humbled to belief in some saving *telos*—is likely to occur not in Peacham, Vermont nor the petunia-ridden enclave of *The New Yorker* poem, but "under the Pyramid" of the TransAmerica Building in San Francisco or drifting within the cybernetic forests and high-finance transactions of Wall Street. Or the postmodern sublime can occur, finally, in worrying, mind-quelling forces released at Los Alamos and Hiroshima, the Apollo 11 moonlanding, nuclear winter, or superpower explorations of black holes and the ozone layer on Mars.

Approaching boundaries of the *liminal,* the American sub/lime still carried the ego of the poet not so much *under* as *up to* or *against* material thresholds of the ego's facticity. This perception of *anxious grandeur* became even more heightened in furiously modernizing, then post-modernizing contexts—though not necessarily to affirm what had been imagined as "God."

Dread-and-Wonder Machines

> No mere conceit of the Age of Enlightenment, the sublime is still with us. The Empire State Building and the World Trade Center are tourist attractions just because they are "productive of the sublime" . . .
>
> —John Ashbery, "God and Man at Yale"

After Burke, Kant, and the eighteenth-century aesthetic recovery of the *Peri Hypsos,* the sublime held out a way for Romantic poets to represent the death of the individual mind yet to prefigure, in an affective calculus of awe and terror, the ego's absorption into some vast ontological ground. Only the retreat into moral idea (Kant) or into the will to abstraction and the euphorics of self-power (Schopenhauer, Nietzsche) could rescue this "self" from affective—if not semiotic—banishment before vast objects which threaten the poet with material powerlessness and the nearness of his own death.

As idealist legacy—if not generic mindset—lurking in Euramerican poetics, the sublime developed as one set of conventions (literary "speech-genre") that might allow the ego—as "strong voice"—to represent a life-and-death struggle between subjectivity and half-visible/invisible forces which increasingly, in different materialities of nature and machine, served to overwhelm this ego. The experience of the *Romantic sublime* subjected this self-preserving stranger to puniness and (seeming) emptiness before vast space. These shifting forces rendered the subject conscious not only of moral grandeur but of his or her imaginary and self-expressive *limits,* tracing new boundaries of the real. The poet stood alone yet as a social representative before vast forms of totality, ontological depths and black holes, atomic figurations of energy and formlessness: a whole natural and technological theater of deformations emerging in ways armchair Kant could barely imagine.

At Niagara Falls or the plastic prairies of shopping malls, geographical immensity and mass thinking became pitted against the puniness of the democratic ego, dreaming as it was of a grandeur to be achieved through natural and corporate mergers that might compound, unto infinitude, this individual's lyric worth. The value of this American self was not so much given (as in Europe or Asia), but made (as in New York City) through perpetual acts of reimagining and self-naming, defensive hyperboles asserted over a very real social abyss and an equally vast cultural emptiness: Walter Whitman become "*Walt Whitman, a kosmos, of Manhattan the son*"; Robert Zimmerman of a mining town become "Bob Dylan, Columbia's heir apparent to Woody Guthrie and Rimbaud."

Tocqueville theorized that a "lofty," self-absorbed literature would someday emerge out of the "antipoetic" materiality and pragmatic jargon of American daily life. "Equality [in the American democracy], then," he wrote, "does not destroy all the subjects of poetry. It makes them fewer but more vast."[9] "More vast" in ways that other awe-struck egos ("mickey-mockers") could approve of or, as models/rivals, emulate and outdo. As the latter-day French theorist of the American sublime as spectacular power, Jean Baudrillard, puts it—evoking the western deserts, interstate highways, stellar spaces and speeds of a commodity-infinitude that are seemingly pulling the globe (France, say) into ready-made icons of Las Vegas and Disneyland: "Astral America. The lyrical nature of pure circulation. As against the melancholy of European analysis. The direct star-blast from vectors and signals, from the vertical and the spatial. . . . Star-blasted, horizontally by the car, altitudinally by the plane, electronically by television, geologically by deserts, stereolithically by the megalopoloi, transpolitically by the power game, the power museum that America has become for the whole world."[10] The desert remains the ground of any American sublime.

If technological explorations have exhausted the earth of sublimity and effectively shorn the moon of animistic aura, there is always the hyperexhilaration of Mars: ". . . the Moon is a long detour, if not a dead end. We've been there. We've even brought some of it back. People have seen the Moon rocks, and, for reasons that I believe are fundamentally sound, they are bored by the Moon. It is static, airless, waterless, dead world. Mars, by contrast, has weather, dust storms, immense volcanoes, seasonally varying polar ice caps, enigmatic landforms and ancient river valleys indicating that massive climatic change has occured on a once-Earthlike world." [11] The American sublime just needs to be relocated, and technology promises to ameliorate the task.

Haunted by a sense of social insignificance and fearing (idealizing) the beauty of rising women, the democratic ego might become more desperate for grandeur. The poet might end up finding it, beyond Big Sky landscapes, in the hugeness of vast cities; in vast wildernesses spreading beyond the Ohio frontier; or even in *the state* itself as an immense staging of corporate grandeur. As Tocqueville claimed of the American people, their "imagination shrinks at the thought of themselves as individuals and expands beyond all limits at the thought of the state. Hence people living cramped lives in tiny houses [log cabins] often conceive public monuments [as in Washington D.C.] on a gigantic scale."

Dissecting such a will to grandeur, Stevens's "The American Sublime" (1935) showed that this monumentalizing sublime came down (beyond that imperious statue of General Jackson in the Capitol, gesturing on a horse), via decreation, to a self-voiding perspective on vast nothingness; a tropological evacuation of the transcendental subject with its prior Church-like infinitudes of the Hudson River, "the weather, / The landscape and that":

And the sublime comes down
To the spirit itself,

The spirit and space,
The empty spirit
In vacant space. [12]

By no means alone in deploying this vocabulary of "spirit" and "space," Stevens's dialectic of outer-inner forces emerged as a way to displace historical struggles for power onto a seemingly objectified landscape or, otherwise stated, as a way of interiorizing these hard-to-represent struggles into a scenario about obtaining an influx of *power*, voice, signifying capital, "originality," selfhood. The poet of modernist supreme fictions had to become the "American sublime" he struggles to de-idealize into tropes of inner vacancy and, thereby, beyond abysmal emptiness, to voice new possibilities for the nation and the self as commensurate grandeurs. Such a cash-value fiction remained resonant with that American will to technocratic domination over the slovenly wilderness, positing an art-jar which might "take dominion everywhere."

In shifting contexts and tonalities of technocratic domination, the lonely poet as "empty spirit" undergoes a decentering that post-modernism better allows us to map as a conflicted state of "onto-logical marginalization" before vast formations of otherness ("vacant space"). This vastness for the nineteenth century primarily meant the counterforce of Nature-writ-large, whereas for poets of postmodernism, this newer sublime entails an experience of tech-nological space and commodity-infinitude which ungrounds and decenters the human agent to a condition of mute subjugation and fresh wonders of accomodation, as in Andy Warhol's bored-but-hyper longing for the Empire State Building in flames.[13]

The dread-and-wonder machinery of the sublime remains a widely circulated *ideologeme* by which post-Whitmanic poets such as Stevens, Kenneth Rexroth, Marianne Moore, and Hart Crane could inform themselves of self-empowerment within claustropho-bic conditions of estrangement if not an increasing sense of subjec-tive diminishment, that is, within formations of "Capital" and the technocratic activism that was dominating nature if not moderniz-ing the globe. The sublime came down to "empty spirit / In vacant space." Yet this self-evacuation could be made to serve the death-of-God poet as the enabling moment of power/knowledge: a blank space of "decreation" in which a post-Romantic sublime could be reoriginated from the intertextual vastness of great poetry as well as from a position of social diminishment.

In a postmodern aesthetic of "vastness"—representing this in-surmountable ("unrepresentable") vastness shattering the arro-gance of selfhood that claimed central agency/mastery—the sub-lime moment has more to do with cybernetics and the dread of nuclear power than with organic physics or pastoral retreats—what William Gass once stigmatized as the nature "lie[s] of old poetry." The lyric ego is terrorized, rather, by speculations about some "vacant space" beyond subjective interiorization, where only a Max Headroom or post-ego Zippy might feel adequate or at home: as Lyotard avers, "Data banks are the Encyclopedia of to-morrow. They transcend the capacity of each of their users. They are 'nature' for postmodern man." [14]

As Hart Crane euphorically/desperately depicted in the double-codings of *The Bridge* (1930), the American sublime has continued its migration from Whitman's New York crowds and democratic en-masses, as well as Thomas Cole's Catskill mountains or Church's volcanic Andes, to mainframes and spacerocketry, as "Stars scribble on our [American] eyes the frosty sagas, / The gleaming cantos of unvanquished space ... the closer clasp of Mars." [15] Crane dialectically mapped this emerging condition of technological "wonderment" in an essay from 1930 entitled "Modern Poetry":

> For, contrary to general [modernist] prejudice, the wonderment ex-perienced in watching nose dives is of less immediate creative prom-ise to poetry than the familiar gesture of a motorist in the modest act of shifting gears. I mean to say that mere romantic speculation on the power and beauty of machinery keeps it at a continual re-move; it can not act creatively in our lives until, like the unconscious nervous responses of our bodies, its connotations emanate from within—forming as spontaneous a terminology of poetic reference as the bucolic world of pasture, plow, and barn. (262)

Such "wonderment" verges uneasily into denaturalized dread. The "unconscious nervous responses of our bodies" to this postmodern technoscape of cars, jets, videos, stereos, rockets, greenhouse ef-fects, super-computers, and so on now pervade postmodern life to such an extent that it seems credible to argue "The End of Nature" as source of myth, metaphor, and health in a magazine propagating nineteenth-century nature poetry well into the 1990s. [16] The "steeled Cognizance" (116) Crane saw projected as American en-gineering hurtling its futuristic worshippers—such as Carl Sagan—"toward endless terminals, Easters of speeding light" (95) can be-get a hallucinatory ecstasy in the poetic ego that is hard to tell, at times, as in Crane's schizoid drifting amid the high technologies and polyethnic masses of New York City, from a cry of self-abolishing despair.

205

The Return of the Sublime

Not only in poets such as Crane, Ai, Robert Glück, Ashbery, or Canada's Christopher Dewdney in the dystopic language-poetry of *Alter Sublime* (1980), but also in the theory-discourse of postmodern cultural critics such as Jameson, Ferguson, White, Hertz, Lyotard, Adorno, Baudrillard, Deleuze, Dick Hebdige, Peter de Bolla, Hélène Cixous, Patricia Yaeger, and Stephen Tyler, the sublime has returned from the Burkean dawn of capitalism to represent these new modes and speeds, these new temporalities of vastness. Moving beyond the poetry-begets-poetry intertextualism of Harold Bloom, this concept of aesthetic vastness returns in the 1980s to help illuminate aspects of *the postmodern condition* through which the awesome/terrific byproducts of technological vastness can reduce the ego to dumbfounded consumption of an infinite array of items.

The symbolist transfigurations of Emersonian nature as transporting agency, still shared to a large extent by Stevens, in which ego-loss before wild objects of otherness entailed empowerment by an "aboriginal" agency of the Over-Soul, have been supplanted by postindustrial imageries and the phasings-in of cybernetic/robotic technologies which threaten to make Romantic "man" obsolete as sovereign (aesthetically centered) subject of such "transports to summer." [17]

The discourse of natural correspondence does (at times grandly) persist in poets such as William Stafford, Galway Kinnell, Robert Bly, Dave Smith, or Bruce Weigl's war-haunted *Songs of Napalm* (1988) as "snowy egrets" rising. It may even survive in the post-nuclear "oblivion ha-ha" of James Tate, or Bill Griffith's media-glutted post-self that is "Zippy," as a little-house-on-the-prairies diction evoking pastoral longings for organic connectedness and self-presence. The sublime remains a lingering ego-stance of the Platonic subject, however, one of the last "grand narratives" in which the consciousness of the self still matters as countervoice and un-name resisting social sublation. Any sublime would remain *unformed*, out-of-reach, an opacity or excess resisting normative assimilation. For, as Kimberly Benston voices this aspiration as a promissory trope haunting "unnaming" scenes of Afro-American literature, the refusal to be named invokes the power of the Sublime, a transcendent impulse to undo all categories, all metonymies, and reifications, and thrust the self beyond received patterns and relationships into a stance of unchallenged authority. In short, in its earliest manifestations the act of unnaming is a means of passing from one mode of representation, to another, of breaking the rhetoric and "plot" of influence, of distinguishing the self from all else—including Eros, nature and community.[18]

The Euramerican sublime turns upon an identification with vast space and power, however imaginary this sense. Frederick Douglass was granted no such Emersonian luxury, however, and his sense of nature remains more a panopticon of bloodhounds, fences, and chains than an enclave of metaphoric release, though (as Benston's terms suggest) there are traces of sublime "un-naming."

The postmodern sublime, however de-essentialized, runs the risk of repeating idealizing power-moves of the Romantic sublime: with its (minute) data bank of strategies for transcendence, leaps towards self-absorption into a totality of nature or knowledge, situating the self as "nodal" center circulating the flow of cosmic energy and information which is—largely considered—"language." Oedipal aggressions and oceanic idealizations threaten the generic territory. Even Régis Debray admitted in the enclave of resistant theorizing wherein "ideas are also forms of combat" that "all of us, Marxists included, are more or less Platonists, [because] that three thousand years of theological idealism cannot be eradicated overnight from the human brain."[19]

The Romantic sublime depended upon a "specular structure" that situates the poet within configurations of mimetic force whereby the ego can figure a model standing for future "originality," or "voice." Sublimation is brought about through identification with an overempowered, typically male ancestor such as Crane's icon of native wonderment, Walt Whitman, "Our Meistersinger [who] set breath in steel," the worship of whom rebegets the infinitude of the private self. Converting a disarrayed sequence to a one-on-one confrontation with the sublime, the poet posits a narcissistic self-image to overcome a lurking sense of overdetermination by vast forces like Vesuvius (nature), Wordsworth or Milton (text), or dynamos (technology) which threaten the subject with the annihilation of his own voice. The fear remains one of "textual blockage," a phase of creative death: the mind humbled into material subjugation as in the middle moment posited by Kant or traumatized compellingly, for reasons of gender and belief, by Emily Dickinson.[20]

The population explosion, or fear of others, implodes in the lyric subject as silence or unnameable dread (*das Unform*): the death of the voice, for example, in Vermont snows in Robert Frost's "Desert Places." In Stevens's "The American Sublime," this figure of male ego-power is General Andrew Jackson, a vulgar American who rose to presidential grandeur through force of will, imposing—like Lincoln or Whitman—his own rude style upon the land: a figure, I think, for those Emersonian power-goals within Stevens himself.

Confronting forces of nature or technology, the Romantic sublime narrows into an agony of the literary subject (ego) competing for signs of authority by resisting such threats: not so much of nature or mass society but of the weight of poetic history itself. This text-centered threat of the fathers (tradition) within the sublime is not so much physical death as rhetorical silence or psychic breakdown. The poet fears a "blockage" induced by intertextual plenitudes that get displaced ("misread") as external determinations or social conditions. Whatever the shocks of textual/material decentering, the trope of the sublime works to recuperate the integrity of the poetic subject, whose ego-confrontation with the cognitive obstacle ("blocking agent") is overcome by identifying with some oedipalized other. Later, in this scenario of self-making, the poet-rival will be scapegoated as superfluous to this subjugating voice of originality, who has humanized (interiorized) sublime power as "strong voice," or the Me-myself of "the great style."

In Stevens's "Man on the Dump," this strong self emerges out of newfound emptiness only as prelude to a fullness of self trumping the ground—however blasted, wasted, or deformed. As "the man on the dump" portrays the glut and glamour of daily life in Hartford,

> The dump is full
> Of images. Days pass like papers from a press . . .
> Now, in the time of spring (azaleas, trilliums,
> Myrtle, viburnums, daffodils, blue phlox),

Between that disgust and this, between the things
That are on the dump (azaleas and so on)
And those that will be (azaleas and so on),
One feels the purifying change. One rejects
The trash.[21]

Stevens proclaims a new sense of wilderness purity. He enacts the recovery of an imagined ground of American emptiness ("vacant space") without Indians or Miltons, affirming this imaginal abyss by the power of originary voice:

Everything is shed; and the moon comes up as the moon
(All its images are on the dump) and you see
As a man (not like the image of a man),
You see the moon rise in the empty sky.

The intertextuality of myriad images and the threat of a self blasted by Romantic rivals have been overcome, so that the poet can "cry *stanza my stone*," as if the natural sublime has been displaced by the sublime of Stevens's own last stanza.

Dispersing the poetic ego, Stevens yet remains in idealist tune with the American ideology of the sublime. This is depicted in "The Doctor of Geneva" (1921). "Lacustrine" Puritans, quailing in awe before spectacles of waterfalls and oceans in the New World, initiated a technological process that arose as an "unburgherly apocalypse" blotting out the sky if not displacing God:

The doctor of Geneva stamped the sand
That lay impounding the Pacific swell,
Patted his stove-pipe hat and tugged his shawl.

Lacustrine man had never been assailed
By such long-rolling opulent cataracts,
Unless Racine or Bossuet held the like.

He did not quail. A man so used to plumb
The multifarious heavens felt no awe
Before these visible, voluble delugings,

Which yet found means to set his simmering mind
Spinning and hissing with oracular
Notations of the wild, the ruinous waste,

Until the steeples of his city clanked and sprang
In an unburgherly apocalypse.
The doctor used his handkerchief and sighed.[22]

The Calvinist sigh of Stevens's doctor before his sky-blotting sky-scrapers prefigures the object-shattering apocalypse of technology which Thomas Pynchon captures in the war-haunted opening to *Gravity's Rainbow:* "A screaming comes across the sky."[23] After two world wars, it is this postnuclear screaming which the poet is called upon by his high-capitalist culture to map—to "disalienate"—in annotations of "the wild, the ruinous waste."

As poetry refracts this modernist will to mastery over nature, hyper-technologies, vast space, if not the globe itself, the poet invokes tropes of the Romantic sublime as if to undo this environment through "oracular notations of the wild." The subject tries to remain a force of all-centering selfhood, but risks repeating the tropes of a euphoric individualism linking the will-to-power of self and place. Prior to its modern and postmodern refigurations, what is the political genealogy embedded in this discourse of the "Romantic sublime"?

As broadly refigured within conventions of Western Romanticism, the natural sublime becomes the *mise-en-scène* of a mental flight, transcendence, a fall upward in which the mind can stage what Kant outlined as "the feeling of a momentary checking of the vital powers and a consequent stronger outflow of them":[24] "Sublimity, therefore, does not reside in anything of nature, but only in our mind, in so far as we are conscious that we are superior to nature within, and therefore also to nature without us (so far as it influences us). Everything [both "mathematical" in extent and "dynamic" in force] that excites this feeling in us, e.g., the *might* of nature which calls forth our forces, is called then (although improperly) sublime" (104). After a century's speculation in "confused seas of English theories of the sublime" (Samuel Monk) leading to Edmund Burke, and their teleological summation in Kant, the sublime comes down to a delusion of agency.[25] It stages a mock capitulation of the subject before some vasty thing-in-itself which threatens to induce ethical accomodation and political complacency.

210

From the Enlightenment onward, Kant's analytic of the "Romantic sublime" had legitimated the transcendence of external determinations on the grounds of "supersensible" faculties assumed as a priori components of the subject. Localizations of power need not be resisted as such because, in this aesthetic illusion of autonomy, the self is superior to any power-plays of nature on prior grounds which mock the sublime of volcanoes, generalissimos, and galactic calculations, as of rules. Freedom stirs in the subject when sensing—in the shock of the sublime—an affinity to nature which can ethically *always be overcome.*

A rhetorical demystification of this "Romantic sublime" as hyperbole of the idealist subject is certainly called for. But such a reading of the "fictional logic of the sublime" can reiterate a scenario of transcendence which locks nature into place only as a veiled figure for the reification of a society which cannot be overcome—except subjectively, in fictions of supremacy.[26] The sublime is unmasked as a fiction of self-empowerment, a hyperbole of ideal agency better segregated from the lyric into the genres of "allegory" and "satire" where it can be overcome through the ascesis of perpetual self-irony.

The Romantic sublime rehearses this basically Kantian epistemology of liberalism in which (1) ideal agency is shown to be unattainable, a kind of rational raving of the overbelieving subject, just as (2) the social totality in which this sublime experience occurs is ultimately unrepresentable to the senses: Reason (in Kant's "dynamic" and/or "mathematical" sublime) displays itself in the mind's capacity to think a totality that it cannot represent, and to think a superiority to nature that it cannot naturally achieve. The legacy of this neo-Kantian sublime becomes a *fictive* experience of self-empowerment which changes nothing but the self-image of the ego before a vast totality ("nature") which eludes the critique of subjective representation or, consequently, the possibility of collective change. God, Nature, and Capital converge as unmappable horizons, reified boundaries of an all-too-eternal real. The sublime intuition of power may camouflage, as Romantic trope, this deeper intuition of *social powerlessness.* As such, the sublime enacts Romantic ideology.

In the more dialectical interpretation of the sublime as proposed by Lyotard and Jameson, or in Adorno's *Aesthetic Theory,* how-

ever, the *critique* element of the sublime as symbolic resistance to
social power cannot be elided within a vocabulary of liberal accom-
odation or rhetorical perpetuity: as Adorno rephrases Kant's all-
too-Romantic dilemma, "By situating the sublime in the awesome-
ness of sheer magnitude, i.e., in a dimension of power, he [Kant]
betrayed an unmitigated complicity with domination."[27]

Sublime art should seek, then, through an imagery of excess and
liberation, to reverse this social subjugation to the "administered
world" with its totalizing commodity reign. For Adorno, as later
for Lyotard, "Radical negativity, as bare and non-illusory as the
illusion promised by the sublime, has become the heir of the sub-
lime" (284). Such a sublime does not come naturally, however, but
must be brought to literature through social forces encountered,
resistances overcome, codes challenged and decreated. This sublime
resists forces that would, "in venom and wonder," deform. The
spell the idealist sublime puts upon nature as a subjugating force
should not remain the spell society puts upon the self-aggrandizing
subject as always-already unfree; it should betoken, as symbolic
practice, a premonition of freedom.

In ethical recuperations, the energy released by the sublime ex-
perience does not so much become this liberating *premonition* of
forces destabilizing naturalized codes of nature, state, and subject,
but remains *admonitory*, rather, of stabilizing forces encoding the
self with teleological messages and eruptions of "reverential awe"
which are hard to tell finally, as in Edmund Burke's not so latently
political sublime, from displacements of state terror.[28] In Burke's
Loyalist normalizing of sublime terror, premonitions of subjective
liberation in the energy of the sublime must give way to admoni-
tions of submission before nature, God, and the awesome/awful
King.

Burke's psychologizing of the sublime, founded as it is in "sen-
sible images" of *power* as "a capital source of the sublime" (70),
can be read as a mechanism which allegorizes the dread of political
power. Burke's sublime depends upon the circulation of terror in a
hierarchy of pain, bespeaking the underlying power of a natural/
social totality which can materialize itself in "sensible images" of
domination, submission, and figurative annihilation (68), which
Burke invokes in his portrayal of *sublime terror* as the image of
public execution of hapless Damiens, the regicide, in 1757 (39).
The sublime serves as a way of scarifying the body into submission

212

before "vast forces" which materialize the pain and death of the individual subject as he stands terrorized before lions and tigers, noise, falling rocks, the "*dread majesty*" of the British king, or that ultimate and seemingly redundant political sovereign, God himself (66–68).

As in the sublimity of William Livingston's *Philosophic Solitude,* the "production of the sublime effect" cannot be separated from the political/aesthetic *production of the body* (via recoding of the liberal soul) taking place under formations of capital, which as Foucault has notably argued (expanding upon the same image of Damiens), "becomes a useful force only if it is both a productive body and a subjected body."[29] The pre-Romantic constitution of the sublime by Burke in 1757 can be seen, beyond local aesthetics, to cooperate in the political constitution of an awestruck body, a subjected body on which dread power can be inscribed as so many admonitory affects in which sublime "terror [reigns] quite throughout the progress" (Burke, 70).

Producing the sublime as an effect of "deadly terrors" before the dread hands, feet, and anvils of the Deity, Burke is reproducing a liberal subject for whom "timidity with regard to power" is "natural" and indeed "inhere[s] in our constitution" (67). Considered from the perspective of the American sublime, Burke's dynamic of "terror" becomes a way of articulating yet warding off subversive energies and terrors that are soon to be unleashed in the revolutions of America and France, despite his sublimations which would moralize the Longinian code into an affect of monological stability before God and King.

So phrased, or deconstructed, the sublime threatens to become one of the dead metaphors of liberal "theory." The sublime functions not so much as the will to theorize social totality as the compulsion to abandon the delusions of theory as idealist fiction. The social formations under capital render approaches to theorizing freedom not only unnecessary but impossible. Going beyond these oedipal unmaskings or rhetorical deconstructions of the Romantic sublime, however, a more radical "vocation of the sublime" emerges as the Kantian heritage to French theorists of the genre such as Lyotard and to negative dialecticians such as Adorno.

This "Romantic sublime" summons postmodern artists into a perpetual revolution of form and language destabilizing the real, an ever-open horizon of "representing the unrepresentable" which

Lyotard has installed as the latent dynamic of the avant-garde: "not to supply reality but to invent allusions to the conceivable which cannot be presented." In "Answering the Question: What Is Postmodernism?", the postmodern sublime of art turns upon this deformative intuition of *indeterminacy* and semiotic play, positing a wild art destabilizing and decreating normative productions of "reality." This language-game perspective on the sublime, driven as it is by "the incommensurability of reality to concept" and of social material to the free play of technique, demands of the postmodernist a struggle with the materiality of that which can be conceived but not fully presented.[30] If the sublime can rigidify into private delusion or imperial disaster, it still can empower the destabilizing wild-signs of a Jackson Pollock or a John Ashbery which would challenge more naturalized conventions of the "beautiful" and the "real." In Lyotard's claim from *The Postmodern Condition*, "it is in the aesthetic of the sublime that modern [and postmodern] art (including literature) finds its impetus and the logic of the avant-gardes finds its axioms" (77). This would-be *postmodern sublime* must be cleansed, furthermore, of any nostalgias and ego-delusions of technocratic nature-mastery.

Not so much a moral *admonition* as a trans-social force of *premonition* unleashed in the subject as nodal point in a discursive movement, this sublime is driven towards formal and social liberation: the postmodern sublime is enlisted as a symbolic praxis destabilizing reigning ideas of "order" and of "beauty" which collective narratives of the self assume as limit, form, decorum, and history.[31]

Jameson's related deformations of the sublime under Capital as a hysterical/euphoric "disposition of the subject"—blissed out before feats of postmodern commodification and communication—have supplemented epistemological accounts of the sublime as some outworn Augustan habit or moribund discourse bespeaking, in Weiskel's phrase, a "pursuit of the infinitude of the private self." The sublime totality, for Jameson, bespeaks multinational sublation:

> What can be retained from this [Burke's] description is the notion of the sublime as a relationship of the individual subject to some fitfully or only intermittently visible force which, enormous and systema-

214

tized, reduces the individual to helplessness or to that ontological marginalization which structuralism and poststructuralism have described as a 'decentering' where the ego becomes little more than an 'effect of structure' (262).

This is the post-Marxist sublime of infinite mirror-glass, neon hyper-realism, steel "hyperspaces." Not purely textual, this force materializes not so much in the spectacles of Mount Saint Helen's eruption or in the great earthquake of Mexico City in 1985, but in megastructures (*"public monuments on a gigantic scale"*) such as the Sears Tower or the Los Angeles Bonaventura Hotel, which can represent, in Jameson's totalizing phrase, the "new world space of multinational capital."

This dissemination of Capital into urban skyscrapers is now so ordinary, so "vernacular" in its disposition of everyday space that we take it for granted as given, as was a California redwood tree for Whitman, Niagara Falls for Margaret Fuller, or superstars like Marilyn Monroe (or Chairman Mao) for Andy Warhol. Sublime awe/terror seems a sensible response to Mike Davis's description of urban development in downtown Los Angeles whereby "truly vast pools of mobile capital" are being deployed in multiblock structures like "the forthcoming California Plaza (3,200,000 square feet of office space, 220,000 of retail, 750 residential units, a 100,000 square foot museum, and a five-acre park—being built by $1.5 billion of expatriate Canadian funds)." [32]

As contemporary moviegoers must realize, the postmodern sublime of ego loss is no longer evoked by the spacious "purple-mountains'-majesty" foothills of the Dakotas, but by spectacular visitations of special effects, as in the finale of science fiction movies like *Star Wars* or *Close Encounters of the Third Kind,* wherein the natural sublime has been superseded by icons expressive of a technological sublime. As John Rieder has argued in "Embracing the Alien: Science Fiction in Mass Culture,"

It is no exaggeration to say that special effects have become the hegemonic element of contemporary, high-budget SF films. Special effects allow filmmakers to realize fantasies with spectacular sensuous immediacy. Special effects sequences thus take on the character of epiphanies, moments of total phenomenal absorption in which the audience feels itself momentarily redeemed from time and individuality.[33]

An example of this postmodern sublimity is the ego-transcendence of Norman Mailer's persona, "Aquarius," as he stands dumbfounded, all language of "metaphor" and "dream" superseded, before the corporate structures of NASA in *Of a Fire On the Moon* (1969):

> So, it was probably the Vehicle Assembly Building which encouraged Aquarius to release the string of the balloon and let his ego float off to whatever would receive it. It was not that he suddenly decided to adopt the Space Program, or even approve it in part, it was just that he came to recognize that whatever was in store, a Leviathan was most certainly ready to ascend the heavens—whether for good or ill he might never know—but he was standing at least in the first cathedral of technology, and he might as well recognize that the world would change, that the world *had* changed, even as he had thought of pushing and shoving on it with *his* mighty ego.[34]

The effect upon the ego of the Apollo-Saturn vehicles and their moonshot apparatus is exactly one of "decentering": an ongoing displacement in which Mailer's vocabularies of moral measurement and individual heroics have been superseded, in a mood that has been ominously foreshadowed by the suicide of Papa Hemingway in chapter 1, "A Loss of Ego."

In this situation of monumentalized awe invading social space with megastructures of God and Capital, and discursive infiltrations of a sign-glutted "ecstasy of communication," the sublime returns from Euramerican poetics as an ideologeme rephrasing the dialogue between the exhilarated/desperate subject and spectacular by-products which would awe him into technocratic belief.[35] Given these vast structurations of the subject, the sublime can become a vocabulary of resistance *and* accomodation: a way of articulating forces which would render postmodern man a mute epiphenomenon, transported into that media-induced "stupor" of Baudrillard's simulacrous self, who is dwarfed by the silent majority as by images of nuclear war.

216

John Ashbery's Postindustrial Sublime

> The urge towards [American] grandeur is there, co-existing
> with the intent to subvert it, through a deadpan, no-comment
> rendering. It is true that just plain solemnity will no longer do;
> the days of Bierstadt are no more.
> —John Ashbery, "1976, And All That"

Though other poets might easily be invoked, John Ashbery's mask
of the postindustrial poet as some kind of weirded-out, sign-
juggling Orpheus can capture this shifting mood as a landscape of
bliss/terror which threatens the "whole continent with blackness"
in "Syringa," from the interiorized world of *Houseboat Days*
(1977):

> Orpheus like the glad personal quality
> Of the things beneath the sky. . . .
>
>   The singer [Ashbery/ Orpheus] thinks
> Constructively, builds up his chant in progressive stages
> Like a skyscraper, but at the last minute turns away.
> The song is engulfed in an instant in blackness
> Which must in turn flood the whole continent
> With blackness, for it cannot see.[36]

This free-floating ego becomes dwarfed by the threat of cosmic
"blackness," descending upon the subject seemingly without origin,
end, or traceable name.

We confront a transcendentalist nostalgia for the natural sub-
lime in Stevens, whose responsiveness to nature (in Florida, say)
would mingle rhetoric with forces of nature in a kind of sublime
babble defying interpretation. Ashbery amps up this lush, decon-
textualized intermingling of codes. Nature is reduced to an occa-
sional flower or the boon companion of semiotic madness: "Alone
with our madness and favorite flower [. . .] the talking engines of
our day." We abide within this "disturbed landscape" as the will
to signify an alternative universe to that of the commodified
one which the Interior Paramour felt at home in, "As the immense
dew of Florida / Brings forth hymn and hymn / From the
beholder. . . ."[37]

217

With Ashbery we are in some decreative, wry, *camp sublime,* as Jameson suggested in a broader context, defining postmodernism as "cultural dominant": a sublime made out of cultural bric-a-brac and junk, that "hysterical sublime" of parodic mastery and camp double-coding noted by Susan Sontag in 1966.[38] The sublime object had brought man to the limits of figuration and the power of the mind to represent forces he could only invoke as "*God.*" The poet was thrown back on invocations of some mental immensity by which to resist "the violence without." Yet that nostalgic invocation of some "idea of order" or style of majesty would be arbitrary clutter, for Ashbery, within the image-flux of history.

As in the junkheap splendors of *April Galleons,* Ashbery perdures as one of those postmodern artists whose "work seems somehow to tap the networks of reproductive process and thereby to afford us some glimpse into a postmodern or technological sublime." [39] This work would defamiliarize the promiscuous consumer, if only to disalienate the ego from the immediate environment. Ashbery represents the self of postmodern space in schizoid richness: as at once euphoric and unnerving, what Jameson terms the "two-fold movement of euphoria and alienation (or perhaps I should say schizophrenization)." In this "postmodern sublime" as the cultural logic of High Capitalism, the hallucinatory intensity of New York City instigates both hyperrealism and an apolitical despair threatening to break in to this enclave of "ontological marginalization" like some heroine in need of rescue by Orlando Furioso, who may be coked-out and watching the sign-flow on MTV.

Even in an innocuous little poem like "Down By the Station Early in the Morning," from *A Wave* (1984), the sublime experience of self-evacuation opening to emptiness ("confirming the new value the hollow core has again") is occasioned not by a *natural landscape,* but by an *urban wrecking ball* which destroys (in reverie?) the library, and dismantles the alienation of "perceptual dysfunction you've [Ashbery?] been carrying around for years":

                                        And so each day
Culminates in merriment as well as deep shock like an electric one,

As the wrecking ball bursts through the wall with the bookshelves
Scattering the works of famous authors as well as those
Of more obscure ones, and books with no author, letting in

Space, and an extraneous babble from the street
Confirming the new value the hollow core has again, the light
From the lighthouse that protects as it pushes away.[40]

Discontinuous, like Times Square zen, Ashbery's poem bares the stigmata of a luridly postmodernized sublime: a threatening urban context of massive energy and mass image, a rapid sliding from merriment to shock in one line (an earlier line is even more disjunctive: "The result is magic, then terror, then pity at the emptiness"), the irruption of shock "babble" and static from the environment, along with *kitschman* proclamations of an expansive "space" of sublimity which can still glue outer (street) and inner (library) into one "hollow core" resonant with the concealed/revealed light of being.

Ashbery represents this as a sublime "emoting" over lost urban objects as well as the outcome of hyperdisjunctive signs and unstable affects. Yet he proclaims the result as "Emoting all over something that is probably mere reportage / But nevertheless likes being emoted on." If the poem is mere "reportage," the simulacrum of news, yet it is reportage of where and how sublimity can still happen in 1984: under the technological sign of the (indifferent) wrecking ball of urban capital destroying texts, kitsch, and monuments like historical debris.

This "technological sublime" is not so much a *name* as a *site;* the place where the spectacle of Capital produces its idols of production/reproduction, signs of collective colonization of urban and global space and the electronically infiltrated unconsciousness ("From there it's a big, though necessary leap to / The more subtly conceptual conditionings"), its superpower "cathedrals" of the space age. The American sublime has been effectively taken out of the heavens, out of the moon and stars, out of mountains and volcanoes, only to be installed in Apollo rocketry, into the computerized cockpit per se, where national power circulates and "satellites" us in a project we trust is idealistic research and not a "Star Wars" narrative written banally into history.

The euphoric/dreadful source of this postmodern sublime is not merely technology per se as icon of material vastness but more unspeakable totalities of commodity-infinitude and sign-glut, for example. The sublime occurs as a semiotic overload or the exhilarating threat of that "whole new decentered global network of the third stage of capitalism itself" which Jameson and Daniel Bell term *postindustrial* or *multinational* and which Baudrillard nominates as *The Age of the Simulacrum.* This astral sublimity is energized by a Disney-like capacity to generate infinite images (ad-poems) which "liquidate reference" and "satellite" the real into dead metaphor.[41] This postmodern sublime merges into states of acquiescense before a transpersonal system disconnected from any ideology of the godhead, yet proclaiming the wonders of new-found emptiness, as Ashbery's nervous, egoless, latter-day transcendentalism (by the wrecking ball) suggests.

Although "America *en masse*" may remain unavailable for representation, or cannot regenerate new moods and myths of egocentric vastness, this very Whitmanic will-to-sublimity continues its quest to affirm boundlessness and strong selfhood, beyond social mediation, as measured within structurations not so much of "God" but of "Capital." Seemingly lost is that "space" of critical distance, of the radical "foco" which Stevens preserved (as semiotic enclave) in the late fifties: "To say that everything has become a pseudo-event or an image or a spectacle is to imply this proposition about the expansion of culture generally." [42]

If Emerson had elided human agency into transactions of nature, enacting his will-to-dominate the commodity into "symbol," a more high-capitalistic poetics elides nature into robotry and then researches the stars and moons of Mars for further sites of real estate. The immense dew of Cape Canaveral brings forth hymn and hymn from trailer camps watching the conquest of space. As Ashbery writes, getting "radiant drunk" in "So Many Lives," we can make a hobby of such rapture and love, "just as long as we continue to uphold / The principle of private property":

> It's rapture that counts, and what little
> There is of it is seldom aboveboard,
> That's its nature,
> What we take our cue from.
> It masquerades as worry, first, then as self-possession
> In which I am numb, imagining I am this vision
> Of ships stuck on the tarpaper of an urban main, . . . [43]

220

This American exhilaration ("It's rapture that counts") may be hard to tell from *anxiety,* the threat of self-loss rather than self-possession. The postmodern self "masquerades" to avoid the threat of the "urban main" which no reverie can undo, as the poet nurtures "some fable / To block out that other whose remote being / Becomes every day a little more sentient and more suavely realized." Such a sublime goes underground or becomes marginalized to a site of privacy, "radiant drunk" with being—that locus of "ontological marginalization" which we have described as aftereffect of the technocratic situation Ashbery assumes as dread in "So Many Lives":

> At night, coal stars glinting,
> And you the ruby lights hung far above on pylons
> Seeming to own the night and the nearer reaches
> Of a civilization we feel as ours,
> The lining of our old doing.

This post-Whitmanic sublime, with its zany reversals of tone and "seeming" unions which the half-parodic language undercuts, is not representable at all: Ashbery in each crazed line opens the mental climate of the poem to "the omnipresent possibility of being interrupted / While what I stand for is still almost a bare canvas." [44] What the poet stands for generally is some kind of decreative emptiness as ground of any sublime at all, "a kind of tragic euphoria / In which your spirit sprouted." [45]

Ashbery disalienates this "disturbed landscape" of "the human genre" for whom serenity is threatened and the landscape an ancient dream of stolid grandeur, collectively out of reach. The poem becomes a bric-a-brac landscape, a storage place of rapture and junk, a destabilized collage of possibility in which "knowing can have this / Sublime rind of excitement, like the shore of a lake in the desert / Blazing with the sunset," eluding "explanation." [46]

Beyond the Natural Sublime

Even a poem propagating pastoral correspondences, such as Galway Kinnell's "Shroud" (*New Yorker,* 9 Sept. 1985), cannot help

221

but register in the rural enclave of Vermont the shock of the nuclear horizon, the totalizing threat of global extinction which surrounds us like a deadly parody of all prior sublimes. Surely the "sheet or shroud large enough / to hold the whole earth" being woven by little goldfinches and milkweeds in New England serves as Kinnell's sublimated metaphor for the nuclear threat which would do away with all such creativity, whether of poet, soldier, or of bird:

> Lifted by its tuft
> of angel hairs, a milkweed
> seed dips and soars
> across a meadow, chalking
> in outline the rhythm
> that waits in air all along,
> like the bottom hem of nowhere.
> *Spinus tristis,* which spends
> its days turning gold
> back into sod, rises and falls
> along the wavy line the seed
> just waved through the sunlight.
> What sheet or shroud large enough
> to hold the whole earth
> are these seamstresses' chalks
> and golden needles
> stitching at so restlessly?
> When will it ever be finished?

The lyric "stitching" of the poet and bird are threatened with eschatological finishing, beyond their own designs, in the technological weaving of a planetary "shroud."

Louis Simpson's "The Hour of Feeling" from *Searching for the Ox* (New York: Morrow, 1976) depicts a more crazed version of Wordsworth's *natural sublime,* situating the "blessed power" of exhilarated/anxious rapture not in Tintern Abbey but amid the skyscrapers and neon blandishments of capital that is New York City:

> Thanks to the emotion with which she spoke
> I can see half of Manhattan,
> the canyons and the avenues.

222

There are signs high in the air
above Times Square and the vicinity:
a sign for Schenley's Whiskey,
for Admiral Television,
and a sign saying Milltag, whatever that means.

I can see over to Brooklyn and Jersey,
and beyond there are meadows,
and mountains and plains.

This opening of the self to immensity is not stimulated by a benev-
olent sister—as is Wordsworth's "To My Sister" (1798), which the
poem builds upon—but by a paranoid stranger Simpson met
(briefly) in a New York city publishing house (the "she" of the
poem), whose "sheer intensity" of terror allows her to "read a
deeper significance / into everything, every whisper . . ." The implo-
sion of significance in this "schizoid" postmodern sublime is
founded not so much in euphoria as in a free-floating anxiety which
cannot totalize the agency of a vast, unstable fear.

Simpson's lyric would map, in chatty miniature, a mindscape of
disalienation. The poem depicts an "hour of feeling" in which the
real conforms to subjective linkages of whiskey sign and TV ad
with the ancient (that is, preindustrial) substance of meadows,
mountains, and plains. As Simpson comments on the troubled
woman in this poem, "The insane view held by this woman was,
in its way, an act of poetic imagination. She wished to make events
in the real world conform to her vision of things. The doctor's name
for her condition was paranoia."[47] Her paranoia, emerging as an
atmospheric *unity* of feeling in a dwarfed self, is made to serve the
American poet as parodic admonition/premonition of a postmod-
ern sublime situated in the cosmic aura and panic semiotics of
capital.

Another nervously sketched landscape of the *technological sub-
lime,* Robert Lowell's "The Mouth of the Hudson" (1964) opens
with the Thomas Cole-like voice of a nature-watcher, out to espy
birds and mountains for intimations of grandeur by the shores of
the Hudson River. This self is soon invaded by whiffs of toxicity,
the impact of technological processes impinging upon the unstable
self of the poet (Lowell had just been released from hospitalization
for a nervous breakdown). He can infer in the "sublime Hudson"

not progressive infinitude but a chemical entropy to serve as a vast metaphor for the disintegration of "America" and his own—post-Whitmanic—identity. In such vernacular landscapes, the American sublime must now take place, in all its affective schizophrenia of astonishment and terror, glut and glamour:

> A single man stands like a bird-watcher,
> and scuffles the pepper and salt snow
> from a discarded, gray
> Westinghouse Electric cable drum.
> He cannot discover America by counting
> the chains of condemned freight-trains
> from thirty states. They jolt and jar
> and junk in the siding below him.
> He has trouble with his balance.
> His eyes drop,
> and he drifts with the wild ice
> ticking seaward down the Hudson, . . .
>
> Chemical air
> sweeps in from New Jersey,
> and smells of coffee.[48]

Confronting the "sulphur-yellow sun / of the unforgivable landscape," Lowell laments the ecological deformity pockmarking Thomas Cole's God-drenched locus of the American sublime.[49]

If this industrial totality of freight trains and factories is broken, as is any corresponding *wholeness* in psyche or continent, the poet attempts to conceptualize the totality in which such private suffering takes place, *as self-induced:*

> His eyes drop,
> and he drifts with the wild ice
> ticking seaward down the Hudson,
> like the blank sides of a jig-saw puzzle.

"Mouth of the Hudson" waxes desperate at closure and verges into a sign of Lowell's psychic instability. Yet consider John Updike's sketch of the postindustrial horizon of downtown Los Angeles, where in this Babylon of spectacular images and specular icons of capital, "The lone pedestrian stares, scooped at by space":

224

Lo, at its center one can find oneself
atop a paved and windy hill, with weeds
taller than men on one side and on the other
a freeway thundering a canyon's depth below.
New buildings in all mirror-styles of blankness
are being assembled by darkish people while
the tan-bricked business blocks that Harold Lloyd
teetered upon crouch low, in shade, turned slum.

The lone pedestrian stares, scooped at by space.
The palms are isolate, like psychopaths.
Conquistadorial fevers reminisce
in the adobe band of smog across the sky,
its bell of blue a promise that lured too many
to this waste of angels, of ever-widening gaps.[50]

Conventional in form—as befits a *New Yorker* poet's gentrified
warding off of Californian "vulgarity" ("being assembled by dark-
ish people")—Updike's poem epitomizes states of *urban dread* I
have called the "venom and wonder" of American sublimity. The
poem depicts evacuation of selfhood ("oneself," as if outside the
self, caught in quiet structures of alienation), a life-world organized
around automobiles and skyscrapers, blankly imperious buildings,
glut-and-glamour images in which all is a copy-of-a-copy, the terror
and "psychopathic" isolation of palm and ego in gap-filled space.
This mood takes place under air pollution which serves as one sign
of "conquistadorial" betrayal of the sublime covenant.

In "Invitation to Miss Marianne Moore," Elizabeth Bishop more
inventively succeeds not only in transferring the soaring, bragging
euphoria of Walt Whitman and Hart Crane to a female genealogy
of empowerment but in situating her invocation of this sublimity
within a cityscape that measures the damages wrought by this
American will to technocratic mastery:

From Brooklyn, over the Brooklyn Bridge, on this fine morning,
    please come flying,
In a cloud of fiery pale chemicals,
    please come flying,
to the rapid rolling of thousands of small blue drums
descending out of the mackerel sky,

over the glittering grandstand of harbor-water,
please come flying.[51]

Icon of the American sublime since its construction in 1883, the Brooklyn Bridge would still link the local and the cosmic, the natural and the urban into a euphoric trajectory of uplift and flight. But Moore's passage into sublimity has to be qualified with decreations, as Bishop cannily depicts, "negative constructions" warding off arrogance and filth:

With dynasties of negative constructions
darkening and dying around you,
with grammar that suddenly turns and shines
like flocks of sandpipers flying,
please come flying.

Out of ecological filth and urban disaster, can the American poet still "come flying"?

As sites mingling affluence and disaster, cities like Los Angeles, New York, and Detroit now function within configurations of postmodern immensity as sublime heroes of the future. Americans must live within, defy, and risk their lives and livelihoods within these glut-and-glamour totalities as experiential maps, coded with venom and wonder, terror and consumption. Desperately supple urban restructurings would foreshadow yet prevent a toxic, violent, or nuclear catastrophe that seems casual and likely like mass murder, oil spills, freeway disaster, Hollywood gossip, or daily news. Theorists or poets of these lived-in urban spaces become "political economists with their space suits on" trying to map out and preserve enclaves of survival within a system of glut, glamour, and greed consuming wilds of nature and delusions of image-truth like God's superannuated unconscious.[52]

Postmodern poets try to theorize these emergent modes of American sublimity—commodity-infinitude, simulacrous immensity, mass death, nuclear weaponry, black holes, the colonization of outer space into tourist attractions, viral infiltration—within an urban space like Los Angeles or Robocop's Motor City that is itself another instance of mass empowerment gone off the deep end into waste, death, disaster.

226

Whatever the spell of these cities as sites of new-fangled immensity, nuclear power, nonetheless, seems to emanate from the innermost depths of American poetics articulating self-rapture and national empowerment like a first fate, a fact of nature. Poets, too, stand implicated in this fascination with icons of national superiority, self-sublation into nature and God, the death of European history back into the primal scene of the desert—poets and scientists conjuring the technology of the Over-Soul set in the sublime solitude of Los Alamos.

With the landscape of natural correspondence recoded into a "grid" of nuclear forces, and space become a terrain of toxic "singularities" and greenhouse effects one forgets in order to write at all, the poet would still consume his or her myriad sublime objects: waterfall, train, dynamo, bridge, skyscraper, nuclear umbrella, New York City, abstract space, the Hotel Bonaventura, the Hudson River, Chairman Mao, or a soup can. Yet in so doing the poet risks ratifying the American will to use nature/technology in sublime acts of beholding and subjugating space. "The rhetoric of the technological sublime" may be tired, qualified, but it is still holding on; and retreat to pastoral enclaves looks more evasive, given the nuclear context of America policing the globe along with that other vastness-haunted nation of supreme fiction, Russia.

Building upon postmodern notions of material/spiritual decentering that take place under formations of postwar American power, in the final chapter I will theorize "the nuclear sublime" as an admonition/premonition of boundlessness situated in the aura of atomic energy: the nuclear sublime as it emerges from venomous/wondrous depths of American poetics.[53] Beyond leaf-tropes over nothingness, as in Steven's "The Rock," one of the examples adduced will be William Carlos Williams's poem from 1955, "Asphodel, That Greeny Flower," with its insight into the life-and-death struggle between the troping imagination and the atomic force unleashed at Hiroshima: *the bomb puts an end to all that.* Can the sublime remain *das Unform*, as Dick Hebdige claims in theorizing the liberating potential of postmodern culture-glut amid global forces of "Americanisation," "that which is without form, hence that which is monstrous and unthinkable"?[54]

NINE

Towards the Nuclear Sublime

Representations of Technological Vastness in Postnuclear America

Congratulations on Los Alamos. Was Los Alamos a place be-
fore the bomb? My notions of the southwest are vague but I
should think you would have definite sensations about living
in a place completely Post Bomb.

—Flannery O'Connor

The Awful, yet Sublime doctrine of MAD [Mutual Assured
Destruction] is *unthinkable* . . .

—E. P. Thompson

The Sublime Scenario at Alamogordo

W HEN BRIGADIER GENERAL THOMAS FARRELL groped to de-
scribe (in an official government report) the subjective effect of the
first atomic explosion at Alamogordo, New Mexico, at 5:29:50
A.M. on 16 July 1945, he found himself, like many a would-be
writer of the sublime before him, at a loss for adequate terms and
tropes—stupefied, dwarfed, reaching for hyperbolic endterms like
doomsday and *blasphemous* and resorting to spaced-out adjectives
such as *tremendous* or *awesome* that nineteenth-century Americans
had reserved for more manageable spectacles of God's grandeur
such as Niagara Falls or the Grand Canyon. Though a military man
and no poet, as Farrell registered this history-shattering event in
language, he struggled to command some rhetoric of ultimacy be-
fore nuclear "effects [that] could well be called unprecedented,
magnificent, beautiful, stupendous and terrifying":

228

No man-made phenomenon of such tremendous power had ever oc-
curred before. The lighting effects beggared description. The whole
country was lighted by a searing light with the intensity many times
that of the midday sun. It was golden, purple, violet, gray and blue.
It lighted every peak, crevasse, and mountain range with a clarity
and beauty that cannot be described but must be seen to be imag-
ined. It was the beauty the great poets dream about but describe
most poorly and inadequately. Thirty seconds after the explosion
came, first the air blast pressing hard against people and things, to
be followed almost immediately by the strong, sustained awesome
roar which warned of doomsday and made us feel that we puny
things were blasphemous to dare tamper with the forces heretofore
reserved to The Almighty. Words are inadequate tools for the job of
acquainting those not present with the physical, mental, and psycho-
logical effects. It had to be witnessed to be realized.[1]

Standing on the brink of the postmodern as *postnuclear,* Farrell's
confrontation with figurative inadequacy and inexpressibility
comes about because a terrifying *abyss* has suddenly opened be-
tween cognition (the language of the self) and its corresponding
object (nature here dematerialized or sublimated into atomic en-
ergy). The self, furthermore, seems sublated by technologies mo-
dernity has wrought.

In more aesthetic terms, this widening gap between the General's
strongest language and death-inducing forces of nature was what
Longinus and myriad neo-Romantic critics after him had privileged
as the rapture (*hypsos*) of the sublime. This sublime force of energy
released in numinous dread is precisely what General Farrell *mis-
labels* (in his awe-stricken government report) the "beauty the great
poets dream about but describe most poorly and inadequately."
Such a scenario of sublime confrontation had been used by a host
of writers (in various genres) to induce—symbolically, if not mate-
rially—the death of the ordinary self that, paradoxically, would
awaken a language of passionate elevation that might go on speak-
ing beyond the grave, achieving literature's "great time" as exalted
textuality.[2] Farrell is awe-struck not so much into belief (as was
Thomas Gray at the Grand Chartreuse, 1737) as into *uncertainty,*
however, concerning the moral/political consequences of such force
in American hands.[3]

Thinking the Limit—The Nuclear Sublime

If the Romantic sublime after the theorizing of Kant and Hegel came to represent a dialectic between some "quantitative magnitude" of nature and the mind's resistance to such prepotency of force through verbal and cognitive strategies of self-transcendence, how can any "poetic sublime" overcome the *nuclear sublime?* The mind confronts a force of atomic energy so vast and final in its disclosures of power that it renders the vaunted "supreme fiction[s]" of the Romantic imagination ludicrous or mute.[4] The postnuclear age ushered in by such dynamisms of the superpowers after World War II can be said to constitute the poet-as-subject by the mingled awe and terror of this thermonuclear force that seemingly cannot be bounded nor sublated.

This all-too-present sublimity of a magnitude defying expression and reducing the American poet to helplessness before the vastness of creation is no longer the prairies of the midwest or Niagara Falls (as barely displaced signs of a pragmatic mandate to accrue national power), but the technological projects of NASA and the nuclear arsenal which quietly, like a gray landscape, comprise the deconstructive horizon of postmodern American poetry. As John Elder argues to a chorus of literary worthies in "Seeing Through the Fire: Writers in the Nuclear Age," "The most urgent tasks facing writers today are to communicate our common danger and to invent a vocabulary of response."[5]

If such an eschatological awareness of nuclear energy deployed in "some thermonuclear / Game of chicken" goes without saying in the discourse of the mass media, it has yet to be acknowledged as subtext of force threatening the tones and codes of postmodern American poetry with technologically decentering formations of awe/terror.[6] Yet as Jane Cooper contended in a protest of "Poets Against the End of the World" held in New York City on 26 May 1982, "It seems to me almost impossible to address the nuclear threat directly, yet—whether we like it or not—that threat is an undercurrent in all our work now." As the loomingly real force of 2,000,000,000,000,000,000,000,000 atoms of plutonium are split apart via nuclear fission in one millionth of a second, this nuclear power can threaten the most solid and greeny pastoral lyric, as Seamus Heaney reveals in commenting upon one of his own poems

230

evoking mores of a beloved Irish countryside: "It struck me that 'The Birthplace', which had no intention of being a 'nuclear' poem, nevertheless touches upon our inability to trust too far a language of continuity: words, especially hallowed words, can now turn into weightless chimeras."[7]

This nuclear sublime, whether sensed as complex presence or hinted at as unarticulated absence, comprises the terror of a technological determination within the Cold War period, reducing the subject to languagelessness and bodily sublation, as in the space-shrunken green cabinet depicted in Robert Lowell's poem on the arms buildup under Kennedy, "Fall 1961":

All autumn, the chafe and jar
of nuclear war;
We have talked our extinction to death.
I swim like a minnow
behind my studio window.

Our end drifts nearer,
the moon lifts,
radiant with terror.
The state
is a diver under a glass bell.[8]

This latent *dread* of nuclear annihilation from which, as Lowell urges, "A father's no shield / for his child," can undermine older vocabularies of domestic continuity and stability, overwhelming such tenderness with lurking anxiety about any possible future, given such a horizon of infinite force that holds even "the state" and moon captive to technocratic productions of greatness. The fallout shelter lingers as one pathetic token of such earthy pastoralism, consumer haven against powers-that-be.

Once again, amid the suburban abundancies and greenhouse prophecies of the 1980s, isn't "this [nuclear] Horror starting already to scratch its way in?", as W. H. Auden portrays the "void" of atomic power threatening Cold War consciousness in "If On Account of the Political Situation."[9] Such a landscape of dread, as *the* horizon of power enframing postmodern American poetry, materializes itself in daily banalities such as the pious representations of the Strategic Defense Initiative, as in this morning's newspaper account of hyperimaginative nuclear weapons for outer space which the Energy Department is developing "under" (*sic*) the desert wilderness of Nevada:

> The technologies envision exploding a bomb, perhaps in outer space, and then channeling its phenomenal force into some kind of destructive directed-energy lasers, microwaves or a cloud of "hypervelocity pellets," according to official documents (*The Honolulu Advertiser*, 26 Feb. 1986).

If we can shrug off this latest landscape of technological sublimity from the annals of "Star Wars" research, we daily abide, as E. P. Thompson maps, within a steady state of terror and awe before a "technology of destruction" that defies rational control by dwarfed human agents. Such communities must somehow find a language with which to contend against the dialectical force of *Mutual Assured Destruction* [MAD] and the anti-archival threat that "all politics and all culture will cease." [10]

If the *natural sublime* made Niagara Falls and Lake Ontario function as collective symbols of material force and liberal empowerment in Emerson's America, it did so by articulating a dialogue between idealist man and his own more latent Godhead within an ideology of power over the desert/garden wilderness. This force has been broadly superseded in postmodern American poetics by an implied dialogue between man and technology. Such a dialogue of sublimity occurs within the durable thematics of a naturalized system which is the vast "always-already-given" the subject must contend with through gestures of alienation, (failed) transcendence, nature retreat, decreation, theory flight, silence—that whole Romantic vocabulary of subjective critique.

For in the wake of national superpowers still dispersing and deploying—as icons or signs—multimegatons of Cold War force, the sense of the nuclear sublime has become the American commonplace or common sense of an *unspeakable* force that cannot be—by any power of the imagination, however transcendental—overcome: "Witnesses of atomic explosions even at the kiloton level universally report a mingled sense of awe and horror. The multimegaton weapons simply surpass the capacity of human imagination and comprehension." [11] Such mind-quelling images and sense-

deadening effects must now superintend the vatic hyperboles of po-
etry—its "Whitmanic" claims to transport and elevation—during
what George Oppen has depicted as the *sensorium communis* of
the "Time of the Missile":

My love, my love,
We are endangered
Totally at last. Look
Anywhere to the sight's limit: space
Which is viviparous:

Place of the mind
And eye. Which can destroy us,
Re-arrange itself, assert
Its own stone chain reaction.[12]

The landscape of this love lyric, set in the wharfs and crannies of
New York City, can offer no retreat from the nuclear grid. There is
strength and size in these American numbers, but little environmen-
tal relief from "its own stone chain reaction."

Consider—as instance of this postmodern nuclear sublime—the
uncanny representation in William Pitt Root's "The Day the Sun
Rises Twice," one of the more allusive (and least polemical) descrip-
tions of sublime terror/wonder from *Nuke-Rebuke: Writers & Art-
ists Against Nuclear Energy & Weapons* (1984):

The day the sun rises twice
the primitive dream of fire comes true,
fire that burns forever,
fire no water on earth can quench,
fire whose light pins shadows to the stones,
fire whose killing edge turns flying birds to ash.

Aeons after the last of the one-eyed prophets
has chanted into the permanent darkness
no archeologist shall unearth,
countless minute embers will linger among the omens.

I make this black mark on the silence now
because none shall write
and none shall remain to read
when the clouds rise in our eyes

against those suns rising around us
like the thousand trees of life all clad in flames.[13]

Like the last "one-eyed prophet" of some nuclear abyss, Root cap-
tures the anti-archival power of nuclear energy that, as global
fire-force, threatens to efface *both* supreme fictions: the Native
American dream of supernatural animism (stanza 1) and the Judeo-
Christian dream of redemptive prophecy (stanza 2). Root's paratac-
tic language and allusive imagery all-too-gleefully capture the infi-
nite power yet impending nothingness of this nuclear sublimity, as
in the final line, which revisions the once-hopeful language of fire
and sun from the Bible as the death of earth and its symbolizations:
"like the thousand trees of life all clad in flames."

Root's poem lucidly images forth what Jacques Derrida has
termed (in a conference on "Nuclear Criticism" at Cornell) the "re-
mainderless cataclysm" of nuclear power as a massive "missive/
missile" that threatens to efface not only subjective traces but entire
reference systems whose annihilated "black mark[s]" once pro-
vided pre-Hiroshima structures of purpose and hope (*telos*): "The
hypothesis of total destruction watches over deconstruction, it
guides its footsteps."[14] In a postnuclear age whose critical reflex is
some version of deconstructive deferral or decreative nihilism, tex-
tual chatterings over the nuclear void, would Frost's speaker in
"Fire and Ice" (1920) so smugly embrace the rapt *desire* of "Some
[who] say the world will end in fire"?[15]

Yet, as Bob Perelman captures our lingering idealist faith in pro-
jects of material technology, however nuclearized or spiritualized
their fires, in "Statement" (1984):

The Pentagon inhales the mystery religion
Of its hydrogen bomb, fried regions'
Penetralia in recompense for attacks
On theory or shy good looks, orchestrated
To an overall bland finale
To logic-stories.[16]

Hence this terror of the nuclear sublime can dwarf a "Language
Poet" of the 1980s such as Perelman with the sense of his own
referential insignificance ("Hey you! I say to the H-bomb"), as such

avant-garde tactics of language-play against the "fetish of the refer-
ent" get sublated by corporate American projects that threaten po-
etic autonomy with more atomic imperatives—"It's lights out at
the fetish factory":

> Eleven million children (picture it)
> (Don't stop) standing on the surface of the earth
> (Scarface) looking at a lightbulb.
> The plot? I don't know you.
> ("Institutions and the Individual Application," in *To the Reader*)

In "Meanwhile," from *The First World* (1986), Perelman depicts
the American urban self as a latter-day Bartleby, one of a million
nuclearized "worst-case scenarios walking down Sixth Street /
head under arm talking, preferring not to, to the / whole city at
once, scheduled to be burnt in the / trash . . ."[17] A seemingly sys-
temic and free-floating *paranoia* often infiltrates Perelman's tones
and terms, like some disillusioned Melville, resulting in an atomis-
tic and discontinuous syntax suspicious of narrative. Yet a benign
technology still promises the Third World another New World, one
made over in the image of ranch-style progress:

> Once the missiles have done their imaginary work
> the solid ranch-style earth
> will truly be heaven:
> rich people and no poor people.
> Industry is to be back on its feet in four days, according
>   to one government projection.

With post-nuclear poets "picturing" power and searching for
terms to domesticate this astonishing force through homey but in-
adequate metaphors of *mushroom, lightbulb, flower,* or *umbrella,*
it is no wonder that, as Terrence Des Pres contends in a compelling
essay on the nuclear landscape as "Self/Landscape/Grid," "the
'American sublime,' as critics call it, has been missing in our poetry
at least since late Stevens. The sublime, as observers like Burke and
Kant and Schopenhauer insist, arises from terror, terror beheld and
resisted, the terror of revolution for Wordsworth, of the abyss for
Whitman, of nuclear annihilation for any poet today who would
make a language to match our extremity."[18] If, to invoke Burke's *A*

Philosophical Enquiry into the Origin of Our Ideas of the Sublime and Beautiful, we love what we can fictively dominate (the beautiful), whereas we admire what subjugates us (the sublime) because this very superior force of nature or human otherness can inspire a force of resistance that releases inner resources of self-preservation and trope, can the nuclear sublime still afford this same leisurely empowerment of selfhood? Can Los Alamos displace Niagara as a figure of national empowerment?

In a ground-breaking essay on "The Nuclear Sublime," Frances Ferguson (1984) has called attention to the way this discourse of an idealist sublime still recurs in a nuclear author such as Jonathan Schell when envisioning end-time scenarios in *The Fate of the Earth* (1982). He goes on to recuperate subjective freedom from the dominations of nature and, even more so in her view, from the claustrophobic imposition of human masses and future citizens now invoked as the nuclear *unborn.*[19] Yet we need to wonder whether or not, at some point within postnuclear history, quantitative changes in speed and force could produce qualitative changes in the subject. That is, even within this recycled discourse of the sublime, can't we find new formations and affects commensurate with (if not resistant to) this space-age threshold of nuclear force? It may already be the case that, as Fredric Jameson has theorized of "quantum leaps" produced by changes in technology and the semiautonomous productions of culture in the 1960s, postmodern history can be the site of "a [dialectical] passage from quantity to quality in which the *same* force, reaching a certain threshold of excess, in its prolongation now produces qualitatively distinct effects and seems to generate a whole new system [which he theorizes as the by-now-global dispensation of the *postmodern*]."[20]

Schopenhauer at Vesuvius

Looking back for models of sublime empowerment in Schopenhauer's *The World as Will and Representation,* the sovereign subject ("genius") confronted a vast object or force of the natural sublime and "[was] not oppressed but exalted by its immensity."[21] Scaring itself (in imagination) with what Robert Frost called "desert places" of immensity between stars, the self could thereby experience consciousness as simultaneously determined by material forces that threaten the body with aggression and death and yet, by dialectical contrast, exalted into an awareness of transcendental freedom. Through sublimity, the will of libidinous individuality is fleetingly abolished. In this self-quieting of the sublime, the "world-as-will" must give way to the "world-as-representation," that is, to a representative knowledge that selfhood both partakes of yet transcends the world of violent force, however dynamic or deadly.

The sublime of nature presents what we would now term an ideological apparatus that better allows the "pure will-less subject of knowledge" (178) to be "raise[d] out of the endless stream of willing" (196), that is, lifted from the flux of history as dominion of appetite, desire, and hostile force (197). Such material objects can be overcome when the subject "forcibly" tears away from confronting hostile objects of will and instead "may quietly contemplate, as pure, will-less subject of knowing," those very objects that terrorize the will: "In that case, he is then filled with the feeling of the *sublime;* he is in the state of exaltation, and therefore the object that causes such a state is called *sublime*" (201–2). The natural object, in effect, no longer exists.

Though such sublime "exaltation" can come about for Schopenhauer's subject "in any environment" (197), it became a commonplace after the Augustan appropriation of Longinus in critics such as Burke and Kant that this "impression of the *sublime*" was most powerfully stimulated by pain-inducing landscapes of dynamic force wherein "they [sublime objects] may threaten it [the will as body] by their might that eliminates all resistance, or their immeasurable greatness [that] may reduce it to nought" (201). In this Western struggle against totalizing determinations, the natural sublime begets the resistance to a force that must be subjectively overcome through mighty language and psychic stance ("by a conscious and violent tearing away from the relations of the same object to the will"), that is, by a subject-altered "representation" of that same vast object. "Exaltation" follows from a change in semiotic perspective, as the object as sign-of-will gives way to the object as sign-of-idea, that is, as sign of this free play of interior representation. For, if the mind becomes emancipated from "all willing and its cravings" (203), it also becomes emancipated from the prior domination of the material object in this very act of subjective symbolization, as the world-as-will (form) gives way to the world-as-representation (idea). As often in Romantic poetics, the sublime object of materiality is overcome by this change in perspective (trope).

For example, when confronting "agitated forces of nature" at sea or in the mountains, by a waterfall or near lightning, the trumping power of a Whitman-like *double self* soon becomes manifest:

> Simultaneously, he feels himself as individual, as the phenomenon of will, which the slightest touch of these forces can annihilate, helpless against powerful nature, dependent, abandoned to chance, a vanishing nothing in face of stupendous forces; and he also feels himself as the eternal, serene subject of knowing, who as the condition of every object is the supporter of this whole world, the fearful struggle being only his mental picture or representation; he himself is free from, and foreign to, all willing and all needs, in the quiet comprehension of the Ideas. This is the full impression of the sublime. (205)

As the poet-as-subject confronts the remainderless power of the "nuclear sublime," can this serve the writer as another instance of a "mental picture or representation"? That is, is the sovereign "subject of pure knowing" still free to transcend the world of hostile force and terrified bodies by a semiotic turn of ideation, mental transformation, by a retreat from history into affirmations of neo-Platonic essence? Will "the quiet comprehension of the Ideas" such as those of iambic pentameter, heroic ode, and democratic ballot survive the "agitated forces" of thermonuclear megatonnage, as million-personed individuality gets lost ("extinguished") into the monistic Godhead of Schopenhauer's beloved Vedas?: "I am all this creation collectively, and besides me there exists no other being" (206).

In the modernist scenario of "Esthétique du Mal" (1944), Wallace Stevens represents himself as a writer in Naples, distantly contemplating Vesuvius while "reading paragraphs on the sublime." Confronting this volcanic agent of the natural sublime, Stevens yet recognizes the threat to self-preservation of a merely private *catastrophe:* "Vesuvius might consume / In solid fire the utmost earth and know / No pain (ignoring the cocks that crow us up / To die)."

The pain of material annihilation threatens the poet with an image of his own death, and he draws back: "This is a part of the sublime / From which we shrink." Nevertheless, Stevens goes on to assert, in the qualifying phrase "except for us," the endurance of the humanist subject beyond time's annihilation through fire: "And yet, except for us, / The total past felt nothing when destroyed." The human agent remains the site of history, discourse, archive of past and future, maker of the Longinian affect if not of the sublime landscape he in self-pitying terror beholds.[22]

Like Emerson, who thought of the American poet as an "endless seeker with no past at [his] back," or Henry Ford who abolished the legacy of European history as so much "bunk," Stevens seemingly delights in this abolition of history to nothingness through wild natural force: "The total past felt nothing when destroyed." "The Man on the Dump" (1938), for example, delights in the decreation of floral landscapes (space) and immense time (history) to sheer junk ("One rejects the trash"), reduces it *all* to emptiness, as this provides Stevens a blank slate of "nothingness" whereupon the belated American poet can assert tropes of original seeing: "You see the moon rise in the empty sky."[23] But now, after the World War II fires which Stevens was abstractly confronting through Vesuvius had ended at Hiroshima, American writers have to contemplate a nuclear fire that threatens this all-too-languaged subject with utter tracelessness, the physical abolition of any past or future. "The total past felt nothing when destroyed" is not hyperbole, as the technological fire exists at such a megaton level of destructiveness.

Poetry as Sublime Intertext

At the risk of participating in a simulacrum of nuclear terror that I would avoid by evoking it as hypothetical future, it still needs to be stressed that nuclear power threatens to abolish the master narratives of the archive, the total past wherein human grandeur has been stored in traces of sublime textuality. Terror without end or capable structuring reduces the human agent to powerlessness, an underlying current of apolitical helplessness: a death of the future has, in effect, already happened, as many now despair of bringing children into such a threatened life-world. Could the natural sub-

limity of something like the *aurora borealis* reduce our "puny sput-
niks and missiles" to size, hence return them to the human dimen-
sion, as William Carlos Williams avowed in 1958?[24] That is, will
not textual sublimity outlast or outdo (symbolically) the power of
nuclear technology? Or, in lieu of nuclear disaster, will the green-
house effect serve to end the comforts of environmental sublimity?

Asserting the fictive supremacy of *Paterson* over the natural
landscape, Williams shocked his audience in 1951 by bluntly af-
firming, "The very inner casings of Egyptian sarcophage, made of
paper sheets, are ungummed in the improbable hope that a shred
of papyrus found there may contain even a few words from a poem
by Sappho. If England is destroyed by Russian bombs it will hardly
be a matter of importance to history so long as the works of Shake-
speare be not lost."[25] Even the mighty texts of Shakespeare cannot
withstand the nuclear fires we have invented, that nuclear winter
which threatens all flowers, empires, and all springs. As Williams
best intuited in his own imagery: "The bomb puts an end to all
that." Caught between a stance of pious expostulation evoking
more terror or a zany one of "giddy incompetence" suggesting a
lightheaded amazement at any assumption of technocratic mastery
or plot, we must somehow go on to articulate or image forth this
end-game genre of the nuclear sublime, with all our collective re-
sources of language and wit.[26]

For cultural genres and disciplines fascinated up to the frames
and limits of representation and all-but-blocked in expressive
power by this "fabulously textual" (Derrida) or "simulacrous"
(Baudrillard) nature of nuclear terror, the nuclear sublime can func-
tion as the collective attempt "to think the unthinkable" or "to
represent the unpresentable" in discursive arenas such as poems,
films, novels, and speculative essays.[27] Somehow, reemerging as a
global concept, it is as if the "nuclear sublime" is a force/concept/
trope of such magnitude that it has taken the cognitive double-take
of forty years (1945–1985) for writers of the United States, USSR
and other countries even to begin to articulate responses of suffi-
cient "resistance." This search for a new concept, for a nuclear way
of thinking that can envision if not contain such force must con-
tinue on in the 1990s, under an administration that still invokes the
nuclear sublime as force and sign of American supremacy or as a
geopolitical bargaining chip with Russia. (If an "antinuclear" po-

sition exists, it is, at this point, off the map of Cold War history, in the discursive exile of *theory:* witness New Zealand or the Big Island of Hawaii, dangling in the Pacific with overridden moral or local objections to shoring nuclear arms.)

The hope of such cultural work, it seems to me, is that by employing the means not of technological production but of semiotic (re)production, the poet can offer symbols of discursive resistance. By destabilizing the business-as-usual language of the "modern administered world," the aim of cultural work such as Perelman's language-defamiliarizing poems or the sentence-massiveness of Ron Silliman's *Ketjak,* for example, would be to allow that—as Adorno argues of "the sublime in nature and art"—"the uncommunicable is communicated and . . . [therefore] the hold of reified consciousness is thus broken" (see note 4). Yet as Walter Benjamin warned in the shellshocked fragments of *One-Way Street* (1928), observing the "frenzy of destruction" released by the aerial technology of World War I, "If it [the technology of war] is not gripped to the very marrow by the discipline of this power, no pacifist polemics will save it." [28]

Hence, building upon the counter-hegemonic visions Adorno sees in the literature of modernism, "Radical negativity, as bare and non-illusory as the illusion [of freedom] promised by the sublime, has become the heir of the sublime." [29] Yet the figures of sublimity which such art would maintain by representing that which eludes formal presentation, in all puniness and insignificance, can come to seem merely comic or pathetic, a humanistic product of High Textuality and "Supreme Fiction" void of "pretensions to power and greatness" in a totally threatened life-world. This may be because a radical polarization of spirit and matter seems a *fait accompli* of the Cold War, in which the unleashed elemental forces of the atom no longer bode the emancipation of the human subject, as the natural sublime did for Kantian idealism or for Schopenhauer's euphoric will-to-transcendence. If the struggle to represent the sublime has become a constituent element of a genuinely historicized postmodern art, as Adorno and Lyotard argue, can the nuclear sublime as an elemental force of nature still stand for—"represent"— the innermost grandeur of the human spirit in all its power of critical resistance ("radical negativity")? [30]

If the sublime has returned to help articulate an affective calculus of awe and terror before the nuclear threat, has this hyperbole also returned in the subject as a Euramerican *ideologeme* to act out (hence reproduce) another strategy of symbolic self-transcendence yet of systemic accomodation before configurations of technological vastness? Yes, Kant stipulated that no man-made objects or products of human technology can be considered sublime,[31] but do we still need this transcendentalist vocabulary of the natural sublime to effect another (idealist) accomodation to material domination? From a perspective of isolate moral *outrage* as a woman, Denise Levertov evokes this totality of technological silencing confronting the humanist subject: "And was there ever a time as urgent? Never. Never have we faced extinction, the extinction of all future, all consciousness." Given this politically engendered *terror,* Carolyn Forché argues that American "poets of the Nuclear Age" cannot find an adequate language, root-metaphors, or narratives to ward off such threats to representative witnessing: "There is no metaphor for the end of the world and it is horrible to search for one."[32]

Considering the likelihood of such species-extinction and biosphere shutdown, Bruce Boone conjectures in "Writing and an Anti-Nuclear Politics" that American poets risk an ongoing "blockage": "There's a bigness here that's just too staggering, makes itself less available imaginatively."[33] Hence Boone concludes, as did Adorno, that there will be a swerve from contending against this sublimity into tactics of irony and meta-irony: "In this quandary humor often arises." It is by now a commonplace that since the material closure of 1945, nuclear jokes have proliferated as gallows humor under the "Doomsday Clock" of *The Bulletin of the Atomic Scientists:* "On a clear day you can see the end of the world. . . . I have to hurry up and finish shopping, it's four minutes to midnight on the Doomsday Clock." Boone offers the 1955 Hollywood film *Kiss Me, Deadly* as at least a preposterously unconscious attempt by Cold War filmmakers to represent the signifying closure of the nuclear sublime ("the mushroom cloud as the meaning of a society that's turned against sexuality, other cultures (racism), art, women, and finally—itself"). Decrying a boredom worse than the bomb for surviving characters in *Trinity Site,* a dull play on the nuclear topic, Frank Rich warns, "Of all the forms of fallout produced by the atomic bomb, few are more persistent, if less noxious,

Home With the Bomb in Amarillo, Texas (1986), the banal production and stockpiling of nuclear weapons at Pantex has resulted in a consensus of "end-time thinking" in Amarillo, for which the ruling metaphor remains that of a forthcoming Nuclear Armageddon in which elected Americans—those primarily of the Reaganite/Falwell faith—will be sublimely "raptured" from their bodies, united with the Godhead as the fallen earth burns into infinite damnation, flesh and all.[38] Even the accidental meltdown of the Chernobyl Nuclear Power Facility in the Ukraine (26 April 1986), with clouds of radiation pouring over Scandinavia and Eastern Europe while scientists struggle to contain these pre-visible waves of nuclear fire and cellular death, now seems just a rude foreshadowing to the "logic-story" nuclear plants such as Pantex have invented to produce the death of the earth and self. Before such "radioactive / Waters mixed in the salad dressing," the vaunted "Envelope-language [of Being] means nothing," as depicted in Perelman's mock-statist poem "Don't Drink the Water, Eat the Food, or Breathe the Air."[39]

Paul Boyer and Jonathan Schell have both observed that this emerging attempt by writers "to represent the unrepresentable" and "say the unsayable" in the discourse of the 1980s now suggests, at last, a collective effort to bypass the Cold War repression of technological monsters and "subversive demons" of race, class, and history from the American political unconscious. Directly or allegorically, artists are imagining nuclear images and affects, in the limited efficacy of a symbolic praxis.[40] Yet this confrontation with subjective and species annihilation takes place on a global scale that can make the vaunted Vesuvius of Longinus or Matthew Arnold's Aetna look like Romantic tinker toys. Such an intrinsically dialogical subject or poetic "hero," as represented by diverse voices, demands more (from readers) than thematic repetition or retreat into a higher brand of formalism. For, as citizens of a postnuclear superpower whose impact willy-nilly approaches "hegemonic," we must challenge the sublime mythos that God-blessed Americans of elected Rapturism are empowered to overcome material rivals on a scale of nuclear superiority via *intimidation* (the semiotic production of even more fear). We must challenge the ethos that the American sublime somehow mandates liberal culture to place that annual "new pennant up the flagpole / In a predicated romance" in which the New Frontier of space is ours for discovery and posses-

than the mindless anti-bomb melodrama" (*San Fr*
icle, 18 June 1986).

If nuclear thinkers are often (in Robert Schee
"hostage to their own rhetoric," the nuclear sublir
alize the gap between force and sign, between dyn;
hyperbolic imagination, between global death
computer-simulations.[34] Derrida situates this nucl
an "absolute épochè," as that force released unde
constructive nihilism forever making manifest the
of culture's "juridico-literary archive": "The terr
the nuclear conflict can only be the signified refere
referent (present or past) of a discourse or a text
such daily derealizations, a personal "gap" can wi
threat of nuclear contamination and the polite ev;
domestic life, as captured in this scarified lyric fror
Hello La Jolla (1978):

> When each glass of milk is a miniature suicide
> The flowers of Oaxaca have a place on the shelf.
> ("The Blue and the Green: Drugs and the Market")[3]

If this dwarfing of the subject and his or her cul
of difference and hope seems just another human
need to stress the literalness of the environmental
ert Creeley's plain-style rejoinder to the world-we
low's Thesis, That We Think Our Era's Awful I
In It":

> Not only that you're going to die in it,
> but that it will kill you! There is
>
> no way you'll get out of it, away from it,
> alive. Neither money nor hope
>
> nor any other damn thing will make the least diffei
> And there won't even be a you left
>
> to contest this most meager provision,
> your life. You think that's bad? . . . [37]

Gloomy as this privatized "worst-case analysis"
is, however, as A. G. Mojtabai depicts in *Bles*

sion like so many Miranda moons of Uranus (Ashbery, "The Task"). Can even a nuclear war remain winnable with enough soil, shovels, and native spunk—with enough *rapture?*[41]

Signs of Postnuclear Resistance: Beyond Hiroshima

Despite increasing signs of resistance, this massive force of sublimity engendered by the productive apparatus and power formations of the Cold War has materialized itself since 1945 in dynamisms of terror of which nuclear explosion is the ultimate instance, the undoing of prior poetic "heliotropes" of light: as William Carlos Williams perceived in the post-Hiroshima 1950s, *"The bomb puts an end to all that."* Social historian Paul Boyer in *By the Bomb's Early Light* (1985) has aptly described the postnuclear limits of American literary expression of the bomb, from 1945–1950, with the eery catchphrase of sublime inexpressability: "words fail." [42] As Williams depicted in a moving lyric to his elderly wife, "Asphodel, That Greeny Flower" in *Journey to Love* (1955), the atom bomb has forever altered American, if not global, consciousness of space and structure—those human conceits of erotic figuration such as "gems" and "flowers" as timelessly efficacious over the "profound depth" of natural destructiveness:

> The bomb puts an end
> > to all that.
>
> I am reminded
> > that the bomb
> > > also
>
> is a flower
> > dedicated
> > > howbeit
>
> to our destruction.[43]

Confronting the death of love in his wife, Williams yet invokes this timely image to terrify Flossie back into love's tenuous fold; for the atom bomb had released a sublime force of deadliness forever latent in nature and now dwarfing the Romantic subject with "its childlike / insistence."

Deconstructing molecular "limits that prove to be liminal," nuclear fission had unleashed a force that brought the mind up to the *limin* (threshold) of any form as such, devastating the ontological substance of things, rendering objects unstable and resonant with subatomic emptiness—sublimating matter into fire and air, or sheer emptiness.[44] Yet the nuclear bomb is no "flower" of loveliness, and Williams's (deconstructive) trope knows it. For the bomb puts an end to *all that:* eternalizing tropes of love as "flower" and "sun" and so forth, the enduring Renaissance metaphors of "light" which proliferate in this late poem as a force of language circulating wildly to ward off nuclear "heat" and death, of his wife if not of the earth.

Fascinated by the hypnotic image in *Life* magazine of the detonated bomb as "mere picture" of global death, threatening to annihilate loving subjects such as Doctor Williams and his embittered wife, "we cannot wait / to prostrate ourselves before it" into the worship of what Williams depicts as a mechanical death-god. Here was an icon of that massively destructive energy which Robert Oppenheimer's war project had unleashed, rather than "desert music," at wilderness test sites in Alamogordo, New Mexico.

By-product of technological ingenuity and of "a kind of / hardheaded pragmatism standing in the empty spaces" (Perelman, "Person"), America's use of the atomic bomb had historically originated in *fear,* of the Germans and Japanese and later of the Russians, as the militant apparatus if not of death then of an incapacitating truce founded in lifelong intimidation ("deterrence").[45] Oppenheimer's personal scenario of awe/terror before the explosion of the first atom bomb in New Mexico on 16 July 1945 can function as a primal scene of postnuclear sublimity, registering the subjective trace of infrared energy, as the ego gets absorbed (raptured) into a nuclear godhead evoking transcendental scriptures of God-the-destroyer (*Shiva*): "Like the others [on the Manhattan Project], Oppenheimer was stunned by the sheer magnitude of the blast. A passage from the Hindu scripture came to his mind as the mushroom cloud [code-named "Trinity"] rose up toward the heavens: 'I am become death, shatterer of worlds.'"[46]

As in Schopenhauer's dynamic of the sublime, if such a spectacle of cosmic force attracts the dwarfed subject in its magnitude and release of the latent infinitude within nature, it also repulses as the material agent of pain and death on an unprecedented scale, disclosing a new vastness defying the body's measurement ("picturing"), by ton or heat gradient or ethical norm. In Ai's dramatic-monologue from *Sin,* fittingly enough, Oppenheimer becomes another of those nature-subduing American visionaries, in love with the transcendental annihilation of his ego, now done up on a cosmic scale.[47] Wendy Rose would invoke Oppenheimer's anti-reifying insight: *"It's amazing how the tools, the technology trap one."*[48]

Didactically *parodying* the high-Whitmanic celebration of the American self as egocentric model for poetic loftiness, with its euphoric geography of magnitude and its ethos of productive liberation, Allen Ginsberg's "Plutonian Ode" (1978) shows how romantically inadequate upbeat stances of prophetic sublimity would now be before the dread-and-wonder machines of American nuclear power plants. Whatever the lure of Whitman, technological activism is refused poetic vindication:

> Father Whitman I celebrate a matter that renders Self
>   oblivion!
> Grand Subject that annihilates inky hands & pages'
>   prayers, old orators' inspired Immortalities,
> I begin your chant, openmouthed exhaling into spacious
>   sky over silent mills at Hanford, Savannah River,
>   Rocky Flats, Pantex, Burlington, Albuquerque,
> I yell thru Washington, South Carolina, Colorado,
>   Texas, Iowa, New Mexico,
> where nuclear reactors create a Thing under the
>   Sun, where Rockwell war-plants fabricate this death
>   stuff trigger in nitrogen baths,
> Hanger-Silas Mason assembles the terrified weapon
>   secret by ten thousands, & where the Manzano Moun-
>   tain boasts to store
> its dreadful decay through two hundred forty millenia
>   while our Galaxy spirals around its nebulous core.[49]

This litany of American place names and crowds which had filled Whitman with such exuberance and sense of social promise in 1855 is ironized in Ginsberg's nuclear *ode* (a sublime genre) as the idealized apparatus of planetary death; for, while spacious skies hover infinitude over the Rocky Mountains, plutonium factories such as the one Ginsberg protests (with chants, mantras, even invoking poet-shamans like Blake and Whitman) at Rocky Flats yet manufacture a death-inducing substance (named after the death-god, Pluto) with a staying power of 240,000 years, "matter that renders Self oblivion!" Yet haunted by such sublimity, American poets seem drawn to self-oblivion.

As Perelman writes, more deconstructively, in "Seduced By Analogy," "Inside the box is plutonium. / The concept degrades, explodes, / Goes all the way, in legal parlance." Postnuclear American poets, then, must now exist in a steady state of "ontological marginalization," as in the ghostly antireferential poems of Ashbery or the Berkeley "Language Poets," which generate parodic or dystopic tropes of freedom ("freeplay") and language-massiveness all too perilously pronounced, as Ashbery urged, "on the margin / In our technological society." [50]

In an oblique, tonally sensitive approach to the ironies of nuclear power, George Uba, an Asian-American poet teaching at Cal State Northridge, mocks pious domestications of the nuclear sublime by speaking in a classroom discourse whose norms have already been constituted by technocratic data of nuclear terror. In "How Do You Spell 'Missile'?: Preliminary Instructions in the Nuclear Age," a grammar-school teacher speaks calmly in the naturalized hyperboles and cool mentality of the Pentagon:

Today we will speak in megatons.
Say salvo, ballistics, and payload.
How much makes a capacity?
How far a neutral zone?
Use target as a verb.

Today we will color in pencil.
Lead for all the cities,
Lead for the flowers, the trees,
And the name, newly learned,
Scrawled in the corner unsteadily.

Today we will count backwards:
Five Four Three Two One
Last is the thumb.[51]

The free-space of the American classroom has been infiltrated by discourse of this naturalized sublime, draining away terror, the teacher's bland speech already colonized by the lesson plans of euphoric technology, which can calmly plan ("target as a verb") the leaden annihilation of cities, landscapes, and human subjects: "Last is the thumb." Uba's poem serves as parodic image of the discursive dehumanization from which even awe and terror have been banished, transformed into mere signals of mathematical numbness like the "technologese" voice of NASA describing the terrifying explosion of the Challenger with its five tiny astronauts dissolving over Cape Canaveral in January of 1986: "*Obviously . . . we have had a malfunction.*"

In Jim Schley's quite New-Englandy anthology, *Writing in a Nuclear Age* (1984), Galway Kinnell's "The Fundamental Project of Technology" (41) registers a more overtly moralized response to the World War II deaths at Nagasaki as one consequence of the global project of technology, what Heidegger will call the "enframing" of science. For the naturalist Kinnell, for whom the (Emersonian) discourse of nature in rural Vermont still offers a symbolic counter to the world of urban commodification, this burden of contemporary *terror* can be traced to the idolatry of technology which, in Faust-like Puritanical deployment, would annihilate the impure ("animal") body of decay and death:

To de-animalize human mentality, to purge it of obsolete
evolutionary characteristics, in particular death,
which foreknowledge terrorizes the contents of skulls with,
is the fundamental project of technology; however,
the mechanisms of *pseudolgica fantastica* require,
to establish deathlessness it is necessary to eliminate
those who die; a task attempted when a white flash
    sparkled.

Kinnell's verb *sparkled,* as the poem's refrain (which he takes from Tatsuichiro Akizuki's *Concentric Circles of Death*), may describe the camera flash from the ubiquitous Japanese cameras at the memorial site—as does the shallow, pop imagery of Mary Jo Salter's "Welcome to Hiroshima" [52]—but it hardly captures the nuclear rupture which had annihilated thousands in an instant. Better at verbalizing the affect of the nuclear sublime is the arhythmic, heart-disturbing fourth stanza, which records in dehumanized images the "infra-screams bitter-knowledge's speechlessness / memorized, at that white flash, inside closed-forever mouths." Before the massive power embodied in what Hart Crane called this "steeled Cognizance" of American technology, Kinnell (like Schell in *The Fate of the Earth*, 95) can only invoke childlike "ignorance," some humble stance of naive unknowing that remains founded in a "surplus of gratitude" before God-engendered formations of the natural sublime. Kinnell retreats from machine worship into maxims of earth piety:

> Awareness of ignorance is as devout
> as knowledge of knowledge. Or more so.

Robert Hass, another urbane poet who invokes images from depths of wilderness-nature, has contended of the domestic terror induced by nuclear *images:* "Images are powers: it seems to me quite possible that the arsenal of nuclear weapons exists, as Armageddon has always existed, to intensify life." [53] Whatever the origins of this image circulating in the "new Cold War" discourse of the Reagan administration, with its trump card from the world of science fiction called *Star Wars*, Hass contends that the image of the nuclear sublime may heighten that collective, Zenlike sense of nature's *perishability*, our biological transiency, and hence the sense of the crucial role human responsiveness plays in a poetry of "praise" (his incarnational stance) and humility before the earth. Similarly, William Stafford confesses a heightened "feeling of wonderment about everyday places and events and people" in the midwest, paradoxically emanating from the same nuclear threat: "The persuasion that all of those around you may be swept away at once—not just one at a time, with adjustments in between—builds a special perceiving of those friends, these days." [54] Or this threat of nuclear oblivion can lead to a giddy, nihilist mood James Tate has colorfully called his "oblivion ha-ha."

Like a more imagistic John Hersey, Marc Kaminsky has culled various journals and the literature of survivors in Japan to preserve mnemonic images of the nuclear explosion of 6 August 1945, resulting in the flat, shattered monologue of a German Missionary in *The Road From Hiroshima* (1984):

A terrible flash
rushed from east to west
and became everywhere
at once . . .

I can't explain
it was not shock
or horror
I became mute with

I could see streets
in the distance
a few buildings
standing

here and there
but Hiroshima didn't exist
I saw
Hiroshima did not exist.[55]

Fleeing along this road from Hiroshima, as we all are, a Japanese soldier cannot leave behind him these speechless fragments, these burning images of pine trees and fallen power lines, and lastly of "the hands of a baby / black arms lifted to the sky / her fingers on fire / burning with ten blue flames" (88). Hiroshima seemingly *locks the mind in awe,* and survivors must repress what they cannot directly articulate, as in the retrospective dream-language of Marguerite Duras's *Hiroshima Mon Amour* (1959).[56]

Whether invoked as memory (Kaminsky) or as future vision (Root), the "special perceiving" of the nuclear sublime can serve as a trope allowing the technologically dwarfed subject to evoke the wonder/terror of the atomic bomb and, to a lesser degree, of the corporate moonlanding apparatus—not to mention the ABM of the Star Wars scenario—which have estranged the (American) moon into an effect which, as a poststructuralist might affirm, has "satellitiz[ed] the real" into a simulation of terror.[57] Even the

251

moon, territorialized as a new frontier of the American Manifest Destiny to challenge the vastness of outer space, has become the site of a golf game and a TV setting forever lost, as Norman Mailer copiously argues in *Of a Fire on the Moon,* to the lunatic metaphors of poetry.

As Lowell senses the nuclear radiance in 1961, "Our end drifts nearer, / the moon lifts / radiant with terror." By contrast, Gertrude Stein's early stance of aesthetic aloofness and political resignation in "Reflection on the Atomic Bomb" (1946), however ironic, seems to me morally untenable, a modernist illusion of private superiority smugly sustained: "They asked me what I thought of the atomic bomb. I said I had not been able to take any interest in it. . . . What is the use, if they [atomic bombs] are really as destructive as all that there is nothing left and if there is nothing there is nobody to be interested and nothing to be interested about." [58] Such aesthetic ironies sound arch and hollow, echoing in vacant space.

In *Of a Fire on the Moon* (1969), Norman Mailer represents his "loss of the ego" before the cathedral-like environment of NASA as one consequence of a highly idealized appropriation of space that makes poetry into obsolete Indian "fire," some artisanal craft worthy of another era when "lunacy" was valued as symbolically productive. Articulating (at turns critically and rhapsodically, as if in a *schizoid* flux between praise and panic) this "unmapped continent of America's undetermined heart" (90), Aquarius/Mailer stands dumbfounded before configurations of technological sublimity readying in the Florida wilds:

> All over America in the summer the night fields were now filled with Americans sleeping on air mattresses which reposed on plastic cloth floors of plastic cloth tents—what a sweet smell of Corporate Chemical, what a vat and void to mix with the balmy fermy chlorophylls and pollens of nature! America the Sanitary, and America the Wild, went out to sleep in the woods, Sanitary-Lobe and Wild-Lobe nesting together neatly, schizophrenic twins in the skull of the good family American.[59]

The spectacle such Americans worship in the wilds is no longer the dynamics of Niagara Falls (now chemically toxic anyway) nor the therapeutic Hudson River, but the launching of Saturn V as corporate display of "guts and grease, plumbing and superpipes, Lucifer or the Archangel grinding the valves" (67); that is, an updated instance of an American sublime which dwarfs to puniness Mailer's vaunted male ego before the collective Dynamo.

As Robert Lowell depicted the aftermath of World War II in "For the Union Dead," these technological formations which are deforming the once-moral values of Boston can survive even the nuclear "boiling" of Hiroshima:

> There are no statues for the last war here;
> on Boylston Street, a commercial photograph
> shows Hiroshima boiling
>
> over a Mosler Safe, the 'Rock of Ages'
> that survived the blast. Space is nearer.[60]

Instead of the bronze statue of Colonel Shaw and his negro soldiers battling for emancipation in the Civil War, we discover the commercial monuments of Capital: a Mosler Safe (whose emblem is taken from the natural sublime), underground garages, gigantic cars, TV sets, a dilapidated aquarium to preserve some token link with nature. The dead soldiers serve as relics of an outdated moral agency and New England ethos, held over from the days of Emerson and James: "Their monument sticks like a fishbone / in the city's throat."

American Rapturism

Considered from a perspective of American poetics, this buildup towards a nuclear sublime results partly from the dynamics of American Rapturism and the will to transcend limits, as well as from the progress of a cultural system—Capital—manifesting spectacles of its own technological benevolence, the homey idealism of power embedded in our *minutemen, discoverers,* and *peacekeepers.* Given the build-up of idealized weaponry by superpowers in a "New Cold War" discourse, the nuclear sublime—as boundary-threatening force—in effect deconstructs an ideology of nation-state power that would attempt to localize this vastness of space or energy as a national property overcoming rivals through stockpiling "Missiles/Missives." Acts of ideological critique are called for to rupture the romantic sacralization of power and force, if only to sketch in the nuclear totality in which such poems as Ashbery's in *Double Dream of Spring* get written "on the margin/ In our technological society."

Even the most solipsistic poetry does not produce its visions of sublimity apart from larger social forces and dreams, extra-literary tones and themes. Smallness of voice and wryness of concern may simply be a retreat into that which is near at hand, "desert places" closer to the heart, as in the urban multi-voicedness of Faye Kicknosway's *All These Voices* (1986). Yet as Bob Perelman depicts in "Things" (1986), in such a vast system of nuclear dread even "the [postmodern] city doesn't fit in the eye":

> And who is this "they"
> who have terrorized all sentient let's not say "beings"
> with the plurality of their buildings
> the notions in their texts set up
> to test you and me (proud little ones & twos)?
>   (*The First World*, 37)

Fredric Jameson has theorized the result of this technological sublimity as inducing a state of "ontological marginalization" and subjective "decentering" before vast totality: as he claims, representing the unrepresentable, "it is no longer necessary [as in Burke and Kant] to evoke the deity to grasp what such a transindividual system might be." [61] This "transindividual system" which dwarfs the self to credulous capitulation within "glacial showrooms" (Perelman) emanates not from above but from megastructures of Capital. What Jameson claims in a recoding of Burke's sublime (as hyperbole of the self under Capital) is a transvaluation of anxiety before an "artificial sublime" into an ideologically necessitated rapture. The creation of a "Romantic sublime" (as in Stevens) functions to preserve the *pyrrhic* victory of the imagination, dwarfed as it is by configurations not so much of landscape but of technoscape, as in the mixed blessings we confront as nuclear energy. As Jameson laments,

> And indeed, in a situation of radical impotence, there is really little
> else to do than that, to affirm what crushes you and to develop one's

capacity for gratification in an environment which increasingly makes gratification impossible (262).

Contemporary poets of the "deep" and "leaping" image, with their mystique of images served up from unconscious depths and animistic states of mineral/animal being, in part offer merely a nostalgic retreat from the technology-glutted environment of the postmodern into subjective sanctuaries of symbol-worship—which can, ironically, leave the (reified) social totality they complain of all too palpably in place. Robert Bly's politicized surrealism can proffer "leaping images" from psychic depths, as if a priori indictments of some "reptilian" Cold War mentality of the 1950s. As can be seen in Kinnell or Charles Simic, such poets do not just recirculate the discourse of nature as surplus metaphor to be had, as in Emerson, from goldfinches and Vermont ponds. Kinnell's "The Fundamental Project of Technology" voices a Romantic endictment of American enterprises harming the globe, in a stance of vatic pronouncement akin to the "bioregional" poetics/politics of Gary Snyder's *Axe Handles* or Ginsberg's chant against the arms race in *Plutonian Ode*.

In reading such nostalgic poems, however, a fear remains that what Deleuze/Guattari call the *schizoid* subject of Capital has been constructed in such a way as to counter technological anxiety by experiencing a flow of ecstasies before libidinous objects of desire, "being born of the states that it consumes and being reborn with each new state." [62] Given enough material *shocks* and an expanding environment of commodity-infinitude, as I have claimed, the sublime poem works for this "desiring-machine" poet as a structure which produces/reproduces the desire for another unifying experience, another uplift into rapture, the transport of the "body without organs." The poem moves to produce an ecstasy of language ("jouissance"), an excess, by multiplying surface or depth images intended to heal the daily dose of self-division engendered by the forces of a system which furiously stimulates private states of need. This free subject of sublimity is freed merely to consume more libidinal items, nature-signs, which are implicitly determined not by ethical or political but by exchange values: in the words of John Cage, "U.S.A. thinks the Free World is U.S.A.'s / world, is determined to keep it free, / U.S.A.-determined." [63]

Even the "immense dew" of Florida in 1919, say, can generate in Wallace Stevens a "hymn and hymn" to the American ground as self-empowering site of forces "meet for the eye" of this nomadic lawyer from Connecticut, as in "Nomad Exquisite":

> As the immense dew of Florida
> Brings forth hymn and hymn
> From the beholder, . . .
>
> And blessed mornings,
> Meet for the eye of the young alligator,
> And lightning colors
> So, in me, come flinging
> Forms, flames, and the flakes of flames.[64]

Such an American sublime can be promiscuous in the objects which it would consume (dew, palm, alligator, lightning) within this sublime genre as instantiation of a national power commensurate with the "immense dew" produced in natural and technological environments. Stevens is caught up in "forms, flames, and the flakes of flames." Such fireworks in the self are (abstractly) reminiscent of the emergent war technology which was the context of Stevens's formation as an avant-garde poet, 1914–1923, as he sought to write *The Grand Poem: Preliminary Minutiae*.

With ecstatic contact with the physical cosmos broken, or at least reduced to an "optical connection" through technology, oneness with nature was consigned "to the individual as the poetic rapture of starry nights." In World War I, to cite Walter Benjamin's example, "Human multitudes, gases, electrical forces were hurled into the open country, high-frequency currents coursed through the landscape, new constellations rose in the sky, aerial space and ocean depths thundered with propellers, and everywhere sacrificial shafts were dug in Mother Earth" in the attempt to mingle with cosmic forces, as in the experience of subjective mastery that was the sublime. But with this crucial difference: "This immense wooing of the cosmos was enacted for the first time on a planetary scale, that is, in the spirit of technology."[65] The *physis* of technology has created merely a paroxysm of cosmic unification, generating millions of self-fragmenting fits that, for Benjamin, resemble "the bliss of the epileptic" broken open by force of annihilation.

256

Under a homey nuclear umbrella that the imagination must forget about to write at all, this "desiring-machine" poet would consume his or her myriad sublime objects of ecstasy (waterfall, train, dynamo, bridge, skyscraper, New York City, abstract space, the Hotel Bonaventura, the Hudson River, Chairman Mao, infinite soup cans), yet in so doing mimic the American will to proclaim the wonders of nature or technology (our second nature) in another providential act of beholding/subjugating space. As Leo Marx has observed of American industrial transformations effected in the 1830s and 1840s, "Canals, steam boats, mechanized power machinery, locomotives, and the telegraph were repeatedly cited as evidence that the human mind could penetrate the surface of nature, unlock its secrets, and therefore put more and more natural processes to use for human purposes." [66] This triumph of technological sublimity represented, in effect, the cash-value idea of "history as 'progress' "—a *progress* associated in the United States less with political liberation from repressive hierarchies, as Marx goes on to claim, and more with technocratic ideals of efficiency, maximal profit, the lure of high-energy research into fission/fusion.

As Stevens theorized in figures of "majestic" architecture, "noble" statues, as well as "loftiest syllables among loftiest things," "the American sublime" has been increasingly transferred from configurations of nature to transactions of culture and our own urban (secondary) environment of architecture seen as a vast subjugating force. (This theme was anxiously depicted by Henry Adams in "The Dynamo and the Virgin" [1907], of course, and even in the wry aesthetics of *The American Scene* [1907] by Henry James, depicting—on his return to New York City—the money-making skyscrapers of Wall Street blotting out his childhood cathedrals.)

Even more so, a suprapersonal mode of social formation now confronts the poet/subject as a vast system with immense staying power and decentric majesty, dwarfing individual interpretation or eliding agency. And Whitman, ironically enough, was the Homer of such an American sublime, omniverously converting shocks of urban anxiety to cosmic exhilaration through feats of "representational idolatry" before the machinery of the new, as in "Locomotive in Winter" with its futuristic evocation of American power allegorically incarnate in machinery. In the "whit manic" sublime which can "encompass a hurricane with / a single eye"—to use the

257

pun of A. R. Ammons in *Sphere* (1974)—the pain of masses and machineries which can dominate has been (re)experienced as the pleasure of subjective annihilation via symbolic agency and submission of the ego to some technological totality which is assumed to be progressive and self-rectifying: as if benevolent icons of cultural materialism were linking technology to the signatures of the Godhead from Whitman's "Passage to India" to Crane's "Brooklyn Bridge." [67]

Yet doesn't the nuclear sublime *undo* such a large, mythy, power-infatuated tone and stance? In "The Uncreation" (1986), Robert Pinsky warily posits the evacuation (uncreation) of the many-troped globe in terms of the destruction of music, especially human lyricism, that "great excess of song that coats the world." [68] If this is a *displaced* response to the threat of nuclear apocalypse, as I think it is, Pinksy's tone can remain blithe for two reasons: (1) this global end is imagined as another *watery* death, not one of fire; and (2) he posits his own "supreme fiction" in which the gods survive this watery fallout with a stockpile of *their* lyricism: "after the flood the bland Immortals will come / As holy tourists to our sunken world." These Gods reawaken the impulse of song in nature, "humming oblation to what our mouths once made." That is, this remainderless abyss is not fully remainderless: lyrics and mythologies survive their glutted human makers, restored in the mouths of Gods who sing "a choral blast audible in the clouds" and in the mouths of whales, surviving emblems of grandeur. The "white mythology" of Moby Dick still signals towards a natural sublime, but one emptied of human presence.

A more terrifying response to the nuclear sublime has been evoked by Pinsky in the opening poem to *History of My Heart* (1984): as a history-dwarfing artifact absorbing the puny heart, "The Figured Wheel" portrays a vast image of structural over-determination miming a material/spiritual force that grinds up *all* subjects, tropes, and mythologies in its bland, indifferent turning. This futuristic post-machine emerges out of the blessed American ground—its loftiest tropes of making:

> The figured wheel rolls through shopping malls and prisons
> Over farms, small and immense, and the rotten little downtowns.

Covered with symbols, it mills everything alive and grinds
The remains of the dead in the cemeteries, in unmarked graves and
    oceans.

Sluiced by salt water and fresh, by pure and contaminated rivers,
By snow and sand, it separates and recombines all droplets and grains,
Even the infinite sub-atomic particles crushed under the illustrated,
Varying tread of its wide circumferential track.[69]

Whatever this sublimely indifferent force is, it grinds up best and
worst, large and small, into some pulpy festive icon that can incor-
porate *both* a genocidal and a nuclear holocaust, as in these lines
alluding to the arctic terms of *Fate of the Earth:* "So that the wheel
hums and rings as it turns through the births of stars / And through
the dead-world of bomb, fireblast and fallout / Where only a few
doomed races of insects fumble in the smoking grasses." Given this
state of biological annihilation out of which "Even in the scorched
and frozen world of the dead after the holocaust" the Wheel goes
on accreting fresh ornaments and gaudy tropes, Pinsky turns giddy
at the closure of the poem, absorbing his "sweet self" and family
into the wheel's material/spiritual progress—but towards what?
This wheel of figurative sublimity rolls over the globe, evacuating
American selfhood, a mute godhead karmically chewing up its be-
nign makers:

And over the haunts of Robert Pinsky's mother and father
And wife and children and his sweet self
Which he hereby unwillingly and inexpertly gives up, because it is
There, figured and pre-figured in the nothing-transfiguring wheel.

"The Figured Wheel" is one of those postmodern poems which se-
riously attempts to come to representative terms, beyond coy affir-
mations of subjecthood, with Williams's trope-evacuative threat to
poetry: *the bomb puts an end to all that.*

Writing from an Ashbery-like position of social marginalization
and generic diminishment, the critic of Romantic poetry can feel
compelled to produce another vision of *subjective transcendence*
and *higher morality* (based on symbol-making) from within the dis-
cursive heart of American Romanticism. Yet given what has been

mapped as the deconstructive/destructive context of the nuclear
horizon, some measure of negative critical distance, of *ideo-
logiekritik*[70] is called for, unless the poet/critic aspires to write the
sublime epic of some forthcoming nuclear spectacle in which the
Deus Absconditus withdraws in atomic fire, America defeats its
long-lost technological rival, but no First World is left to represent
dialogically—in films like "Atomic Cafe," sublime poems like "The
Figured Wheel," protest lyrics such as "Eve of Destruction" and
Bob Dylan's "Masters of War" or "Jokerman"—spreading *with
venom and wonder* to the Third World of empty space. "Oblivion
ha-ha" will resound in "vacant space" as the world gropes to
emerge beyond the hypocenter and Atomic Dome at Hiroshima.

"Poetically Man Dwells"

To invoke the chastening vocabulary of Martin Heidegger, "tech-
nology" (largely considered) has become the prevailing way of
knowing in this century of Western modernity, a way of approach-
ing the veiled disclosures of Being: "Will we see the lightning-flash
of Being in the essence of technology? The flash that comes out of
stillness, as stillness itself?"[71] These questions from "The Turning"
(1949) remain *open* ones for the epoch of modern science because
what technology has effected is an all-pervasive *aletheia* of "en-
framing" which challenges nature to be no more and no less than
a "standing-reserve" (*Bestand*) of calculable forces, subservient to
instant economic use. In this "revealing that rules in modern tech-
nology" as a "challenging [*Herausfordern*], which puts to nature
the unreasonable demand that it supply energy that can be ex-
tracted and stored" ("The Question Concerning Technology"),
even man becomes "taken as standing-reserve." That is, technology
quietly *technologizes* feats of human knowing, reducing the mind
to robotic gestures as an analogous force of nature, another "cal-
culable complex of the effects of forces" and not the *house* or wit-
ness of Being in the furtive dwellings of language.[72]
 Whether American poetry turned *pastoral* in green retreat or
sublime in heated-up confrontations with technology, after the
"Taylorization" of labor in America, human activity proved to be
more broadly measurable and controllable by serializing tech-

niques that had proved successful in the manipulation of physical objects.[73] By now, as "children of *Sputnik*" and the arms proliferation, American and Russian technocrats have blithely enframed a nuclear force so massive that by 1981 there were ten tons of TNT available to destroy each person on the planet (*Ground Zero*, 60–69; see note 7). Tree-lined or blissed-out, American poetry must quail before such a prospect: the *landscape-as-nuclear-grid* was invented partly by the empowering genius of its own material culture.

Take the more hopeful example of a jet airliner, surely an instance of the technological sublime, as anyone who has stood beneath a gleaming Boeing 747 on a runway can attest. If *"Techne* is a mode of *aletheuein,"* what does this "thing" do to the mind that beholds it as sublime disclosure, as an ontological mode of knowing? For Heidegger, what occurs—has already occurred—is a massive and mute reduction of human *poiesis* to a scientific "bringing forth" that enframes and expedites the use value of Nature:

> Yet an airliner that stands on the runway is surely an object. We can represent the machine so. But then it conceals itself as to what and how it is. Revealed, it stands on the taxi strip only as standing-reserve, inasmuch as it is ordered to ensure the possibility of transportation. For this it must be in its whole structure and in every one of its constituent parts, on call for duty, i. e., ready for takeoff.[74]

In effect, what man has done to the machine he has already done to nature and himself, reducing ("challenging") the sublime energies and forces of Being to a calculus of efficiency, pragmatic "use." If what has been gained is imperious flight across the sky, what has been lost is any lingering sense of nature as awesome or humbling, as beyond this technological "challenge" to dominate and control.

Yet perhaps in the nuclear sublime what has been disclosed is the delusive *limit* of this challenge by the technocratic mentality to nature's forces, the danger of reducing knowing to an instrumentality of *techne*. As Heidegger argues in "The Thing" (1950), technology has abolished vast distances of time and space, but it has brought nature no nearer; indeed it has distanced if not abolished the "thinging thing" and "worlding world" as ontological disclosures, as rapt things with *auras* and *depths* beyond uniformity, efficiency, or commodity-exchange:

261

Man stares at what the explosion of the atom bomb could bring with it. He does not see that the atom bomb and its explosion are the mere final emission of what has long taken place, has already happened. Not to mention the single hydrogen bomb, whose triggering, thought through to its utmost potential, might be enough to snuff out all life on earth. What is this helpless anxiety waiting for, if the terrible has already happened?

Atomic weapons demonstrate that the "terrible has already happened" in the sense that the sublime aura (registered in terror and awe) before the things of nature has been detechnologized, abolished in the *aletheia* of a scientific enframing which rules in the Western episteme as calculus of efficiency and force. The technocratic mentality has enframed a nature of *lost natural sublimity*, thereby displacing the aura of infinitude and power into its own ever-innovative machinery. These works embody that "steeled Cognizance" of engineering that is reified into bridges, canals, satellites, nuclear power plants and space rocketry, as Crane depicts in linking the Brooklyn Bridge to the flight of a lark returning to earth:

O Thou steeled Cognizance whose leap commits
The agile precincts of the lark's return.[75]

Henceforth, things as such no longer "presence" in any active or uplifting sense: like the jet on the runway, what they presence is "standing-reserve," mere use. The atom bomb of 1945 is simply another instance of the objectification and conquest of nature into "standing-reserve": "Science's knowledge, which is compelling within its own sphere, the sphere of objects, already had annihilated things as things long before the atom bomb exploded. The bomb's explosion is only the grossest of all gross confirmations of the long-since-accomplished annihilation of the thing: the confirmation that the thing as a thing remains nil. The thingness of the thing remains concealed, forgotten." *Poetry*, as an older way of knowing more in touch with Greek origins of "bringing forth" and "disclosing," must counter such a reduction of the thing into standing-reserve. Confronting technology, however, can poetry still disclose "the lightning flash of Being in the essence of Technology"—as did Whitman and Crane in moments of euphoric dread?

If scientific investigation of the Real has brought us to the brink of disaster, the annihilation of the thing in more than a semiotic sense of *disambiguation,* Heidegger can only hold out for an agrarian instrument—the jug—to epitomize a more Romantic way of dwelling with handcrafted things as presented in the pastoral lyrics of a Hölderlin: "In a gift of water, in the gift of wine, sky and earth dwell. But the gift of the outpouring is what makes a jug a jug. In the jugness of the jug, sky and earth dwell." [76] Yet we live in a futuristic age which has placed not a jar but a nuclear power-plant in the domineered wilderness of Tennessee. Resisting pastoral nostalgia for such a lost agrarian order, postmodern poetry must disclose the consequences of an American *techne,* this way of knowing which has tapped the sublime forces and energies of Nature, turning them into "standing-reserve" on call as globally uniting/deconstructing powers of creation and destruction.

In Heidegger's prescient analysis, "The flash that comes out of stillness, as stillness itself" (49) will be either the still call of Being's presence in reclaimed structures ("dwellings") of *language,* or the stillness of global annihilation. For poetry of the future will have been written within an ever-present nuclear *aletheia* that threatens to efface what Wallace Stevens called—majestically, with a diminishing tone of self-irony—his tropes "of mere being." Stevens was not alone in trying to theorize/represent "in the bronze distance" of Florida (as in Hartford) the sense of limitlessness emerging beyond "The palm at the end of the mind / Beyond the last thought," *rising.*[77]

Notes

Index

Notes

Introduction

1 Bob Perelman, "Clippings," in *Captive Audience* (Great Barrington, Mass.: The Figures, 1988): 32.

2 Wallace Stevens, "The American Sublime," in *The Collected Poems of Wallace Stevens* (New York: Knopf, 1974): 130. While a longer analysis of the de-idealizing tactics of the sublime in Stevens appears in chapter 7, I would like to invoke two interpretive contexts my reading assumes: in *The Voice in the Margin: Native American Literature and the Canon* (Berkeley and Los Angeles: Univ. of California Press, 1989), Arnold Krupat has theorized the way Euramerican authors and literary canons unconsciously repeat the historical "relation of avoidance justified by an imagined absence," effectively evacuating Native American literatures (98–101); and in *Ariel and the Police: Michel Foucault, William James, Wallace Stevens* (Madison: Univ. of Wisconsin Press, 1988), Frank Lentricchia reads "Anecdote of the Jar" as a representative anecdote of the American will to dominate the Cherokee village of "Tanasi" into the social and discursive networks of "Tennessee" (5–17).

3 A painstaking refusal to intermesh the British and German traditions of the sublime either into a Kantian framework of subjective autonomy or into a Freudian hermeneutic of the unconscious subject is deftly outlined in Peter de Bolla, *The Discourse of the Sublime: Readings in History, Aesthetics and the Subject* (Oxford: Blackwell, 1989). Concentrating on a discourse-analysis of 1756–1763 (the Seven Years' War), when Edmund Burke, Alexander Gerard, and Lord Kames framed their influential theories, de Bolla shows how a "discourse on the sublime" merges into enacting a "discourse of the sublime" within a social framework of inflationary credit and a capital-driven "modernity of speculation and excess" (119) and leads, by moral and political reaction (as in Burkean "terror"), to a stolidly British "conceptualization of the subject as the excess or overplus of discourse itself; as the remainder, that which cannot be appropriated or included within the present [aesthetic] discursive network of control" (6). The "unitary subject" of Longinus gets radically refigured and relocated as "excessive discursivity" and tropes of representative

"voice" (32–40) in ways that, to some extent, set the terms for the liberal subject. The Kantian dynamic of the sublime as tactics of "negative presentation" are argued to perdure as a transcultural dynamic in Jean-François Lyotard, "The Sublime and the Avant-Garde," in *The Lyotard Reader,* ed. Andrew Benjamin (Oxford: Blackwell, 1989): 196–211.

4 The status enhancement and social solidarity presumed by such an ascription of "the American sublime" by art critics in the 1970s, as well as the historical confidence necessary for such as assumption of power to emerge in painters like Church and Newman, are touched upon in Judith Huggins Balfe, "Sociology and the Sublime," *New Literary History* 16 (1985): 237–249. The rapid feedback of literary criticism into art-historical interpretations of American sublimity, especially the Emersonian agonistics of Harold Bloom, is apparent in Bryan J. Wolf, "A Grammar of the Sublime, or Intertextuality Triumphant in Church, Turner, and Cole," *New Literary History* 16 (1985): 321–341. See Lawrence Alloway, "The American Sublime," *Living Arts* 2 (1963) for a reading of the American sublime that predates Bloom's or Barbara Novak's appropriations of this art category to an Emersonian frame.

5 Barnett Newman, "The Sublime Is Now," excerpt from "The Ideas of Art, Six Opinions on What Is Sublime in Art?", in *Theories of Modern Art: A Source Book by Artists and Critics,* ed. Herschel B. Chipp (Berkeley and Los Angeles: Univ. of California Press, 1968): 553.

6 Mutlu Konuk Blasing has challenged this logocentric model of nineteenth-century American poetics with a "generic typing" based on rhetorical habits rooted in the four "master-tropes" of Poe, Emerson, Whitman, and Dickinson, and continued in the poetics of Plath and Eliot, Stevens and Bishop, Pound and O'Hara, and Crane and Ashbery. While I find much to argue with in this synchronic typing of poet by dominant trope in *American Poetry: The Rhetoric of Its Forms* (New Haven: Yale Univ. Press, 1987), Blasing's close readings of the "disarticulating syntax" in Dickinson, Crane, and Ashbery would correct Emerson-based reifications of the American sublime. On the basis of a contrast between metaphoric resemblance and synecdochic identity, Emerson and Whitman are read as distinct poetic traditions, neither one of which holds a monopoly over the American sublime, which, given Blasing's assumption that rhetoric as such establishes continuity, not so oddly turns up as a thematic in a chapter on deconstructive irony, "Hart Crane: Inscribing the Sublime."

7 Arguing that the discourse of the sublime comprised a "double thinking" so deeply embedded in Emerson's era that it created a virtual "second scene" of rhetorical transformation, Donald Pease has written that the seemingly ahistorical transcendence of the American sub-

lime generated convictions of guilt (self-dwarfing) and redemption (self-empowerment) implicitly connected to the ethos of Western expansionism: "Of course the actual source of this will [to the sublime, as in Emerson or Cole] emanated neither from the natural landscape nor from some higher will but from man's future power over the landscape expressed in the policy of western expansionism. . . . Should anyone happen to feel guilty about this activity, the sublime, through its capacity to instill in the observer the concomitant feelings of diminution and awe, at once punishes the culprit in advance (through the feelings of being dwarfed by Nature) and exonerates him (through feelings of awe and rapture accompanying the vision of the sublime)" ("Sublime Politics," in *The American Sublime*, ed. Mary Arensberg [Albany: State Univ. of New York Press, 1986]: 46–47). I take Pease's analysis to be one of the best available interpretations connecting tropes of the American sublime to the political unconsciousness of writers such as Emerson and Whitman.

8   If the sublime enlists the self in a power struggle that, resisted or transformed, involves "grim forces of possession and domination," and this genre of empowerment has been traditionally regarded as a male domain, the sublime remains "a genre the woman writer needs." The oedipal battle of ego aggression and reaction formation can be, and has been, refigured by women writers into a pre-oedipal scenario bespeaking interconnection, merger, and erotic community. At least that is the challenge of Patricia Yaeger, who invokes the sublime writing of French feminists as a contemporary example of the genre and then provides a typology of "the female sublime": "failed sublime," "sovereign sublime," and "feminine sublime" are the types she adduces in works by Bishop, Nikki Giovanni, and Eudora Welty. See Patricia Yaeger, "Towards the Female Sublime," in *Gender & Theory: Dialogues on Feminist Criticism*, ed. Linda Kauffman (New York: Blackwell 1989): 191–212, as well as the response by Lee Edelman, "At Risk in the Sublime" (213–24), who questions whether Yaeger is not defining "a lesbian rather than a female sublime." National differences are, in the framework of such gender consolidations, beside the point, as Anglo-American or French examples merge to supply instances of "the Romantic sublime" as a genre of oedipal aggression or pre-oedipal mutuality. My own use of Bradstreet at the origins of an American sublime, however, calls into question such a literary differentiation based exclusively upon gender division.

9   The paradoxes and "double logic" controlling Emerson's appropriation of the Enlightenment sublime into a discourse underwriting *both* utilitarian manipulation and romantic preservation of nature are outlined in Howard Horwitz, "Respecting Nature: Sublime Paradox," in *Essays on Perceiving Nature*, ed. Diane Macintyre DeLuca (Hono-

lulu: Perceiving Nature Conference, 1988): 186–96. The representative structure of Emersonian action—the bipolar way, for example, in which the American sublime both acts upon and is enacted in the language of "Self-Reliance" or "Circles"—is carefully worked out in Richard Grusin, "Revisionism and the Structure of Emersonian Action," *American Literary History* 1 (1989): 404–31. I adduce this analysis and relate it to the sublime to bolster the circular way "representation" has been used in my own argument: Emerson both represents and is represented by the American sublime, a way of structuring the subject both as agent and as discursive effect of larger social transactions such as inventing the sublime.

10 Tactics from Foucault's "Nietzsche, Genealogy, History," in *Language, Counter-Memory, Practice,* ed. Donald Bouchard (Ithaca, N.Y.: Cornell Univ. Press, 1977) are applied to American literary practices in David Latané, "An Interview with Frank Lentricchia," *Critical Texts* 5 (1988): 16. To forestall being accused of positing "the American sublime" to essentialize a neo-pragmatic version of American exceptionality rather than to construct/deconstruct the very nationalistic uses to which such sublimity has been applied, I would also invoke Ernesto Laclau's concept of "the political imaginary": as Laclau argues of such genealogical practices, "It is necessary to pass from a culture centered on the absolute—that therefore denies the dignity of the specific—to a culture of systematic irreverence. 'Genealogy,' 'deconstruction' and other similar strategies are ways of questioning the dignity of the 'presence,' of the 'origins,' of the form" ("Building a New Left: An Interview with Ernesto Laclau," *Strategies* 1[1988]: 22). On such imaginal constructions of the sublime as a totalizing political sublimation, at once courting and resisting any finalized representation into the subject or state, see Slavoj Žižek, *The Sublime Object of Ideology* (London: Verso, 1989): 201–12.

11 The dread and wonder of domination/liberation which the "technological activism" of America represents to contiguous cultures and nation-states such as Canada is outlined, for example, in Arthur Kroker, *Technology and the Canadian Mind: Innis/McLuhan/Grant* (New York: St. Martin's, 1985).

Chapter 1. An American Sublime—"With Venom and Wonder"

1 For deftly individuated readings of the American sublime, see Gary Lee Stonum, "Emily Dickinson's Calculated Sublime" and Joseph

Kronick, "On the Border of History: Whitman and the American Sublime," in *The American Sublime*, ed. Mary Arensberg (Albany: State Univ. of New York Press, 1986). Jean-François Lyotard connects the Kantian sublime of "negative presentation" to avant-garde tactics in "Newman: The Instant" and "The Sublime and the Avant-Garde," in *The Lyotard Reader*, ed. Andrew Benjamin, (Oxford: Blackwell, 1989). "The textual sublime" emerges from variously deconstructive readings in *The Textual Sublime: Deconstruction and Its Differences*, ed. Hugh J. Silverman and Gary E. Aylesworth (Albany: State Univ. of New York Press, 1990): xii.

2   Bob Dylan, *Lyrics, 1962–1985* (New York: Knopf, 1985): 392. Dylan creates American jeremiads that are centered in the sublime hyperbole of "visualization *(phantasia)*" as in "image-production" that lets the poet "*see* [identify with] what he is saying and bring it *visually* before the audience"—as in his space-drenched, paranoaic Zarathustra of home-made grandeur, "Jokerman": "In the smoke of the twilight on a milk-white steed, / Michelangelo indeed could have carved out your features. / Resting in the fields, far from the turbulent space, / Half asleep near the stars with a small dog licking your face" (471). I quote "Longinus" (15.1) here from D. A. Russell's translation of *On Sublimity*, in *Classical Literary Criticism: Translations and Interpretations*, ed. Alex Preminger et al. (New York: Ungar, 1974): 204. (Subsequent citations for Longinus are given in parentheses in the text.)

3   In later chapters, I will foreground the moment when the pragmatic trope of the American sublime decreases itself into a romantic ideology bespeaking technocratic mastery over "nothingness" in the post-Hiroshima era.

4   James Haug, "Cloud Rises Seven Miles from Observers" *Massachusetts Review* 30 (1989): 13. Also see James Haug, *The Stolen Car* (Amherst: Massachusetts Univ. Press, 1989).

5   Geoffrey H. Hartman, *Criticism in the Wilderness: The Study of Literature Today* (New Haven: Yale Univ. Press, 1980): 119. Hartman is worrying the claims to "counter-sublimity" of Harold Bloom. See Harold Bloom, "Mimesis and the Sublime," in the introduction to his *The Art of the Critic: Literary Theory and Criticism, from the Greeks to the Present*, vol. 1 (New York: Chelsea House, 1985). For related concerns set in a more European context, see Marshall Brown, V. Fortunati, and G. Franci, eds., *La Via al Sublime* (Florence: Alinea, 1987); and Margaret Brose, "Leopardi's 'L'Infinito' and the Language of the Romantic Sublime," *Poetics Today* 4 (1983): 47–71.

6   See Harold Bloom, *The Anxiety of Influence: A Theory of Poetry* (London: Oxford Univ. Press, 1973) and "Emerson and Whitman:

The American Sublime," in *Poetry and Repression: Revisionism From Blake to Stevens* (New Haven: Yale Univ. Press, 1976); 235–66, to invoke two examples of his early usages. Josephine Miles formalizes the adjectival diction and phrasal syntax that differentiate a discourse of American poetry in "The Poetry of Praise: An American Mode," in *Eras & Modes in English Poetry* (Berkeley and Los Angeles: Univ. of California Press, 1964): 224–48. The definitive studies remain those of Thomas Weiskel, *The Romantic Sublime: Studies in the Structure and Psychology of Transcendence* (Baltimore: Johns Hopkins Univ. Press, 1976); and Mary Arensberg, ed., *The American Sublime* (Albany: State Univ. of New York Press, 1986). Subsequent citations for Weiskel and Arensberg are given in parentheses in the text. On figurative *aporias* of any "Longinian" poetic, see Neil Hertz, *The End of the Line: Essays on Psychoanalysis and the Sublime* (New York: Columbia Univ. Press, 1985); and, in a scholarly twist on this whole genre, Daniel T. O'Hara reads critics such as Bloom, Hartman, and Paul de Man ("Nietzsche's Teacher") as seeking to individuate a "Critic's Sublime" in their own right, in *The Romance of Interpretation: Visionary Criticism from Pater to de Man* (New York: Columbia Univ. Press, 1985).

7   Would Japan nominate the *haiku* or *tanka* as globally sublime? Would Great Britain, island of Shakespeare and Milton, foreclose all future sublimes from the English language? Would Canadian poets like Michael Ondaatje or Margaret Atwood brag of their country's wilderness bulk as self-made sublimity or automatic epic? As a poetic form, however, the sublime gets nationally inflected and historically differentiated.

8   Thomas Weiskel, *Romantic Sublime*, 3; on the "beyond" of any idealist sublime, see Walter Jackson Bate's still-compelling analysis, *The Burden of the Past and the English Poet* (London: Chatto, 1971): 127–34; and for a maximally deconstructive approach to the dynamic of the Romantic sublime, see Paul de Man, "Phenomenality and Materiality in Kant," in *The Textual Sublime*, 90–91.

9   Ralph Waldo Emerson, "Considerations By the Way," in *Conduct of Life* [1860], *Complete Works of Ralph Waldo Emerson*, ed. Edward Waldo Emerson (Boston: Houghton Mifflin, 1904): 256.

10 General Farrell's disturbing evocation of the bomb at Los Alamos is discussed in the last two chapters of this book, on the "postmodern" and "nuclear sublime."

11 Pierre Bourdieu's decoding of "taste," cultural "distinction" and literary "style" as signs of symbolic power and social prestige is used in Dick Hebdige, "The Impossible Object: Towards a Sociology of the

Sublime," *New Formations* 1 (1987): 47–76. Along these lines of so-
cial demystification, Bloom's model of poetic selfhood has been re-
coded by Gary Shapiro as reflecting an "entrepreneurship" model of
capitalist vocation: "The pattern of that tradition [of the Anglo-
American sublime] is one in which there is an unrelenting pressure on
the aspiring poet to create his own poetic capital by overcoming the
achievements of his precursors. Competition and individual success
become the presiding values of poetry as they do in civil society"
(217). Even critics can be seen to open "a new economic frontier"
through new metaphors and estranged diction. See Gary Shapiro,
"From the Sublime to the Political: Some Historical Notes," *New Lit-
erary History* 16 (1985): 213–35.

12 Jerome C. Christensen, "The Sublime and the Romance of the Other"
Diacritics 8 (1978):10–23. A compelling critique of Bloom's canoni-
cal claim that "poetry is [the] property" of *becoming major* that can
only take place through an oedipal ego-struggle with intertextual
greatness is argued by Louis A. Renza, in pastoral and regional terms
of resistance, in *"A White Heron" and the Question of Minor Liter-
ature* (Madison: Univ. of Wisconsin Press, 1984): 11–18.

13 Fredric Jameson, *The Political Unconscious: Narrative as a Socially
Symbolic Act* (Ithaca, N.Y.: Cornell Univ. Press, 1981): 30. (Jameson
echoes the "anti-hermeneutic" of Deleuze/Guattari, which would en-
act "the text" as a symptom of desiring-production mechanisms of
"Capital.") Parenthetical page references appear in the text for sub-
sequent citations.

14 Walt Whitman, *The Collected Writings: Comprehensive Reader's Edi-
tion,* ed. Harold W. Blodgett and Sculley Bradley (New York: Norton,
1968): 711. On the will to sacralize the American continent into an
incarnation of sublimity/entrepreneurial individualism, see Myra Jeh-
len's critique, *American Incarnation: The Individual, The Nation,
and the Continent* (Cambridge: Harvard Univ. Press, 1986): "The
sublime—that is to say, the world beyond, the realm of the transcen-
dent, infinity—functions in this cosmology [of American self-
realization, as in the ethos of Emerson or F. O. Matthiessen] as a
moral imperative, an objective correlative for the infinity of human
aspiration" (232).

15 This Longinian claim to self-transcendence underlies the definition of
the humanistic sublime in Weiskel's *Romantic Sublime* (see note 6):
3. The deconstructive war upon the figurative legacies and idealist
habits of the American sublime comprises the main concern of chap-
ter 7, "Wallace Stevens: Decreating the American Sublime." A dy-
namic fusing *humilitas-sublimitas* is related to "woundings" of the

sublime ego in James D. Bloom, *The Stock of Available Reality: R. P. Blackmur and John Berryman* (Lewisburg, Ohio: Bucknell Univ. Press, 1984), chapter 4, "The American Sublime."

16 Terry Eagleton, *Literary Theory: An Introduction* (Minneapolis: Univ. of Minnesota Press, 1983): 15.

17 Perry Miller, *The Life of the Mind in America, from the Revolution to the Civil War* (New York: Harcourt, 1965): 321. Subsequent citations are identified by parenthetical page references in the text.

18 As an analysis of techniques of "speed" and productive expenditures, Cecilia Tichi's *Shifting Gears: Technology, Literature, Culture in Modernist America* (Chapel Hill: Univ. of North Carolina Press, 1987) is argued from within an idealist mythology of American power. More attuned to the ideology of poetic form is Marjorie Perloff's *The Futurist Moment: Avant-Garde, Avant Guerre and the Language of Rupture* (Chicago: Univ. of Chicago Press, 1986) which tracks "the exhilaration that greeted the new technology" and intoxication with the sublime energies of industrialization (through world war) into "proto-Fascist" politics (29).

19 Bryan Jay Wolf, *Romantic Re-Vision: Culture and Consciousness in Nineteenth-Century American Painting and Literature* (Chicago: Univ. of Chicago Press, 1982): 245. (Page references for subsequent citations are given in parentheses in the text.) On the sublime as an allegory of national power deployed at home as in the remote Andes, see Franklin Kelly, *Frederic Edwin Church and the National Landscape* (Washington, D.C.: Smithsonian, 1988): as Kelly quotes from *The Knickerbocker* of July 1861, "None need be told that Church is great—that he is national." On the national obsession with "*long* poems" of phrasal aggregation, numinous place, and self-magnification into an "I, Maximus" voice, see James E. Miller, Jr., *The American Quest for a Supreme Fiction: Whitman's Legacy in the Personal Epic* (Chicago: Univ. of Chicago UP, 1979). As Marjorie Perloff observes of the droll, city-worn, *retro*-Whitmanic inclusiveness that generates the post-hipster poetry in Andrei Codrescu's anthology, *American Poetry Since 1970: Up Late* (New York: Four Walls Eight Windows, 1987), "The *most exciting* years in American poetry? To make such extravagant claims is in keeping with the contemporary urge to MAKE IT, if not NEW, at least BIG" (*American Book Review* 10 [May–June, 1988]: 12). American garrulousness and inclusiveness of form may obtain even in the swarming "talk poems" of David Antin, who mocks more epic or bric-a-brac poems "organized around something like sears by and large" ("Radical Coherency", in Codrescu, 195).

20 Robert Frost, "The Most of It," *The Poetry of Robert Frost*, ed. Ed-

274

ward Connery Latham (New York: Holt, Rinehart & Winston, 1974): 338.

21 Ron Silliman, *Lit* (Elmwood, Conn.: Potes & Poets Press, 1987): 26. I draw upon critiques of this by-now-reified imagery of the psychosexual surreal in Paul Breslin, "How to Read the New Contemporary Poem," *American Scholar* 47 (1978): 357–70, and Robert Pinsky, *The Situation of Poetry: Contemporary Poetry and Its Traditions* (Princeton: Princeton Univ. Press, 1976): 162–65. One assumption, immune to critique, becomes, as Pinsky claims, that "perception is more to be trusted than reflection, former ideas are obstacles, and the large, blank, irreducible phenomena are the truest incarnations of reality" (165).

22 Karl Marx and Frederick Engels, *The German Ideology,* ed. C. J. Arthur (New York: International, 1970): 47.

23 Walter Benjamin, *Charles Baudelaire: A Lyric Poet in the Era of High Capitalism* (London: NLB, 1973): 154. Benjamin's over-reading of poetic imagery is outlined—as are other critics' refigurings of the sublime mode—in Paul H. Fry, *The Reach of Criticism: Method and Perception in Literary Criticism* (New Haven: Yale Univ. Press, 1983), chapter Five, "The Instance of Walter Benjamin: Distraction and Perception in Criticism."

24 Jonathan Culler, *The Pursuit of Signs: Semiotics, Literature, Deconstruction* (Ithaca, N.Y.: Cornell Univ. Press, 1981): 5. Page references for subsequent citations are in parentheses in the text.

25 Barbara Johnson, "The Frame of Reference: Poe, Lacan, Derrida," in *The Critical Difference: Essays in the Contemporary Rhetoric of Reading* (Baltimore: Johns Hopkins Univ. Press, 1980): 119. To incarnate the sublime into heroic selfhood remains, in some respects, the theologically displaced narrative that Harold Bloom is still figuring forth. Bloom's *Ruin the Sacred Truths: Poetry and Belief from the Bible to the Present* (Cambridge: Harvard Univ. Press, 1989) runs the Western tradition of Judeo-Christian sublimity from "the hypothesis of the J author," through Jeremiah, Job, Homer, Dante, Shakespeare, Milton, Blake, Wordsworth, Freud, Kafka, and Beckett, for whom "the isolation and terror of the high sublime returns" as catastrophic creation and post-theological nihilism. This is a heroic cast, exclusively male and delighting in solipsistic grandeur, but this is not the only way to figure forth the emergence and transmission of the American sublime.

26 Louis Althusser, "Ideology and Ideological State Apparatuses (Notes Towards an Investigation)" [1969], in *Lenin and Philosophy,* trans. Ben Brewster (New York: Monthly Review Press, 1971): 162. Alex Callinicos invokes Althusser on "ideology" (from *For Marx*) in *Al-*

thusser's Marxism (London: Pluto Press, 1976): "An ideology is a system (with its own logic and rigour) of representations (images, myths, ideas, or concepts, depending on the case) endowed with a historical existence and role within a given society" (61). The sublime would function as one such "image," inside, yet distant from, the all-compelling hold of American ideology. For a critique of Althusser's ascription to art of special status "as a displayer of ideological contradictions," see Catherine Gallagher's more Foucauldian claim that "under certain historical circumstances, the display of ideological contradictions is completely consonant with the maintenance of oppressive social relations," in her "Marxism and the New Historicism," in *The New Historicism,* ed. H. Aram Veeser (New York: Routledge, 1989): 43–44.

27   See Louis Althusser, "A Letter on Art in Reply to André Daspre," in *Lenin and Philosophy,* 222–23 and 237. My analysis of the sublime as a dialogical genre also assumes the contextualized semiotics of V. N. Vološinov [and M. M. Bakhtin], *Marxism and the Philosophy of Language,* trans. Ladislav Matejka and I. R. Titunik (Cambridge: Harvard Univ. Press, 1986): "Behavioral ideology is that atmosphere of unsystematized and unfixed inner and outer speech which endows our every instance of behavior and action and our every 'conscious' state with meaning" (91). Any poem, as a more formalized ideological creation, maintains a dialogue with such a climate of social ideas, images, habits and pseudo-ideas, "just as any literary work or cognitive idea is dead without living, evaluative perception of it" (91).

28   Gayatri Spivak, "The Politics of Interpretations," in *The Politics of Interpretation,* ed. W. J. T. Mitchell (Chicago: Univ. of Chicago Press, 1983): 347.

29   Sacvan Bercovitch, "American as Canon and Context," talk revised as "Afterword" to *Ideology and Classic American Literature* (Cambridge: Cambridge Univ. Press, 1986): 418–39.

30   I quote from Henry Reeve's first translation of Alexis de Tocqueville, *Democracy in America,* vol. 2 ([New York: Langley, 1840]; New York, Knopf, 1945): 3; throughout the book, except for my phrase "puny democratic ego," which tropes upon Tocqueville's explanation of why American authors turn to "an inflated style" as a way to magnify "a very puny object: namely, himself" (77), I will quote from George Lawrence's translation (New York: Harper, 1966). Subsequent citations from this edition are identified by parenthetical page references. The potentially *violent* force of the American sublime that Tocqueville praises/laments is located not so much in Niagara Falls, nor in locomotives, but in the tyranny of social opinion and mass conformity: ". . . the omnipotence of the majority driving the minor-

ities to desperation and forcing them to appeal to physical force" (240). Like an early Baudrillard, however, he is rather amazed, traveling westward in a frontier mail coach, by the sheer mobility of information and transportation across the vacant American vastness, now become the sublime of Interstate-40: "It is hard to imagine how incredibly quickly ideas circulate in these empty spaces" (279). This puny American ego, given to "vast" conceptions and "lofty" ideals in poetry, is *threatened* by this desert emptiness as well as by self-dwarfing democratic masses: "He is seen but for a moment wandering on the verge of two abysses, and then is lost" (455). In a way, for Tocqueville, America is an open-air prison.

31 Weiskel, *Romantic Sublime,* 6. Theorizing the sublime as an oedipal structure of feeling and trope that evolved in the eighteenth and nineteenth centuries to cope with the boredom and anxiety of industrial alienation if not the death of God, Weiskel hedges on applying "the Dynamical Sublime" to newer technologies of force: "Black holes, we might all agree, are in the present state of knowledge an occasion for the sublime; but how about the ungraspable magnitude of the hydrogen bomb?—possibly that too" (35).

32 Jean-François Lyotard confusingly collapses the modern into the postmodern sublime in "Answering the Question: What is Postmodernism?," in *The Postmodern Condition: A Report on Knowledge,* trans. Geoff Bennington and Brian Massumi [and Régis Durand] (Minneapolis: Univ. of Minnesota Press, 1984): 71–82: "I think in particular that it is in the aesthetic of the sublime that modern art (including literature) finds its impetus and the logic of avant-gardes finds its axioms" (p. 77). Gary Shapiro summarizes this turn in cultural criticism from solacing aesthetics of "the beautiful" (as in the well-wrought urns of New Criticism) to struggles to represent "the sublime" (as in Heidegger, Benjamin, Bloom, and Lyotard) in "From the Sublime to the Political," *New Literary History,* 16 (1985): "Today there is a widely held impression that only criticism oriented toward the sublime is really interesting, regardless of its political tendency" (217). Even American *ethnography* in the 1980s, for example, has shifted its narratives away from scientist closure and formal totalization of other cultures ("the beautiful") towards representing the "unnameable" of non-Western cultures through "'writing at the limit' ["the poetic sublime"], where we seek to push against limits imposed by conventions of syntax, meaning, and genre," (Stephen. A. Tyler, "Post-Modern Ethnography: From Document of the Occult to Occult Document," in *Writing Culture: The Poetics and Politics of Ethnography,* ed. James Clifford and George E. Marcus [Berkeley and Los Angeles: Univ. of California Press, 1986]: 137).

33 See Terrence Des Pres, "Self/Landscape/Grid," in *Writing in a Nuclear Age,* ed. Jim Schley (Hanover, N.H.: New England Univ. Press, 1984): 11. Lamenting the absence of "greatness" in literary studies caused by the spread of poststructural critiques (which would undermine any canon ascribing "sublime" status to authors such as Whitman or works such as *Moby Dick*), Walter Jackson Bate contends, like Longinus at Harvard—,"No one believes in greatness." See James Atlas, "The Battle of the Books," *New York Times Magazine* (5 June 1988): 85. But at such a decontextualized level of ideality—where "sublimity" will only equal the essentiality of "literary greatness" and vice versa—"the sublime" becomes useless as a criterion of cultural value, genre, or interpretive device.

    Though I will recur to Bate's burden-of-the-past model of sublimity, giving a more pragmatic twist to such idealism, I would keep the "corporate knowledge" embedded in the American *sublime* particularistic. As Charles Bazerman observed of Geoffrey Hartman's idea of criticism as a knowledge-producing discourse: "Terms such as *topos, apostrophe, sonnet, turn, enjambment,* and *sublime* are the critic's basic conceptual equipment, learned as part of professional training. On another level, however, the literary terms are more than technical, for each reverberates with former uses and examples. One can know and understand *deoxyribose* on the basis of modern chemistry alone, but to understand the *sublime* one must not only have read Longinus and be familiar with the ensuing critical debate to modern times, one must have read and experienced a wide range of poems that embody the development and variation of that concept" ("What Written Knowledge Does: Three Examples of Academic Discourse," *Philosophy of the Social Sciences* 11 [1981]: 361–87: 376).

34 For postmodern deconstructions of *Nihonga*—the theory of Japanese exceptionality, style, and imperial culture as "number one"—see the special issue of *South Atlantic Quarterly* 87 (1988) edited by Masao Miyoshi and H. D. Harootunian on "Postmodernism and Japan." Our own case of *Americanga* cannot claim Cold War exemption from such moral/political deconstructions. Moving beyond theories of American exceptionality, there still remains within American Studies the need for a broader sense of cultural outsidedness (*vnenakhodimost*) and speculations essaying the boundaries and deformations of a post-Hiroshima sublimity that is all-too-American in origin as in outreach.

35 Walt Whitman, preface to *Leaves of Grass: A Facsimile of the First Edition,* ed. Richard Bridgman (San Francisco: Chandler, 1968): iv–v.

Chapter 2. Preliminary Minutiae: Pluralizing the Genre of the American Sublime

1   Terms particularizing the American sublime in my opening paragraph are taken from poems by Wallace Stevens: "The Idea of Order at Key West" (1934), "Evening Without Angels" (1934), and "The American Sublime" (1935), in *The Collected Poems of Wallace Stevens* (New York: Knopf, 1974); 128, 136, 130. "High speech" is how Amiri Baraka defines the charged-up language of poetry in Ron Mann's performance video, *Poetry in Motion*. Jeffers' poem on "great-enough," overlaying natural *and* technological sublimes, is called "Phenomena," from *Roan Stallion, Tamar, and Other Poems* (New York: Boni, 1925); 91. Andy Warhol responds, "bored but hyper," to the postmodern sublime of volcanoes and flaming skyscrapers in *Vesuvius by Warhol* (Napoli: Electa, 1985): 35–36, as well as in a series of paintings on Vesuvius exploding.

2   Situating poetry on a continuum with everyday language, Bakhtin contends that language-genres are inherited *forms of seeing and interpreting* that provide the subject with a set of formal dispositions and tonalities which "throughout the centuries of their life [have] accumulate[d] forms of seeing and interpreting particular aspects of the world" (M. M. Bakhtin, *Speech Genres & Other Late Essays,* trans. Vern W. McGee [Austin: Univ. of Texas Press, 1986]: 5). As Bakhtin contends, "There exist *speech genres* (everyday, rhetorical, scientific, literary, and so forth). Speech genres are typical models for constructing a speech whole" (127) and, as such, situate the "dialogue" of utterance and response. However "exalted" or "high-thinking" the *tone* of American poetry might get, Robert Frost argued [c. Jan. 1918, Amherst] that it should abide "within the colloquial": "All writing, I don't care how exalted, how lyrical, or how seemingly far removed from the dramatic, must be as colloquial as this passage from [Emersons's] "Monadnoc" comes to. I am as sure that the colloquial is the root of every good poem as I am that the national is the root of all thought and art" (*Selected Letters of Robert Frost,* ed. Lawrence Thompson [New York: Holt, Rinehart & Winston, 1964]: 228).

3   Frances Basham, Bob Ughetti and Paul Rambali, *Car Culture* (New York: Delilah, 1984): 111.

4   Martin Heidegger, *Nietzsche,* vol. 1, *The Will to Power as Art,* trans. David Farrell Krell (New York: Harper, 1979): 115–23: "'the effect of artworks is *arousal of the art-creating state,* rapture'" (117); Friedrich Nietzsche, *Untimely Meditations,* trans. R. J. Hollingdale (Cambridge: Cambridge Univ. Press, 1983): 94–95.

5 Ralph Waldo Emerson, "Self-Reliance," in *Selections from Ralph Waldo Emerson,* ed. Stephen E. Whicher (Boston: Houghton, 1960): 164. Page references for subsequent citations appear in parentheses in the text. A reader's sublime results from dispossession, blockage, and self-silencing before the "alienated majesty" of the other's language (which sounds no better than your own, indeed may be your own best words): "In every work of genius we recognize our own rejected thoughts; they come back to us with a certain alienated majesty" (147). Emerson's stand serves as a productive belief in the power of self-reliance—the conviction that the utterance of the other is one with the language of the inner self—and echoes Longinus's much-quoted claim in *Peri Hypsos* that, in such passages, it is "as if instinctively, our soul is uplifted by the true sublime; it takes a proud flight, and is filled with joy and vaunting, as though it had itself produced what it has heard."

6 Ezra Pound depicts the struggle to forge a classically sublime style in "Hugh Selwyn Mauberly" (1920), breaking with more Victorian commodity-forms and American vulgarity—hence, this grandeur is "wrong from the start." James Clifford claims that such levelings of the sublime into an interplay of high and low tonalities and defamiliarized images became "characteristic of global modernity": " 'Culture,' having barely survived this postwar barrage [of Surrealism and Dada, etc.], was now resolutely lower case, a principle of relative order in which the sublime and the vulgar were treated as symbols of equal significance" ("On Ethnographic Surrealism," *Comparative Studies in Society and History* 23 [1981]: 539–64, 548). On the hollow or de-transcendentalized sublimity of Mallarmé's *azur,* see Louis Wirth Marvick, *Mallarmé and the Sublime* (Albany: State Univ. of New York Press, 1986): 51, 125.

7 George Oppen, "An Adequate Vision: From the Daybooks" [selected by Michael Davidson], *Ironwood* 26 (1985):26.

8 George Oppen, *Of Being Numerous* [1968], in *Collected Poems of George Oppen* (New York: New Directions, 1975): 151. On Oppen's sublime, see Kevin Oderman, "Earth and Awe: The One Poetry of George Oppen," *Sagetrieb* 3 (1984): 63–73, and Michael Heller, *Conviction's Net of Branches: Essays on the Objectivist Poets and Poetry* (Carbondale: Southern Illinois Univ. Press, 1985).

9 From a list of "Ten American Shrines" from *Roadside America* by Jack Barth, Doug Kirby, Ken Smith and Mike Wilkins, published in *Harper's* 273 (Sept. 1986): 21.

10 *"Mock* discursive"/"mock descriptive" are terms used by Robert Pinsky in *The Situation of Poetry: Contemporary Poetry and Its Traditions* (Princeton: Princeton Univ. Press, 1976), for example, describ-

ing "New York poets" (93, 135). Two of Pinsky's points on the
modernist sublime bear repeating: (1) *contra* Imagism, there occur "a
series of strategies for retaining or recovering the elevation of Victo-
rian diction" (26); and (2) many postmodern poems (his examples
are from Louise Bogan, Frank O'Hara, Charles Wright, Theodore
Roethke, and Sylvia Plath) remain grounded in Romantic conventions
of *wonder* as a form-shattering emotion, wedded to nature as pres-
ence: " 'Wonder' is an inclusive name for our most significant feelings
in response to nature, an abrupt and non-referential awe. It is an emo-
tional term, as 'description' is a rhetorical term. Wonder is non-
referential in the sense that as a feeling it seems unrelated, by cause
or analogy, to the rest of life" (118). Kenneth Koch's mock-
Whitmanic poem is from *The Pleasures of Peace and Other Poems*
(New York: Grove, 1969): 35.

11 Marvin Bell, "In America," in *These Green-Going-to-Yellow* (New
York: Atheneum, 1981); 26; Rainer Maria Rilke, "Die Erst Elegie"
[1911–1912] in *Duino Elegies;* Philip Levine, "Last Words," in *Sweet
Will* (New York: Atheneum, 1985); Diane Wakoski, "A Snowy Win-
ter in East Lansing," *Sulphur* 16 (1986):89. I would add, as qualifi-
cation, that Philip Levine is quite capable of forging a down-to-earth
sublime mode, as in a wondrous poem like "They Feed They Lion"
which paratactically, like Whitman, lifts Motown Detroit into an em-
blem of its mythic (football) totem, the NFL's Detroit Lions rising up
out of working-class ghettoes:

Out of burlap sacks, out of bearing butter,
Out of black bean and wet slate bread,
Out of the acids of rage, the candor of tar,
Out of creosote, gasoline, drive shafts, wooden dollies
They lion grow.

12 Robert Pinsky, *An Explanation of America* (Princeton: Princeton
Univ. Press, 1979): 42–58.

13 Mikhail Bakhtin, " 'Notes' (1970–1971)," in *Bakhtin: Essays and
Dialogues on His Work*, ed. Gary Saul Morson (Chicago: Univ. of
Chicago Press, 1986). Also see Michael Davidson, "Discourse in Po-
etry: Bakhtin and Extensions of the Dialogical," in *Code of Signals:
Recent Writings in Poetics,* ed. Michael Palmer (Berkeley: North At-
lantic Books, 1983): 143–50; and Rob Wilson, "Lexical Scapegoat-
ing: The Pure and Impure of American Poetry," *Poetics Today* 8
(1987): 45–63.

14 Walt Whitman, "By Blue Ontario's Shore," in *Leaves of Grass: Com-
prehensive Reader's Edition,* ed. Harold W. Blodgett and Sculley
Bradley (New York: Norton, 1968): 340–55 (subsequent citations

are by page references in text); Margaret Randall, ed., *Risking a Somersault in the Air: Conversations with Nicaraguan Writers* (San Francisco: Solidarity, 1984): 8–9; Kuo Mo-Jo, "The Good Morning" [1920], *Selected Poems From The Goddesses* (Peking: Foreign Languages Press, 1978): 20.

15 On the gender-influenced yet highly individualized relationship obtaining between Dickinson's poetry and the "corporeal anxieties" that mark the sublimity of Emerson, and the Romantic sublime more generally, see Joanne Feit Diehl, "In the Twilight of the Gods: Women Poets and the American Sublime," in Arensberg, *The American Sublime* (Albany: State Univ. of New York Press, 1986) and Gary Lee Stonum, *The Dickinson Sublime* (Madison: Univ. of Wisconsin Press, 1990). Terms of "native wonderment" and "unvanquished space" reflect Crane's tormented interiorizing of Whitman's sublime in the "Cape Hatteras" section of *The Bridge* (1930), in *The Complete Poems and Selected Letters and Prose of Hart Crane,* ed. Brom Weber (Garden City, N.Y.: Doubleday, 1966): 88–95.

16 Charles Newman, *The Post-Modern Aura: The Act of Fiction in an Age of Inflation* (Evanston: Northwestern Univ. Press, 1985): 25; Alan Williamson, *Introspection and Contemporary Poetry* (Cambridge: Harvard Univ. Press, 1984): 190.

17 I draw these terms of aesthetic sublimity from Stephen Westfall, "Ripp's Romantic Theater," *Art in America* 74 (Jan. 1986): 107–8. Westfall argues that in the sublime, "the individual is annihilated before the sublime vista, the spectacle of nature's indifference"; but, paradoxically, we sense "the presence of the artist behind the curtain, pulling the levers" (108)—acknowledging these outmoded conventions of grandeur. In some ways, Charles Altieri's critique of "the scenic mode" as a reigning period style of postmodernism grounded in roadside epiphanies and an ethos of domestication attempts to demystify this sublime as rhetorically suspect: "[David] Young and [William] Stafford are engaged in renegotiating a difficult passage between two destructive forces; on one side lies the interminable self-consciousness that cripples so much of contemporary writing and on the other the false sublimity and vacuous prophecy of what passed as speculative poetic thought a decade ago" (*Self and Sensibility in Contemporary American Poetry* [Cambridge: Cambridge Univ. Press, 1984]: 35). On a politicized "neo-sublime" refiguring concepts of environmental space—"nature"—see Domenique G. Laporte, *Christo* (New York: Pantheon, 1986). In a helpful article on Mark Rothko called "Biography," *Representations* 16 (1986): 42–49, David Antin muses on "the American sublime as aesthetic construct": "In his 1963 article 'The American Sublime,' Lawrence Alloway sketches out the

rhetoric of the 1950s abstract sublime, with its repository of luminos-
ities, atmospheres, and veils, but like all rhetorics this one was some-
what equivocal, and its signifiers in the judgment of many, perhaps
finally even Rothko himself, overlapped the rhetoric of the beautiful
. . ." (45).

18   Frank O'Hara, "The Day Lady Died," *Lunch Poems* (San Francisco:
City Lights, 1964): 27; Ann Waldman, *Makeup on Empty Space*
(West Branch, Iowa: Toothpaste Press, 1984): 45–49. For a deft read-
ing of Frank O'Hara that situates him in the Whitmanic tradition of
synecdochic representation and cosmic identity, see Mutlu Konuk
Blasing, *American Poetry: The Rhetoric of Its Forms* (New Haven:
Yale Univ. Press, 1987), chapter 9, "Frank O'Hara: The Speech of
Poetry." Blasing's concept of the American sublime, derived from the
psychosexual poetics of Harold Bloom and the deconstructive rheto-
ric of Paul de Man, remains too general and evaporated of historical
meaning to be of much use: "Emerson's sublime [as allegorized in
Poe] is the American version of the romantic nostalgia for a union of
the subject and the object" (24).

19   Adrienne Rich, "North American Time," *Your Native Land, Your
Life* (New York: Norton, 1986): 36. The countersublimity emerging
from "the desire for feminine power" is theorized as a pre-oedipal
poetry in which "the other is not obliterated or repressed" in Patricia
Yaeger, "Toward a Female Sublime," in *Gender & Theory: Dialogues
on Feminist Criticism,* ed. Linda Kauffman (Oxford: Blackwell,
1989): 191–212.

20   I here assume the socially situated approach to genre and poetic style
("voice") developed against Russian Formalism by M. M. Bakhtin
and P. M. Medvedev, *The Formal Method in Literary Scholarship,*
trans. Albert J. Wehrle (Cambridge: Harvard Univ. Press, 1985); see,
especially, V. N. Vološinov and M. M. Bakhtin, "Discourse in Life
and Discourse in Art (Concerning Sociological Poetics)" [1926], in
Freudianism: A Marxist Critique, trans. I. R. Titunik (New York:
Academic Press, 1976). Also see V. N. Vološinov, *Marxism and the
Philosophy of Language,* trans. Ladislav Matejka and I. R. Titunik
(Cambridge: Harvard Univ. Press, 1986), especially 65–98.

21   Jack Spicer, *Language* [1964], in *The Collected Books of Jack Spicer,*
ed. Robin Blaser (Santa Barbara: Black Sparrow, 1980): 217.

22   Ron Silliman, "Spicer's Language," in *Writing/Talks,* ed. Bob Perel-
man (Carbondale: Southern Illinois Univ. Press, 1985): 171.

23   Ron Silliman, in "Poetry/Poetics: A Symposium in Practice and
Theory" [ed. Morgan Wines], *Occident* 8 (1974): 184.

24   Robert Hass, "George Oppen: A Tribute," *Ironwood* 13 (1985): 39;
his comment applies to Robert Duncan, "Often I Am Permitted to

Return to a Meadow," in *The Opening of the Field* (New York: Grove, 1960): 7.

25 Lowell's struggle against an imperially sublime mode and an Ahab-like will-to-power, ending in a renunciation of "rhetorical sublimity and religious myth in a quest to enter a demystified present" is detailed in James E. B. Breslin, *From Modern to Contemporary: American Poetry, 1945–1965* (Chicago: Univ. of Chicago Press, 1984): 112–114. "Beyond the Alps" is from *Life Studies & For the Union Dead* (New York: Noonday, 1964), and "Waking Early Sunday Morning" is from *Near the Ocean* (New York: Farrar, 1967): 24.

26 I quote from unpublished poems collected in *"What Odd Expedients" and Other Poems by Robinson Jeffers*, ed. Robert Ian Scott (Hamden, Conn.: Archon, 1981): "The Engines," "Pleasures," and, lastly, "City Destroyers." Jeffers contends in "An Extinct Vertebrate," "Even Niagara becomes ridiculous" when contemplated for ego-gain; the motto of this antihuman sublimity became "You can dissolve man from your mind" (49–56). On Andy Warhol's mock-sublime, see note 1.

27 Michael Amnasan, "The Eclipsing Function of Full Comprehension," *Poetics Journal* no. 6 (1986): 104–8.

28 Friedrich von Schiller, *Naive & Sentimental Poetry/On the Sublime*, trans. Julius A. Elias (New York: Ungar, 1966): 201–2.

29 Robert Glück, "Allegory," *Ironwood* 12 (1984): 112–18.

30 Stevens, "Of Hartford in a Purple Light," in *The Palm at the End of the Mind*, ed. Holly Stevens (New York: Vintage 1972): 169.

31 Stevens, "The Poems of Our Climate," in *Collected Poems*, 193.

32 On this utopian displacement of American sublimity from the environment into language-spaces of self-determination or "style," see Richard Poirier, *A World Elsewhere: The Place of Style in American Literature* (London: Chatto, 1967), chapter 2, "Is There an I for an Eye?: The Visionary Possession of America."

33 Ralph Waldo Emerson, "Self-Reliance," in *Selections*, ed. Whicher, 158.

Chapter 3. "Enrapted Senses": Anne Bradstreet's "Contemplations"

1 See Frank Dauster, *The Double Strand: Five Contemporary Mexican Poets* (Lexington: Univ. of Kentucky Press, 1987): ix, 165–67 on this conflicted tonality between voice and rival traditions in poets such as Jaime Sabines and Bonifaz Nuño. On the "restless ambition" to articulate modes of elected community in the United States, I draw upon

the reflections on democratic "equality" by Tocqueville as well as the portrayal of Puritan/Capitalist "election" given in Max Weber, *The Protestant Ethic and the Spirit of Capitalism,* trans. Talcott Parsons ([1904–1905] New York: Scribner's, 1959): 51–71, and Christopher Kendrick, *Milton: A Study in Ideology and Form* (New York: Metheun, 1986) on the Puritan "sanctification" of everyday work and the reaccenting of "grand style" genres. Contrasting incarnational tropes applied to the United States with less raptly inflected and garrison-ridden wilds of Canada or conquistadorial South America, Myra Jehlen captures the conversionary narrative underwriting the American sublime in these terms, suggestive of ever-rebeginning poets as diverse as Bradstreet or Stevens positing and sublimating "vacant space": "The prior vacancy of the continent was their crucial founding fiction, both asserted directly and implicit in the self-conscious narrativity with which the story of America 'began.' To be born an American is simultaneously to be born again. Americans assume their national identity as the fulfillment of selfhood rather than its point of origin, so that they travel their lives in a state of perpetual landing" (*American Incarnation: The Individual, the Nation, and the Continent* [Cambridge: Harvard Univ. Press, 1986]: 9). (Jehlen, not untypically, makes no mention of Bradstreet in her narrative of American self-invention in chapters called "Starting with Columbus" and "The Mammouth Land.")

2   In "Literary Characteristics of Democratic Centuries," (in *Democracy in America,* vol. 2, trans. George Lawrence [New York: Harper & Row, 1966]), Alexis de Tocqueville warned self-equalized yet grandeur-hungry democratic authors in "these vast wildernesses" and textually empty "forests of the New World" not only that "the concept of [pantheistic] unity becomes an obsession" (417) in cultural productions but also that "aristocratic jargon" and a high-style might be cultivated as a counterforce to social emptiness. Seeking self-advancement and distinction, such American writers would end up "transplant[ing] into democracy thoughts and ways of writing current in the aristocratic nation [Great Britain or France] which they [literary Americans] have taken as their model" (438–39): "Wanting to talk a language different from the vulgar, they will end up with a brand of aristocratic jargon which is hardly less far from pure speech than is the dialect of the people" (440). As contemporary example, see the emblem-book of John Hollander, *Types of Shape* (New York: Atheneum, 1969), with its "Eskimo Pie" and "Swan and Shadow" and "Vanished Mansard"; or, from Emerson's no less conversionary era, the antisublimity and critical wit that is James Russell Lowell's *A Fable for Critics* (1848). Not all poetry aspires to represent, nor needs

to be, the American sublime of Emerson or Whitman. Emily Dickinson's individuated struggle to displace masters and rivals of the "Romantic sublime" can be situated in dialogue with British poets like Elizabeth Barrett Browning and Wordsworth or can occur in forms as unlikely and unprecedented as the Calvinist hymnal, as Gary Lee Stonum argues in *The Dickinson Sublime* (Madison: Univ. of Wisconsin Press, 1990): 34–52. Such displacements, at least at such a later date, proved helpful to the mimetic struggle to voice a female sense of poetic mastery, "Till I take vaster attitudes—/ And strut upon my stem—/ Disdaining Men, and Oxygen, / For Arrogance of them—" (144). Bradstreet's sublime is by no means as canny or ironic as is Dickinson's self-emptying rhetoric in "Of Bronze—and Blaze—."

3 A. R. Ammons, *Sphere: The Form of a Motion* (New York: Norton, 1974): 65–75.

4 Steere's poem is reprinted in Harrison T. Meserole, *Seventeenth-Century American Poetry* (Garden City, N.Y.: Anchor Books, 1968): 252–65; on the shift in sensibility registered by Steere's work, see Donald P. Wharton, "The American Poetry of Richard Steere," *American Poetry* 3 (1986): 2–12. Contrasting the poem with the more *metaphysical* mode of Edward Taylor, Wharton wonders, "Or is it, as some have suggested, a mirror of the change in Puritan sensibility toward eighteenth-century sentimentality, latitudinarianism, and rationalism" (11)? My claim is that this sublime mode or sensibility of subjective excess came early and stayed late. On the heteroglossic mixtures of genres, tones, and modes in Bradstreet's era, see Peter White, ed., *Puritan Poets and Poetics: Seventeenth-Century American Poetry in Theory and Practice* (University Park, Pa.: Pennsylvania State Univ. Press, 1985).

5 Margaret Atwood, Introduction to *The New Oxford Book of Canadian Verse in English* (Toronto, London, New York: Oxford Univ. Press, 1982): xxx. Historically countering yet extending Harold Bloom's anxiety-driven model of "the American sublime," David Laurence's "William Bradford's American Sublime" (*PMLA* 102 [1987]: 55–65) traces a recurring American trope which would convert "sublimation of anxiety into exultation" (57) even into the history-writing of Bradford's *Of Plymouth Plantation,* chapter 9. Even more so concerning Bradstreet, I would agree with Laurence's larger, all but Kantian claim on the "involuntary solipsism" (62) which he ascribes to the American "*scene of writing*" and its oppressive physicality: "The sublime occurs as a defensive maneuver. When nature's sheer materiality threatens to give the lie to the supremacy of reason, feeling [what Bradstreet calls "feeling knowledge"] comes to the rescue" (57).

6 Anne Bradstreet, "To My Dear Children," in *The Works of Anne*

Bradstreet, ed. Jeannine Hensley (Cambridge: Harvard Univ. Press, 1967): 243. (Subsequent references in text are to this edition.) Bradstreet's euphoric tonality in response to the vastness of nature, "That there is a God, I see" soon suffers—interestingly enough in psychosexual terms—from a "block" due to "sickness and weakness" when she goes on to think of a God revealed "in His word" yet so subjected to conflicting interpretations and to worldly hypocrisies (244). In other words, the textual sublime of the Bible is not so comforting to her, at times, as is the felt sublime of the vast cosmos. A helpful reading of Bradstreet's poetic as paradigmatic of New World conditions— marginality, exemption, privacy, subversion—that paradoxically enable a woman to become "an American poetic voice" is detailed in Patricia Caldwell, "Why Our First Poet Was a Woman: Bradstreet and the Birth of an American Poetic Voice," *Prospects* 13 (1988): 1–35. The "sublime" is not a criterion in Caldwell's historical description, however, though it well could be.

7 John Ashbery later posits an "other tradition" evading tradition-centered anxiety. See Marjorie Perloff on this American will to stylistic innovation and a perpetual revolution of form/self: "'No More Margins': John Cage, David Antin, and the Poetry of Performance," in *The Poetics of Indeterminacy: Rimbaud to Cage* (Princeton: Princeton Univ. Press, 1981): and, in more futuristic modes, "The Word as Such: L = A = N = G = U = A = G = E Poetry in the Eighties," in *The Dance of the Intellect: Studies in the Poetry of the Pound Tradition* (Cambridge: Cambridge Univ. Press, 1985).

8 Nathaniel Ward, "Introductory Verses" to *The Tenth Muse, The Works of Anne Bradstreet,* 4.

9 In Erich Auerbach's compelling speculations on the breakdown of aristocratic/stylistic hierarchies, a new sublime is entailed by the very incarnation of Christ as *logos* equating *humilitas* to *sublimitas*—a dynamic of high-in-low that will not be fully realized, poetically at least, until the democratized vernacular of *Leaves of Grass* shows how this can be done in the plurally Christian United States. See *Mimesis: The Representation of Reality in Western Literature* (Princeton: Princeton Univ. Press, 1953): 151–56, and 110: "Here we may recall the discussion concerning the sublime character of the sentence *dixit-que Deus: fiat lux, et facta est lux* (Genesis 1:3) which Boileau and Huet carried on in the seventeenth century in connection with the essay *On the Sublime* attributed to Longinus. The sublime in this sentence from Genesis is not contained in a magnificent display of rolling periods nor in the splendor of abundant figures of speech but in the impressive brevity which is in such contrast to the immense content and which for that very reason has a note of obscurity which fills the listener with a shuddering awe."

10　On such paradigmatic self-displacements in woman writers, see Gayatri Chakravorty Spivak, "Displacement and the Discourse of Woman," in *Displacement: Derrida and After,* ed. Mark Krupnik (Bloomington: Indiana Univ. Press, 1983): 186.

11　Wendy Martin, *An American Triptych: Anne Bradstreet, Emily Dickinson, Adrienne Rich* (Chapel Hill: Univ. of North Carolina Press, 1984): 10; also see the utopian claims based upon gender differentiation in Carolyn Karcher, "A Female Counter-Poetic," *American Quarterly* 37 (1985): 133–39. Oddly enough, while there are fine discussions of "Women Poets and the American Sublime" by Joanne Feit Diehl and others in Mary Arensberg, ed., *The American Sublime* (Albany: State University of New York Press, 1986), there is not *one* reference to the poetry of Bradstreet. Emily Dickinson is fit into the preexisting, male-centered model, with certain adjustments due to gender and singularity; this model of *text as anxious psyche* largely derives from Harold Bloom, *The Anxiety of Influence: A Theory of Poetry* [New York: Oxford Univ. Press, 1973], on "Daemonization or the Counter-Sublime" as this effects post-Miltonic selfhoods willing sublimity, such as Emerson-Whitman or Stevens-Ashbery.

12　John Woodbridge, "To My Dear Sister, the Author of these Poems," in *The Works of Anne Bradstreet,* 4–6.

13　See Adelaide Amore, *A Woman's Inner World: Selected Poetry and Prose of Anne Bradstreet* (Washington, D.C.: University Press of America, 1982); Alicia Suskin Ostriker, *Stealing the Language: The Emergence of Woman's Poetry in America* (Boston: Beacon Press, 1986): 16–22; and Cheryl Walker, *The Nightingale's Burden: Women Poets and American Culture Before 1900* (Bloomington: Indiana Univ. Press, 1982).

14　Patricia Yaeger, "Toward a Female Sublime," *Gender & Theory: Dialogues on Feminist Criticism,* ed. Linda Kauffman (Oxford: Blackwell, 1989): 199–201. On the dynamics of sublime possession overriding such gender considerations, see Paul H. Fry, "The Possession of the Sublime," *Studies in Romanticism* 26 (1987): 187–208.

15　This interplay between a poetics of sensuous image (drawn from nature) and more abstract Biblical figurations from Puritan theology is mapped in Richard Daly, *God's Altar: The World and the Flesh in Puritan Poetry* (Berkeley and Los Angeles: Univ. of California Press, 1978), a work that contends against more modernist notions that Puritans strictly abhorred the world's body and wrote a poetry of typical tropes and predetermined types. Wharton (see note 4) makes similar claims against this assumed hegemony of "plainness."

16　On this *raping*/rapture of Bradstreet's senses and related aesthetic considerations, see Norman Grabo, "The Veiled Vision: The Role of

288

Aesthetics in Early American History," *American Studies: Essays on Theory and Method,* ed. Robert Meredith (Columbus, Ohio: Merrill, 1968).

17 Richard Baxter, *The Saints' Everlasting Rest; Or, A Treatise On The Blessed State of the Saints in Their Enjoyment of God in Heaven* ([London: 1649–1650]; Glasgow: Khull, Blackie, 1822): 272–90. Baxter's language is close to the poetic movement enacted in "Contemplations": "Compare also the excellencies of heaven, with those glorious works of creation, which our eyes now behold. What wisdom, power, and goodness, are manifested therein!" (277). I take devotional self-help handbooks such as Baxter's to provide discursive models of "self" and Christian "interiority," in Michel Foucault's epistemic sense: "What is called Christian interiority is a particular mode of relationship with oneself, comprising precise forms of attention, concern, decipherment, verbalization, confession, self-accusation, struggle against temptation, renunciation, spiritual combat, and so on" (*The Use of Pleasure,* vol. 2 of *The History of Sexuality,* trans. Robert Hurley [New York: Vintage, 1986]: 63). The sublime has to be empowered yet policed as a devotional force in the subject.

18 Passage from Guillaume Du Bartas, *Bartas: His Devine Weekes and Works* as translated and disseminated into English traditions by Joshua Sylvester, ([London: Humfrey Lownes, 1605]; Gainesville, Florida: Scholar's Facsimiles, 1965): 6–8.

19 Bradstreet, "To Her Most Honoured Father," Preface to *The Tenth Muse,* and "In Honour of Du Bartas, 1641," from *The Works of Anne Bradstreet,* 13, 15, 192–94.

20 Perry Miller, *The New England Mind: The Seventeenth Century* ([1939]; Boston: Beacon Press, 1961): 18–27. Also see Norman Pettit, *The Heart Prepared: Grace and Conversion in Puritan Spiritual Life* (New Haven: Yale Univ. Press, 1966); and, on the new currency of such Longinian "transport," Theodore E. B. Wood, *The Word 'Sublime' and Its Context, 1650–1760* (The Hague: Mouton, 1972).

21 See Larzer Ziff, *Puritanism in America: New Culture in a New World* (New York: Viking, 1973): 13, depicting the Puritan sensibility as this reflects social/personal factors of conversionary self-making if not proto-democratic tendencies in the election of self and, by extension, in this new country. (See page references in text for subsequent citations.)

22 Perry Miller, ed. *The American Puritans: Their Prose and Poetry* (Garden City, N.Y.: Doubleday, 1956): 265. Aesthetic "transport" before discourse and nature, it seems to me, was not wholly alien to Puritan conceptions of literary style. Michael Wigglesworth early considered the affective power of language in his "The Prayse of Elo-

quence" (1650) oration at Harvard, before he poeticized the gloomier legalities of Calvinist doctrines in *The Day of Doom* (1662). Wigglesworth claimed, like Cicero and Longinus defending a language-inspired *ekstasis,* that the mind of orator and auditor alike can be "quickened" and "elevated" to mutual rapture: "His mind is transported with a kind of rapture, and inspired with a certain oratoric fury, as if the oratour together with his words had breathed his soul and spirit into those that hear him" with a controlling *power* ("eloquence") which works like "a mighty river augmented with excessive rains or winter snows swelling above its wonted channel [and] bear's down banks and bridges, overflows fields and hedges, sweeps away all before it, that might obstruct its passage . . ." This hardly "*plain style*" document on "Puritan Literary Theory" is reprinted in Perry Miller and Thomas H. Johnson, eds, *The Puritans: A Sourcebook of Their Writings,* vol. 2 (New York: Harper, 1963): 674. As Ziff describes the experience of *conversion,* this word-inspired rapture informed the core of Puritan sensibility: "Behind the uttered words of the preacher vitalizing the revealed word of the Bible, hovers the word itself, the Holy Spirit that will enter the soul of man and help him in his [her] unbelief" (*Puritanism in America,* 29). In other words, *sublime eloquence* could be made to serve the production of faith-states, just as the sublimity of nature could be made to intensify these faith-states of "transport" in Du Bartas, Bradstreet, and Milton's "Il Penseroso." The sublime registered and legitimated the emerging language of such rapture, "transport" at once serving God and the New World community of newly empowered and more mobile selves.

23 John Milton, *Areopagitica and Of Education,* ed. George H. Sabine (Northbrook, Ill.: AHM Pub., 1951): 68. Milton's Puritan curriculum in the "sublime art" of rhetoric/poetics surprisingly included, even before Boileau's influence, Longinus. On Miltonic *sublimity* in epic and pastoral genres (as in a quasi-nature lyric like "Il Penseroso"), which spread early into Puritan New England for better and worse (as Josephine Miles claims in several studies of this sublime diction-syntax), see Christopher Ricks, *Milton's Grand Style* (London: Oxford Univ. Press, 1963) on "Syntax and Sublimity."

24 See Bloom, *Anxiety of Influence,* 99–112. Bloom has not, to my knowledge, ever critically considered the poetry of Bradstreet, though she does suffer from certain stigmata of any would-be American sublime as he has theorized it.

25 Bradstreet's literary rapture has often been compared to Keats's "Ode to a Nightingale" (1819), where melancholy thoughts are subsumed in aesthetic ecstasy through an in-and-out union with nature; see Alvin H. Rosenfield, "Anne Bradstreet's 'Contemplations': Patterns of

Form and Meaning," *New England Quarterly* 43 (1970): 79–96. Gaston Bachelard theorizes the liberating claims of such brazenly "poetic" images and outlines a dialectic of *immensity* and *miniatureness* that might well serve an American poet of world (male) and household (female) such as humble-sublime Bradstreet (*The Poetics of Space* [Boston: Beacon, 1964], for example, 52).

26 Du Bartas, *Devine Weekes,* 175–76 (note 18).

27 Josephine Miles situates this diction and syntax of "Contemplations" in the (Protestant or Whig) tradition of *sublime* stylistics as propagated by Du Bartas and the phrasal accumulations of Walt Whitman; see "The Poetry of Praise: An American Mode," in *Eras & Modes in English Poetry* (Berkeley and Los Angeles: Univ. of California Press, 1964): 230–33. Though no compelling study of Bradstreet's poetic tradition yet exists, Alessandra Contenti does focus on familiar lyrics in "Anne Bradstreet, Il Petrarchismo E Il 'Plain Style,'" *Studi Americani* (1968):7–27; and Austin Warren, at a loss for apt terms, defines her Du Bartas-based tradition as the "Baroque," in *New England Saints* (Ann Arbor: Univ. of Michigan Press, 1956): 6–8. Also see Jane Donahue Eberwein, "The 'Unrefined Ore' of Anne Bradstreet's Quaternions," *Early American Literature* 9 (1974): 19–26; Anne Hildebrand, "Anne Bradstreet's Quaternions and 'Contemplations,'" *Early American Literature* 8 (1973): 117–25; William J. Irvin, "Allegory and Typology 'Imbrace and Greet': Anne Bradstreet's "Contemplations," *Early American Literature* 10 (1975): 30–46; Pattie Cowell and Ann Stanford, eds., *Critical Essays on Anne Bradstreet* (Boston: G. K. Hall, 1983); and Eileen Margerum, "Anne Bradstreet's Public Poetry and the Tradition of Humility," *Early American Literature* 17 (1982): 152–60. Two strong poets in their own right who come to terms with Bradstreet's tradition are Adrienne Rich, in "Anne Bradstreet and Her Poetry," the forward to *The Works of Anne Bradstreet,* ed. Jeannine Hensley; and Ann Stanford in *Anne Bradstreet: The Worldly Poet* (New York: Burt Franklin, 1974). For a contrary view that Bradstreet's imagery represents "the shrinking of poetic sensibilities from the harsh America scene," see John Seelye, *Prophetic Waters: The River in Early American Life and Literature* (New York: Oxford Univ. Press, 1977): 314–15. Admittedly, Bradstreet (as was the more strictly *colonizing* Columbus) was *awed* by a "nightingale" which did not yet exist in the American landscape, only in her European-coded imagination of transport (probably miming the Calvinist "nightingale" of Du Bartas). This tiny bird is no mountain or ocean, but oddly occasions the mood of sublime rapture, as (male) birds can in Whitman or even in the more habitually estranged Dickinson. On gender-differences obtaining in the perception of "land-

scape" as locus of male appropriation or female appreciation, see Annette Kolodny, *The Land Before Her: Fantasy and Experience of the American Frontiers, 1630–1860* (Chapel Hill, N.C.: Univ. of North Carolina Press, 1984). Bradstreet's warfare between "being self-aggrandizing one moment and self-effacing the next" is helpfully connected to gender determinations and Puritan strictures in Cheryl Walker, *The Nightingale's Burden: Women Poets and American Culture before 1900*, 1–20. That Bradstreet both courted and renounced power, fame, sublimity, and worldly success under the camouflage of modesty and anxiety seems undeniable. For Walker, however, the Philomela of American poetry, as figured in Bradstreet's "Contemplations," emerges from the beginning as a "women's tradition" of disempowered ambivalence (15), entailing a separatist regime of furtive privacy rather than public embodiment, as in Whitman or Emerson.

28   John Rogers, "Upon Mrs. Anne Bradstreet, Her Poems, Etc.," *The Works of Anne Bradstreet*, 10.

Chapter 4. William Livingston's *Philosophic Solitude* and the Ideology of the Natural Sublime

1   In addition to David S. Shields's helpful essay, "The Religious Sublime and New England Poets of the 1720s," *Early American Literature* 19 (1984/85): 231–48, on Colonial disseminations of the more Biblically iconic *religious sublime,* also see Donald P. Wharton, "The American Poetry of Richard Steere," *American Poetry* 3 (1986):3–12, for a reading analogous to mine on the latitudinarian tones of sublime wonder in Richard Steere's last poem (*circa* 1710), "Earth Felicities, Heavens Allowances." Scholarship on the eighteenth-century sublime remains immense, but Marjorie Hope Nicolson, *Mountain Gloom and Mountain Glory: The Development of the Aesthetics of the Infinite* (New York: Norton, 1963) and Samuel Holt Monk, *The Sublime: A Study of Critical Theories in XVIII-Century England* (Ann Arbor: Univ. of Michigan Press, 1960) still provide the theological/ critical underpinnings of various (and often overlapping) genres. Like Shields, David B. Morris, in "Gothic Sublimity," *New Literary History* 16 (1985): 299–319, and *The Religious Sublime: Christian Poetry and Critical Tradition in 18th-Century England* (Lexington: Univ. of Kentucky Press, 1972) would separate the truth-beholden genre of the *religious sublime* from the uncanny free-for-all of the

gothic sublime: "The long tradition of *le merveilleux chrétien* had sanctioned the poetic use of angels, spirits, and devils so long as they did not violate Christian theology. Poetry, critics believed, demanded the marvelous, and Christian marvels carried the presumption of truth, as opposed to the fictive mythologies of pagan writers" in "Gothic Sublimity," (309). More deconstructively, see Steven Knapp, *Personification and the Sublime: Milton to Coleridge* (Cambridge: Harvard Univ. Press, 1985) on the sublime as a self-delusive trope of liberal empowerment; and Ernest Tuveson, *The Imagination as a Means of Grace: Locke and the Aesthetics of Romanticism* (Berkeley and Los Angeles: Univ. of California Press, 1960) on the emerging use of the *natural sublime* in Locke's epistemology, long dominant in America. John Adams, *Poems on Several Occasions, Original and Translated* (Boston: D. Gookin, 1745): 18.

2   On the neo-Longinian tradition in England, also see T. R. Henn, *Longinus and English Criticism* (Cambridge: Cambridge Univ. Press, 1934); Theodore E. B. Wood, *The Word 'Sublime' and Its Context, 1650–1760* (The Hague: Mouton, 1972); and Tuveson (1960), who traces conventional imagery of the "natural sublime" to increasingly subjective truth-claims of Lockean epistemology (56–71). I take the post-Lockean *conversion psychology* of the Great Awakening, as outlined for example in Alan Heimert, *Religion and the American Mind From the Great Awakening to the Revolution* (Cambridge: Harvard Univ. Press, 1966) to be another determining social context for American lyrics legitimating "sacred rapture." On the conjunction of Christian ideology and the emerging worldliness of the capitalist self seeking to create its own vocation of sublimity in "fresh woods and pastures new" of middle-class faith, as in less literary markets, see Christopher Kendrick, *Milton: A Study in Ideology and Form* (New York: Methuen, 1986). I will draw upon Edmund Burke, *A Philosophical Enquiry into the Origins of our Ideas of the Sublime and Beautiful,* ed. J. T. Boulton (Notre Dame: Univ. of Notre Dame Press, 1968). That the disruptive force of the sublime can be politically ambidextrous and remains up for critical grabs in this revolutionary era is outlined in Jonathan Arac, "The Media of Sublimity: Johnson and Lamb on *King Lear,*" *Studies in Romanticism* 26 (1987): 209–20.

3   Livingston's letter to Welles is quoted in Milton Klein's introduction to his edition of William Livingston, *The Independent Reflector: or Weekly Essays on Sundry Important Subjects More Particularly adapted to the Province of New-York* (Cambridge, Mass.: Belknap Press, 1963): 24–25. (For subsequent citations, page references appear in the text.)

4   In addition to John A. Krout, "William Livingston," *Dictionary of American Biography,* ed. Allen Johnson et al. (New York: Scribner's, 1928—), I draw upon Milton M. Klein, "The Rise of the New York Bar: The Legal Career of William Livingston," *William and Mary Quarterly* 15 (1958): 334–58, and Dorothy Rita Dillon, *The New York Triumvirate: A Study of the Legal and Political Careers of William Livingston, John Morin Scott, William Smith, Jr.* (New York: Columbia Univ. Press, 1949) for biographical information on Livingston's consistently leftist politics. The Anglican or losing viewpoint in this controversy is narrated in Peter N. Carroll, *The Other Samuel Johnson: A Psychohistory of Early New England* (Rutherford, N.J.: Fairleigh Dickinson Univ. Press, 1978).

5   Frank Shuffelton's essay, " 'Philosophic Solitude' and the Pastoral Politics of William Livingston," *Early American Literature* 17 (1982): 43–53, is the best interpretation of Livingston's poetics in relation to his Whig politics; it is helpful in showing how Locke's conception of "liberty" provided an imported foundation for any American "Whig" pastoral, as in Thoreau's ethic of self-making. (For subsequent citations, page references appear in the text.)

6   The eighteenth-century genre of the "sublime poem" has been lushly documented in scholarly works such as those of Martin Price, "The Sublime Poem: Pictures and Powers," *Yale Review* 58 (1969): 194–213; Josephine Miles, "The Sublime Poem," *Eras & Modes in English Poetry* (Berkeley and Los Angeles: Univ. of California Press, 1964): 48–77; other (culturally delayed) American applications are traced in Eugene L. Huddleston, "Topographical Poetry in the Early National Period," *American Literature* 38 (1966): 303–22, and Henry M. Sayre, "Surveying the Vast Profound: The Panoramic Landscape in American Consciousness," *Massachusetts Review* 24 (1983):723–742. In addition to Anne Bradstreet's "Contemplations," the work of another American poet may have influenced Livingston's stance towards using the natural sublime for self-empowerment: the Maryland nature-poet Richard Lewis (c. 1700–1734), whose poems "A Rhapsody" and "A Journey from Patapsco to Annapolis" (1731), for example, with similar feelings of exaltation before shifting natural vistas and local sites of power, situate the poet on "a solitary walk" (and, better yet, horseride!) all the better that the ego can "my CREATOR'S praise proclaim; / Tho' my low verse ill suits the noble theme." Though Lewis seeks more "pleasing" scenes and "soothing" balms and charms of wild nature to fight off recurring fits of self-abasement more than he gives himself to wondrous moods of transport and self-exaltation, his ego-lonely strategy of contemplating nature is much

the same as Livingston's: "Here, might a Philosophic Poet's Mind, / Fit objects for her Contemplation find." At the end of "A Journey from Patapsco to Annapolis," Lewis is so filled with "holy horror" before the "dread majesty" of God as measured against his own puniness and uncertain speculation that he even fears losing the self in the immensity of the natural sublime: "TREMENDOUS GOD! may I not justly fear / That I, unworthy object of thy care, / Into this world from thy bright presence tost, / Am in the immensity of nature lost!" Lewis's poems are reprinted in Richard Beale Davis, C. Hugh Holman, and Louis D. Rubin, Jr., eds., *Southern Writing, 1585–1920* (New York: Odyssey, 1970): 213–25. I thank the editors of *Early American Literature* for this regional analogy.

7   Pomfret's influence on American landscape poetry is discussed in Edwin T. Bowden, "Benjamin Church's *Choice* and American Colonial Poetry," *New England Quarterly* 32 (1959):170–184. On Pomfret's middle-class vision of "the small independent freeholder," see Raymond Williams, *The Country and the City* (New York: Oxford Univ. Press, 1973): 25, and more generally on class tensions increasingly embedded in the pastoral. Auden's contrast of utopian/arcadian pastoral is reprinted in Bryan Loughrey, ed., *The Pastoral Mode: A Casebook* (London: Macmillan, 1984): 90.

8   As Klein writes of the early printing history of *Philosophic Solitude*, "A partial investigation reveals, in addition to New York editions of 1747, 1769, and 1790, a Boston edition of 1762 and a Trenton edition of 1782. The poem was reproduced in part in *The New-England Magazine*, 1 (August, 1758): 50–51, reprinted serially in the *Boston Magazine*, 2 (March–June, 1785): 107–9, 147–48, 189–90, 227–28, and included in the *Columbian Muse, A Selection of American Poetry, from Various Authors of Established Reputation* (New York, 1794): 16–33; *American Poems, Selected and Original* (Litchfield, 1793): 154–75; and the *Young Gentleman and Lady's Monitor . . .* (New York, 1790): 325–42" (Klein, "Introduction," in *Independent Reflector*, 10, n. 30).

9   The "reader's sublime," as an ambivalent complex of self-exaltation and external blockages that must be overcome to achieve imaginative "originality," in any neo-Romantic sense, is traced in Julie Ellison, "Emerson's Sublime Analysis," *Bucknell Review* 28 (1983):42–62, as stimulating the will-to-greatness in Emerson's sublime-hungry career that proves central to capitalizing America.

10 Mather Byles, "Bombastic and Grubstreet Style: A Satire" [1727], in *The Puritans: A Sourcebook of Their Writings*, Vol. 2, ed. Perry Miller and Thomas H. Johnson (New York: Harper, 1963). The Byles piece

is reprinted in Miller and Johnson from *American Magazine 2* (January 1745); it appeared originally in *New England Weekly Journal*, no. 5 (24 April 1727).

11   On the proto-sublimity of the nature lyric, as transmitted through the Protestant poetics of Du Bartas's "La Semaine" and "L'Uranie" (which influenced, among others, Anne Bradstreet and Milton), see Barbara Lewalski, *Protestant Poetics and the Seventeenth-Century Religious Lyric* (Princeton: Princeton Univ. Press, 1979): 9, 231–32, 349–54. The *displacement* of Protestant poetics into later, more secular forms is also traced as figurative legacy in Mason I. Lowance, Jr., *The Language of Canaan: Metaphor and Symbol in New England from the Puritans to the Transcendentalists* (Cambridge: Harvard Univ. Press, 1980); see especially "Joel Barlow and the Rising Glory of America," 208–46.

12   On less pious constructions of an American sublime as ideological influence upon diverse poets, see post-Whitmanic studies of this sublime in poets diverse as Dickinson and Bishop in Mary Arensberg, ed., *The American Sublime* (Albany, New York: State Univ. of New York Press, 1986); and James D. Bloom on the "American Sublime" as contested in Blackmur and Berryman in Bloom's *The Stock of Available Reality: R. P. Blackmur and John Berryman* (Lewisburg, Ohio: Bucknell Univ. Press, 1984).

13   Walter Jackson Bate, *From Classic to Romantic: Premises of Taste in Eighteenth-Century England* (New York: Harper, 1961): 99.

14   John Locke, *An Essay Concerning Human Understanding,* ed. Peter H. Nidditch (Oxford: Clarendon Press, 1975): 210.

15   Ernest Tuveson, "Space, Deity, and the 'Natural Sublime,'" *Modern Language Quarterly* 12 (1951):20–38 (28).

16   Wallace Stevens, "Nomad Exquisite," *The Palm at the End of the Mind: Selected Poems and a Play,* ed. Holly Stevens (New York: Vintage, 1972), 44.

Chapter 5, William Cullen Bryant: Domesticating the Natural Sublime

1   William Cullen Bryant, *Prose Writings of William Cullen Bryant,* [1884], ed. Parke Godwin, vol. 1 (New York: Russell, 1964): 51–53. I will quote Bryant's poems from *Poetical Works of William Cullen Bryant, Collected and Arranged by the Author* (New York: Appleton, 1878). Bryant works out a brief defense of this newer sublimity, closer

to the vernacular, in *A Library of Poetry and Song* (New York: 1872): xxviii–xxx. On Bryant's poetry generally, see *Under Open Sky: Poets on William Cullen Bryant*, ed. Norbert Krapf (New York: Fordham Univ. Press, 1986); Robert A. Ferguson, "William Cullen Bryant: The Creative Context of the Poet," *New England Quarterly* 53 (1980):431–63; and Donald A. Ringe, *The Pictorial Mode: Space & Time in the Art of Bryant, Irving & Cooper* (Lexington: Univ. of Kentucky Press, 1971): 11–25.

2 John Trumbull's *Essay* is reprinted in George Perkins, ed., *American Poetic Theory* (New York: Holt, Rinehart & Winston, 1972): 3–8.

3 John Trumbull, *An Essay on the Use and Advantages of the Fine Arts* (New Haven: T. and S. Green, 1770): 13–16.

4 Bryant, *Prose Writings*, 40.

5 Ibid., 158. Elements of Common Sense aesthetics in Bryant's poetics have been well documented: see, for example, William Palmer Hudson, "Archibald Alison and William Cullen Bryant," *American Literature* 12 (1940): 59–68; Albert F. Mclean, Jr., *William Cullen Bryant* (New York: Twayne, 1964): 29, 43, 125; and Rebecca Rio-Jelliffe, *The Poetry of William Cullen Bryant: Theory and Practice* (Ph.D. diss., Univ. of California, Berkeley [1964]: 94–106). On the "affective" criticism which paved the way for the Longinian musings of Bryant and Poe, see Gordon McKenzie, *Critical Responsiveness: A Study of the Psychological Current in Later Eighteenth-Century Criticism* (Berkeley and Los Angeles: Univ. of California Publications in English, vol. 20, 1949).

6 Bryant, *Prose Writings*, 5–6.

7 Ibid., 8, 15.

8 Henry David Thoreau, "Walking," [complete essay first published in *Atlantic Monthly*, 1862], in *Walden and Other Writings*, ed. Brooks Atkinson (New York: Modern Library, 1950): 611–12.

9 See Harold Bloom's cautionary comments on the failed, insufficiently anxious, or reactive attempts of *any* American "counter-sublime" before the agonistic complex of Emerson/Whitman in his "Whitman's Image of Voice: To the Tally of My Soul," in Harold Bloom, ed., *Walt Whitman: Modern Critical Views* (New York: Chelsea House, 1985): 127–31. On these romantic modes of "address[ing] the torrent" of such natural vastness in a new diction, see Geoffrey H. Hartman, "Blessing the Torrent: On Wordsworth's Later Style," *PMLA* (93):196–203, from whom I borrow the phrase "to domesticate the sublime" as applied to Wordsworth's picturesque sketches or reflective sonnets (197). We do know that Anne Bradstreet's sublime nature lyric, "Contemplations," was much admired in Bryant's Romantic

era; for example, the *American Quarterly Review* 2 (1827):482–509 reprinted "with surprise" this poem, calling it "the most favorable specimen of Mrs. Bradstreet's language and poetic talent."

10 Bryant, *Prose Writings*, 5, 39.

11 Ibid., 40. On "new modes of sublimity" developed as discourses of visual grandeur in American painting and poetry, see Charles L. Sanford, "The Concept of the Sublime in the Works of Thomas Cole and William Cullen Bryant," *American Literature* 28 (1957):434–48; James T. Callow, *Kindred Spirits: Knickerbocker Writers and American Artists* (Chapel Hill: Univ. of North Carolina Press, 1967); and on the Emersonian optics of vast space/inner light, see Barbara Novak, *American Painting in the Nineteenth Century* (New York: Praeger, 1969) and *Nature and Culture* (New York: Oxford Univ. Press, 1980). A synchronic typology of nineteenth-century American poetry is outlined in Mutlu Konuk Blasing, *American Poetry: The Rhetoric of Its Forms* (New Haven: Yale Univ. Press, 1987); bypassing Bryant, she links four "master tropes" to rhetorical protocols inhering in four enduring types of American poetry: (1) Emerson (metaphor/analogy); (2) Whitman (synecdoche/anagogy); (3) Poe (metonymy/allegory); and (4) Emily Dickinson (irony/literalism).

12 Written while living in Bryant's home in Cummington, Massachusetts, Wilbur's poem ("A Wall in the Woods: Cummington") negotiating Bryant's "homiletic woods" and romantic metaphors is from *The New Yorker*, 5 June 1989, 40.

13 The patriotically upbeat lyric, "To Know No Boundaries," as Merrill Lynch proclaims in vastness-haunted ads for market deregulation and bullish faith in the 1980s, still assumes subtexts of Romantic piety such as Bryant's sublime of American *boundlessness* linked to self-expansive power. The *Marlboro Man*, smoking in the vastness of some western American godhead, is another pious example. Whatever the vague, grandly ideological appeal of such primal sublimity, however, the purple-mountain majesty of "America, the Beautiful" has yet to replace the grand war-mongering of "The Star-Spangled Banner" as our national anthem.

14 Gary Lee Stonum, *The Dickinson Sublime* (Madison: Univ. of Wisconsin Press, 1990): 72. Eschewing national inflections, Stonum reads the lure of this "Romantic sublime" as a "three-phase structure" that entails (as in Thomas Weiskel's reading of Kant's sublime) a subjective drama of normalcy, trauma, and reaction structuring the greatest Anglo-American poetry of the nineteenth century. Dickinson, unlike the more public Bryant or Whitman, hesitates to give this sublime any achieved, positive, or consensual content as the material constituting American identity or comprising "heroic mastery." Negotiating ter-

rors of otherness, the sublime subjects Dickinson to "a drama of sub-jectivity, in most instances an interiority certainly representing her own, and then she opens the theater out to the diverse and incalcu-lable subjectivities of unknown readers" (144).

15 Gerard Manley Hopkins, "God's Grandeur," in *The Poems of Gerard Manley Hopkins,* ed. W. H. Gardner and N. H. MacKenzie (London: Oxford Univ. Press, 1970): 66.

16 For a reading of the way Bryant's poetry mingles landscapes of gran-deur with moralized cognition as well as anticipates "the metaphoric and symbolic modes of later poetry," see Rebecca Rio-Jelliffe, "Bryant's 'Thanatopsis' and the Development of American Litera-ture," in *American Poetry to 1914,* ed. Harold Bloom (New York: Chelsea House, 1987): 121–33. In my reading, the moral policing of the natural sublime by Bryant looks back to Livingston and forward to Henry Wadsworth Longfellow much more than to the discursive excesses of Poe or Dickinson. Still, in his hyperconventionality, Bryant installed the sublime landscape into a domestic commonplace and prepared for the journalizing associations of the sublime in Whitman.

Chapter 6. Walt Whitman: The American Sublime as "Song of Myself"

1 I invoke the sociological dialectic of individuality and social/geo-graphical largeness that becomes worked into "habits of the [Ameri-can] heart" (p. 264) in Alexis de Tocqueville, *Democracy in America* trans. George Lawrence ([1835/1840]; New York, Harper, 1966): on "vast egotism" (p. 742); on how, out of diverse regions and lan-guages, the democratic individual "can form the picture of one vast democracy in which a nation counts as a single citizen" (454); on the "antipoetic" daily life of an American (454), rooted as it is in money-making concerns, even delusions of sociological grandeur (509); and on "vast wildernesses" of the interior continent to the west (21).

2 I will parenthetically cite subsequent references from Walt Whitman, *Leaves of Grass: Comprehensive Reader's Edition,* ed. Harold W. Blodgett and Sculley Bradley (New York: Norton, 1968).

3 M. M. Bakhtin, *Speech Genres and Other Late Essays,* trans. Vern W. McGee (Austin: Univ. of Texas Press, 1986): 5. Dialogically situated, such "speech-genres" (or "literary" ones) provide social models for constructing and accenting a speech-whole and tone (127).

4 Wallace Stevens, *Letters of Wallace Stevens,* ed. Holly Stevens (New York: Knopf, 1966): 871. Stevens' letter to Joseph Bennet of February

8, 1955, admits that Whitman's poetry "in which he collects large numbers of concrete things" as well as "gatherings of precious Americana" reflects an America fast vanishing, "disintegrating as the world of which he made himself a part, disintegrates" (ibid).

5 Gary Lee Stonum contrasts the heroic mastery of Whitman with the "hesitant sublime" of Dickinson in *The Dickinson Sublime* (Madison: Univ. of Wisconsin Press, 1990): 171–72. Whatever the pressures of time, temperament, or the legacy of Emerson, gender considerations have to be more fully taken into consideration, surely, as determining the radically different orientations of these two poets. See the contrasting sublimities posited, for example, in Joanne Feit Diehl, "In the Twilight of the Gods: Women Poets and the American Sublime," in *The American Sublime,* ed. Mary Arensberg (Albany: State Univ. of New York Press, 1986): 173–214, who reads in woman-to-woman encounters and a poetics of erotic expenditure a way of overcoming the "radical solipsism" of the "Emersonian sublime." Diehl's claim, furthermore, is that "gender blocks the identifications Emerson [or Whitman] so fluently assumes" (174).

6 This idea of *Leaves* as "only a language experiment" is taken from Whitman's notes for a lecture on "American" language, written mainly between 1851 and 1861, which were edited by Horace Traubel as *An American Primer* ([1904]; San Francisco: City Lights, 1970); Whitman is quoted from the "Foreword." Whitman's axiom: "All the greatness of any land, at any time, lies folded in its names" (31). Whitman's godlike claim to *atextualized* originality is quoted in Richard Bridgman, ed., *Leaves of Grass: A Facsimile of the First Edition,* (San Francisco: Chandler, 1968): xxviii.

7 See Tocqueville, *Democracy in America:* 456, on "Why American Writers and Speakers Are Often Bombastic"—especially when they turn from the "clear and dry" language of business and "attempt a poetic style." On Whitman's defensive confrontations with the sublime as an abyss of self-threatening language, see Joseph Kronick, "On the Border of History: Whitman and the American Sublime," in *The American Sublime,* ed. Mary Arensberg (Albany: State Univ. of New York Press, 1986): 51–82, and Harold Bloom, "Emerson and Whitman: The American Sublime," in *Poetry and Repression: Revisionism from Blake to Stevens* (New Haven: Yale Univ. Press, 1976): 235–66.

8 See Tocqueville, *Democracy in America.,* on "vast wildernesses" west of Detroit (21) and on the American selves of capitalist mobility in his "Letter to Chabrol" (9 June 1831): "Here the whole world seems made of malleable [and mobile] stuff that man can shape and fashion to please himself: a huge field, of which only the smallest part has

been hastily explored, is here open to human industry" (732). In such a labor-sanctified world open to self-possibility, Tocqueville goes on to explain how the imagination of such democratic egos easily conflates American self-making with money-making, as the sublime *under* Capital becomes (as in our own day's *bottom-line* thinking) the sublime mobility *of* Capital: "In America nothing is easier than to make oneself rich, so of course the human spirit, which needs some dominant passion, ends by directing its every thought toward hopes of profit; as a result, this people at first sight seems to be a company of traders come together for purposes of business, and as one delves deeper into the national character of the Americans, one finds that their one test of the value of everything in this world depends on the answer to this single question: 'How much money does it bring in?'" (732). On the social consequences of this democratic ethos, see Donald Pease, "Walt Whitman and the Vox Populi of the American Masses," in his *Visionary Compacts: American Renaissance Writings in Cultural Context* (Madison: Univ. of Wisconsin Press, 1987); see Pease also on the Emersonian "possession" of the material sublime as nature becomes dematerialized (223–27).

9   On this genealogical dispersion of authority into vast intertextuality and social codes, see Edward Said's "A Meditation on Beginnings," in *Beginnings: Intention and Method* (Baltimore: Johns Hopkins Univ. Press, 1975), specifically on Nietzsche's rhetorical deconstruction of the "Homeric question" (56–58). On self-transfiguring energies of the "great style" and ego-rapture become form-engendering force, see Friedrich Nietzsche, *The Will to Power,* trans. Walter Kaufmann and R. J. Hollingdale (New York: Vintage, 1968), especially "The Will to Power as Art" (419–53). On the self-publishing of ["Walter"] Whitman and his complex biographical/nationalistic origins, see *Leaves of Grass: A Facsimile of the First Edition,* ed. with introduction by Richard Bridgman (San Francisco: Chandler, 1968): xxix–xxxix. Subsequent references will appear parenthetically.

10 See the speculations of Richard Maurice Bucke on Whitman's "rebirth" occurring in the 1850s, in *Cosmic Consciousness* ([1901] New York: Dutton, 1969). On the "expansive" and "healthy-minded" set of "over-beliefs" posited by Whitman, converting solitude into *voluntary* wholeness ("his gospel has a touch of bravado and an affected twist"), see William James, who situates Whitman's imaginings within the Protestant cash-value ethos of self-help and self-cure through self-suggestion, in *The Varieties of Religious Experience* ([1902] New York: Collier, 1961: 85.

11 See Martin Price, Review of David B. Morris's *The Religious Sublime* [1972] in *Modern Language Quarterly* 35 (1974):85–87. Whitman's

language-shaping does exactingly transfigure older poetry in this *sublime mode,* as the stylistic studies of Josephine Miles in *Eras & Modes in English Poetry* (Berkeley and Los Angeles: Univ. of California Press, 1964) have claimed, wherein Whitman's *adjectival* diction and *phrasal* syntax (parataxis) has been described as "Poetry of Praise: An American Mode." The anxiety-engendering influence of Romanticism upon Whitman has been seen to generate the necessarily repressive, self-defensive *hyperbole* of an "American sublime" by Harold Bloom in many studies, notably in *Poetry and Repression* (New Haven: Yale Univ. Press, 1976) and "Whitman's Image of Voice: To the Tally of My Soul," in *Walt Whitman: Modern Critical Views,* ed. Harold Bloom (New York: Chelsea House, 1985): 127–42. Identifying with yet displacing models of prior grandeur such as Emerson, Whitman defends against prior sublimity with tropes of countersublimity, reversing *late* into *early, empty* into *full,* lonely into *united, abyss* into *language* and so on.

12 See this generic description in Martin Price, "The Sublime Poem: Pictures and Powers," *Yale Review* 58 (1969):194–213.

13 Without agreeing with Richard Howard's assumption that American poets "address themselves to the current, to the flux, to the process of experience rather than to its precepts," or social constructs of sublime self-interpellation, I would say that his title, *Alone with America: Essays on the Art of Poetry in the United States Since 1950* (New York: Atheneum, 1969), captures the primal scene and will to individuation of the American sublime as a Puritan and Romantic legacy (xiii).

14 Tocqueville, *Democracy in America,* 456.

15 On the "bliss" that might result from abolishing this gender difference as customarily reified into bipolar opposition, see Jacques Derrida, "Voice ii," *boundary2* (1984):85; and Lee Edelman, "At Risk in the Sublime: The Politics of Gender and Theory," in *Gender & Theory: Dialogues on Feminist Criticism,* ed. Linda Kauffman (Oxford: Blackwell, 1989): 213–24, who evaluates feminist and homoerotic claims to refigure, rather than to recapitulate, an oedipal or "oppositional sublime."

16 Nietzsche, *Will to Power,* 420, 444–48.

17 On Whitman's sublimity founded in "*impure*" dictions from foreign countries, ethnic and regional dialects, or slang from lower-class vernaculars, in contrast to the aesthetic purity and de-ideologizing of the sublime in Poe, see Rob Wilson, "Lexical Scapegoating: The Pure and Impure of American Poetry," *Poetics Today* 8 (1987): 45–63.

18 Bloom's astutely *sublimating/desublimating* comment on Stevens is from *Wallace Stevens: The Poems of Our Climate* (Ithaca: Cornell

Univ. Press, 1977): 74. In contrast to the formal stylistics of Josephine Miles in *Eras & Modes in English Poetry* which effectively *"sublimate"* Whitman by registering his language in his own idealized terms, critical *"desublimation"* occurs when Edwin Haviland Miller, for example, connects Whitman's oceanic imagery with drives of homoerotic fantasy in *Walt Whitman's Poetry: A Psychological Journey* (New York: New York Univ. Press, 1968), or when Stephen Black in *Whitman's Journey into Chaos: A Psychoanalytic Study of the Poetic Process* (Princeton: Princeton Univ. Press, 1975) connects the language of achieved form to "sublimations" of autoerotic impulse.

19 On the American conjunction of "expressive individualism" (as in Whitman) and "utilitarian individualism" (as in Franklin) producing *lonely* citizens who seek to merge with other persons, with nature, or with the cosmos as a whole to overcome a bitter sense of economic competition of *each against all,* see Robert Bellah et al., eds., *Habits of the Heart: Individualism and Commitment in American Life* (Berkeley and Los Angeles: Univ. of California Press, 1985): 32–41 and 334. Also see Donald Pease on American literature's supplemental production, now and again, of "visionary compacts," in "Visionary Compacts and the Cold War Consensus," in his *Visionary Compacts* (see note 8). As Pease exposes the solipsism lurking in the imperialist unconscious of the American sublime, as prefigured in Emerson's "Nature," sublimity "results from an intensification of the interval, an excess—paradoxically enough—of relation. Or rather the Emersonian sublime arises with the breakdown of a continuous 'determinate' relation between self and other until only the connection between remains" (224). The sublime exists, then, both to ward off and to secure American individualism, just as this trope of sublimity (in Emerson at least) materializes and dematerializes the very location of Capital's higher power into a figure of thought.

20 My use of "interpellated" here to describe the Whitmanic subject of the sublime would allude to the way ideology constructs and refracts the subject through habits and practices of day-to-day, spontaneous belief. As a set of representational practices and codes, "the *structure* and mechanisms of [American] ideology are no more immediately *visible* to the people subjected to them than the *structure* of the relations of production, and the mechanisms of economic life produced by it, are visible to the agents of [literary] production" (Louis Althusser, "Theoretical Practice and Theoretical Formation," in *Philosophy and the Spontaneous Life of the Scientists & Other Essays,* ed. Gregory Elliott (London and New York: Verso, 1990): 26. As such, poets of the American sublime like Whitman *practice* this ideology; they do

not know it, nor in any full way can they claim to resist or recognize its innermost encodings into democratic modes of economic/symbolic domination.

21 Susan Sontag, "On Style," in *Against Interpretation* (New York: Dell, 1966): 25.

22 Jerome J. McGann, "Formalism, Savagery, and Care; or, The Function of Criticism Once Again," *Critical Inquiry* 2 (1976): 616.

23 Harold Bloom, "John Ashbery: The Charity of the Hard Moments," *Salmagundi* (1973): 111. Bloom's reading of "Song of Myself" as a crisis-poem of poetic vocation representing Whitman's struggle with "father" Emerson for phallo-poetic priority is argued in *Poetry and Repression: Revisionism from Blake to Stevens,* 248–66.

24 See Bridgman, Introduction to *Leaves of Grass* (see note 9): xxx.

25 Walt Whitman, "Democratic Vistas," in *Prose Works 1892,* vol. 2, ed. Floyd Stovall (New York: New York Univ. Press, 1964): 398.

26 *The Uncollected Poetry and Prose of Walt Whitman,* vol. 2, ed. Emory Holloway (Gloucester, Mass.: Peter Smith, 1972): 85.

27 In "A Backward Glance O'er Travel'd Roads" (1888), Whitman admitted his debt to sublime poetry of the intertextual *past,* even from "European feudalism's rich fund of epics, plays, ballads": "Another and separate point must now be candidly stated. If I had not stood before those poems with uncover'd head, fully aware of their colossal grandeur and beauty of form and spirit, I could not have written *Leaves of Grass*" (567–68).

28 Walt Whitman, *Prose Works 1892,* 731.

29 This comment applies to "Winter" from James Thomson, *The Seasons: to which is prefixed the life of the author* by P. Murdoch (New York: R. & W. A. Bartow, 1820). On modes of "The Aweful Sublime" of descriptive poetry all too popular in American poetry before Whitman, see Ralph Cohen, *The Unfolding of The Seasons* (Baltimore: Johns Hopkins Univ. Press, 1970): 295–315.

30 Walt Whitman, *Whitman's Manuscripts: Leaves of Grass (1860): A Parallel Text,* ed. Fredson Bowers (Chicago: Univ of Chicago Press, 1955): 3.

31 David Humphreys, "Preface to the Ninth Edition of the Poem on the Happiness of America" (1789), quoted in Leon Howard, *The Connecticut Wits* (Chicago: Univ. of Chicago Press, 1943): 249. Humphrey's own poetry was more predictably based, as a line claims, in "See[ing] nature's grandeur awfully unfold."

32 Thomas McGuane, in *Alive and Writing: Interviews with American Authors of the 1980s,* conducted by Larry McCaffery and Sinda Gregory (Urbana: Univ. of Illinois Press, 1987): 221.

33 Emerson's letter acknowledging Whitman as a "great power" of

"large perception" (mailed from Concord, 21 July 1855) is reprinted in *Walt Whitman,* ed. Francis Murphy (Middlesex, England: Penguin, 1969): 29. In the same letter, Emerson assumed the sublime influence of American geography upon the would-be "poet": "Yet America is a poem in our eyes; its ample geography dazzles the imagination, and it will not wait long for metres." Even commonplace images of Capital ("Banks and tariffs, . . ."), as of nature, "rest on the same foundations of wonder" that had once inspired Homer; see "The Poet," *Selected Writings of Ralph Waldo Emerson,* ed. William H. Gilman (New York: Signet, 1965): 324.

34 On the "topographical fallacy" assumed by such a nationalized sublime, see Benjamin T. Spencer, *The Quest For Nationality: An American Literary Campaign* (Syracuse: Syracuse Univ. Press, 1977): 13.

35 Walt Whitman, *Faint Clews and Indirections* ed. Clarence Gohdes and Rollo G. Silver (Durham, N.C.: Duke Univ. Press, 1949): 53.

36 Walt Whitman, *Prose Works, 1892,* vol. 1, ed. Floyd Stovall (New York: New York Univ. Press, 1963): 231–33.

37 Walt Whitman, *Walt Whitman's Workshop: A Collection of Unpublished Manuscripts,* ed. Clifton Joseph Furness (New York: Russell, 1964): 189.

38 Whitman, *Prose Works,* 2:397.

39 Ibid., 398–99.

40 Ibid., 2:412, 404.

41 Ibid., 678.

42 Walt Whitman, *An American Primer,* ed. Horace Traubel (Boston: Small, Maynard, 1904): viii–ix.

43 Leo Spitzer, "*Explication de Texte* Applied to Walt Whitman's Poem 'Out of the Cradle Endlessly Rocking,'" *Essays on English and American Literature* (Princeton: Princeton Univ. Press, 1962).

44 While documenting widespread pastoral reactions to technology in the nineteenth century, Leo Marx first called attention to the escalating "rhetoric of the technological sublime" in *The Machine in the Garden: Technology and the Pastoral Ideal in America* (New York: Oxford Univ. Press, 1964): 195–207, 222–25. An example he cites from Charles Caldwell, "Thoughts of the Moral and Other Indirect Influences of Rail-Roads" (1832), remains prophetic, it seems to me, of modernist and postmodernist domestications of American technology into icons of sublime domination/release: "Objects of exalted power and grandeur elevate the mind that seriously dwells on them, and impart to it greater compass and strength. Alpine scenery and an embattled ocean deepen contemplation, and give their own sublimity to the conceptions of beholders. The same will be true of our system of Rail-roads. Its vastness and magnificence will prove communicable,

and add to the standard of the intellect of our country" (195). Confronting such feats of sublime engineering as instances of American empowerment, then, American poets are enlisted to shift the locus of the sublime godhead from waterfalls and deserts to bridges, rockets, and skyscrapers whereby they can, like the waterfall-diver risking death in *Paterson,* abolish the ego, affirm God and country, and fleetingly (amid such self-dwarfing sublimity) matter.

45 Virginia Woolf, *A Room of One's Own* ([1929]; New York: Harcourt, 1957): 68–69.

46 Walt Whitman, *Uncollected Poetry,* vol. 2, 66.

47 Walt Whitman, *The Correspondence,* vol. 4, ed. Edwin Haviland Miller (New York: New York Univ. Press, 1969): 164.

48 On this pondering of "the Prairies" as a source of statistical (and "dynamic") immensity, see Whitman, *Prose Works 1892* 1:221. British imperial quests to discover remote landscapes so as to intensify waning sublime sensations ("All that expands the spirit, yet appals") are discussed in Chauncey C. Loomis, "The Arctic Sublime" in *Nature and the Victorian Imagination,* ed. U. C. Knoepflmacher and G. B. Tennyson (Berkeley and Los Angeles: Univ of California Press, 1977): 95–112. The "Romantic sublime" of Emerson, Thoreau, and Whitman gets broadly refigured in the visionary/capitalist discourse of travelogues, photographs, and government reports mapping the sublime as the will to possession in the Gilded Age: see David Wyatt, *The Fall into Eden: Landscape and Imagination in California* (Cambridge: Cambridge Univ. Press, 1986), chapter 2, "Muir and the Possession of Landscape."

49 The Emersonian dynamics of this claim are exposed in Donald Pease, "Sublime Politics," in *The American Sublime,* ed. Mary Arensberg (Albany: State Univ. of New York Press, 1986): 46–47. As Oliver Wendell Holmes warily argued in 1840, reviewing a Washington Allston exhibition, "The mountains and cataracts, which were to have made poets and painters, have been mined for anthracite and damned for power" (*North American Review* 50 [1840]:358–59). Ratifying both aesthetic and technological uses of nature as equally compelling, the ideology of the sublime trapped Americans such as Whitman into a contradictory discourse on expanding national "power." The natural sublime amplified and expressed, at a symbolic remove, the divided American will to contemplate/dominate this greater power. Although in Whitman's New York state, for example, and especially in the Lower Hudson Valley, as Raymond J. O'Brien argues, "the doctrine of sublime scenery was the underlying ideal called upon to justify [environmental] preservation" during the nineteenth century and was even assumed in the battle to prevent Storm King Mountain from

being turned into a Con Edison hydroelectric plant in 1980, the equally compelling American claim to tap into, develop, and dominate this natural power of the Hudson River Valley was no less rooted in the dynamics of the "technological sublime." These competing claims of aesthetic/therapeutic preservation and economic/utilitarian domination of natural sublimity are carefully documented in Raymond J. O'Brien, *American Sublime: Landscape and Scenery of the Lower Hudson Valley* (New York: Columbia Univ. Press, 1981). That the majestic force of the American sublime, as manifest at Niagara Falls, would be used both to stimulate aesthetic mastery in artists such as Thomas Cole and Frederic Edwin Church and to ratify commercial energies of electricity, tourism, circus feats, quarrying, hydraulic works, and so on is the fall-from-Eden scenario traced in Elizabeth McKinsey, *Niagara Falls: Icon of the American Sublime* (Cambridge: Cambridge Univ. Press, 1985).

Chapter 7. Wallace Stevens: Decreating the American Sublime

1 Jacques Derrida, *La Verité en Peinture* (Paris: Flammarion, 1978): 146. My epigraph is taken from Steven's response to a *Partisan Review* questionnaire on "The Situation in American Writing," *Opus Posthumous* ed. Milton J. Bates (New York: Knopf, 1989): 310. The proto-deconstructive metaphorics of the "negative sublime" as encountered, instigated, and resisted at borders/margins of textuality in Stevens are outlined in Michael T. Beehler, "Kant and Stevens: The Dynamics of the Sublime and the Dynamics of Poetry," in *The American Sublime,* ed. Mary Arensberg (Albany: State Univ. of New York Press, 1986): 131–52, and Paul A. Bové, "Fiction, Risk, and Deconstruction: The Poetry of Wallace Stevens," in his *Destructive Poetics: Heidegger and Modern American Poetry* (New York: Columbia Univ. Press, 1980): 181–216. The latter work compellingly charts Stevens attempt to overcome nothingness as weak willing (irony).

2 This "French" Kant's analytic of the sublime (in the *Third Critique*) is situated in terms implicating both aesthetic and political values ("judgments") and language-games ("rules") of new formations in David Carroll's analysis of Jean-François Lyotard's *Le Différend* and Jean-Luc Nancy's "L'Offrande sublime," in *Paraesthetics: Foucault, Lyotard, Derrida* (New York: Metheun, 1987): 155–84. Lyotard's ascription (even *prescription*) of an "aesthetic of the sublime" to modernism/postmodernism generally, as a formal mandate in the aes-

thetics of the West, remains paramount: "As for a politics of the sublime, there is none. If there were, it could only be Terror. But in politics, there is an aesthetics of the sublime" (quoted by Carroll from *Le postmoderne expliqué aux enfants* [1986], 180). See Jean-François Lyotard, "The Sublime and the Avant-Garde," in *The Lyotard Reader* ed. Andrew Benjamin (Oxford: Blackwell, 1989), 196–211.

3   Walt Whitman, "Song of Myself," *Leaves of Grass: Comprehensive Reader's Edition,* ed. Harold W. Blodgett and Sculley Bradley (New York: Norton, 1968): 56. Searching for "a romantic that is potent" (183), Stevens argues persistently for some American difference of temperament and style that remains neither British nor French in genealogy: "Nothing could be more inappropriate to American literature than its English source since the Americans are not British in sensibility" ("Adagia," in *Opus Posthumous,* 201).

4   On the fading aura of the natural sublime as deployed into technological and commercial formations, see Elizabeth McKinsey, *Niagara Falls: Icon of the American Sublime* (Cambridge: Cambridge Univ. Press, 1985), part 5. McKinsey ends by invoking the self-conscious sublimity of Stevens as an attempt to recuperate ("recreate") this environmental aura and thereby serve an ecological mandate to preservation (282). On the hold of environmental metaphors, see Frederick Jackson Turner, "The Significance of the Frontier in American History," Annual Report, The American Historical Association (1893): 190–227.

5   Wallace Stevens, *The Collected Poems* (New York: Alfred A. Knopf, 1965): 403.

6   See Wallace Stevens, *Letters of Wallace Stevens,* selected and edited by Holly Stevens (New York: Alfred A. Knopf, 1966): 237. "Owl's Clover," with its unremarked sublimity, is reprinted in *Opus Posthumous,* 86, as is "The Sail of Ulysses" (1954), which provides Beehler's proof-text (see note 1). The Keatsian "poetic angelism" that Stevens warred against if not introjected as a "false sublime" is historicized, in gender and career terms, by Frank Lentricchia, "Writing After Hours," in his *Ariel and the Police: Michel Foucault, William James, Wallace Stevens* (Madison: Univ. of Wisconsin Press, 1988): 158–73. The "economachismo" of the Whitmanic sublime would, I think, more fully haunt and inhabit the reaches of Stevens's American imagination. "Would you be likely to mistake *Leaves of Grass* for something English?" Stevens asks readers of *Modern American Poetry* in 1950 (*Opus Posthumous,* 315).

7   The half-antagonistic relationship between Stevens and these tropes of Transcendental idealism is detailed in the overdeterministic ponderings of Harold Bloom in *Wallace Stevens: The Poems of Our Cli-*

mate (Ithaca: Cornell Univ. Press, 1977). On the familial erotics and rigorous textuality of such post-Romantic quests to interiorize American vastness, see Mary Arensberg, "White Mythology and the American Sublime: Stevens' Auroral Fantasy," (*American Sublime*, 153–72). Her earlier claim is that "Stevens is so belated a poet that for him the sublime is already a fiction, an effect of rhetoric with no reference to an experience outside the text" (16). This may well point "toward the poststructuralist sublime" (17), but such "decreations" have to be filtered through the ideology of the American sublime which, in part, comprises Stevens's "experience" of it. In "Like Decorations in a Nigger Cemetery" (1935), Stevens takes an elegiac stance toward Whitman's sublimity as if it were a *setting sun* which the modernist poet must supplant (that is, *decreate* and *recreate*) with an "incandescent" imagery of particulars and synoptic generalizations befitting this once-great land. Whitman comprises a "first idea" of this American sun—as a force of majesty still blessing and cursing the present.

8 Robert Frost's more muted, New Englandly struggle to domesticate the sublime as a terrain (and trope) not of vast outer space but of inner spaces nearer home and the wounded psyche occurs in "Desert Places" (1934); on this ironical vernacularizing of the sublime, see Richard Poirier, *Robert Frost: The Work of Knowing* (New York: Oxford Univ. Press, 1977): 144–49.

9 Wallace Stevens, "The Noble Rider and the Sound of Words," in *The Necessary Angel: Essays on Reality and the Imagination* (New York: Random House, 1951): 35. Fully "conscious of negations" emerging in the revolutionary 1930s and 1940s, Stevens strove to maintain some "nobility" or "majesty" of language and self-image that would be credible as charismatic aura; which is to say, in less social or class-conscious terms, he courted the grand language and "elevation" of sublimity. But *nobility,* like the sublime, must remain "unfixed" for Stevens, "because if it is defined, it will be fixed and it must not be fixed. . . . To fix it is to put an end to it" (34).

10 Valéry's comment is used in an apology for minimality of craft and mood by Mark Strand, "Notes on the Craft of Poetry," *Antaeus* 30–31 (1978): 346; it is from Paul Valéry, *The Art of Poetry* (New York: Vintage, 1961): 57. A post-Romantic sublime, to be credible as form and pragmatic belief, must, in Stevens's view, survive the scrutiny of critical intelligence *within the poem,* unless it remain narcissism or residual animism: "What we have called elevation and elation on the part of the poet, which he communicates to the reader, may be not so much elevation as an incandescence of the intelligence and so more than ever a triumph over the incredible," as Stevens claims in quasi-Longinian terms of mutual bliss ("The Noble Rider," 60).

11   Wallace Stevens, "The American Sublime," *The Palm at the End of the Mind,* ed. Holly Stevens (New York: Vintage, 1971): 114. Subsequent references to *Palm* will appear in parentheses in the text.

12   Thomas Weiskel's Kantian/Freudian decoding of the sublime as a self-empowering moment of semiotic bewilderment yet of dynastic authority in Wordsworth, Blake, and Stevens, is argued in *The Romantic Sublime: Studies in the Structure and Psychology of Transcendence* (Baltimore: Johns Hopkins Univ. Press, 1976): 3 ff. Hudson River School and Luminist versions of sublime landscapes, with their latently nationalist and Emersonian underpinnings, are discussed in Barbara Novak, *Nature and Culture: American Landscape and Painting, 1825–1875* (New York: Oxford Univ. Press, 1980): 34–44. On the shift in American modernism/postmodernism from representations of a *natural sublime* toward the detextualized or spatial *emptiness* emerging as an "Abstract Sublime," see Kynaston McShine, ed., *The Natural Paradise: Painting in America, 1800–1950* (New York: Museum of Modern Art, 1976): 59–129. In Barnett Newman's "The Sublime Is Now" (1948), the American painter of works such as *Vir Heroicus Sublimis* (1950–1951) struggles to articulate a credible concept of "the sublime" amid postmodern negations such as Hiroshima and Auschwitz, or, as he says, "in a time without a legend or mythos that can be called sublime": "We are freeing ourselves of the impediments of memory, association, nostalgia, legend, myth, or what have you, that have been the devices of Western European painting. Instead of making *cathedrals* out of Christ, man, or 'life,' we are making it out of ourselves, out of our own feelings" (essay excerpted in McShine, *The Natural Paradise,* 120–23). Newman's *Emersonian* affirmation of self-reliance as *the* ground of any American sublime would partially fit for the dynamics of Stevens. He wrought the "cathedral" of a sublime art (his *Harmonium* or *Grand Poem*) out of imagination by first *decreating* ("freeing ourselves of") illusory notions that seek to reify the sublime in the landscape, in the logocentric bread and wine of Christianity, in heroic statues of General Jackson, and so on, as I will detail in this chapter through intertextual allusions to several poems. On the representational tactics of sublime "indeterminacy" in Newman, by way of Kant and Judaic epistemology, see Lyotard, "Newman: The Instant," in *The Lyotard Reader,* 240–49 (see note 2).

13   Stevens, "Noble Rider," 8–11. On the Mills statue, see Joshua C. Taylor, *The Fine Arts in America* (Chicago: Univ. of Chicago Press, 1979): 63. On the will to public monumentality and a visible "elevation" of American style, see Michael North, *The Final Sculpture:*

310

Public Monuments and Modern Poets (Ithaca, N.Y.: Cornell Univ. Press, 1985): 185–227.

14 Alexis de Tocqueville, *Democracy in America,* vol. 2, trans. George Lawrence (New York: Harper, 1966), 436 ("Why the Americans Erect Some Petty Monuments and Others That Are Very Grand").

15 Wallace Stevens, "A Weak Mind in the Mountains," *The Palm at the End of Mind,* ed. Holly Stevens (New York: Vintage, 1971), 155.

16 Walt Whitman, "Preface," 1855, to first issue of *Leaves of Grass,* in *Prose Works 1892,* ed. Floyd Stovall (New York: New York Univ. Press, 1964): 435–36.

17 Stevens encountered this crucial (French) concept of *decreation* in Simone Weil's *Le Pesanteur et La Grâce* where, in his own words, "she says that decreation is making pass from the created to the uncreated," a power of ideological *negation* crucial for Stevens to modern art. The rather necessary (American) movement beyond "decreation" to "recreation" is traced by Roy Harvey Pearce in "Toward Decreation: Stevens and the 'Theory of Poetry,' in *Wallace Stevens: A Celebration,* ed. Frank Doggett and Robert Buttel (Princeton: Princeton Univ. Press, 1980): 286–307. On the adjectival components of the sublime style, imported from Miltonic England to the liberal wilds of America, see Josephine Miles, *Eras & Modes In English Poetry* (Berkeley and Los Angeles: Univ. of California Press, 1964): 48–77, 224–48.

18 Figurative mystifications that obtain in any self-consuming identity between the sublime of nature and the rhetoric of poetry are traced (in Hegelian terms) by Geoffrey H. Hartman, "From the Sublime to the Hermeneutic," in *The Fate of Reading* (Chicago: Univ. of Chicago Press, 1975): 114–23. Also see Hartman's analysis of Wordsworthian poets seeking to "domesticate the sublime" of nature and Milton, "Blessing the Torrent: On Wordsworth's Later Style," *PMLA* 93:196–204.

19 Stevens's post-humanist struggle with such Romantic notions of the sublime is argued (in nicely revisioned Longinian terms) by Helen Vendler, "Wallace Stevens: The False and True Sublime," in *Part of Nature, Part of Us: Modern American Poets* (Cambridge: Harvard Univ. Press, 1980): 1–15: "One quarrel [in Stevens's mind] was between the sublime and the not-sublime; the other was between two forms of the sublime—the received and the new." The limitations of purely "deconstructive accounts" of metaphorical play in Stevens are argued in Charles Altieri, "Wallace Stevens' Metaphors of Metaphor: Poetry as Theory," *American Poetry* 1 (Fall 1983): 27–48, wherein "two styles" of metaphoric language are seen to work in subtle co-

operation, though the terms of *plain* and *sublime* are not used in Altieri's description. On this dialectic of imaginative "poverty" and "the sublime" in modern American poetry, especially Stevens, see Daniel O'Hara, "The Poverty of Theory: On Society and the Sublime," *Contemporary Literature* 26 (1985):335–50.

20 Emerson enunciates this dialectic between inner emptiness (ego) and immensity (geography, history, and what we would now call "intertextuality") that such an ego-relying American sublime entails in "Circles" (1840): "Alas for this infirm faith, this will not strenuous, this vast ebb of a vast flow! I am a God in nature; I am a weed by the wall." On this "Emersonian" over-faith giving way to emergencies of self-affirmation, see Bloom, *Wallace Stevens*, 63–77, 354–57.

21 Walter Jackson Bate counters anxiety towards textual grandeur by defending the ideal-mimetic of the sublime as "a release of what is 'below the threshold' of consciousness for fulfillment in and through the great," in *The Burden of the Past and the English Poet* (London: Chatto, 1971): 129–31. According to this "Longinian" mimetic of greatness, the past functions as a self-empowering agency and provides models of selfhood more than it comprises a legacy haunting *all* literature, even Samuel Beckett's plays, as oedipal recapitulations of "the anxiety of influence."

22 I quote from Stevens's annotated copy of Richards's *Coleridge on Imagination*, with Longinus's comment noted in Stevens's hand on the inside back cover, which can be found in the Stevens Collection of the Huntington Library, San Marino, California. I have examined Stevens's *marginalia* here and in his collected edition of Emerson's works, an "intertext" of American idealism and the will to Capitalist sublimity which he knew and remembered quite well, in intense spots, as he echoed a self-reliant Emersonianism throughout his poems (as Bloom claims).

23 Robert Penn Warren, "Homage to Emerson, On Night Flight to New York," in *Selected Poems: 1923–1975* (New York: Random House, 1976): 153.

24 The contradiction haunting such an Emersonian "*double consciousness,*" whereby American poetics is drawn *both* to *transcendental idealism* and to *pragmatic instrumentalism,* to commodity-transfiguring symbol and to commodity-beholden fact, is argued in Rob Wilson, "Sculling to the Over-Soul: Louis Simpson, American Transcendentalism, and Thomas Eakin's *Max Schmitt in a Single Scull*," *American Quarterly* 39 (1987): 410–30.

25 "St. Armorer's Church from the Outside," *The Collected Poems of Wallace Stevens*, 529–30.

26 Jean-François Lyotard, "The Sublime and the Avant-Garde," 204. As

Lyotard describes this dynamic at work in the paintings of Barnett Newman, "What is sublime is the feeling that something will happen, despite everything, within this threatening void, that something will take 'place' and will announce that everything is not over. That place is mere 'here,' the most minimal occurrence" (245). Given the traditions both Newman and Stevens confront, this avant-garde struggle with Romantic sublimity is not just aesthetically but ideologically mandated.

27 See Milton Bates, *Wallace Stevens: A Mythology of Self* (Berkeley and Los Angeles: Univ. of California Press, 1985): 154.

28 Entry dated Sept. 12–20, 1841, in *Emerson in His Journals,* ed. Joel Porte (Cambridge: Harvard Univ. Press, 1982): 259. In *Ecstatic Occasions, Expedient Forms* (New York: Collier, 1987), an anthology of the "new formalism" emerging in the 1980s, the editor, David Lehman, invokes Stevens's "ecstatic" image of disembodied sky-serpents in "The Auroras of Autumn" ("This is form gulping after formlessness") and A. R. Ammons's in *Sphere* ("The shapes nearest shapelessness awe us most / suggest the god") to argue the American (that is, Emersonian) case *against* inherited forms and small structures. Lehman posits the ongoing lure of such egodwarfing rapture ("formlessness") for *any* American poet, however formalist his or her ultimate reach: "A distrust of received forms seems endemic to American poets. It is predicated on the conviction that depth or complexity of vision, force of passion, profundity of insight, or whatever it is that distinguishes art from mere craft will invariably precede rather than follow from a formal maneuver" (215–17). This view, Lehman claims like many a repressive modernist, found its first exemplar in Whitman's "barbaric yawp"—and its first great theoretical sponsor in Emerson (in "The Poet").

Chapter 8. Postmodern Sublime: New Admonitions/ Premonitions of the Vast

1 *Letters of Thomas Gray,* ed. John Beresford (London: Oxford Univ. Press, 1951): 44–45.

2 *Letters of Wallace Stevens,* ed. Holly Stevens (New York: Knopf, 1981): 291–92.

3 See the project in idealized domination of "the slovenly wilderness" documented in Franklin Kelly, *Frederic Edwin Church and the National Landscape* (Washington, D.C.: Smithsonian, 1988). The modernist infatuation with the "aesthetics of technology" is established in

Lisa M. Steinman, *Made in America: Science, Technology, and American Modernist Poets* (New Haven: Yale Univ. Press, 1987) and Dickran Tashjian, *Skyscraper Primitives: Dada and the American Avant-Garde, 1910–1925* (Middletown, Conn.: Wesleyan Univ. Press, 1975). The latter analysis is helpful on Hart Crane's technological euphoria/dread.

4 Wallace Stevens, "Mr. Burnshaw and the Statue," *Opus Posthumous,* ed. Milton J. Bates (New York: Alfred A. Knopf, 1989): 83.

5 Ralph Waldo Emerson, *Emerson in His Journals,* ed. Joel Porte (Cambridge: Harvard Univ. Press, 1982): 321. While documenting pastoral reactions to technology, Leo Marx notes the shift towards an emerging "rhetoric of the technological sublime" in *The Machine in the Garden: Technology and the Pastoral Ideal in America* (New York: Oxford Univ. Press, 1964): 195–207, 222–25.

6 Wallace Stevens, "Owl's Clover," *Opus Posthumous,* ed. Milton J. Bates (New York: Knopf, 1989): 94.

7 See Arthur Kroker, Marilouise Kroker, and David Cook, eds., *Panic Encyclopedia: The Definitive Guide to the Postmodern Scene* (New York: St. Martin's, 1989): 13–17. A mood of *panic sublimity* emanates from "[living] on the edge of ecstasy and dread"—the North American self dwarfed from political efficacy in a context of high-tech and sign-glut, drifting within an "oscillating *fin-de-millenium* mood of deep euphoria *and* despair."

8 Wallace Stevens, "A Duck For Dinner," in *Opus Posthumous,* 92.

9 Alexis de Tocqueville, "On Some Sources of Poetic Inspiration in Democracies," in *Democracy in America,* vol. 2, trans. George Lawrence (New York: Harper, 1966): 454–55.

10 Jean Baudrillard, *America,* trans. Chris Turner (London and New York: Verso, 1989): 27.

11 Carl Sagan, "The Gift of Apollo," *Parade,* 16 July 1989: 6.

12 Wallace Stevens, "The American Sublime," in *The Collected Poems* (New York: Alfred A. Knopf, 1974): 131. On Stevens's confrontation with modernist "nothingness," see Daniel O'Hara, "The Poverty of Theory: On Society and the Sublime," *Contemporary Literature* 26 (1985): 335–50; and Fredric Jameson on the enclave of "theory" and the "intricate evasions of as" during the Cold War, "Wallace Stevens," *New Orleans Review* 2 (1984): 10–19.

13 On "technological marginalization," see Fredric Jameson, "Baudelaire as Modernist and Postmodernist: The Dissolution of the Referent and the Artificial 'Sublime,'" in *Lyric Poetry: Beyond New Criticism,* ed. Chaviva Hošek and Patricia Parker (Ithaca, N.Y.: Cornell Univ. Press, 1985): 247–63. For Jameson's reformulation of the sublime as an awe interpellating the libidinous subject of multinational

capitalism, see "Postmodernism and Consumer Society" in *The Anti-Aesthetic: Essays on Postmodern Culture,* ed. Hal Foster (Port Townsend, Washington: Bay Press, 1983): 111–25, and "Postmodernism, or The Cultural Logic of Late Capitalism," *New Left Review* 146 (1984): 52–92.

14 Jean-François Lyotard, *The Postmodern Condition: A Report on Knowledge,* trans. by Geoff Bennington and Brian Massumi (Minneapolis: Univ. of Minnesota Press, 1984): 51. Also see the Lyotard issue of *Diacritics* 14 (Fall 1984), especially David Carroll, "Rephrasing the Political with Kant and Lyotard: From Aesthetic to Political Judgments" (74–88); Jean-François Lyotard, "On Terror and the Sublime," *Telos* 67 (1986):196–98; and David Carroll, *Paraesthetics: Foucault, Lyotard, Derrida* (New York: Methuen, 1987): 141–44, 180–84.

15 Hart Crane, "Cape Hatteras," from *The Bridge,* in *The Complete Poems and Selected Letters and Prose,* ed. Brom Weber (Garden City, N.Y.: Doubleday, 1966): 90. The post-Romantic transference of sublimity from objects of nature to forces of technology, which Crane's poetic nervously assumes, is argued in Catherine McKinsey, *Niagara Falls: Icon of the American Sublime* (Cambridge: Cambridge Univ. Press, 1985): "technology at Niagara soon far outweighed nature in its imaginative appeal" (139).

16 See Bill McKibben, "The End of Nature," *The New Yorker,* 11 Sept. 1989: 47–105. The two poems that appear in the same issue are ironically nature-beholden: "John Updike's "To a Box Turtle" and James Schuyler's "Yellow Flowers," which ends, "[you] grunt in delight / at their sunset sweetness // it begins with 'C'// yes: coreopsis."

17 Although Emerson considered the mountains and observatory of Williamstown equally sublime—"Of all tools, an observatory is the most sublime" (*Journals,* 530) as he wrote on 14 Nov. 1865—his concept of the sublime was dominantly instigated by natural objects, large or small, as in this journal entry dated 26–28 April, 1838: "At night I went out into the dark & saw a glimmering star & heard a frog & Nature seemed to say Well do not these suffice? Here is a new scene, a new experience. Ponder it, Emerson, & not like the foolish world hanker after thunders & multitudes & vast landscapes, the sea or Niagara" (*Journals,* 185).

18 On this problematic of naming/unnaming afflicting the emergence of decolonized subjects and nation-states, see Kimberly Benston, "I Am What I Am: The Topos of Un(naming) in Afro-American Literature," *Black Literature and Literary Theory,* ed. Henry Louis Gates, Jr. (New York: Metheun, 1984): 153. On the potential reifying of this ethnic essence/difference (as African, Indian, Korean, American, and

so on) into a transcendent sublimity immune to domination, see Radha Radhakrishnan's deconstruction, "Ethnic Identity and Post-Structuralist Difference," *Cultural Critique* 6 (1987):199–220.

19 Régis Debray, *Strategy for Revolution*, ed. Robin Blackburn (London: Jonathan Cape, 1970): 232–33. On feminist revisionings of the Romantic sublime in poststructuralist theory and poetic practice, see Patricia Yaeger, "Toward a Female Sublime," in *Gender & Theory: Dialogues on Feminist Criticism*, ed. Linda Kauffman (Oxford: Blackwell, 1989): 191–212, who goes beyond her early claim that "the sublime is a risky genre for Bishop to re-invent, or for the feminist critic to reaffirm, because it is an outmoded genre [of oedipal agonistics] that has little relevance for a modernist poetics" (196).

20 Neil Hertz, "The Notion of Blockage in the Literature of the Sublime," in *Psychoanalysis and the Question of the Text,* ed. Geoffrey H. Hartman (Baltimore: Johns Hopkins Univ. Press, 1978): 78. Hart Crane, "Cape Hatteras," *Complete Poems,* 94.

21 Stevens, "Man on the Dump," in *Collected Poems,* 201–3.

22 Ibid., 24.

23 Thomas Pynchon, *Gravity's Rainbow* (New York: Viking, 1973): 3. Though the sky's [nuclear] "screaming" "has happened before, but there is nothing to compare it to now," Pynchon counters this postwar nihilism with Werhner von Braun's idealism in an epigraph to "Beyond the Zero": "Nature does not know extinction; all it knows is transformation." See Marc W. Redfield, "Pynchon's Postmodern Sublime," *PMLA* 104 (1989):152–62.

24 Immanuel Kant, *The Critique of Judgment,* trans. J. H. Bernard (New York: Hafner, 1966): 83.

25 See Samuel H. Monk, *The Sublime: A Study of Critical Theories in XVIII-Century England* (Ann Arbor: Univ. of Michigan Press, 1960): 4–9, 84–100.

26 Steven Knapp, *Personification and the Sublime: Milton to Coleridge* (Cambridge: Harvard Univ. Press, 1985): 3–4, 74–82. On the tragic individualism emerging out of this Romantic sublime, see R. Jahan Ramanzani, "Yeats: Tragic Joy and the Sublime," *PMLA* 104 (1989):163–77.

27 For a critique of the liberating force of the idealist sublime, see T. W. Adorno, *Aesthetic Theory* (London: Routledge & Kegan Paul, 1984), trans. C. Lenhardt, 284, 134–37, 280–84, and 387.

28 See Edmund Burke, *A Philosophical Enquiry into the Origin of Our Ideas of the Sublime and Beautiful,* ed. J. T. Boulton (Notre Dame, Ind.: Univ. of Notre Dame Press, 1968): 70. For a reading of political burdens of the sublime—woman as "the [inmobilized, swooning] beautiful"—see Frances Ferguson, "The Sublime of Edmund Burke,

or the Bathos of Experience," *Glyph* 8 (1981):62–78. For implications of this Burkean tradition, also see the special issue on "The Sublime and the Beautiful: Reconsiderations," *New Literary History* 16 (1985). As Peter de Bolla shrewdly argues of Burke's sublime, mapping the unlegislatable if not unthinkable excess of subjectivity in/as the discourse of the sublime, "Burke, for a number of reasons, among which we must include political aims and ends, stops short of a discourse on the sublime, and in so doing he reinstates the ultimate power of an adjacent discourse, theology, which locates its own self-authenticating power firmly within the boundaries of the godhead," [*The Discourse of the Sublime: History, Aesthetics & the Subject* (Oxford: Blackwell, 1989): 65–72].

29 Michel Foucault, *Discipline & Punish: The Birth of the Prison,* trans. Alan Sheridan (New York: Vintage Books, 1979): 26.

30 The "incommensurability of reality to concept" is Lyotard's ascription of the post-Kantian sublime to avant-garde art generally as a heterogeneous plenitude immune to totalization or ideological reification: see *The Postmodern Condition,* 71–82, as well as the pragmatics of sublime performance worked out in Jean-François Lyotard and Jean-Loup Thébaud, *Just Gaming,* trans. Wlad Godzich (Minneapolis: Minnesota Univ. Press, 1985: "Justice here [in postmodern language games] does not consist merely in the observance of the rules; as in all games, it consists in working at the limits of what the rules permit, in order to permit new moves, perhaps new rules and therefore new games" (100). On the "heterogeneous 'sublime'" that emanates from the postmodern aesthetic of Lyotard and Bakhtin, see Murray Krieger's linkages of literary de-totalizations to social freedoms in "The Literary, the Textual, the Social," in *The Aims of Representation: Subject/Text/History,* ed. M. Krieger (New York: Columbia Univ. Press, 1987): 1–22, as well as Lyotard's essay on the Kantian sublime after Marx in the same collection, "Judiciousness in Dispute: Or Kant After Marx" 23–67. I want to make it clear that I do not subscribe to this opposition of the sublime (aesthetic) to the ideological (political) because, historically speaking, the sublime has been enlisted to support and enact phrases of ideology, theology, the capitalist subject, and the Western nation-state. In some ideal realm, perhaps, the aesthetic sublime is immune to ideological appropriations and instantiations, but this is not how poets of the sublime such as Whitman or Stevens work.

31 Historians of the postmodern moment would rescue the "historical sublime" from more domesticating politics of the beautiful which seek to tame, through orderly machinations of "narrative discipline," what Schiller invokes as "the terrifying and magnificent spectacle of

change which destroys everything and creates it anew." The demotion of the sublime in favor of the beautiful, which pervaded the heritage of German historicism even in radical critics of modernist art such as Herbert Marcuse, needs to be reversed through an alternative narration which claims that, as Hayden White contends, "Romanticism represented the last attempt in the West to generate a visionary politics on the basis of a sublime conception of the historical process" (135). The sublime remains a desublimating mode of narrative history evoking spectacles not of *subjugation* but of *contingency, disorder, chaos*—history becomes a textual wilderness whose meaninglessness or multiple meanings can only be overcome through master-tropings of the narrating subject. See Hayden White, "The Politics of Historical Interpretation: Discipline and De-Sublimation," in *The Politics of Interpretation,* ed. W. J. T. Mitchell (Chicago: Univ. of Chicago Press, 1983): 135, whose essay depends heavily upon Freidrich von Schiller, *Naive and Sentimental Poetry and On the Sublime,* trans. Julias A. Elias (New York: Frederick Ungar, 1975): 210.

32 Mike Davis, "Urban Renaissance and the Spirit of Postmodernism," *New Left Review* 151 (1985): 106–24. On this parodic sublimity within the post-Venturi vocabulary of American architecture, one "actually playing *up* to American megalomania," barbaric yawps, and "grandiose sentiments" (84), see Tom Wolfe, *From Bauhaus to Our House* (New York: Washington Square, 1981): 60–63, 84–108.

33 John Rieder, "Embracing the Alien: Science Fiction in Mass Culture," *Science-Fiction Studies* 9 (1982):26–37. On this collective will to produce a technological heaven in "Tomorrowland," see Louis Marin, "Disneyland: A Degenerate Utopia," *Glyph* 1 (1977):50–66. Mapping the terrain of this *neo*-sublime, Terry Gilliam's film *Brazil* (1984) presents dystopic images which wildly capture this false sublime of technological displacement: "And this ultimately means that something in the vision of *Brazil* reverberates with the late capitalist experience, the subjectivity that engages with urban vastness, with faceless bureaucracy, with the moral decay accompanying the commodification of all social relationships" (Fred Glass, Review of *Brazil, Film Quarterly* 39 [1986]:28).

34 Norman Mailer, *Of a Fire on the Moon* (New York: American Library, 1968): 55. The model here is Henry Adams.

35 For a scathing analysis of the technologies inducing *derealization* through a "sublime" process of simulacrous infinitude and semiotic overload ("the ecstasy of communication"), see Jean Baudrillard, *Simulations,* trans. Paul Foss, Paul Patton and Philip Beitchman (New York: Semiotext(e), 1983); and Baudrillard, "The Ecstasy of Com-

munication," in *The Anti-Aesthetic,* trans. John Johnson 126–33. This disturbing assimilation of commodity structures and values of postmodern art is moralized in Charles Newman, *The Post-Modern Aura: The Act of Fiction in an Age of Inflation* (Evanston, Ill.: Northwestern Univ. Press, 1985). Also see the strategy of re-aestheticized commoditization outlined in Arthur Kroker and David Cook, *The Postmodern Scene: Excremental Culture and Hyper-Aesthetics* (New York: St. Martin's, 1986).

36   John Ashbery, "Syringa," in *Houseboat Days* (New York: Penguin, 1977): 69–71. On the shift from the euphoria of international modernism to more disenchanted modes of postmodernism, as in Ashbery, see Daniel L. Guillory, "Leaving the Atocha Station: Contemporary Poetry and Technology," *TriQuarterly* 12 (1981):165–81.

37   John Ashbery, "Late Echo," *As We Know* (New York: Viking, 1979): 88; Wallace Stevens, "Nomad Exquisite," *The Palm at the End of the Mind,* ed. Holly Stevens (New York: Alfred A. Knopf, 1971): 44.

38   See Susan Sontag, "Notes on 'Camp,' " and "The Imagination of Disaster," in *Against Interpretation* (New York: Dell, 1969), whose "allegorical" analysis of the *mass traumas,* real and imagined in SF genre films of the 50s, situates the depersonalized anxiety/bliss that afflicts New York city poets such as Ashbery (or Ted Berrigan) in these post-nuclear terms: "Ours is indeed an age of extremity. For we live under continual threat of two equally fearful, but seemingly opposed, destinies: unremitting banality and inconceivable [nuclear] terror" (227). "Camp" mock-luxuriated in the commodity infinitude of simulacrous Americana. As Sontag explains, "Nothing in nature can be camp . . . A great deal of Camp suggests Emerson's phrase, 'urban pastoral' " (280).

39   See Fredric Jameson on these postindustrial technologies of "hyperspace" which induce a "waning of affect" and a "euphoria" that comprises a highly unstable ("depthless") sublimity, as when watching the image-glutted videos of Nam Juin Paik as staged in a New York bank lobby, in "Postmodernism, or The Cultural Logic of Late Capitalism," 76–85. For Paik's impact on the desperately mediated politics of postmodern American fiction, see Robert Siegle, *Suburban Ambush: Downtown Writing and the Fiction of Insurgency* (Baltimore: Johns Hopkins Univ. Press, 1989): 20–25. John Ashbery, *April Galleons* (New York: Viking, 1987).

40   John Ashbery, "Down By the Station Early in the Morning," *A Wave* (New York: Viking, 1984): 14.

41   See Jean Baudrillard on "the *satellization of the real,* the putting into orbit of an indefinable reality without common measure to the fan-

tasies that once used to ornament it," in *Simulations,* trans. Paul Foss, Paul Patton, and Philip Beitchman (New York: Semiotext(e), 1983): 149.

42 See Fredric Jameson on "The Abolition of Critical Distance" under Capital, as this obtains in postmodern art, in "Postmodernism, or The Cultural Logic of Late Capitalism," 85–88; Jameson's strategy is to disseminate the "cognitive mapping" of *theory* as a way to "disalienate" such urban space (if not postmodern art).

43 John Ashbery, "So Many Lives," in *A Wave,* 54.

44 John Ashbery, "Around the Rough and Rugged Rocks the Ragged Rascal Rudely Ran," *A Wave,* 15.

45 John Ashbery, "A Wave," *A Wave:* 69.

46 Ibid., 70.

47 Louis Simpson comments on Wordsworthian allusions in "The Hour of Feeling" in Alberta T. Turner, ed., *50 Contemporary Poets: The Creative Process* (New York: Longman, 1977): 284. The effect of American cities upon Whitman in 1871 was no less daunting and exhilarating: "When I pass to and fro, different latitudes, different seasons, beholding the crowds of the great cities, New York, Boston, Philadelphia, Cincinnati, Chicago, St. Louis, San Francisco, New Orleans, Baltimore—when I mix with these interminable swarms of alert, turbulent, good-natured, independent citizens, merchants, young persons—at the idea of this mass of men, so fresh and free, so loving and so proud, a singular awe falls upon me. I feel, with dejection and amazement, that among our geniuses and talented writers or speakers, few or none have yet really spoken to this people, created a single image-making work for them, or absorbed the central spirit and the idiosyncrasies which are theirs—and which, thus, in highest far remain uncelebrated, unexpress'd." "Dejection and amazement" have to give way to sublime representation or remain baffled, democratic, mute (Walt Whitman, *Prose Works,* ed. Floyd Stovall [New York: New York Univ. Press, 1965]: 308–9).

48 Robert Lowell, "The Mouth of the Hudson," in *Life Studies and For the Union Dead* (New York: Noonday, 1969): 10.

49 Cole's "Essay on American Scenery" (1836) remains an influential example of Romantic approaches to nature as a vast field of sublime morals, energies, and inducements to an environmental covenant: it is reprinted in John Conron, ed., *The American Landscape: A Critical Anthology of Prose and Poetry* (New York: Oxford Univ. Press, 1973): 568–78.

50 John Updike, "L.A.," in *Facing Nature* (New York: Knopf, 1985): 12. Examples of this genre could multiply, but I take Robert Pinsky's crazed poem on the astroturfing of his hometown in New Jersey, "The

Destruction of Long Branch," to be exemplary: see *Sadness and Happiness* (Princeton: Princeton Univ. Press, 1975): 51.

51 Elizabeth Bishop, "Invitation to Miss Marianne Moore," in *The Complete Poems 1927–1979* (New York: Farrar, 1984), 82–23. For a reading of this poem's gender dynamics, see Yaeger, "Toward a Female Sublime," 193–94. In such a reading, Bishop's goal would be to surpass "Adamic" sublimity, "not through the old-fashioned sublime of domination, the vertical sublime which insists on aggrandizing the masculine self over others, but instead through a horizontal sublime that moves toward sovereignty or expenditure, that refuses an oedipal, phallic fight to the death with the father, but expands towards others, spreads itself out into multiplicity" (191). This describes, to some extent, the Whitmanic project in sublime expenditure that closes "Song of Myself."

52 See Mike Davis's spooky yet wondrous portrayal of global transformations rezoning Los Angeles into a postmodern "hyperspace," "Homeowners and Homeboys: Urban Restructuring in LA," *ENclitic* 11 (1989):9–16.

53 The recuperation of subjective freedom from threats of nuclear disaster, as well as from claustrophobic overpopulation, has been theorized in Frances Ferguson's ground-breaking essay, "The Nuclear Sublime," *Diacritics* 14 (1984):4–10.

54 Dick Hebdige, *Hiding In the Light: On Images and Things* (London: Routledge, 1988): 197–99, 52–58.

Chapter 9. Towards the Nuclear Sublime: Representations of Technological Vastness in Postnuclear America

1 See David Barash, "Immediate Effects of Nuclear Explosions," *The Arms Race and Nuclear War* (Belmont, Calif.: Wadsworth, 1987): 64. Farrell's report is part of General Leslie R. Groves's "Report on Alamogordo Atomic Bomb Test," ["Top Secret"] Memorandum for the Secretary of War": this document is reprinted as an appendix to Martin J. Sherwin, *A World Destroyed: The Atomic Bomb and the Grand Alliance* (New York: Knopf, 1975): 310–12. I would like to thank Brien Hallett of the University of Hawaii's Peace Institute for well-informed guidance on this crucial subject. General Farrell's description of "the nuclear sublime" intuits what I will call the *postnuclear* rupture of atomic forces in these terms: "All seemed to feel that they had been present at the birth of a new age—the Age of Atomic En-

ergy—and felt their profound responsibility to help in guiding into right channels the tremendous forces which had been unlocked for the first time in history [at the Alamogordo bomb test]" (312). America's emergence into a "Post Bomb" place is shrewdly characterized as such by Flannery O'Connor in a letter to Betty Boyd postmarked 5 Nov. 1949, in *The Habit of Being,* ed. Sally Fitzgerald (New York: Farrar, 1979): 18 (see chapter epigraph).

2   See M. M. Bakhtin, *Speech Genres & Other Late Essays,* trans. Vern W. McGee (Austin: Univ. of Texas Press, 1986): 4.

3   I comment more fully on General Farrell's compound of ideological uncertainty and American piety before the atomic bomb in "Postmodern as Post-Nuclear: Landscape as Nuclear Grid," in *Ethics/ Aesthetics: Post-Modern Positions,* ed. Robert Merrill (Washington, D.C.: Maisonneuve Press, 1988): 169–92. The atomic landscape as an "alter [post-altar] sublime" is compellingly articulated in a work by Canadian "Language Poet," Christopher Dewdney, in *Alter Sublime* (Toronto: Coach House Press, 1980): "The room breaking into flashing white shards of interstellar nothingness" (18).

4   See Theodor Adorno, *Aesthetic Theory,* [1970] trans. C. Lenhardt (London: Routledge, 1984): 280–84, "The sublime in nature and art [and play]." On the long-standing American fascination with such spectacles of national force, see Elizabeth McKinsey, *Niagara Falls: Icon of the American Sublime* (Cambridge: Cambridge Univ. Press, 1985), on Thomas Cole's self-empowering evocation of Niagara Falls: "And Niagara! that wonder of the world!—where the sublime and beautiful are bound together in an indissoluble chain. In gazing on it we feel as though a great void had been filled in our minds—our conceptions expand—we become a part of what we behold!" (211–12). Can Los Alamos figure as such an empowering icon?

5   John Elder, "Seeing Through the Fire: Writers in the Nuclear Age," in *Writing in a Nuclear Age,* ed. Jim Schley (Hanover, N.H.: University Press of New England, 1984): 223. On deconstructive paradoxes pervading the rhetorical overkill of nuclear force, as historically disseminated, see J. Fisher Solomon, *Discourse and Reference in the Nuclear Age* (Norman, Okla.: Oklahoma Univ. Press, 1988). Also see Paul Brians, *Nuclear Holocausts: Atomic War in Fiction, 1895–1984* (Kent, Ohio: Kent State Univ. Press, 1987).

6   Bob Perelman, "Statement," in *To the Reader* (Berkeley: Tuumba Press, 1984): n.p.

7   Jane Cooper "Poets Against the End of the World," in *Poetry and Politics: An Anthology of Essays,* ed. Richard Jones (New York: Morrow, 1985): 306; I draw upon nuclear data from the group Ground Zero [Director, Roger Molander], eds., *Nuclear War: What's In It for*

You? (New York: Pocket Books, 1982): 34; Heaney's comment appears in Schley, *Writing in a Nuclear Age*, 150. Ground Zero is a nonpartisan organization based in Washington, D.C. concerned with the threat of nuclear war.

8   Robert Lowell, "Fall 1961," in *For the Union Dead* (New York: Noonday, 1964): 11.

9   W. H. Auden "If On Account of the Political Situation," in Schley, *Writing in a Nuclear Age:* 1–2.

10 See E. P. Thompson, "Deterrence and Addiction," *Yale Review* 72 (1982):1–18.

11 This is the claim of Ground Zero ([Roger Molander et al., eds.], *Nuclear War*): 60.

12 George Oppen, *The Collected Poems* (New York: New Directions, 1975): 49.

13 William Pitt Root, "The Day the Sun Rises Twice," in *Nuke-Rebuke: Writers & Artists Against Nuclear Energy & Weapons*, ed. Marty Sklar (Iowa City: The Spirit That Moves Us Press, 1984): 103.

14 Jacques Derrida, "No Apocalypse, Not Now (full speed ahead, seven missiles, seven missives)," *Diacritics* 14 (1984):20–31 (21, 27).

15 Robert Frost, "Fire and Ice," *The Poetry of Robert Frost* (New York: Holt, Rinehart & Winston, 1969): 220. This ice-and-fire was first evoked—on an unprecedent scale of technological "destruction"—in World War I.

16 Perelman, *To The Reader*, n.p.

17 Bob Perelman, *The First World* (Great Barrington, Mass: The Figures, 1986): 23.

18 Terrence Des Pres, "Self/Landscape/Grid," in Schley, *Writing in a Nuclear Age:* 11.

19 Frances Ferguson, "The Nuclear Sublime." *Diacritics* 14 (1984):4–10; and "The Sublime of Edmund Burke, Or the Bathos of Experience," *Glyph* 8 (1981):62–78.

20 Fredric Jameson, "Periodizing the Sixties" *Social Text* 3 (1984):178–209 (200).

21 Arthur Schopenhauer, *The World as Will and Representation,* trans. E. F. J. Payne (New York: Dover, 1969): 205. (Subsequent references to this compelling analysis of the will-to-sublimity will appear in parentheses.) The poetic sublime may leave nature intact yet wills domination.

22 Wallace Stevens, "Esthétique du Mal," in *Collected Poems* ([1954], New York: Alfred A. Knopf, 1974): 314.

23 Ibid., 201–3.

24 Paul Mariani, *William Carlos Williams: A New World Naked* (New York: McGraw-Hill, 1981): 738.

25 Ibid., 699.

26 See Richard Klein and William B. Warner, "Nuclear Coincidence and the Korean Airline Disaster," *Diacritics* 16 (1986):2–21. From another point of view on imaging forth the nuclear sublime as a (symbolic) way of preventing its literal occurrence in history, see the interdisciplinary essays collected in Valerie Andrews, Robert Bosnak, and Karen Walter Goodwin, eds., *Facing Apocalypse* (Dallas: Spring Publications, 1987).

27 Derrida, "No Apocalypse," 23. On the related, yet quite differently inflected idea that "There will never be a [nuclear] catastrophe, because we live under the sign of virtual catastrophe [nuclear simulacra]," see Jean Baudrillard, "Panic Crash!," in Arthur Kroker, Marilouise Kroker, and David Cook, *Panic Encyclopedia: The Definitive Guide to the Postmodern Scene* (New York: St. Martin's, 1989): 64. Also see the attempt to think this postnuclear derealization into a "hyperreal" technoscape and simulacrous mediascape in Jean Baudrillard, *Simulations,* trans. Paul Foss, Paul Patton, and Philip Beitchman (New York: Semiotext(e), 1983), especially "Orbital and Nuclear," 58–75.

28 See Walter Benjamin's dread-and-wonder evocation of the new technologies of war, *Reflections: Essays, Aphorisms, Autobiographical Writings,* trans. Edmund Jephcott, (New York: Schocken, 1986): 94.

29 Adorno, *Aesthetic Theory,* 284.

30 This is the kind of question, concerning technological forces of sublimity ("terror, terror beheld and resisted"), which critics and writers such as Terrence Des Pres are asking in anthologies like *Writing in a Nuclear Age* (11), urging American poets to contend with the consequences of a power-infatuated culture. Also see the inadequately theorized portrayal of lyric self against a death-threatening system in Terrence Des Pres, *Praises & Dispraises: Poetry and Politics, the 20th Century* (New York: Viking, 1988). An Emersonian stance—"Here's for the plain old Adam, the simple genuine Self against the whole world"—seems inadequate, that is, to the United State's postnuclear/poststructural situation. See Rob Wilson, "Literary Vocation as Occupational Idealism: The Example of Emerson's 'American Scholar,'" *Cultural Critique* (forthcoming).

31 See Ferguson's analysis of Kant, "The Nuclear Sublime," 6.

32 Denise Levertov appears in Jones, *Poetry and Politics:* 312; Carolyn Forché, "Imagine the Worst," *Mother Jones* (October, 1984): 39.

33 Bruce Boon, talk on antinuclear poetics in Bob Perelman, ed. *Writing/ Talks* (Carbondale, Ill.: Southern Illinois Univ. Press, 1985): 88.

34 Robert Scheer, *With Enough Shovels: Reagan, Bush and Nuclear War* (New York: Random House, 1982): 121.

35 Derrida, "No Apocalypse," p. 23, p. 27.

324

36 Edward Dorn, *Hello, La Jolla* (Berkeley: Wingbow Press, 1978): 25.

37 Robert Creeley, "On Saul Bellow's Thesis . . . ," in Sklar, *Nuke-Rebuke,* 104.

38 This small-town rupturism is depicted in A. G. Mojtabai, *Blessed Assurance: At Home With the Bomb in Amarillo, Texas* (Boston: Houghton, 1986).

39 Perelman, *To the Reader* (1984): n.p.

40 See Paul Boyer, *By the Bomb's Early Light: American Thought and Culture at the Dawn of the Atomic Age* (New York: Pantheon, 1985); Jonathan Schell, *The Fate of the Earth* (New York: Knopf, 1982); and Michael Rogin, "Kiss Me Deadly: Communism, Motherhood and Cold War Movies," *Representations* 6 (1984):1–36.

41 Scheer, *With Enough Shovels,* 18–32. John Ashbery, "The Task," in *The Double Dream of Spring* (New York: Dutton, 1970): 13.

42 Boyer, *Bomb's Early Light,* 243–56.

43 William Carlos Williams, *Pictures from Brueghel and other poems: Collected Poems, 1950–1962* (New York: New Directions, 1962): 165.

44 On "liminal" tactics of literary deconstruction, see the post-Derridean speculations of Geoffrey H. Hartman, *Saving the Text: Literature/ Derrida/ Philosophy* (Baltimore: Johns Hopkins Univ. Press, 1981): 150.

45 Perelman, "Person," in *The First World,* 51.

46 J. Robert Oppenheimer, as quoted in Ground Zero [Roger Molander et al., eds.], (*Nuclear War,* 29).

47 Ai, "The Testimony of J. Robert Oppenheimer," *Sin* (Boston: Houghton, 1986): 64–67; on Ai's ethnically inflected confrontations with American sublimity, see Rob Wilson, "The Will to Transcendence in Contemporary American Poet, Ai," *Canadian Review of American Studies* 17 (1986):437–48.

48 J. Robert Oppenheimer, quoted in *Nuke Chronicles: Art on the End,* ed. Contact II (New York: Contact II Publications, 1985): 10.

49 Allen Ginsberg, *Plutonian Ode and Other Poems, 1977–1980* (San Francisco: City Lights, 1982): 12–13.

50 John Ashbery, "Soonest Minded," *The Double Dream of Spring* (New York: E. P. Dutton, 1970), p. 17.

51 George Uba, "How Do You Spell 'Missile'?" *Breaking Silence: An Anthology of Contemporary Asian American Poets,* ed. Joseph Bruchac (Greenfield, N.Y.: Greenfield Review Press, 1983): 272.

52 Mary Jo Salter, "Welcome to Hiroshima," in *Henry Purcell in Japan* (New York: Knopf, 1985): 59.

53 Robert Hass, "Images," in *Twentieth Century Pleasures: Prose on Poetry* (New York: Ecco, 1984): 303.

54 William Stafford, note to "Next Time," in Schley, *Writing in a Nuclear Age,* 202.
55 Marc Kaminsky, *The Road From Hiroshima* (New York: Simon and Schuster, 1984): 41–43.
56 Marguerite Duras, *Hiroshima Mon Amour* (text for the film by Alain Resnais), trans. Richard Seaver (New York: Grove Press, 1961). For speculations on Duras's postmodernism as distinctly "post-nuclear" in form and affect, see Julia Kristeva, "The Pain of Sorrow in the Modern World," *PMLA* 102 (1987):138–52.
57 See the poetics of semiotic glut and the "Disneyfication" of the American sublime as worked out in Jean Baudrillard, "Simulacra and Simulations," in *Jean Baudrillard: Selected Writings,* ed. Mark Poster (Stanford: Stanford Univ. Press, 1988): 166–84.
58 Gertrude Stein, "Reflection on the Atomic Bomb," in [1946] *Uncollected Writings of Gertrude Stein,* vol. 1, ed. Robert Bartlett Haas (Los Angeles: Black Sparrow Press, 1973).
59 Norman Mailer, *Of a Fire on the Moon* (New York: Signet, 1970): 60.
60 Robert Lowell, "For the Union Dead," in *Union Dead,* 72.
61 See Fredric Jameson, "Baudelaire as Modernist and Postmodernist: The Dissolution of the Referent and the Artificial 'Sublime,'" in *Lyric Poetry: Beyond New Criticism,* ed. Chaviva Hošek and Patricia Parker (Ithaca, N.Y.: Cornell Univ. Press, 1985): 262.
62 See Gilles Deleuze and Felix Guattari, *Anti-Oedipus: Capitalism and Schizophrenia,* [1972], trans. Robert Hurley, Mark Seem, and Helen R. Lane (Minneapolis: Univ. of Minnesota Press, 1983) on "desiring-production" mechanisms of the capitalized ego.
63 John Cage, *A Year From Monday: New Lectures and Writings* (Middletown, Conn: Wesleyan Univ. Press, 1967): 159.
64 Stevens, *Collected Poems,* 95.
65 Walter Benjamin, *Reflections,* 93.
66 Leo Marx, "On Heidegger's Conception of 'Technology' and Its Historical Validity," *Massachusetts Review* 25 (1984):638–52 (645). For a disenchanted view of America's self-representations, see Arthur Kroker, *Technology and the Canadian Mind: Innis/McLuhan/Grant* (Montreal: New World Perspectives, 1984).
67 Again, I am implicitly building upon and supplementing reflections on the "rhetoric of the technological sublime" in Leo Marx's *The Machine in the Garden: Technology and the Pastoral Ideal in America* (New York: Oxford Univ. Press, 1964) and the mythopoesis of modernist technology in Alan Trachtenberg, *Brooklyn Bridge: Fact and Symbol* (Chicago: Univ. of Chicago Press, 1965): "Translating engineering accomplishments into ideas, the poet [Whitman/Crane] com-

pleted the work of [American] history, and prepared for the ultimate journey to 'more than India,' the journey to the Soul: 'thou actual Me'" (150). On competing claims to preserve American sublimity as an aesthetic resource versus the more technological mandate to redistribute this force as an economic resource, see Raymond J. O'Brien, *American Sublime: Landscape and Scenery of the Lower Hudson Valley* (New York: Columbia Univ. Press, 1981), who argues of New York's Storm King that "the mountain will now generate not power but, like so much of the [Hudson] rivershore to the south, a 'psychic income' in the form of recreation and visual enjoyment forever" (282).

68 Robert Pinsky, "The Uncreation." *The New Republic*, 14 April 1986: 38.

69 Robert Pinsky, "The Figured Wheel," in *History of My Heart* (New York: Ecco, 1984): 3–4.

70 See Raymond Geuss, *The Idea of a Critical Theory: Habermas & the Frankfurt School* (Cambridge: Cambridge Univ. Press, 1981); and, more in the American grain of "prophetic pragmatism" as technocratic critique, see Cornel West, *The American Evasion of Philosophy: A Genealogy of Pragmatism* (Madison: Univ. of Wisconsin Press, 1989).

71 Martin Heidegger, *The Question Concerning Technology and Other Essays*, trans. William Lovitt (New York: Harper, 1977): 49; also see the counter-response in *Poetry, Language, Thought,* trans. Albert Hofstadter, (New York: Harper, 1971).

72 Heidegger, *The Question Concerning Technology*, 14, 26–27.

73 Marx, "Heidegger's Conception of 'Technology,'" 649.

74 Heidegger, *The Question Concerning 'Technology,'* 13–17.

75 Hart Crane, "Atlantis," *Complete Poems and Selected Letters and Prose* (Garden City, N.Y.: Doubleday, 1966): 116.

76 Heidegger, *Poetry, Language, Thought,* 172.

77 Wallace Stevens, "Of Mere Being" (1955), in *Opus Posthumous*, 141. For reasons having to do with the genre of the American sublime, I prefer the phrase "bronze distance" (evoking geographical vastness) in the third line (used in *Opus Posthumous*, 1957) to its textual variant, "bronze decor" (suggesting an aura of aesthetic bric-a-brac, or even Ashbery's "camp sublime"), as used in Holly Stevens, ed., *The Palm at the End of the Mind* (New York: Vintage, 1972): 398, 404. Milton J. Bates's expanded edition of *Opus Posthumous* (New York: Knopf, 1989) reverts to "bronze decor" on the basis of a typescript that survives at the Huntington Library (325). In either version, "the palm stands on the edge of space"—threatened by vacant immensity.

Index

Adams, Henry: on the technological sublime, 257, 318*n34*

Adams, John, 94–95

Addison, Joseph: on the natural sublime, 94–96, 103, 109–111, 119

Adorno: Theodor, on the sublime, 206, 211–13, 241

Ai: and the American sublime, 10, 11, 19, 23, 32, 37, 206, 247, 325*n47*

Alison, Archibald, 120

Alloway, Lawrence, 283*n17*

Althusser, Louis: on ideology, 35–36, 275–76*n26*, 303–4*n20*

Altieri, Charles, 282*n17*, 311–12*n19*

American sublime: definition of, 3–5, 8–10, 11, 13–14, 19–20, 23, 26–27, 36, 83–85, 130–32, 139, 151–52, 192, 213, 229, 253–54, 257–58, 268–69*n7*, 303*n19;* in American art history, 6–7, 8, 32, 129–31, 175–76, 268*n4*, 274*n19*, 282*n17*, 298*n11*, 310*n12. See also* Sublime

Ammons, A. R.: and the American sublime, 7, 8, 67, 93, 137, 258

Amnasan, Michael: refiguring the sublime, 60–61

Arensberg, Mary, 7, 27, 308–9*n7*

Arnold, Matthew, 182, 199, 244

Ashbery, John, 8, 19, 23, 35, 37; postmodern sublime of, 201, 206, 214, 217–21, 244–45, 248, 254, 260, 287*n7*

Atwood, Margaret: on early Canadian poetry, 70–71

Auden, W. H., 101, 231

Auerbach, Erich: on sublimity of the humble, 100, 287*n9*

Baillie, John, 95

Bakhtin, Mikhail: on the social ideology of genre, 36, 42, 49, 55–56, 135, 276*n27*, 279*n2*, 283*n20*

Baraka, Amiri: 41, 279*n1*

Barlow, Joel: the aspiration to the sublime of, 55, 113, 117, 119, 135, 165. *See also* Connecticut Wits.

Bate, Walter Jackson: on the sublime mimetic, 24, 107, 185, 278*n33*, 312*n21;* on Locke's sublime, 109

Bates, Milton, 195

Baudelaire, Charles, 34

Baudrillard, Jean: on the postmodern sublime, 200, 202, 206, 216, 220, 240, 251, 318*n35*, 319*n41*, 320*n42;* on nuclear sublime, 324*n27*, 326*n57*

Baxter, Richard: process of sublime contemplation in, 80, 87, 91, 289*n17*

Bell, Daniel, 220

Bell, Marvin, 47, 49

Benjamin, Walter, 34, 241, 256

Benston, Kimberly: on Afro-American sublime, 206–7

Bercovitch, Sacvan: on American ideology, 36–37

Bierstadt, Albert, 20

Bird, Larry, 43

Bishop, Elizabeth: the American sublime of, 8, 13, 19, 23, 51, 225–26, 321*n51*

Blackmore, Richard, 94, 106, 107

Blake, William, 43, 55, 138, 248; Whitman on, 158–59

Blasing, Mutlu Konuk, 268*n6, 283n18,* 298*n11*

Bloom, Harold, x, 7, 9, 24, 25, 39, 69,

Index

Bloom Harold (*continued*)
    119, 206, 273*n11;* oedipalizing the
    sublime, 12, 35, 273*n12;* Emerso-
    nian claims for the sublime, 23, 27,
    70, 144, 147, 268*n4;* on anxiety of
    American sublime, 88, 171, 195,
    271*n5,* 288*n11,* 290*n24;* on Bryant,
    122; on Whitman, 147; on Stevens,
    144, 190; solipsistic sublime of,
    275*n25*
Bly, Robert, 33, 206, 241, 255
Boone, Bruce, 242
Bourdieu, Pierre: 27, 272*n11*
Boyer, Paul, 244–45
Bradstreet, Anne, 6, 10, 19, 27, 37, 67,
    269*n8;* the Puritan sublime of, 71–
    93, 108, 119, 148, 151, 286–87*n6;*
    influence on Livingston, 102, 104–5,
    112
— "Contemplations," 10, 72, 74, 75; as
    a sublime poem, 79–93, 104–105,
    124, 297–98*n9*
— "The Flesh and the Spirit," 86–87
— "In Honour of Du Bartas," 92–93
— "In Honour of that High and Mighty
    Princess Queen Elizabeth," 76–77
Breslin, James: on Robert Lowell, 59
Bryant, William Cullen, 10, 29, 35, 70,
    74; the American sublime of, 117–
    33, 178; compared to Whitman, 126,
    129, 150, 152, 156, 166
— "A Forest Hymn," 127–28
— "Hymn of the City," 129
— "Inscription For the Entrance to a
    Wood," 126–27
— "The Prairies," 120, 128–29, 130,
    146
— "Thanatopsis," 123, 124
— "To a Waterfowl," 28, 122, 125–26
— "To Cole, the Painter, Departing for
    Europe," 129–31, 133
Bucke, Richard M.: on Whitman, 138–
    39, 144
Burke, Edmund: theory of sublime in,
    30, 32, 39, 104, 172, 201, 210, 254,
    316–17*n28;* sublime of terror, 97–8,
    106, 212–14, 235–36, 237, 267*n3*

Burnet, Joseph, 110
Burns, Robert, 174
Byles, Mather: counter-sublime of, 94,
    105–7, 112, 118

Cage, John, 72, 255
camp sublime, 218, 319*n38*
Christensen, Jerome, C., 27
Christo, 52,
Church, Frederic Edwin: as painter of
    the American sublime, 6, 8, 11, 13,
    30, 31, 32, 153, 166, 176, 198, 203,
    205, 274*n19*
Clifford, James, 280*n6*
Cole, Thomas: 8, 31, 32, 176, 205,
    223–24; Bryant's poem on, 129–32;
    use of natural sublime in, 320*n49,*
    322*n4*
Coleridge, Samuel Taylor: 124, 185
Connecticut Wits: aspiration to the
    sublime of, 70, 106, 117–20, 151,
    152, 156. *See also* Barlow, Joel;
    Humphreys, David; Trumbull, John.
Conversion scenario: in Bradstreet, 74–
    75, 83; in Livingston, 104–5, 107–8,
    293*n2;* in Bryant, 121–22, 125; in
    Whitman, 146, 159–61; in Stevens,
    194–96; postmodern transforma-
    tions of, 197–201, 228–29
Cooper, Jane, 230
Crane, Hart: the American sublime in,
    7, 19, 20, 23, 32, 35, 36, 50, 55–56,
    135, 138, 146, 206–7; on sublime of
    technology, 205, 250, 258, 262
Creeley, Robert, 243
Crèvecoeur, J. Hector St. John de, 20,
Culler, Jonathan: on Bloom's sublime,
    34–35

Dana, Richard Henry, Sr., 125
Darío, Reubén, 49
Davis, Mike, 215, 226
de Bolla, Peter, 206, 267*n3,* 316–
    17*n28*
Debray, Régis, 207
Deep Image poetics: 33, 255. *See also*
    Bly, Robert.

330

Index

Index

THE WISCONSIN PROJECT ON AMERICAN WRITERS
A SERIES EDITED BY FRANK LENTRICCHIA

American Puritanism and the Defense of Mourning:
  Religion, Grief, and Ethnology
in Mary White Rowlandson's Captivity Narrative
MITCHELL ROBERT BREITWIESER

F. O. Matthiessen and the Politics of Criticism
WILLIAM E. CAIN

In Defense of Winters: The Poetry and Prose
  of Yvor Winters
TERRY COMITO

A Poetry of Presence: The Writing of
  William Carlos Williams
BERNARD DUFFEY

Selves at Risk: Patterns of Quest in Contemporary
  American Letters
IHAB HASSAN

Reading Faulkner
WESLEY MORRIS WITH BARBARA ALVERSON MORRIS

Repression and Recovery: Modern American Poetry and the
  Politics of Cultural Memory, 1910–1945
CARY NELSON

Lionel Trilling: The Work of Liberation
DANIEL T. O'HARA

Visionary Compacts: American Renaissance Writings in
  Cultural Context
DONALD E. PEASE